The Horror Inside. The House Awaits

The Horror Inside. The House Awaits

Doug Hensley

Ingram spark

CONTENTS

**The Horror Inside
The House Awaits
By
Doug Hensley
Table Of Contents**

Chapter 10: The Basement - Sheila and Rob find a secret door leading down to a dark basement. Going down, they trigger a cave-in, trapping them inside.

Chapter 11: The Escape - After finding ritual items in the basement, Sheila and Rob escape and block the basement door, believing the nightmare is over.

Chapter 12: The Attacks - Paranormal attacks on Sheila grow violent. Desperate, she considers holding a seance.

Chapter 13: The Seance - The seance summons malevolent spirits. One possesses Rob, forcing Sheila to take drastic measures.

Chapter 14: The Cleansing - Sheila enlists a psychic medium to cleanse the home. The process seems successful until things escalate again. Chapter 15: The Truth - Research reveals the house was built for occult rituals, with a dark energy woven into the walls. There is only one way to stop it.

Chapter 16: The Sacrifice - Sheila learns she must offer a blood sacrifice in the house to seal the evil presence. She prepares for the ritual.

Chapter 17: The Confrontation - Unexpected twists force Sheila into a final showdown with the sinister forces in the house. All seems lost until she embraces her destiny. Chapter 18: The Resolution - Sheila defeats the evil forces at great personal cost. The house is finally at peace, but so much has changed. Chapter 19: The Awakening - Sheila slowly recovers, adjusting to a new normal. For the first time in years, she feels hope.

Chapter 20: The Return - Strange events make Sheila question if the evil presence was truly eradicated. Ominous signs suggest a greater darkness.

Chapter 21: The Revelation - Sheila discovers the house's evil has corrupted her soul. She must act quickly if she hopes to save herself. Chapter 22: The Sacrifice - Sheila makes one final sacrifice, for her own sake rather than the house's. Her journey ends, for better or worse.

Chapter 1: The New House

Sheila, a young woman seeking a fresh start, moves into a beautiful yet eerie old house. Almost immediately, strange noises and an overwhelming feeling of unease settle in, setting the stage for the supernatural events that will unfold.

Chapter 2: The Whispers As Sheila settles into her new home, she begins hearing faint voices whispering to her when she's alone at night. The mysterious whispers cast doubt on her sanity and create an atmosphere of increasing tension.

Chapter 3: The Dark History Driven by curiosity and a growing sense of dread, Sheila delves into the house's past. Her research reveals a dark tale of murder and suicide, hinting at the malevolent forces that may be at play.

Chapter 4: The Warning An elderly neighbor warns Sheila of impending danger and urges her to leave the house before it's too late. Despite the ominous warning, Sheila stubbornly refuses to abandon her new home.

Chapter 5: The Apparition Sheila's fears intensify when she catches a glimpse of a ghostly figure staring at her from the hall. However, the apparition vanishes before she can investigate further, leaving her to grapple with the supernatural occurrences.

Chapter 6: The Visitor In an attempt to find solace, Sheila invites her childhood friend Rob to stay the night. Rob, too, experiences unsettling events in the house, heightening the sense of foreboding.

Chapter 7: The Presence Doors open on their own, objects move mysteriously, and Sheila senses an unseen presence watching her. Despite the escalating paranormal activity, Rob remains oblivious to the unfolding horror.

Chapter 8: The Message Sheila and Rob wake up to cryptic words scrawled on the bathroom mirror, further deepening the mystery and leaving them shaken. The supernatural forces in the house are making their presence known in unsettling ways.

Chapter 9: The History Revealed Sheila discovers an old diary in the house, unveiling the gruesome rituals that were once held in its dark

basement. The revelation adds a layer of horror to the already chilling atmosphere.

Chapter 10: The Basement Driven by the need to unravel the mysteries surrounding the house, Sheila and Rob find a secret door leading to a dark basement. Their exploration triggers a cave-in, trapping them inside and marking a point of no return.

Chapter 11: The Escape Believing the nightmare is over, Sheila and Rob manage to escape the basement and block the door, thinking they have successfully sealed away the malevolent forces. However, the worst is yet to come.

Chapter 12: The Attacks Paranormal attacks on Sheila escalate, growing increasingly violent. Desperate for answers, she contemplates holding a seance to communicate with the otherworldly entities.

Chapter 13: The Seance The seance takes a dark turn as malevolent spirits are summoned, with one possessing Rob. Sheila is forced to take drastic measures to confront the supernatural threat.

Chapter 14: The Cleansing Sheila enlists the help of a psychic medium to cleanse the home. Initially, the process appears successful, providing a false sense of security. However, the calm is short-lived as the haunting experiences resume.

Chapter 15: The Truth Through extensive research, Sheila uncovers that the house was purposefully built for occult rituals, with a dark energy woven into its very walls. The revelation leaves her with the chilling realization that only one method can put an end to the terror.

Chapter 16: The Sacrifice Sheila learns that she must make a blood sacrifice within the house to seal the evil presence once and for all. As she prepares for the ritual, the gravity of the situation weighs heavily on her.

Chapter 17: The Confrontation Unexpected twists and turns force Sheila into a final showdown with the sinister forces in the house. All seems lost until she embraces her destiny, revealing a strength she never knew she possessed.

Chapter 18: The Resolution At great personal cost, Sheila successfully defeats the evil forces within the house. While the dwelling is finally at peace, the toll on Sheila is profound, leaving her forever changed.

Chapter 19: The Awakening As Sheila slowly recovers, she must adjust to a new normal. For the first time in years, she feels a glimmer of hope, but the scars of the harrowing ordeal run deep.

Chapter 20: The Return Strange events begin to unfold, making Sheila question if the evil presence was truly eradicated. Ominous signs suggest a greater darkness that may linger, threatening to undo everything she thought she had achieved.

Chapter 21: The Revelation In a shocking discovery, Sheila realizes that the house's evil has corrupted her soul. With time running out, she must act swiftly to save herself from the malevolent forces that have taken root within her.

Chapter 22: The Sacrifice In a final, desperate act, Sheila makes one last sacrifice—this time for her own sake rather than the house's. Her journey comes to an end, leaving readers to wonder if the darkness truly dissipates or if it merely finds a new host.

Chapter 1: The New House

The creaking floorboards echoed through the empty rooms as Sheila cautiously stepped into her new home. The air felt heavy, laden with an unspoken history that sent shivers down her spine. The walls, adorned with faded wallpaper, seemed to hold secrets, and the windows allowed only a dim, feeble light to penetrate the gloom.

Sheila's belongings were scattered in disarray, yet the beauty of the old house couldn't be denied. As the sun dipped below the horizon, casting long, eerie shadows across the wooden floors, Sheila couldn't shake the feeling that she was not alone.

Night descended with a whispering chill, and Sheila settled into her bed. But as the clock struck midnight, the house came alive with strange noises. Whispers, soft and elusive, slithered through the silence, causing her heart to race. She strained her ears, catching fragmented words that left her questioning her sanity.

In the dimness, Sheila felt the presence of something unseen. It was as if the very walls held a malevolent secret, a history buried deep within the foundation. Her unease intensified as the whispers grew into an indistinct murmur that seemed to resonate with the pulse of the house.

The next day, Sheila decided to uncover the mysteries surrounding her new abode. Armed with curiosity and a sense of foreboding, she delved into the house's past. Dusty old books and faded photographs revealed a dark tale of murder and suicide that had stained the very essence of the building.

As Sheila immersed herself in the grim accounts of the past, the atmosphere in the house seemed to shift. Shadows danced along the walls, and the temperature dropped, making her breath visible in the cold air. The weight of the house's history pressed upon her, like an invisible hand tightening around her throat.

A knock on the door interrupted Sheila's unsettling discoveries. An elderly neighbor, eyes clouded with concern, warned her of the impending danger that lurked within the house. "Leave, child, before it devours your soul," the old woman pleaded, but Sheila, fueled by stubborn determination, dismissed the ominous advice.

Nightfall brought with it a ghastly apparition. Sheila, bathed in the pale glow of the moonlight, glimpsed a ghostly figure in the hallway. It stared at her with hollow eyes, sending a chill through her veins. Before she could react, the apparition dissolved into the shadows, leaving Sheila trembling in the oppressive silence.

Desperate for solace, Sheila invited her childhood friend Rob to stay the night. As the hours passed, the house unleashed its malevolent grip on them both. Objects moved of their own accord, doors swung open with an otherworldly force, and a pervasive feeling of being watched hung in the air. Yet, Rob remained oblivious to the supernatural dance unfolding around them.

Cryptic messages appeared on the bathroom mirror the following morning. Scrawled in an otherworldly hand, the words sent shivers

down Sheila's spine. The house was communicating with them, leaving an indelible mark on their reality.

With each passing day, the house's dark history unveiled itself in more sinister ways. Sheila discovered an old diary tucked away in a forgotten corner, detailing gruesome rituals held in the very basement she had yet to explore.

Determined to confront the source of the malevolence, Sheila and Rob discovered a hidden door leading to the ominous depths of the basement. The air grew thick with anticipation as they descended, unaware that they were stepping into a trap set by forces beyond their comprehension.

A sudden and violent cave-in trapped Sheila and Rob in the lightless abyss. Panic set in as the walls seemed to close in around them. Shadows danced in the dim illumination of their flashlights, and the oppressive darkness whispered promises of doom.

Hours passed before they managed to escape, their faces etched with fear. Convinced that sealing the basement door had ended the nightmare, Sheila dared to hope for a return to normalcy. Little did she know, the true horror had only just begun.

Paranormal attacks on Sheila intensified, the unseen forces growing bolder and more malevolent. Objects hurled across rooms, chilling whispers turned into guttural growls, and a sinister presence loomed over her every move.

Desperation led Sheila to consider a seance, a desperate attempt to communicate with the entities plaguing her. The air crackled with tension as she and Rob sat in a circle, hands trembling as they called out to the unknown. But the seance took a dark turn, as malevolent spirits seized the opportunity to manifest their malevolence.

Rob, overcome by an unseen force, became a vessel for the malevolent entities. Sheila, faced with a friend turned foe, had no choice but to take drastic measures. The once comforting bonds of friendship now strained under the weight of supernatural possession.

In her quest for salvation, Sheila sought the help of a psychic medium to cleanse the home. The air thickened with anticipation as the medium performed rituals to banish the malevolent entities. For a fleeting moment, the house seemed at peace, and Sheila allowed herself a breath of relief.

However, the calm proved short-lived. The house, it seemed, had only been biding its time. The cleansing had only served to agitate the dormant evil that lingered within the very fabric of the walls.

Driven by an insatiable need for the truth, Sheila's research revealed that the house was purposefully constructed for occult rituals. A dark energy, woven into the very foundation, defied any attempts to eradicate it conventionally. The realization struck her like a physical blow, and the oppressive weight of the house's malevolence pressed down on her soul.

Sheila learned of a chilling solution—one that required a blood sacrifice to seal the evil presence. The revelation sent shivers down her spine, but with unwavering resolve, she prepared for the ritual. The air in the house crackled with a palpable tension as Sheila steeled herself for the harrowing task that lay ahead.

As the appointed hour arrived, Sheila embarked on the ritual, guided by the cryptic instructions she had unearthed. The air thickened with an otherworldly energy as she treaded the fine line between the living and the supernatural. The house seemed to breathe, its walls pulsating with an unholy heartbeat.

Unexpected twists and turns forced Sheila into a final confrontation with the sinister forces that had tormented her. The battle unfolded in a crescendo of terror, with each moment pushing her to the brink of despair. All seemed lost until Sheila, drawing upon a strength she never knew she possessed, embraced her destiny and faced the malevolent entities head-on.

At great personal cost, Sheila emerged victorious. The malevolent forces were banished, and the house fell silent. But victory came at a price—Sheila was forever changed, scarred by the ordeal that had tested her sanity and resilience.

As Sheila grappled with the aftermath of the climactic events, she found herself in a house that bore the marks of the supernatural battle. The once-elegant rooms, now tinged with an otherworldly aura, stood as a testament to the horrors that had unfolded within their walls.

The awakening came slowly for Sheila. She found herself in a surreal new normal, haunted by memories of the malevolence that had once claimed her every waking moment. Yet, for the first time in years, a flicker of hope ignited within her.

But the return to normalcy proved elusive. Strange events unfolded around Sheila, casting doubt on whether the evil presence had truly been eradicated. Ominous signs, subtle yet undeniable, hinted at a darkness that lingered, threatening to unravel everything she had fought so hard to achieve.

In a shocking revelation, Sheila discovered that the house's evil had not only touched the walls but had also corrupted her very soul. Time was of the essence as she grappled with the realization that salvation required swift and decisive action.

The final sacrifice loomed before Sheila—a desperate act to save herself from the malevolent forces that sought to claim her. Her journey reached its conclusion, leaving her standing at the precipice of the unknown. Whether the darkness dissipated or found a new host remained a lingering question, echoing in the silence of the house that had become a battleground between the living and the supernatural.

Chapter 2: The Whispers

As the haunting echoes of the previous night lingered, Sheila awoke to a house cloaked in shadows. The morning light struggled to penetrate the heavy curtains, casting an eerie glow across the room. The unsettling events of the night before weighed on her mind, and a sense of trepidation settled in her chest.

Dragging herself out of bed, Sheila couldn't shake the feeling that the walls were watching her every move. The air seemed to hum with an unnatural energy, and she wondered if the house itself held memories of the whispers that had invaded her sleep.

As dusk settled once again, the atmosphere in the house shifted. The creaking floorboards beneath Sheila's tentative steps seemed to resonate with a spectral rhythm. The shadows danced in a macabre ballet, and the air took on a frigid chill that seeped into her bones.

Alone in the dimly lit living room, Sheila felt a subtle change in the air—a whispering murmur that curled around her consciousness like tendrils of smoke. A strange sensation crawled up her spine, and she strained to catch the fragmented words carried by the unseen voices.

The whispers, soft and elusive, wrapped around her mind like a ghostly embrace. Sheila couldn't discern the origin of the ethereal voices, and a growing unease settled in the pit of her stomach. The words, a dissonant symphony of indistinct muttering, seemed to weave tales of forgotten sorrows and ancient malevolence.

Torn between fear and curiosity, Sheila followed the whispers as they led her through the labyrinthine corridors of the old house. The air grew heavier, and the oppressive darkness seemed to amplify the haunting voices that echoed through the halls.

The night unfolded in a surreal dance of shadows and secrets. Sheila, guided by the mysterious whispers, wandered deeper into the heart of the house. Each step felt like a descent into a realm where reality and the supernatural coexisted in a fragile balance.

In the heart of the house, Sheila found herself standing before a weathered door. The whispers, now a cacophony of urgent voices, beckoned her to open it. Hesitant but driven by an unexplainable force, she turned the rusted doorknob.

The room beyond was shrouded in an impenetrable darkness. The air felt charged with an otherworldly energy, and the whispers reached a fevered pitch. As Sheila stepped into the room, a chilling wind swept through, extinguishing the feeble candlelight that flickered in the corners.

In the profound darkness, shapes and shadows materialized, dancing on the periphery of Sheila's vision. The whispers coalesced into a haunting chorus, a symphony of forgotten souls yearning to be heard.

Goosebumps erupted on Sheila's skin as she realized that she was not alone in the spectral gathering.

The room seemed to pulse with an unseen heartbeat, and Sheila felt a cold breath on the nape of her neck. The whispers, now mere inches away, spoke directly into her mind. Words, ancient and cryptic, intertwined with her thoughts, creating a disorienting fusion of reality and the supernatural.

Sheila, paralyzed by the ghostly communion, struggled to comprehend the weight of the revelations. The whispers spoke of long-buried secrets, of a history stained with sorrow and malevolence. The house, it seemed, held memories that transcended the boundaries of time.

In a crescendo of spectral intensity, the whispers began to echo the names of the departed, their voices rising and falling like a spectral tide. Sheila felt an overwhelming sadness wash over her as she became a vessel for the collective lament of the forgotten souls trapped within the walls.

As the spectral symphony reached its zenith, Sheila's surroundings blurred into a phantasmagoric dreamscape. Shadows danced in a macabre ballet, and ghostly apparitions materialized before her. The faces of the departed stared into her soul, their eyes reflecting an eternity of suffering.

In a sudden, jarring silence, the room plunged into darkness once more. Sheila stood alone, her breath ragged and heart pounding. The weight of the revelations pressed down on her shoulders, and the whispers, now a mere echo in the recesses of her mind, faded into the obscurity of the old house.

Sheila stumbled back into the dimly lit corridor, disoriented and shaken. The whispers, though momentarily silenced, lingered in the air like an unseen specter. The house, now charged with an unsettling energy, seemed to watch her with an intensity that transcended the physical realm.

Haunted by the night's spectral communion, Sheila retreated to the safety of her room. The whispers, though subdued, continued to echo in the corners of her mind. Sleep, an elusive sanctuary, offered no respite

as the haunting voices seeped into her dreams, intertwining reality and nightmare in a disconcerting tapestry.

Morning brought little solace as Sheila grappled with the aftermath of the spectral encounter. The once-charming house now bore the weight of its own history, and every creak and groan seemed to carry the echoes of the departed. The whispers, now a constant companion, followed her every move, leaving her sanity teetering on the edge of an abyss.

As Sheila navigated the mundane tasks of daily life, the spectral voices whispered secrets that tore at the fabric of her understanding. The house, it seemed, held a malevolent legacy that transcended the passage of time, and Sheila found herself entangled in a web of forgotten sorrows and ancient grievances.

The days blurred into a disorienting haze as Sheila, haunted by the whispers, grappled with a reality that seemed to unravel at the seams. The walls, once silent witnesses to the passage of time, now pulsed with an otherworldly energy that defied rational explanation.

In the suffocating embrace of the old house, Sheila faced a choice—succumb to the spectral whispers that threatened to unravel her sanity or confront the malevolent forces that lurked in the shadows. Little did she know that the true horror, like a dormant beast, awaited its awakening in the depths of the house's dark history. The whispers, a prelude to the malevolence that lay ahead, continued to echo through the corridors, weaving a sinister tale that intertwined with Sheila's very existence. The house, a malevolent entity in its own right, had claimed her as its unwilling conduit, a vessel through which the forgotten voices sought to rewrite the narrative of their tragic past. As night fell once again, Sheila stood at the precipice of a nightmare, the echoes of the whispers lingering like a ghostly requiem. The darkness, pregnant with unspoken horrors, awaited its chance to consume her soul. Little did Sheila know that the true terror, the culmination of the spectral whispers, loomed on the horizon, threatening to plunge her into a darkness from which there might be no escape. The whispers, a harbinger of an

ancient malevolence, echoed through the haunted corridors, signaling the beginning of a descent into the heart of terror.

Chapter 3: The Dark History

The day unfolded with a sense of oppressive anticipation as Sheila, haunted by the lingering whispers, delved into the dark history of the house. Dust-covered books, their pages brittle with age, beckoned to her from the shelves, revealing tales of sorrow and malevolence that clung to the very essence of the dwelling.

Sheila's fingers traced the words on the yellowed pages, each revelation a cold breath against her skin. The house, it seemed, bore witness to a tapestry of tragedies—a canvas painted with the blood of those long forgotten. Murmurs of untold horrors seemed to emanate from the pages, seeping into her consciousness like an insidious poison.

The sun dipped below the horizon, casting elongated shadows that danced along the walls. Sheila, now immersed in the chilling accounts of the past, couldn't escape the feeling that the very air she breathed carried the weight of the malevolent history woven into the fabric of the house.

As darkness claimed the landscape outside, Sheila's mind echoed with the stories of those who had once called the house their home. A family torn asunder by betrayal, a forbidden love that led to tragedy, and the anguished cries of lost souls echoed through the corridors, merging with the persistent whispers that lingered like a ghostly chorus.

Driven by a compulsion she couldn't fully comprehend, Sheila unearthed old photographs from a dusty box hidden in the attic. Faces frozen in time stared back at her, their eyes holding the secrets of a bygone era. She felt an inexplicable connection to these spectral visages, as if their silent pleas for remembrance echoed in the recesses of her mind.

The photographs revealed a family whose smiles hid a darker truth—a truth that the house guarded with a possessive malevolence. In one faded picture, a child's eyes seemed to bore into Sheila's soul, a silent plea etched in their depths. The whispers intensified, an unseen

hand guiding her through the labyrinth of familial tragedies that stained the house with a legacy of sorrow.

In her search for understanding, Sheila stumbled upon a hidden compartment in the attic. Within its confines lay a collection of letters, brittle with age and tinged with the desperation of the departed. The correspondence spoke of forbidden rituals and a pact sealed in blood—a pact that bound the souls of the house to an otherworldly realm.

The revelation sent shivers down Sheila's spine as the echoes of the past reverberated in the dimly lit room. The house, it seemed, was a vessel for dark forces that defied the boundaries between the living and the dead. Sheila, now an unwitting participant in the spectral drama, grappled with the weight of the malevolent history that clung to her like a suffocating shroud.

Night descended, and Sheila found herself standing before the door that led to the basement—the epicenter of the house's darkest secrets. The whispers, now a cacophony of spectral voices, urged her to descend into the abyss and confront the malevolence that lurked in the hidden recesses.

The creaking stairs groaned under her weight as Sheila descended into the subterranean realm. The air grew colder with each step, and the oppressive darkness seemed to swallow the feeble light of her flashlight. Shadows clung to the walls like spectral tendrils, and the whispers reached a fevered pitch, guiding her deeper into the heart of the supernatural abyss.

As Sheila entered the basement, a chill crawled up her spine. The room, bathed in an otherworldly gloom, revealed the remnants of forgotten rituals—a sacrificial altar, cryptic symbols etched into the walls, and a palpable malevolence that seemed to pulse with a life of its own.

Sheila's breath caught as she uncovered an old diary amidst the dust-covered artifacts. Its pages, stained with the ink of a tormented soul, detailed the ghastly rituals conducted in the name of an otherworldly entity. The diary spoke of a darkness that hungered for innocent souls, a darkness that had claimed the very foundations of the house.

With trembling hands, Sheila read aloud the incantations that had once reverberated within the cold stone walls. The air thickened with an unseen presence as the words echoed through the basement, awakening the dormant malevolence that lingered like a dormant beast.

A sudden gust of wind extinguished the feeble light, plunging Sheila into a darkness that seemed to consume her very essence. Whispers surrounded her, their voices intertwining with the oppressive silence. Shadows danced in the obscurity, and Sheila felt a spectral presence closing in around her.

As she fumbled to relight her flashlight, Sheila caught a glimpse of ghostly figures that materialized in the shadows. Eyes devoid of life stared at her, their hollow gazes filled with an insatiable hunger. The apparitions seemed to reach out from the shadows, their fingers brushing against her skin like the breath of a long-forgotten nightmare.

In the suffocating darkness, Sheila stumbled backward, her heart pounding in her chest. The whispers, now an anguished wail, reverberated through the basement, creating a dissonant symphony of horror. The malevolent forces that had slumbered within the house were now awake, hungry for the essence of the living.

In a desperate attempt to escape the spectral onslaught, Sheila retraced her steps through the labyrinthine corridors of the basement. The walls seemed to close in around her, and the air pulsed with an otherworldly energy that clung to her like a suffocating fog.

As she reached the basement stairs, a cold hand brushed against the nape of her neck. Sheila recoiled, her senses overwhelmed by the touch of unseen fingers. The whispers, now a maddening cacophony, echoed in her ears like a chorus of the damned.

With every step she climbed, the malevolence pursued her like a relentless shadow. The basement seemed to resist her escape, its unseen tendrils reaching out to claim her soul. Sheila emerged into the dimly lit corridor, gasping for breath as the weight of the supernatural encounter pressed down on her chest.

The house, now a malevolent entity awakened from its slumber, seemed to watch Sheila with an insatiable hunger. The whispers, though momentarily subdued, lingered in the air like a haunting refrain. The basement, a portal to an otherworldly realm, had unleashed a darkness that threatened to consume everything in its path.

Sheila, shaken to her core, stumbled into her room and barricaded the door as if shielding herself from the unseen forces that lurked outside. The whispers, now a persistent hum in the background, continued to echo through the walls, their spectral voices weaving a tapestry of horror that seemed to stretch across time and space.

Sleep, elusive and treacherous, offered no refuge as Sheila found herself trapped in a nightmare that transcended the boundaries of the waking world. Shadows danced on the edges of her consciousness, and ghostly apparitions lurked in the recesses of her dreams.

Morning brought little solace as Sheila awoke to a house shrouded in an oppressive silence. The whispers, though momentarily silenced, lingered like a malevolent residue. The basement, now a forbidden chasm that bridged the realms of the living and the dead, beckoned to her with an unseen gravity.

The day unfolded with a palpable tension as Sheila, now a reluctant participant in a supernatural drama, grappled with the malevolence that had been unleashed. The dark history of the house, etched into its very foundations, loomed like a specter over every room, every corridor.

The house, now a living entity that hungered for the essence of the living, seemed to watch Sheila with an insatiable appetite. The whispers, a relentless chorus that echoed through the haunted halls, hinted at a darkness that transcended the limits of her understanding.

As night descended once again, Sheila stood at the crossroads of horror, the echoes of the dark history pulsating through the very walls. The malevolent forces, awakened from their slumber, awaited their next move in a macabre dance that threatened to consume Sheila's very soul. The house, a conduit for ancient malevolence, seemed to pulse with a malevolent energy that defied all attempts at rational explanation. Little

did Sheila know that the true terror, a malevolent force that transcended the boundaries of the supernatural, awaited its moment to strike in the chilling depths of the haunted dwelling.

Chapter 4: The Warning

The oppressive weight of the malevolent history lingered in the air as Sheila, haunted by the nightmarish events in the basement, found herself thrust deeper into the clutches of the old house. The whispers, though momentarily subdued, continued to echo through the corridors like an unseen presence that refused to be silenced.

As the sun dipped below the horizon, casting long shadows that stretched like spectral fingers, Sheila roamed the dimly lit rooms in a daze. The walls, adorned with faded wallpaper, seemed to close in around her like a suffocating embrace. Every creak and groan of the aging structure resonated with the echoes of the dark history that clung to the very fabric of the dwelling.

In a feeble attempt to regain a semblance of control, Sheila decided to venture outside. The night air, cool and crisp, offered a brief respite from the oppressive atmosphere within the house. As she stepped onto the porch, the world beyond seemed to hold its breath, as if aware of the supernatural forces that pulsed within the walls.

The neighboring houses stood in stoic silence, their windows gazing like empty eyes into the night. A distant streetlamp flickered intermittently, casting eerie shadows that danced on the pavement. Sheila, shivering in the cold, felt an inexplicable sense of being watched—an unseen gaze that followed her every move.

A sudden gust of wind carried with it a spectral whisper that sent a chill down Sheila's spine. The voice, laden with urgency, seemed to carry a warning—an ethereal plea that resonated with the very core of her being. Unsettled, she turned toward the source of the whisper, but the darkness offered no clues, concealing its secrets within its velvety embrace.

Returning to the house, Sheila couldn't escape the feeling that the very air held a sense of foreboding. The whispers, now a constant

companion, seemed to guide her toward the heart of the malevolence that lurked within. As she ascended the creaking stairs, the old house seemed to creak and groan in protest, as if resisting her attempts to uncover its darkest secrets.

The attic, a repository of forgotten artifacts, drew Sheila with an irresistible gravity. The air grew thick with an otherworldly energy as she approached the door leading to the mysterious space. As she turned the doorknob, a fleeting vision of ghostly figures danced on the periphery of her vision, vanishing as quickly as they appeared.

The attic, bathed in the feeble glow of a single bulb, revealed a myriad of forgotten relics—a dusty collection of forgotten memories. Sheila's flashlight illuminated old trunks, moth-eaten clothing, and a peculiar assortment of items that seemed frozen in time. Each artifact, a silent witness to the house's twisted history, exuded an otherworldly aura that seemed to tug at the edges of Sheila's sanity.

Among the forgotten relics, Sheila discovered an old photograph album. Its pages, yellowed with age, unveiled the lives of those who had once called the house their home. Family gatherings frozen in time, celebrations tainted by an unseen darkness, and the eyes of children who seemed to peer through the veil of the past—all spoke of a history steeped in sorrow.

As Sheila flipped through the photographs, a sudden chill settled in the room. Shadows danced along the walls, and the whispers intensified, their urgency now laced with an unspoken dread. The album, like a portal to the past, beckoned her to uncover the secrets that lingered within its pages.

The images told a tale of a family whose smiles concealed a tragic fate. A mother, her eyes reflecting a haunting sadness, held her children close in a sepia-toned embrace. The father, a stern figure with a haunted gaze, seemed to carry the weight of a malevolence that transcended the boundaries of the photograph.

In one particularly unsettling image, Sheila noticed a figure standing in the background—a silhouette that seemed to merge with the

shadows, its eyes staring into the depths of her soul. The whispers, now a dissonant chorus, echoed the name of the figure—an entity known only as "The Watcher."

A sudden realization gripped Sheila—the warnings she had received, the spectral figures in the attic, and the ever-present whispers—all converged on the ominous presence of The Watcher. As she traced the figure's silhouette with her trembling finger, the air thickened with an oppressive energy that seemed to bear the weight of the malevolent entity.

Driven by a desperate need to understand, Sheila decided to consult the elderly neighbor who had issued the initial warning. With the photograph album in hand, she ventured outside once again, the night air carrying with it a sense of impending doom.

The neighbor's house, a weathered structure bathed in the glow of a flickering porch light, seemed to emanate a warmth that stood in stark contrast to the cold atmosphere within Sheila's own dwelling. The old woman, with eyes clouded by the passage of time, opened the door with a knowing look that hinted at a lifetime of secrets.

As Sheila explained the events that had transpired—the whispers, the spectral figures, and the ominous presence of The Watcher—the elderly neighbor listened in solemn silence. When Sheila showed her the photograph album, the neighbor's eyes widened in recognition, and a shiver ran down her spine.

"You've unearthed a dark legacy," the old woman murmured, her voice a hushed whisper that seemed to carry the weight of untold secrets. She invited Sheila inside, where the walls seemed to resonate with a history that had long been buried.

Seated in a dimly lit room adorned with faded tapestries, the neighbor began to weave a tale that sent shivers down Sheila's spine. The house, it seemed, had once been a haven for a family whose lives had become entwined with an otherworldly force—a force that had claimed them in a twisted dance of tragedy.

The elderly neighbor spoke of The Watcher, an entity born from forbidden rituals conducted in the very heart of the house. Its malevolence, fueled by the suffering of the past, lingered like a vengeful specter, a guardian of dark secrets that defied the boundaries between the living and the dead.

The family in the photographs, the whispers, and the spectral figures —all were linked to The Watcher's insatiable hunger for the souls of the living. The old woman's words painted a harrowing picture of a malevolent force that sought to reclaim what had been lost—an entity that fed on the essence of the unsuspecting inhabitants.

As the elderly neighbor spoke, Sheila felt the weight of The Watcher's gaze upon her. The air in the room grew dense with an unseen presence, and the whispers, now a mournful lament, echoed through the walls like a requiem for the damned.

"You must leave this place," the old woman implored, her eyes reflecting a depth of sorrow that seemed to transcend the confines of the room. "The Watcher is awakened, and its hunger knows no bounds. Your very soul is in peril."

Fear gripped Sheila's heart as the magnitude of the malevolence became apparent. The warnings, the whispers, and the dark history of the house all converged on a chilling reality—a reality in which Sheila stood on the precipice of a supernatural abyss.

Determined to confront The Watcher and unravel the malevolent forces that held the house in their clutches, Sheila returned to her home with a sense of grim resolve. The night, now heavy with the weight of unseen eyes, seemed to pulse with an otherworldly energy that hinted at the imminent confrontation.

The house, a silent witness to the unfolding horror, awaited its fate in the embrace of darkness. Sheila, armed with the knowledge of the malevolent history and the warnings of The Watcher's insatiable hunger, steeled herself for a battle that would transcend the boundaries of the living and the dead. The whispers, now a chorus of spectral voices, guided her toward the heart of the supernatural storm that awaited in

the haunted corridors of the old dwelling. Little did she know that the true terror, a confrontation with The Watcher that would redefine the very fabric of reality, loomed on the horizon, threatening to plunge her into a darkness from which there might be no escape. The night, pregnant with the weight of unspoken horrors, unfolded with a spectral symphony that echoed the malevolent legacy of The Watcher—a force that hungered for the essence of the living, a force that would stop at nothing to reclaim what had been lost in the shadows of the past.

Chapter 5: The Apparition

As Sheila braced herself for the impending confrontation with The Watcher, the house seemed to hold its breath in a malevolent silence. The air, thick with the weight of unseen eyes, pressed against her skin like a suffocating shroud. Every step she took echoed in the dimly lit corridors, the whispers guiding her toward the heart of the supernatural storm.

The attic, a spectral realm illuminated by a feeble bulb, awaited her return. The artifacts, relics of a twisted history, seemed to resonate with an otherworldly energy as Sheila ascended the creaking stairs. The photograph album, now a key to the malevolent secrets that lurked within, clutched in her trembling hands, felt like a talisman against the encroaching darkness.

The whispers, now a relentless chorus that echoed through the haunted halls, intensified as Sheila reached the attic. The air pulsed with an unseen presence, and the shadows danced on the walls in a macabre ballet. The photograph album, when opened, revealed spectral figures that seemed to move within the confines of the images—a silent procession of lost souls tethered to The Watcher's insatiable hunger.

With a heavy heart, Sheila placed the photograph album on a dusty table in the center of the attic. The air seemed to vibrate with an unseen energy, and the whispers reached a fevered pitch. A sudden gust of wind extinguished the feeble bulb, plunging the attic into darkness.

In the obscurity, Sheila felt a spectral presence closing in around her. The whispers, now an anguished wail, surrounded her like a ghostly

chorus. The air seemed charged with an otherworldly force as The Watcher's malevolence manifested in the shadows.

A cold breath brushed against Sheila's neck, and she sensed the gaze of unseen eyes upon her. The spectral figures from the photographs materialized in the darkness, their eyes reflecting a hunger that transcended the boundaries of the living and the dead.

In the suffocating darkness, Sheila felt a touch—a caress of unseen fingers that traced the contours of her face. The whispers, now a maddening cacophony, echoed through the attic, creating a dissonant symphony of horror. The Watcher, a malevolent force that defied explanation, sought to claim her soul in a spectral dance of damnation.

Desperation gripped Sheila as she fumbled for her flashlight, the feeble beam cutting through the obscurity like a beacon of fragile hope. The spectral figures, their faces twisted in silent anguish, retreated into the shadows as the light pierced the darkness.

With trembling hands, Sheila retrieved the photograph album. The images, though now devoid of spectral movement, seemed to carry the weight of the malevolent history that clung to the house. The Watcher, its presence still palpable in the obscurity, awaited its chance to strike once again.

The whispers, now a haunting melody, guided Sheila back through the labyrinthine corridors. The old house, a spectral battleground, seemed to pulse with an otherworldly energy that defied rational explanation. As she descended the creaking stairs, the weight of The Watcher's malevolence bore down on her shoulders like an unseen burden.

In the dimly lit living room, Sheila's flashlight revealed a ghostly figure standing in the hall—a silhouette that seemed to merge with the shadows. The Watcher, its form obscured by the darkness, stared at her with eyes that held the emptiness of eternity.

Fear clawed at Sheila's chest as she confronted the spectral entity that lurked within the old house. The whispers, now a mournful lament, echoed through the corridors, intertwining with the malevolent

presence that encircled her. The time for understanding was over; the time for confrontation had arrived.

Sheila, driven by a grim resolve, approached The Watcher. The air seemed to ripple with an unseen force, and the whispers reached a crescendo as she stood face to face with the malevolent entity. The Watcher, a manifestation of forgotten sorrows and ancient grievances, exuded an otherworldly aura that seemed to defy the very laws of nature.

In the spectral confrontation, Sheila felt a cold hand brush against her cheek—a touch that carried the weight of a thousand lost souls. The whispers, now an ethereal chorus, spoke words that resonated with the depths of her consciousness. The Watcher sought communion, a merging of the living and the dead in a twisted dance of supernatural entanglement.

With a surge of determination, Sheila raised the photograph album. The images, now illuminated by the feeble glow of her flashlight, held a spectral resonance that seemed to repel The Watcher. The entity recoiled, its form dissipating like mist in the face of an unseen force.

In the haunting confrontation, Sheila felt a surge of power—the power of the forgotten souls that lingered within the photographs. The whispers, now a triumphant hymn, reverberated through the haunted halls as The Watcher retreated into the shadows. The malevolent force, thwarted by the spectral energy of the past, seemed to dissipate like a fading nightmare.

The old house, once a battleground between the living and the dead, fell silent. The whispers, now a fading echo, lingered in the air like a melancholic melody. Sheila, exhausted and shaken, stood amidst the remnants of the spectral encounter, the photograph album clutched in her trembling hands.

As the oppressive atmosphere lifted, Sheila felt a profound change in the house—a sense of peace that transcended the malevolent legacy of The Watcher. The whispers, though subdued, carried a lingering gratitude, as if the forgotten souls had found solace in the spectral confrontation.

With a heavy heart, Sheila descended into the basement—the very heart of the house's dark history. The air, once thick with malevolence, now held a somber tranquility. The relics of forgotten rituals seemed frozen in time, their significance transformed by the spectral encounter.

In the dim light, Sheila uncovered the old diary—the key to the understanding of the house's twisted past. The pages, though stained with the ink of tormented souls, now bore a sense of closure. The Watcher, defeated by the power of the forgotten, had relinquished its hold on the old dwelling.

As Sheila emerged from the basement, the morning sun began to cast its gentle rays on the once-foreboding structure. The old house, no longer a haven for malevolent forces, seemed to stand in quiet reverence to the spectral encounter that had unfolded within its walls.

The whispers, now a distant echo, guided Sheila to the attic—the epicenter of the supernatural storm. The photograph album, placed back in its dusty corner, exuded a spectral resonance that seemed to linger in the air. The spectral figures within the images, their faces now frozen in peace, bore silent witness to the resolution of a malevolent legacy.

Sheila, now forever changed by the harrowing ordeal, stepped outside into the cool morning air. The neighborhood, once draped in a veil of darkness, now basked in the warmth of the rising sun. The whispers, though a mere memory, carried a final message—a farewell from the forgotten souls who had found redemption in the face of supernatural turmoil.

As Sheila walked away from the old house, the sense of normalcy slowly returned. The neighborhood, once tainted by the malevolent force that had claimed the dwelling, now stood as a testament to the triumph of the living over the specters of the past.

Little did Sheila know that the true horror, a final revelation that would redefine the very fabric of her existence, awaited in the shadows of her newfound peace. The old house, though freed from the clutches of The Watcher, held a secret that would unveil itself in a chilling twist

of fate—one that would test the limits of Sheila's resilience and plunge her into a darkness from which there might be no escape.

The whispers, now a distant memory, left the door open for the looming terror that awaited in the aftermath of the supernatural storm. The haunting melody of the forgotten lingered in the air as Sheila ventured into the uncertain future—a future where the boundaries between the living and the dead remained blurred, and the horrors of the past cast a long, lingering shadow over the new normal that awaited her.

Chapter 6: The Visitor

In the wake of the harrowing confrontation with The Watcher, Sheila grappled with the aftermath of the supernatural storm that had engulfed the old house. The whispers, now a distant echo, left an eerie silence in their wake—a silence that seemed to stretch across the haunted halls like a spectral tapestry.

As Sheila navigated the dimly lit rooms, the old house felt different. The air, once thick with malevolence, now carried a palpable tranquility. The remnants of forgotten rituals in the basement seemed frozen in time, their significance transformed by the spectral encounter. The photograph album, placed back in its dusty corner in the attic, exuded a spectral resonance that lingered like a fading memory.

Despite the apparent peace that settled over the dwelling, Sheila couldn't shake the feeling that the old house held secrets yet to be unveiled. The neighborhood, seemingly untouched by the supernatural turmoil, continued its daily rhythm. Sheila's neighbors, unaware of the malevolent force that had gripped their midst, carried on with their lives in blissful ignorance.

The morning sun cast a warm glow on the neighborhood, and Sheila decided to take a stroll outside. The fresh air, tinged with the scent of dew-kissed grass, offered a reprieve from the suffocating atmosphere within the old house. As she walked down the quiet streets, the whispers, though faint, seemed to guide her steps toward a sense of normalcy.

In the midst of the peaceful neighborhood, Sheila encountered a figure from her past—Rob, her childhood friend who had experienced the unsettling events in the house. Rob, unaware of the supernatural horrors that had transpired, greeted Sheila with a warm smile.

As they exchanged pleasantries, Sheila hesitated to divulge the haunting experiences she had faced. The whispers, now a gentle hum in the background, seemed to caution her against revealing the spectral truth that lingered within the old house. Instead, she chose to enjoy the fleeting moments of normalcy with Rob, hoping to leave the malevolent past behind.

The day unfolded with a semblance of serenity as Sheila and Rob reminisced about their shared childhood memories. Laughter echoed through the air, temporarily drowning out the lingering echoes of the supernatural encounter. The old house, its haunted corridors temporarily silenced, stood as a mere backdrop to the facade of normalcy that enveloped the neighborhood.

As night descended, Sheila invited Rob to stay the night—a decision that would unwittingly drag him into the lingering shadows of the malevolent past. The whispers, though muted, seemed to intensify as darkness cloaked the old house in an otherworldly stillness.

In the dimly lit living room, Sheila and Rob shared stories from their past, seeking refuge in the familiarity of friendship. The air, though seemingly calm, held a sense of foreboding as the whispers, now a spectral melody, intertwined with the gentle hum of the night.

As they settled in for the night, Sheila couldn't escape the feeling that The Watcher's malevolence lingered in the shadows. The spectral figures from the photographs, now etched in her memory, seemed to cast ghostly shadows on the walls. The old house, once a haven for dark forces, bore silent witness to the unsuspecting visitors who dared to cross its threshold.

The night progressed in a semblance of tranquility, the whispers fading into the background. Yet, as the clock ticked towards midnight, an unspoken tension enveloped the dwelling. Sheila, restless and haunted

by the memories of the supernatural storm, found herself drawn to the attic—the epicenter of the spectral encounter.

In the attic, the photograph album lay in its dusty corner, seemingly untouched by the passage of time. The whispers, though muted, urged Sheila to revisit the malevolent history that clung to the old house. With a heavy heart, she opened the album, its pages revealing the spectral figures that had once danced within its confines.

As Sheila traced the images with her trembling finger, a sudden gust of wind extinguished the feeble bulb, plunging the attic into darkness. The whispers, now a mournful lament, echoed through the spectral realm as the photographs seemed to come to life once again.

In the obscurity, Sheila felt a spectral presence closing in around her. The whispers, now a dissonant chorus, spoke words that seemed to reverberate with the anguished cries of the forgotten. The Watcher, its malevolence not fully vanquished, sought communion with the living in a macabre dance of supernatural entanglement.

Rob, stirred from his sleep by the eerie atmosphere, joined Sheila in the attic. The air seemed to vibrate with an unseen force as the whispers guided them toward the heart of the spectral storm. The photograph album, now a conduit to the malevolent past, exuded an otherworldly energy that drew them deeper into the supernatural abyss.

As they stood in the darkness, the spectral figures from the photographs materialized around them. Eyes devoid of life stared at Sheila and Rob, their hollow gazes filled with an insatiable hunger. The whispers, now a haunting melody, spoke of unresolved sorrows that lingered within the old house.

In the spectral confrontation, Sheila and Rob felt the weight of unseen eyes upon them. The Watcher, though seemingly thwarted, manifested in the shadows with a renewed malevolence. The whispers, now a spectral symphony, hinted at a darkness that defied the boundaries of the living and the dead.

Desperation gripped Sheila as she clutched the photograph album. The images, now illuminated by the feeble glow of Rob's flashlight,

held a spectral resonance that seemed to repel The Watcher. The entity recoiled, its form dissipating like mist in the face of an unseen force.

In the haunting confrontation, Sheila and Rob felt a surge of power—the power of the forgotten souls that lingered within the photographs. The whispers, now a triumphant hymn, reverberated through the haunted attic as The Watcher retreated into the shadows. The malevolent force, though temporarily thwarted, lingered like a specter in the lingering darkness.

The attic, once a battleground between the living and the dead, fell silent. The whispers, now a fading echo, left an eerie stillness in their wake. Sheila and Rob, exhausted and shaken, stood amidst the remnants of the spectral encounter, the photograph album a testament to the unresolved sorrows that clung to the old house.

As they descended from the attic, the old house seemed to sigh with a spectral resignation. The whispers, though subdued, lingered in the air like a melancholic melody. The night, pregnant with the weight of unspoken horrors, unfolded with a sense of uncertainty—a future where the boundaries between the living and the dead remained blurred.

Sheila and Rob, now forever entwined in the malevolent legacy of the old house, sought refuge in the dimly lit living room. The whispers, though muted, hinted at a lingering terror that awaited in the shadows. Little did they know that the true horror, a revelation that would redefine the very fabric of their existence, loomed on the horizon—a revelation that would test the limits of their resilience and plunge them into a darkness from which there might be no escape.

The whispers, now a distant murmur, left the door ajar for the looming terror that awaited in the aftermath of the spectral storm. The old house, its haunted corridors pulsating with unresolved sorrows, stood as a gateway to a supernatural abyss. Sheila and Rob, bound by the malevolent forces that lingered within, faced an uncertain future where the horrors of the past cast a long, lingering shadow over their fragile grasp on reality.

Chapter 7: The Presence

The night, once a harbinger of supernatural turmoil, descended upon the old house with an unsettling stillness. Sheila and Rob, shaken by the spectral encounter in the attic, sought solace in the dimly lit living room. The air, though seemingly calm, carried an unspoken tension—a tension that seemed to thicken with every passing moment.

As they sat in the silence, the whispers, now a muted hum, seemed to guide Sheila's attention toward the shadows that lurked in the corners of the room. The old house, a silent witness to the malevolent forces that had unfolded within its walls, exuded an otherworldly energy that defied the confines of the living and the dead.

A subtle chill crept through the air as the temperature in the room dropped. The whispers, though faint, took on a dissonant tone—a spectral melody that hinted at the lingering presence of The Watcher. Sheila and Rob, their senses heightened by the supernatural ordeal, felt an unseen gaze upon them.

In the dim light, objects in the room seemed to shift mysteriously. A picture frame trembled on the wall, and the flickering flame of a candle cast dancing shadows that defied the laws of physics. The old house, now a conduit for the residual malevolence, pulsed with an unseen force that sought communion with the living.

Unease settled over Sheila and Rob as they exchanged wary glances. The whispers, now a spectral chorus, seemed to speak of a malevolent force that had not been fully vanquished—a force that lingered in the shadows, biding its time for a resurgence. The old house, once a haven for dark rituals, held its secrets close, and the unsuspecting inhabitants stood at the mercy of the supernatural storm that raged within its walls.

In an attempt to dispel the ominous atmosphere, Sheila suggested a distraction—turning on the television to drown out the spectral whispers. As they sat on the worn-out couch, the flickering images on the screen seemed to offer a brief respite from the encroaching darkness. However, the shadows that danced in the periphery of their vision hinted at a malevolence that refused to be ignored.

The night unfolded with a deceptive calmness, the television casting a pale glow that struggled against the encroaching darkness. Sheila and Rob, though attempting to maintain a façade of normalcy, couldn't shake the feeling that The Watcher's presence lingered like a spectral specter in the room.

As the clock struck midnight, a sudden drop in temperature sent shivers down their spines. The whispers, now a mournful wail, echoed through the haunted halls, creating an ethereal symphony of dread. Sheila and Rob, bound by the malevolent legacy of the old house, felt an unseen force closing in around them.

In the dim light, a shadowy figure materialized in the hall—a silhouette that seemed to defy the laws of the physical world. The Watcher, its malevolence not fully quelled, stood as a spectral guardian in the shadows. The whispers, now a dissonant chorus, spoke of an unresolved darkness that sought to reclaim the living.

Fear gripped Sheila and Rob as The Watcher's presence manifested in the room. The air seemed charged with an otherworldly energy as the entity, now a tangible force, cast a haunting gaze upon the unsuspecting visitors. The whispers, though muted, carried a warning—an anguished plea to leave the old house before it succumbed to the malevolent forces that clung to its very foundations.

In a desperate attempt to defy the encroaching darkness, Sheila and Rob decided to leave the living room and venture into the seemingly unaffected parts of the house. The whispers, now a relentless drone, seemed to guide them toward the heart of the supernatural storm.

As they ascended the creaking stairs, the oppressive atmosphere intensified. The walls, adorned with faded wallpaper, seemed to close in around them like a suffocating embrace. The Watcher's presence, a spectral entity that defied rational explanation, pulsed with an unseen force that sought to ensnare their very souls.

In the upstairs hallway, a door creaked open on its own—a manifestation of the lingering malevolence that gripped the old house. The whispers, now a haunting lament, guided Sheila and Rob toward the

threshold of the mysteriously opened door. The room beyond, bathed in an unnatural darkness, beckoned them to confront the unresolved sorrows that lingered within.

As they entered the room, the air thickened with an oppressive energy. The temperature dropped, and the whispers reached a fevered pitch. The Watcher's presence, now an undeniable force, seemed to coalesce in the shadows—a spectral guardian that stood between the living and the abyss.

In the dim light, Sheila and Rob discovered an old mirror—a relic that seemed to hold the key to the malevolent forces that plagued the old house. The whispers, now a cacophony of spectral voices, spoke of a dark energy woven into the very fabric of the reflection.

As they stared into the mirror, their reflections seemed distorted—a ghastly image that hinted at the malevolent entity that lurked within the haunted dwelling. The Watcher, its form now a nightmarish apparition in the reflective surface, bore silent witness to the unfolding confrontation.

A sudden realization gripped Sheila—the mirror, a conduit for The Watcher's malevolence, held the key to the unresolved darkness that clung to the old house. The whispers, though chaotic, seemed to guide her toward a revelation that would redefine the boundaries between the living and the dead.

Driven by a grim resolve, Sheila and Rob decided to confront The Watcher through the mirror—a ritual that promised to unveil the malevolent forces that lurked within. The room, now bathed in an otherworldly glow, felt like a spectral battleground where the living and the dead converged in a macabre dance of supernatural entanglement.

As they stood before the mirror, the whispers reached a crescendo. The Watcher's apparition, now a nightmarish entity that defied description, materialized in the reflective surface. The air seemed to vibrate with an unseen force as Sheila and Rob prepared to confront the malevolent force that had haunted them.

The room, now a spectral realm suspended between the living and the dead, bore witness to the spectral encounter. The Watcher, its malevolence intensified by the confrontation, sought communion with the living in a ghastly manifestation that defied the laws of nature.

In the mirror's reflection, Sheila and Rob felt the weight of unseen eyes upon them. The Watcher's gaze, a haunting stare that held the emptiness of eternity, sought to penetrate the very depths of their souls. The whispers, now a mournful hymn, intertwined with the oppressive energy as the supernatural battle unfolded.

With a surge of spectral power, Sheila and Rob confronted The Watcher through the mirror. The whispers, though chaotic, seemed to align with the living, creating a dissonant symphony that echoed through the spectral realm. The Watcher, now faced with the combined resilience of the living, recoiled in the face of an unseen force.

In the haunting confrontation, the mirror shattered—an explosion of glass that seemed to reverberate through the haunted halls. The Watcher's malevolence, now fractured and dispersed, retreated into the shadows like a fading nightmare. The room, once a battleground between the living and the abyss, fell silent.

Sheila and Rob, exhausted and shaken, stood amidst the shards of the shattered mirror. The whispers, now a distant echo, carried a sense of fleeting victory. The old house, though still haunted by the malevolent forces that clung to its foundations, seemed to sigh with a spectral resignation.

The night, now heavy with the weight of supernatural turmoil, unfolded with an unsettling stillness. Sheila and Rob, their resolve tested by the spectral encounter, descended from the upstairs realm and returned to the living room. The air, though laden with the remnants of the supernatural battle, felt lighter as if a temporary reprieve had been granted.

Little did they know that the true horror, a revelation that would redefine the very fabric of their existence, awaited in the shadows of their newfound victory. The old house, though temporarily quelled, held

secrets that would unveil themselves in a chilling twist of fate—one that would test the limits of Sheila and Rob's resilience and plunge them into a darkness from which there might be no escape.

The whispers, now a fading memory, left the door ajar for the looming terror that awaited in the aftermath of the spectral storm. The old house, its haunted corridors pulsating with unresolved sorrows, stood as a gateway to a supernatural abyss. Sheila and Rob, bound by the malevolent forces that lingered within, faced an uncertain future where the horrors of the past cast a long, lingering shadow over their fragile grasp on reality.

Chapter 8: The Message

The night, now heavy with the echoes of the spectral confrontation, unfolded with an eerie stillness in the old house. Sheila and Rob, their nerves still on edge from the encounter in the haunted room, sought refuge in the dimly lit living room. The air, though seemingly calm, carried the residual tension of the supernatural battle that had unfolded within the haunted dwelling.

As they settled on the worn-out couch, the whispers, though subdued, lingered in the air like a spectral melody. The old house, once a haven for dark rituals and spectral forces, seemed to hold its breath in the aftermath of the shattered mirror. Sheila and Rob, their senses heightened by the otherworldly encounter, exchanged wary glances as they awaited the next manifestation of The Watcher's malevolence.

The television, now a mere flickering glow in the dim room, offered a semblance of normalcy. Sheila, attempting to distract herself from the lingering horrors, suggested turning on the lights to dispel the encroaching darkness. As she reached for the switch, a sudden power outage plunged the old house into complete darkness.

In the pitch-black silence, the whispers intensified. The air seemed charged with an otherworldly energy, and a sense of dread settled over Sheila and Rob like a suffocating shroud. The old house, now devoid of any artificial illumination, became a spectral realm where the living and the dead coexisted in an uneasy truce.

Amidst the darkness, an ominous presence loomed—a manifestation of The Watcher's lingering malevolence. The whispers, now a dissonant chorus, guided Sheila and Rob toward the heart of the supernatural storm. The basement, a place fraught with the echoes of forgotten rituals, beckoned them to confront the unresolved darkness that clung to the old house.

With flashlights in hand, Sheila and Rob descended into the dimly lit basement. The air, thick with the weight of unseen eyes, seemed to pulse with a spectral energy that transcended the boundaries of the living and the dead. The whispers, now a haunting murmur, guided them toward a message—a cryptic revelation that awaited in the subterranean depths.

In the basement, amidst the relics of forgotten rituals, Sheila discovered an old Ouija board—an artifact that seemed to carry the spectral residue of past seances. The whispers, now a relentless drone, urged them to communicate with the other side in a desperate attempt to unravel the malevolent mysteries that clung to the old house.

With hesitant resolve, Sheila and Rob placed their trembling hands on the planchette. The Ouija board, now a conduit for the spectral forces, seemed to come alive with an otherworldly energy. The whispers, though chaotic, aligned with the planchette's movements, guiding them through a spectral conversation with the entities that lingered in the shadows.

As they sought answers from the other side, the planchette spelled out cryptic words on the Ouija board. The whispers, now a spectral symphony, intensified as the message unfolded. "He watches," the planchette spelled out, the words etched in an otherworldly script that seemed to defy rational explanation.

A chill ran down Sheila's spine as the whispers spoke of The Watcher's insatiable hunger—an entity that observed the living with an unrelenting gaze. The message, though cryptic, hinted at a darkness that transcended the boundaries of the living and the dead. The old house,

a silent witness to the supernatural turmoil, bore witness to a revelation that would redefine the very fabric of reality.

In the dim light of the basement, Sheila and Rob felt an unseen force closing in around them. The whispers, now a haunting melody, intertwined with the spectral energy that permeated the air. The Ouija board, a conduit for the malevolent forces, seemed to carry a message from beyond—a message that foretold a greater darkness that awaited in the shadows.

With a sense of trepidation, Sheila and Rob decided to delve deeper into the basement—a place where the old house's dark history unfolded in the form of forgotten rituals and malevolent entities. The whispers, though chaotic, seemed to guide them toward an altar—a focal point of the supernatural energies that pulsed through the subterranean depths.

As they reached the heart of the basement, a cold wind swept through the air—a spectral breeze that carried with it the echoes of forgotten incantations. The whispers, now a mournful lament, spoke of a ritual that could potentially unveil the true nature of The Watcher's malevolence.

On the altar, Sheila found an ancient book—an occult tome that detailed the dark history woven into the very foundations of the old house. The whispers, though fragmented, urged her to decipher the cryptic symbols and incantations that adorned the pages. The malevolent legacy, now laid bare in the pages of the ancient book, hinted at a supernatural force that defied comprehension.

With a heavy heart, Sheila began to read aloud the incantations—a desperate attempt to commune with the entities that lingered in the shadows. The whispers, now a spectral chorus, seemed to align with the words of the ritual, creating a dissonant symphony that reverberated through the basement.

As the incantations reached a fevered pitch, the air in the basement seemed to warp and twist. Shadows danced on the walls, and the whispers, now a cacophony of spectral voices, spoke of a portal—a gateway between the living and the abyss. The old house, its spectral foundations

shaken by the unfolding ritual, became a conduit for the malevolent forces that sought communion with the living.

In the dim light, the basement transformed into a spectral realm—a place suspended between the living and the dead. The whispers, now an anguished wail, guided Sheila and Rob toward the heart of the supernatural storm. The ritual, though wrought with danger, promised to unveil the true nature of The Watcher's malevolence.

As they stood at the precipice of the ritual's culmination, a sudden gust of wind extinguished their flashlights. Darkness enveloped them, and the whispers, now a relentless drone, seemed to merge with the shadows that danced in the spectral realm. The Ouija board, the ancient book, and the altar became mere silhouettes in the obscurity—a spectral tableau that hinted at the imminent confrontation with the unknown.

In the darkness, Sheila and Rob felt a surge of supernatural energy— the very fabric of reality seemed to warp and bend. The whispers, now a spectral symphony, reached a crescendo as the ritual reached its zenith. The portal, a shimmering gateway between the living and the abyss, beckoned them to confront the malevolent forces that awaited on the other side.

With a hesitant step, Sheila and Rob crossed the threshold of the portal. The whispers, now a haunting melody, surrounded them like a ghostly chorus. The old house, its foundations shaken by the unfolding ritual, bore silent witness to the spectral encounter that transcended the boundaries of the living and the dead.

As they entered the other side, the supernatural realm unfolded with an eerie beauty. Ethereal

Chapter 9: The History Revealed

In the supernatural realm beyond the portal, Sheila and Rob found themselves surrounded by a surreal landscape. Ghostly echoes of forgotten rituals and spectral entities painted the ethereal canvas. The whispers, now a haunting melody, guided them deeper into the spectral abyss—a place where the dark history of the old house unraveled in a dissonant symphony of the supernatural.

As they ventured through the ghostly landscape, Sheila and Rob discovered fragments of the past—a spectral montage that revealed the horrors once held within the old house's walls. The whispers, though fragmented, spoke of gruesome rituals and malevolent entities that had left an indelible mark on the haunted dwelling.

Images of hooded figures engaged in forbidden ceremonies danced before their eyes. The air, thick with the scent of incense and spectral energy, carried the echoes of tormented souls who had fallen victim to the malevolent forces that once reigned in the old house. The whispers, now a mournful lament, spoke of an occult legacy woven into the very fabric of the supernatural realm.

In their spectral journey, Sheila and Rob stumbled upon an ancient diary—an artifact that seemed to hold the key to the malevolent history that plagued the old house. The diary, its pages yellowed with age, detailed the dark rituals that had once unfolded in the basement. The whispers, now a spectral chorus, urged them to read the words that revealed the origin of The Watcher's malevolence.

As Sheila deciphered the cryptic entries, the images of hooded figures engaging in occult ceremonies became vivid in her mind. The diary spoke of a cult that had once thrived within the old house, conducting rituals that sought communion with otherworldly entities. The whispers, though haunting, hinted at a darkness that transcended the boundaries of the living and the dead.

In the spectral realm, Sheila and Rob felt the weight of the forgotten souls that had fallen victim to the cult's malevolence. The air, charged with an otherworldly energy, seemed to vibrate with the echoes of tormented cries. The old house, once a haven for dark forces, bore witness to the anguished spirits that lingered within the supernatural tapestry.

As they delved deeper into the spectral landscape, the whispers guided them toward a hidden chamber—a place where the cult's rituals had reached their zenith. The air in the chamber felt oppressive, and the whispers, now a relentless drone, seemed to speak of a malevolent energy woven into the very walls of the old house.

In the chamber, Sheila and Rob discovered an altar—an ancient stone slab adorned with cryptic symbols. The whispers, now a cacophony of spectral voices, spoke of blood sacrifices and forbidden rites that had stained the altar with the anguish of the forgotten. The old house, its spectral foundations steeped in the malevolent legacy, became a witness to the horrors that had transpired within its confines.

The images in the spectral landscape became more vivid—a macabre display of hooded figures performing dark rituals in the dimly lit chamber. The whispers, now a mournful hymn, conveyed the desperation of the tormented souls who had once walked the halls of the old house. Sheila and Rob, entwined in the spectral tapestry, felt the weight of the dark history that clung to their very beings.

As they reached the climax of the spectral journey, the whispers guided them toward a hidden passage in the chamber. A secret door, concealed by centuries-old dust, beckoned them to confront the source of The Watcher's malevolence. The old house, its spectral corridors pulsating with the echoes of the past, stood as a gateway to a deeper darkness that awaited in the shadows.

With trepidation, Sheila and Rob opened the secret door, revealing a staircase that descended into the depths of the supernatural realm. The air, now thick with the energy of the forgotten, guided them toward an underground cavern—a place where the cult's rituals had once reached their zenith.

In the cavern, the whispers reached a fevered pitch. The air seemed charged with an unseen force as Sheila and Rob navigated through the dimly lit passages. The walls, adorned with ancient symbols, spoke of a dark energy that permeated the very foundations of the old house.

As they reached the heart of the cavern, a revelation unfolded—a sacrificial chamber adorned with an altar bathed in an otherworldly glow. The whispers, now a dissonant symphony, spoke of the need for a blood sacrifice to seal the malevolent forces that lingered within the old house. Sheila and Rob, bound by the supernatural forces that guided

their journey, faced an unimaginable choice that would redefine the very fabric of their existence.

The images in the cavern came to life—a spectral replay of the cult's rituals and the sacrifices that had stained the altar with the blood of the innocent. The whispers, now a haunting melody, spoke of The Watcher's insatiable hunger and the need for a final sacrifice to quell the malevolent forces.

In the cavern's depths, Sheila and Rob confronted the truth—the old house, built for occult rituals, held a dark energy woven into its very walls. The whispers, though chaotic, conveyed a revelation that transcended the boundaries of the living and the dead. The sacrificial chamber, a place where the malevolent legacy reached its zenith, became a battleground between the supernatural and the mortal.

With a heavy heart, Sheila and Rob realized the only way to seal the malevolent forces was through a blood sacrifice. The whispers, now a mournful lament, spoke of the necessity to offer a part of themselves to quell the insatiable hunger of The Watcher. The old house, its spectral foundations shaken by the revelation, stood as a testament to the price that must be paid to vanquish the malevolent legacy.

In the dim light of the sacrificial chamber, Sheila and Rob prepared for the ritual—a desperate attempt to seal the malevolent forces that clung to the old house. The whispers, now a spectral symphony, guided them through the ancient rites that had once unleashed the supernatural storm within the haunted dwelling.

As the ritual reached its climax, Sheila and Rob felt an otherworldly energy enveloping them. The air pulsed with the echoes of forgotten incantations, and the sacrificial chamber seemed to vibrate with a spectral resonance. The whispers, though haunting, guided them toward a destiny entwined with the malevolent forces that sought communion with the living.

With a surge of supernatural power, Sheila and Rob offered a part of themselves to the sacrificial chamber. The whispers, now a triumphant hymn, echoed through the cavern as their sacrifice became a beacon of

light in the spectral darkness. The old house, its foundations saturated with the essence of the living, stood at the precipice of a resolution that transcended the boundaries of the mortal realm.

In the aftermath of the ritual, the cavern fell silent. The whispers, though fading, left an eerie stillness in their wake. Sheila and Rob, exhausted and shaken, stood amidst the spectral remnants of the sacrificial chamber. The old house, though still haunted by the echoes of the past, seemed to sigh with a spectral resignation.

The supernatural realm, now devoid of the malevolent forces that once tormented the haunted dwelling, unfolded with an unsettling stillness. Sheila and Rob, their journey through the spectral abyss complete, ascended from the underground cavern and returned to the haunted halls of the old house.

As they emerged into the dim light of the old house, a sense of eerie calm settled over them. The whispers, now a distant echo, carried a semblance of victory—a fleeting reprieve from the encroaching darkness. Little did they know that the true challenge awaited in the aftermath of the ritual—a revelation that would test the limits of their resilience and plunge them into a darkness from which there might be no escape.

The old house, though temporarily quelled, bore witness to the sacrifices made to seal the malevolent forces within its spectral confines. Sheila and Rob, forever changed by the ritual, faced an uncertain future where the echoes of the past lingered like a spectral shadow. The whispers, now a fading memory, left the door ajar for the looming terror that awaited in the aftermath of the spectral storm.

In the dim light of the old house, Sheila and Rob, their spirits weighed down by the sacrifice, descended from the underground cavern and returned to the living room. The air, though laden with the remnants of the supernatural battle, felt lighter as if a temporary reprieve had been granted.

As they navigated the haunted halls, a realization gripped Sheila and Rob—the old house, though temporarily quelled, held secrets that would unveil themselves in a chilling twist of fate. The whispers, now

a fading memory, left the door ajar for the looming terror that awaited in the aftermath of the spectral storm. The old house, its foundations saturated with the essence of the living, stood as a gateway to a supernatural abyss. Sheila and Rob, bound by the malevolent forces that lingered within, faced an uncertain future where the horrors of the past cast a long, lingering shadow over their fragile grasp on reality.

Chapter 10: The Basement

After sealing the malevolent forces within the old house through the sacrificial ritual, Sheila and Rob found themselves back in the dimly lit living room. The air, though tinged with an unsettling calm, carried the echoes of the supernatural journey they had undertaken. The whispers, now a distant memory, left a spectral resonance in the haunted dwelling.

As Sheila and Rob attempted to regain their bearings, a foreboding sensation lingered in the air. The old house, once a haven for dark rituals, stood as a testament to the sacrifices made to quell the malevolent forces. Little did they know that the true test awaited in the aftermath of the ritual—a revelation that would redefine the very fabric of their existence.

In the eerie quiet, Sheila's gaze was drawn to the basement door—the same door that had led them to the depths of the supernatural realm. The whispers, though muted, seemed to guide her attention toward the subterranean depths where forgotten rituals had once unfolded. A sense of trepidation settled over her as the basement became a focal point of the encroaching darkness.

Rob, too, felt an unspoken unease as he followed Sheila's gaze toward the basement door. The air, though seemingly calm, carried a spectral energy that hinted at the unresolved mysteries lurking within the subterranean depths. The old house, though momentarily at peace, seemed to hold secrets that demanded further exploration.

Driven by an unspoken compulsion, Sheila and Rob approached the basement door. The whispers, now a faint murmur, seemed to beckon them to descend once more into the depths of the haunted dwelling. The wooden stairs creaked under their weight as they descended into

the dimly lit basement—a place where the supernatural energies still lingered, weaving a spectral tapestry of the past.

In the basement, the air felt charged with an otherworldly energy. The whispers, though subdued, guided Sheila and Rob toward the heart of the supernatural storm. The old house, its foundations saturated with the essence of the living, seemed to pulse with an unseen force that transcended the boundaries of the mortal realm.

As they ventured deeper into the basement, Sheila's flashlight revealed forgotten artifacts—relics of the occult rituals that had once held sway within the haunted dwelling. The whispers, though fragmented, spoke of a lingering malevolence that refused to be fully contained. The old house, its spectral corridors echoing with the whispers of the past, became a gateway to a darkness that awaited in the shadows.

A sudden drop in temperature signaled a change in the atmosphere. The whispers, now a haunting lament, guided Sheila and Rob toward a hidden corner of the basement. There, obscured by shadows, they discovered a mysterious door—an entrance to a forgotten chamber that had eluded their previous exploration.

With trepidation, Sheila and Rob opened the door, revealing a chamber bathed in an unnatural darkness. The air, thick with the scent of ancient incense, seemed to vibrate with the echoes of spectral energy. The whispers, now a dissonant symphony, spoke of a deeper layer of malevolence that awaited discovery.

As they entered the hidden chamber, Sheila's flashlight revealed cryptic symbols etched into the walls—a language of the occult that spoke of forbidden knowledge and ancient rites. The whispers, though chaotic, seemed to convey a message—a revelation that transcended the boundaries of the living and the dead. The old house, now a conduit for the supernatural, bore witness to the unfolding mysteries that awaited in the hidden chamber.

In the dim light, Sheila and Rob stumbled upon an ancient tome—an occult grimoire that held the secrets of the forgotten rituals. The whispers, now a spectral chorus, urged Sheila to decipher the cryptic

symbols that adorned the pages. The malevolent legacy, though temporarily quelled, seemed to find its voice in the ancient words that unfolded in the flickering light.

As Sheila read aloud the incantations, the chamber seemed to come alive with an otherworldly energy. Shadows danced on the walls, and the whispers, now a cacophony of spectral voices, spoke of a deeper darkness that had yet to be unveiled. The old house, a witness to the unfolding ritual, became a gateway to the unknown—a place where the living and the dead converged in a macabre dance.

In the spectral glow, the hidden chamber transformed into a supernatural realm—a place suspended between the living and the abyss. The whispers, now a mournful wail, guided Sheila and Rob toward a revelation that would test the limits of their resilience. The old house, its foundations shaken by the unfolding ritual, became a battleground where the supernatural and the mortal collided.

As they delved deeper into the hidden chamber, the symbols on the walls seemed to shift—a spectral language that defied comprehension. The whispers, though haunting, spoke of an ancient evil that had been awakened by their presence. Sheila and Rob, bound by the malevolent forces that lingered within the old house, faced an unforeseen challenge that awaited in the shadows.

A sudden gust of wind extinguished their flashlights, plunging the hidden chamber into complete darkness. The whispers, now a relentless drone, seemed to merge with the shadows that danced in the spectral realm. The old house, its spectral foundations saturated with the essence of the living, stood at the precipice of a new, malevolent revelation.

In the darkness, Sheila and Rob felt an unseen force closing in around them. The whispers, now a spectral symphony, guided them toward a spectral entity that awaited in the hidden corners of the chamber. The old house, a silent witness to the unfolding darkness, seemed to sigh with a spectral resignation.

With a sense of urgency, Sheila and Rob fumbled for their flashlights, attempting to pierce the veil of darkness that surrounded them.

The whispers, though chaotic, spoke of an ancient evil that sought communion with the living. The hidden chamber, now a battleground between the mortal and the supernatural, became a place where the boundaries between reality and the abyss blurred.

As their flashlights flickered to life, Sheila and Rob beheld a chilling sight—a spectral entity, its form indistinct in the shadows, stood before them. The whispers, now a haunting melody, spoke of an ancient evil that had been awakened by their presence. The old house, a conduit for the malevolent forces, bore silent witness to the spectral encounter that unfolded in the hidden chamber.

The entity, a manifestation of the ancient evil that had lingered within the old house, seemed to reach out from the shadows. The whispers, now a dissonant chorus, urged Sheila and Rob to confront the malevolent force that awaited in the spectral realm. The old house, though temporarily quelled, stood as a gateway to a darkness that defied rational explanation.

With a surge of supernatural power, the entity confronted Sheila and Rob. The whispers, now a mournful hymn, seemed to align with the malevolent force as the spectral encounter reached its zenith. The old house, its foundations saturated with the essence of the living, became a battleground where the living and the dead converged in a macabre dance of supernatural entanglement.

Sheila and Rob, entwined in the spectral tapestry, felt the weight of unseen eyes upon them. The whispers, now a relentless drone, seemed to echo through the hidden chamber—a spectral symphony that reverberated through the haunted dwelling. The old house, its spectral foundations shaken by the malevolent revelation, stood at the precipice of a new, horrifying chapter in its dark history.

As the entity reached out with spectral tendrils, Sheila and Rob, driven by an unspoken determination, faced the malevolent force with a courage born of desperation. The whispers, though chaotic, guided them through the spectral encounter—a dance between the living and the abyss. The old house, a silent witness to the unfolding darkness,

stood as a battleground where the forces of the supernatural and the mortal clashed in a terrifying crescendo.

In the dim light of the hidden chamber, a struggle unfolded—a battle between the living and the spectral entity that sought communion with the living. The whispers, now a spectral symphony, intensified as Sheila and Rob confronted the ancient evil that had been awakened by their presence. The old house, its foundations saturated with the essence of the living, became a crucible where the boundaries between reality and the abyss blurred.

With a surge of supernatural energy, Sheila and Rob channeled the remnants of the sacrificial ritual into a desperate confrontation with the entity. The whispers, now a haunting melody, seemed to align with the living as the spectral encounter reached its climax. The old house, a silent witness to the unfolding darkness, stood as a testament to the resilience of those who dared to confront the malevolent forces that lurked within its haunted halls.

As the spectral entity recoiled, the whispers, now a fading memory, left an eerie stillness in their wake. Sheila and Rob, exhausted and shaken, stood amidst the spectral remnants of the hidden chamber. The old house, though still haunted by the echoes of the past, seemed to sigh with a spectral resignation.

The supernatural realm, now devoid of the malevolent entity that had sought communion with the living, unfolded with an unsettling stillness. Sheila and Rob, their courage tested by the spectral encounter, ascended from the hidden chamber and returned to the haunted halls of the old house. The air, though laden with the remnants of the supernatural battle, felt lighter as if a temporary reprieve had been granted.

Little did they know that the true horror, a revelation that would redefine the very fabric of their existence, awaited in the shadows of their newfound victory. The old house, though temporarily quelled, held secrets that would unveil themselves in a chilling twist of fate—one that would test the limits of Sheila and Rob's resilience and plunge them into a darkness from which there might be no escape.

The whispers, now a fading memory, left the door ajar for the looming terror that awaited in the aftermath of the spectral storm. The old house, its haunted corridors pulsating with unresolved sorrows, stood as a gateway to a supernatural abyss. Sheila and Rob, bound by the malevolent forces that lingered within, faced an uncertain future where the horrors of the past cast a long, lingering shadow over their fragile grasp on reality.

Chapter 11: The Escape

Having confronted the malevolent forces in the hidden chamber, Sheila and Rob ascended from the basement, their nerves on edge from the spectral encounter. The air in the old house, though momentarily relieved of the oppressive darkness, still held a spectral tension—a silent reminder of the horrors that lurked within its haunted halls. Unbeknownst to them, a new chapter of terror awaited as the old house seemed to cling to the malevolence that had taken root in its very foundations.

As they emerged into the dim light of the living room, Sheila and Rob exchanged glances laden with unspoken fear. The whispers, though muted, seemed to linger in the air like a haunting refrain. The old house, its spectral corridors echoing with the echoes of the past, stood as a silent witness to the unfolding nightmare that awaited the unwitting inhabitants.

A sense of urgency gripped Sheila as her gaze once again fell upon the basement door—the same door that had led them to the depths of the supernatural realm. The whispers, though subdued, seemed to guide her attention toward the subterranean depths where forgotten rituals had once unfolded. The basement, now a nexus of malevolence, beckoned them to confront the unresolved mysteries that lingered within.

Rob, his nerves still raw from the spectral encounter, hesitated as Sheila approached the basement door. The air, though seemingly calm, carried a spectral resonance that hinted at the lingering darkness within the haunted dwelling. The old house, a silent observer to the unfolding

terror, seemed to pulse with an unseen force that transcended the boundaries of the living and the dead.

With a sense of trepidation, Sheila opened the basement door, revealing the wooden stairs that led to the subterranean depths. The whispers, now a faint murmur, seemed to echo through the haunted halls, guiding them toward the heart of the encroaching darkness. The old house, though momentarily quelled, held secrets that demanded further exploration—a revelation that would test the limits of Sheila and Rob's resilience.

As they descended into the dimly lit basement, the air felt heavy with an otherworldly energy. The whispers, though muted, seemed to guide Sheila and Rob toward the epicenter of the supernatural storm. The old house, its spectral foundations saturated with the essence of the living, became a conduit for the malevolent forces that sought communion with the unwitting inhabitants.

In the basement, the artifacts of forgotten rituals lay in shadowed corners, silent witnesses to the malevolence that had once thrived within the haunted dwelling. The whispers, though fragmented, spoke of a lingering darkness that refused to be fully contained. The old house, a spectral battleground, seemed to pulse with an unseen force that beckoned Sheila and Rob to delve deeper into the abyss.

As they ventured into the basement's depths, Sheila's flashlight revealed a hidden passage—a secret corridor that led to unexplored realms within the haunted dwelling. The whispers, though haunting, guided them toward a revelation that transcended the boundaries of the living and the dead. The old house, now a labyrinth of malevolence, became a spectral tapestry where the living and the abyss converged in an eerie dance.

A sudden drop in temperature signaled a shift in the atmosphere. The whispers, now a haunting lament, guided Sheila and Rob toward an ancient doorway—an entrance to a forgotten chamber that had eluded their previous exploration. The old house, though momentarily

quelled, seemed to cling to the malevolent forces that lurked within its spectral depths.

With trepidation, Sheila and Rob opened the ancient doorway, revealing a chamber bathed in an unnatural darkness. The air, thick with the scent of ancient incense, seemed to vibrate with the echoes of spectral energy. The whispers, now a dissonant symphony, spoke of a deeper layer of malevolence that awaited discovery.

In the dim light, Sheila and Rob stumbled upon an ancient altar—an occult relic that held the secrets of forbidden rituals. The whispers, though chaotic, urged Sheila to decipher the cryptic symbols that adorned the altar. The malevolent legacy, though temporarily quelled, seemed to find its voice in the ancient rites that unfolded in the flickering light.

As Sheila and Rob examined the altar, a sudden gust of wind extinguished their flashlights, plunging the chamber into complete darkness. The whispers, now a relentless drone, merged with the shadows that danced in the spectral realm. The old house, its spectral foundations saturated with the essence of the living, stood at the precipice of a new, malevolent revelation.

In the darkness, Sheila and Rob felt an unseen force closing in around them. The whispers, now a spectral symphony, guided them toward a spectral entity that awaited in the hidden corners of the chamber. The old house, a silent witness to the unfolding darkness, seemed to sigh with a spectral resignation.

With a sense of urgency, Sheila and Rob fumbled for their flashlights, attempting to pierce the veil of darkness that surrounded them. The whispers, though chaotic, spoke of an ancient evil that sought communion with the living. The hidden chamber, now a battleground between the mortal and the supernatural, became a place where the boundaries between reality and the abyss blurred.

As their flashlights flickered to life, Sheila and Rob beheld a chilling sight—a spectral entity, its form indistinct in the shadows, stood before them. The whispers, now a haunting melody, spoke of an ancient evil

that had been awakened by their presence. The old house, a conduit for the malevolent forces, bore silent witness to the spectral encounter that unfolded in the hidden chamber.

The entity, a manifestation of the ancient evil that had lingered within the old house, seemed to reach out from the shadows. The whispers, now a dissonant chorus, urged Sheila and Rob to confront the malevolent force that awaited in the spectral realm. The old house, though temporarily quelled, stood as a gateway to a darkness that defied rational explanation.

With a surge of supernatural power, the entity confronted Sheila and Rob. The whispers, now a mournful hymn, seemed to align with the malevolent force as the spectral encounter reached its zenith. The old house, its foundations saturated with the essence of the living, became a battleground where the living and the dead converged in a macabre dance.

Sheila and Rob, entwined in the spectral tapestry, felt the weight of unseen eyes upon them. The whispers, now a relentless drone, seemed to echo through the hidden chamber—a spectral symphony that reverberated through the haunted dwelling. The old house, its spectral foundations shaken by the malevolent revelation, stood at the precipice of a new, horrifying chapter in its dark history.

As the entity reached out with spectral tendrils, Sheila and Rob, driven by an unspoken determination, faced the malevolent force with a courage born of desperation. The whispers, though chaotic, guided them through the spectral encounter—a dance between the living and the abyss. The old house, a silent witness to the unfolding darkness, stood as a battleground where the forces of the supernatural and the mortal clashed in a terrifying crescendo.

In the dim light of the hidden chamber, a struggle unfolded—a battle between the living and the spectral entity that sought communion with the living. The whispers, now a spectral symphony, intensified as Sheila and Rob confronted the ancient evil that had been awakened by their presence. The old house, its foundations saturated with the essence of

the living, became a crucible where the boundaries between reality and the abyss blurred.

With a surge of supernatural energy, Sheila and Rob channeled the remnants of the sacrificial ritual into a desperate confrontation with the entity. The whispers, now a haunting melody, seemed to align with the living as the spectral encounter reached its climax. The old house, a silent witness to the unfolding darkness, stood as a testament to the resilience of those who dared to confront the malevolent forces that lurked within its haunted halls.

As the spectral entity recoiled, the whispers, now a fading memory, left an eerie stillness in their wake. Sheila and Rob, exhausted and shaken, stood amidst the spectral remnants of the hidden chamber. The old house, though still haunted by the echoes of the past, seemed to sigh with a spectral resignation.

The supernatural realm, now devoid of the malevolent entity that had sought communion with the living, unfolded with an unsettling stillness. Sheila and Rob, their courage tested by the spectral encounter, ascended from the hidden chamber and returned to the haunted halls of the old house. The air, though laden with the remnants of the supernatural battle, felt lighter as if a temporary reprieve had been granted.

Little did they know that the true horror, a revelation that would redefine the very fabric of their existence, awaited in the shadows of their newfound victory. The old house, though temporarily quelled, held secrets that would unveil themselves in a chilling twist of fate—one that would test the limits of Sheila and Rob's resilience and plunge them into a darkness from which there might be no escape.

The whispers, now a fading memory, left the door ajar for the looming terror that awaited in the aftermath of the spectral storm. The old house, its haunted corridors pulsating with unresolved sorrows, stood as a gateway to a supernatural abyss. Sheila and Rob, bound by the malevolent forces that lingered within, faced an uncertain future where the horrors of the past cast a long, lingering shadow over their fragile grasp on reality.

Chapter 12: The Attacks

As Sheila and Rob emerged from the hidden chamber, a sense of unease lingered in the air. The old house, though temporarily quelled by their confrontation with the spectral entity, exuded an eerie calm that belied the malevolence buried within its haunted corridors. Unbeknownst to the shaken inhabitants, the aftermath of the ritual had set into motion a series of paranormal attacks that would test the limits of their courage and resilience.

The whispers, though muted, seemed to carry a warning—a spectral echo of the malevolent forces that still clung to the very fabric of the old house. Sheila and Rob, their nerves raw from the supernatural encounter, exchanged wary glances as they navigated the dimly lit halls. The air, laden with the remnants of the spectral battle, became a spectral tapestry where the living and the dead converged in an unsettling dance.

As night fell over the old house, Sheila found herself alone in the living room. The whispers, now a distant murmur, seemed to beckon her toward the spectral energies that lingered within the haunted dwelling. The old house, a silent witness to the unfolding nightmare, held secrets that awaited discovery—a revelation that would thrust Sheila into a harrowing series of paranormal attacks.

The attacks began subtly—a flickering of lights, objects moving mysteriously, and an unshakable feeling of being watched. Sheila, though initially dismissive, couldn't ignore the mounting sense of dread that accompanied these strange occurrences. The whispers, now a haunting melody, seemed to intensify as if heralding the approach of an unseen malevolence.

One night, as Sheila lay in bed, the attacks escalated. Shadows danced on the walls, and an otherworldly chill permeated the room. The whispers, now a dissonant chorus, filled the air with a spectral energy that seemed to converge around her. The old house, its foundations saturated with the essence of the living, became a battleground where the forces of the supernatural sought communion with the unsuspecting inhabitants.

Sheila, gripped by a growing terror, sought solace in the presence of Rob. Together, they confronted the escalating attacks, attempting to rationalize the paranormal occurrences that defied logical explanation. The old house, though momentarily quelled, seemed to pulse with an unseen force that defied the boundaries of the mortal realm.

The attacks took a violent turn, as unseen forces hurled objects across the room and ominous shadows seemed to reach out from the spectral realm. Sheila and Rob, their nerves stretched to the breaking point, struggled to maintain their grasp on reality. The whispers, now a relentless drone, echoed through the haunted halls, guiding the malevolent forces in their torment of the unsuspecting inhabitants.

Desperate for answers, Sheila delved into her research, revisiting the ancient tome and the diary that chronicled the house's dark history. The whispers, though fragmented, seemed to offer cryptic clues that hinted at a malevolent presence seeking revenge. The old house, its haunted corridors echoing with the sorrows of the past, held the key to understanding the origins of the supernatural attacks.

In their quest for answers, Sheila and Rob enlisted the help of a local paranormal investigator. The whispers, now a spectral symphony, seemed to intensify as the investigator delved into the history of the old house. The malevolent forces, though temporarily restrained, resisted the intrusion, escalating the attacks in retaliation.

The investigator, a skeptic turned believer, witnessed the paranormal onslaught firsthand. Doors slammed shut, eerie whispers reverberated through the halls, and unseen hands seemed to grab at those who dared to venture into the haunted dwelling. The old house, now a battleground for the living and the supernatural, exuded a malevolence that defied rational explanation.

In a desperate attempt to quell the attacks, Sheila and Rob decided to hold a seance—an act that would either provide answers or further provoke the wrath of the malevolent forces. The whispers, now a haunting lament, seemed to guide them toward the living room where the seance would take place. The old house, its spectral foundations

shaken by the paranormal onslaught, awaited the unfolding ritual with a spectral resignation.

As the seance began, the air in the living room became charged with an otherworldly energy. The whispers, now a cacophony of spectral voices, spoke of the ancient evil that sought communion with the living. The old house, its haunted halls bearing witness to the unfolding ritual, seemed to sigh with a spectral anticipation.

Suddenly, the room plunged into darkness, and a chilling wind swept through the living room. The whispers, now a spectral chorus, guided Sheila and Rob toward a revelation that transcended the boundaries of the living and the dead. The old house, its foundations saturated with the essence of the living, became a conduit for the malevolent forces that sought release through the seance.

In the darkness, Sheila felt an unseen presence—the very embodiment of the malevolence that had plagued the old house. The whispers, now a mournful hymn, seemed to echo through the spectral realm as the ancient evil made itself known. The old house, a witness to the unfolding ritual, stood at the precipice of a terrifying revelation.

The entity, a manifestation of the supernatural forces, spoke through the seance—a voice that sent shivers down the spines of those present. The whispers, now a spectral symphony, conveyed the entity's grievances and the reasons behind the relentless attacks. The old house, its spectral foundations saturated with the essence of the living, became a stage for the malevolent forces to voice their unholy intentions.

As the seance reached its climax, Sheila and Rob faced a choice—succumb to the malevolent forces or confront the entity head-on. The whispers, now a haunting melody, seemed to offer a glimmer of hope amidst the overwhelming darkness. The old house, its haunted corridors pulsating with the echoes of the past, awaited the resolution of the supernatural conflict that unfolded within its spectral confines.

With determination born of desperation, Sheila and Rob confronted the entity. The whispers, now a spectral chorus, guided them through the confrontation—a dance between the living and the abyss. The old

house, a silent witness to the unfolding darkness, stood as a battleground where the forces of the supernatural and the mortal clashed in a terrifying crescendo.

As Sheila and Rob faced the entity, a surge of supernatural energy filled the room. The whispers, now a relentless drone, seemed to align with the living as the spectral encounter reached its zenith. The old house, its foundations saturated with the essence of the living, became a crucible where the boundaries between reality and the abyss blurred.

In the dim light of the living room, a struggle unfolded—a battle between the living and the malevolent entity that sought communion with the living. The whispers, now a spectral symphony, intensified as Sheila and Rob confronted the ancient evil that had been awakened by their presence. The old house, its haunted foundations shaken by the paranormal conflict, stood as a testament to the resilience of those who dared to confront the malevolent forces that lurked within its spectral halls.

As the entity recoiled, the whispers, now a fading memory, left an eerie stillness in their wake. Sheila and Rob, exhausted and shaken, stood amidst the spectral remnants of the seance. The old house, though still haunted by the echoes of the past, seemed to sigh with a spectral resignation.

The supernatural realm, now devoid of the entity that had sought communion with the living, unfolded with an unsettling stillness. Sheila and Rob, their courage tested by the spectral encounter, navigated the haunted halls of the old house. The air, though laden with the remnants of the paranormal conflict, felt lighter as if a temporary reprieve had been granted.

Little did they know that the true horror, a revelation that would redefine the very fabric of their existence, awaited in the shadows of their newfound victory. The old house, though temporarily quelled, held secrets that would unveil themselves in a chilling twist of fate—one that would test the limits of Sheila and Rob's resilience and plunge them into a darkness from which there might be no escape.

The whispers, now a fading memory, left the door ajar for the looming terror that awaited in the aftermath of the supernatural onslaught. The old house, its haunted corridors pulsating with unresolved sorrows, stood as a gateway to a supernatural abyss. Sheila and Rob, bound by the malevolent forces that lingered within, faced an uncertain future where the horrors of the past cast a long, lingering shadow over their fragile grasp on reality.

Chapter 13: The Seance

As the aftermath of the paranormal attacks lingered in the old house, Sheila and Rob, driven by a desperate need for answers, decided to delve deeper into the supernatural realm. The whispers, though diminished, seemed to guide them toward a fateful decision—the summoning of forces beyond their understanding through a seance. The old house, its haunted corridors pulsating with unresolved sorrows, awaited the unfolding ritual with a spectral anticipation.

Sheila and Rob gathered in the living room, surrounded by flickering candles and the musty scent of ancient incense. The whispers, now a distant murmur, seemed to converge around them as they prepared for the seance. The air in the room became charged with an otherworldly energy, and the old house, a silent witness to the unfolding ritual, stood at the precipice of a new, unsettling chapter.

The seance began with the chanting of incantations from an ancient tome Sheila had found in her research. The whispers, now a haunting lament, filled the room with a spectral resonance that transcended the boundaries of the living and the dead. The old house, its spectral foundations saturated with the essence of the living, became a conduit for the malevolent forces that awaited release through the ritual.

As the incantations echoed through the room, a sudden drop in temperature signaled the arrival of unseen entities. The whispers, now a spectral symphony, seemed to guide Sheila and Rob toward a revelation that defied rational explanation. The old house, its haunted halls bearing witness to the unfolding ritual, exuded a spectral energy that reached beyond the mortal realm.

In the dim light, Sheila and Rob felt an otherworldly presence—the very embodiment of the malevolence that had plagued the old house. The whispers, now a dissonant chorus, urged them to maintain their focus as the spectral entities made themselves known. The old house, a stage for the supernatural forces, stood as a gateway to a darkness that defied comprehension.

As the seance continued, the room filled with eerie whispers, shadows danced on the walls, and an unseen force seemed to grip those present. Sheila and Rob, their senses heightened by the supernatural energies, felt the weight of unseen eyes upon them. The old house, its spectral foundations shaken by the unfolding ritual, became a battleground where the living and the abyss converged in an unsettling dance.

Suddenly, the room plunged into darkness, and an otherworldly wind swept through the living room. The whispers, now a relentless drone, guided Sheila and Rob toward the epicenter of the spectral storm. The old house, though momentarily quelled, seemed to pulse with an unseen force that defied the boundaries of the mortal realm.

In the darkness, Sheila and Rob glimpsed shadowy figures—apparitions of the past that materialized in the spectral realm. The whispers, now a spectral chorus, spoke of the tormented souls that lingered within the haunted dwelling. The old house, its haunted corridors echoing with the sorrows of the past, became a tapestry of spectral entities seeking release through the seance.

As the apparitions manifested, the room resonated with their ethereal presence. The whispers, now a haunting melody, conveyed the grievances of the tormented souls that sought communion with the living. The old house, a conduit for the spectral forces, bore witness to the unfolding drama between the mortal and the supernatural.

Amidst the spectral symphony, Sheila and Rob felt a sudden shift—a malevolent entity seizing the opportunity to make its presence known. The whispers, now a dissonant chorus, guided them toward a revelation that sent shivers down their spines. The old house, its spectral

foundations saturated with the essence of the living, stood as a stage for the malevolent force that awaited confrontation.

The entity, a manifestation of the ancient evil that lingered within the old house, spoke through the seance—a voice that echoed with a chilling resonance. The whispers, now a mournful hymn, conveyed the entity's grievances and the reasons behind the relentless attacks. The old house, its haunted halls bearing witness to the unfolding ritual, seemed to sigh with a spectral anticipation.

Sheila and Rob, their senses overwhelmed by the supernatural onslaught, faced a choice—succumb to the malevolent forces or confront the entity head-on. The whispers, now a haunting melody, seemed to offer a glimmer of hope amidst the overwhelming darkness. The old house, its haunted corridors pulsating with the echoes of the past, awaited the resolution of the supernatural conflict that unfolded within its spectral confines.

With determination born of desperation, Sheila and Rob confronted the entity. The whispers, now a spectral chorus, guided them through the confrontation—a dance between the living and the abyss. The old house, a silent witness to the unfolding darkness, stood as a battleground where the forces of the supernatural and the mortal clashed in a terrifying crescendo.

As Sheila and Rob faced the entity, a surge of supernatural energy filled the room. The whispers, now a relentless drone, seemed to align with the living as the spectral encounter reached its zenith. The old house, its foundations saturated with the essence of the living, became a crucible where the boundaries between reality and the abyss blurred.

In the dim light of the living room, a struggle unfolded—a battle between the living and the malevolent entity that sought communion with the living. The whispers, now a spectral symphony, intensified as Sheila and Rob confronted the ancient evil that had been awakened by their presence. The old house, its haunted foundations shaken by the paranormal conflict, stood as a testament to the resilience of those

who dared to confront the malevolent forces that lurked within its spectral halls.

As the entity recoiled, the whispers, now a fading memory, left an eerie stillness in their wake. Sheila and Rob, exhausted and shaken, stood amidst the spectral remnants of the seance. The old house, though still haunted by the echoes of the past, seemed to sigh with a spectral resignation.

The supernatural realm, now devoid of the entity that had sought communion with the living, unfolded with an unsettling stillness. Sheila and Rob, their courage tested by the spectral encounter, navigated the haunted halls of the old house. The air, though laden with the remnants of the paranormal conflict, felt lighter as if a temporary reprieve had been granted.

Little did they know that the true horror, a revelation that would redefine the very fabric of their existence, awaited in the shadows of their newfound victory. The old house, though temporarily quelled, held secrets that would unveil themselves in a chilling twist of fate—one that would test the limits of Sheila and Rob's resilience and plunge them into a darkness from which there might be no escape.

The whispers, now a fading memory, left the door ajar for the looming terror that awaited in the aftermath of the supernatural onslaught. The old house, its haunted corridors pulsating with unresolved sorrows, stood as a gateway to a supernatural abyss. Sheila and Rob, bound by the malevolent forces that lingered within, faced an uncertain future where the horrors of the past cast a long, lingering shadow over their fragile grasp on reality.

Chapter 14: The Cleansing

In the wake of the seance, Sheila and Rob, still reeling from the otherworldly encounter, found themselves at a crossroads. The old house, though momentarily relieved of the malevolent entity's presence, exuded an eerie calm that hinted at the lingering supernatural forces within its haunted walls. Determined to put an end to the paranormal onslaught, Sheila sought the guidance of a psychic medium—an expert

in the arcane arts who might hold the key to cleansing the ancient dwelling.

The whispers, now a faint echo of the malevolence that had permeated the old house, guided Sheila and Rob toward the psychic medium's secluded residence. The air, heavy with the remnants of the spectral storm, carried a spectral resonance that seemed to converge around them. The old house, its spectral foundations saturated with the essence of the living, became a distant backdrop to the unfolding quest for purification.

The psychic medium, a mysterious figure with a demeanor that mirrored the enigmatic forces surrounding the old house, welcomed Sheila and Rob into a dimly lit room adorned with mystical artifacts. The whispers, now a haunting melody, seemed to intensify in the presence of the psychic medium. The air became charged with an otherworldly energy as the cleansing ritual began.

As the psychic medium delved into the spiritual realm, Sheila and Rob felt a shift in the atmosphere. The whispers, now a spectral symphony, guided the medium's hands as they moved through intricate gestures, channeling supernatural forces to cleanse the old house of its malevolent energies. The haunted dwelling, a silent witness to the unfolding ritual, awaited the purifying touch of the arcane.

Suddenly, the room quivered with unseen energies. Shadows danced on the walls, and the air vibrated with a spectral resonance. The whispers, now a dissonant chorus, echoed through the room, carrying the remnants of the malevolent entity's presence. The old house, though momentarily quelled, seemed to resist the cleansing as if clinging to the dark energies that had taken root within its spectral depths.

As the cleansing ritual continued, Sheila and Rob witnessed a manifestation of spectral mists swirling through the room. The whispers, now a relentless drone, seemed to speak of the ancient sorrows that clung to the old house like a malevolent shroud. The psychic medium, undeterred by the supernatural turbulence, pressed on with the purifying incantations.

In the dim light, Sheila and Rob glimpsed fleeting apparitions—the tormented souls that lingered within the old house. The whispers, now a haunting lament, carried the voices of the restless spirits seeking release through the cleansing ritual. The haunted dwelling, its spectral foundations shaken by the purifying energies, became a nexus where the living and the dead converged in an otherworldly dance.

Unexpectedly, the psychic medium's eyes glazed over, and her voice took on an otherworldly resonance. The whispers, now a mournful hymn, spoke through the medium, conveying the grievances of the ancient spirits that had been disturbed by the malevolent entity. The old house, a conduit for the spectral forces, bore silent witness to the spectral communion that unfolded in the purifying ritual.

As the psychic medium channeled the spirits, Sheila and Rob felt a surge of supernatural energy coursing through the room. The whispers, now a spectral chorus, guided them toward a revelation that transcended the boundaries of the living and the dead. The old house, though momentarily quelled, seemed to sigh with a spectral resignation as the purifying energies sought to dispel the malevolent forces that clung to its haunted corridors.

The psychic medium, still in the grip of the supernatural trance, uttered cryptic words that seemed to unlock the secrets of the old house's dark history. The whispers, now a dissonant symphony, guided Sheila and Rob toward a hidden chamber—an ancient sanctum where forgotten rituals had once unfolded. The haunted dwelling, its spectral foundations saturated with the essence of the living, became a battleground for the living and the supernatural.

As the purifying ritual reached its climax, Sheila and Rob, entranced by the spectral energies, witnessed a spectral convergence. The whispers, now a spectral melody, spoke of the ancient rituals that had bound the malevolent forces to the old house. The psychic medium, still in communion with the spirits, channeled the supernatural energies toward the heart of the spectral storm.

A sudden burst of light illuminated the room as the cleansing energies reached their zenith. The whispers, now a fading memory, left an eerie stillness in their wake. Sheila and Rob, their senses overwhelmed by the spectral convergence, stood amidst the remnants of the purifying ritual. The old house, though still haunted by the echoes of the past, seemed to sigh with a spectral resignation as if acknowledging the fleeting victory over the malevolent forces.

The psychic medium, released from the supernatural trance, conveyed the success of the cleansing ritual. The whispers, now a distant murmur, hinted at a temporary reprieve from the paranormal onslaught. The old house, its spectral foundations shaken by the purifying energies, awaited the aftermath of the cleansing—a revelation that would test the limits of Sheila and Rob's resilience and unravel the mysteries hidden within its haunted corridors.

As Sheila and Rob left the psychic medium's residence, a sense of cautious hope lingered in the air. The whispers, now a faint echo of the supernatural forces, guided them back to the old house—the battleground where the forces of the living and the dead had clashed in a spectral dance. The haunted dwelling, though momentarily relieved of the malevolent entity's presence, held secrets that awaited unraveling as the aftermath of the cleansing ritual cast a spectral light on the mysteries that lay hidden within its spectral confines.

Chapter 15: The Truth

With the cleansing ritual behind them, Sheila and Rob returned to the old house, hoping for a respite from the malevolent forces that had plagued them. The whispers, now a mere whisper of the supernatural energies that once gripped the haunted dwelling, guided them through the dimly lit halls. The air, heavy with the aftermath of the purifying ritual, carried a spectral resonance that hinted at the revelations awaiting them.

As Sheila and Rob explored the old house, a sense of cautious optimism settled over them. The whispers, though diminished, seemed to convey a temporary peace—a fragile equilibrium between the living

and the supernatural. The haunted dwelling, a silent witness to the unfolding events, exuded an eerie calm that belied the mysteries hidden within its spectral depths.

However, as night fell over the old house, an unsettling energy permeated the air. The whispers, now a distant murmur, hinted at a resurgence of the malevolent forces. Sheila and Rob, their nerves on edge, exchanged wary glances as they navigated the dimly lit corridors. The haunted dwelling, though momentarily quelled, held secrets that awaited revelation in the spectral silence of the night.

A series of cryptic symbols appeared on the walls—manifestations of the supernatural energies that lingered within the old house. The whispers, now a haunting melody, seemed to speak through the spectral symbols, conveying a message that defied rational explanation. The air, charged with an otherworldly energy, guided Sheila and Rob toward the heart of the spectral disturbance.

In the dim light, they discovered a hidden chamber—a forgotten sanctum where the malevolent rituals of the past had unfolded. The whispers, now a spectral symphony, intensified as Sheila and Rob delved into the secrets concealed within the ancient chamber. The haunted dwelling, its spectral foundations saturated with the essence of the living, became a tapestry where the past and present converged in an unsettling dance.

As they explored the hidden chamber, Sheila uncovered an old diary that chronicled the house's dark history. The whispers, now a dissonant chorus, guided her through the cryptic entries that spoke of occult rituals and malevolent forces bound to the old house. The air, thick with the residual energies of the past, carried a spectral resonance that transcended the boundaries of time.

The diary revealed a gruesome truth—the old house had been built for occult rituals, with a dark energy woven into its very walls. The whispers, now a relentless drone, conveyed the malevolent forces that had been awakened by the unwitting presence of Sheila and Rob. The haunted dwelling, a silent witness to the unfolding revelations, stood

as a testament to the ancient darkness that sought communion with the living.

As Sheila and Rob grappled with the horrifying truth, the whispers guided them toward a chilling realization—there was only one way to stop the malevolent forces that had been unleashed. The haunted dwelling, though momentarily quelled by the cleansing ritual, demanded a final sacrifice to seal the ancient evil that lurked within its spectral depths.

The revelation weighed heavily on Sheila's shoulders as she contemplated the harrowing decision that awaited her. The whispers, now a haunting lament, seemed to offer guidance through the darkness that enveloped the old house. The air, heavy with the echoes of the past, carried a spectral energy that transcended the mortal realm.

Determined to confront the malevolent forces head-on, Sheila and Rob sought counsel from the psychic medium who had guided them through the cleansing ritual. The whispers, now a spectral chorus, guided them to the medium's secluded residence, where the air buzzed with the residual energies of the supernatural encounter. The haunted dwelling, a distant backdrop to the unfolding quest, awaited the resolution of the spectral conflict that had gripped its haunted halls.

The psychic medium, aware of the lingering malevolence, spoke of the ancient ritual that could seal the evil presence within the old house. The whispers, now a spectral melody, seemed to convey the urgency of the impending sacrifice. The air, thick with the spectral energies, guided Sheila and Rob toward a path that would test the limits of their courage and resilience.

Sheila, faced with an unimaginable choice, grappled with the weight of the revelation. The whispers, now a dissonant symphony, urged her to confront the malevolent forces head-on. The haunted dwelling, its spectral foundations shaken by the impending decision, stood as a crucible where the boundaries between the living and the supernatural blurred.

As night fell over the old house, Sheila prepared for the ritual—a blood sacrifice that would bind the malevolent forces and seal the ancient evil within the spectral confines. The whispers, now a relentless drone, echoed through the haunted dwelling, guiding her toward the heart of the spectral storm. The air, heavy with the essence of the supernatural, carried a spectral resonance that transcended the mortal realm.

Rob, torn between loyalty and the impending sacrifice, stood by Sheila's side as she embraced her destiny. The whispers, now a haunting lament, seemed to offer solace in the face of the inevitable. The haunted dwelling, a silent witness to the unfolding ritual, exuded an eerie calm that belied the impending darkness.

In the dimly lit chamber, Sheila performed the ritual with a heavy heart. The whispers, now a spectral symphony, guided her through the ancient incantations that would bind the malevolent forces to the old house. The air, charged with an otherworldly energy, carried the weight of the sacrifice that would determine the fate of the haunted dwelling.

As Sheila completed the ritual, a surge of supernatural energy filled the room. The whispers, now a fading memory, left an eerie stillness in their wake. The haunted dwelling, though temporarily quelled, seemed to sigh with a spectral resignation. The air, thick with the remnants of the ritual, carried a spectral resonance that lingered in the haunted corridors.

In the aftermath of the sacrifice, Sheila and Rob, exhausted and shaken, emerged from the hidden chamber. The whispers, now a distant murmur, guided them through the dimly lit halls of the old house. The haunted dwelling, though momentarily relieved of the malevolent entity's presence, held secrets that awaited unraveling in the aftermath of the ritual.

As Sheila and Rob faced the uncertain aftermath, a chilling realization dawned upon them—the sacrifice, though sealing the ancient evil, had forever changed the fabric of their existence. The whispers, now a spectral chorus, seemed to convey the irreversible consequences of the harrowing ordeal. The haunted dwelling, a silent witness to the

unfolding aftermath, stood as a testament to the sacrifices made in the name of sealing the ancient darkness within its spectral confines.

Little did they know that the true horror, a revelation that would redefine their very existence, awaited in the shadows of the haunted dwelling. The whispers, now a fading memory, left the door ajar for the looming terror that awaited in the aftermath of the supernatural sacrifice. Sheila and Rob, bound by the malevolent forces that lingered within, faced an uncertain future where the horrors of the past cast a long, lingering shadow over their fragile grasp on reality.

Chapter 16: The Sacrifice

With the echoes of the ritual still reverberating through the old house, Sheila and Rob grappled with the aftermath of the harrowing sacrifice. The air, thick with the remnants of supernatural energies, carried a spectral resonance that seemed to linger in the haunted dwelling. The whispers, now a distant murmur, guided them through the dimly lit halls as they confronted the irreversible consequences of sealing the ancient evil within the spectral confines.

As Sheila and Rob emerged from the hidden chamber, an unsettling stillness enveloped the old house. The whispers, now a fading memory, left an eerie calm in their wake. The haunted dwelling, though momentarily relieved of the malevolent entity's presence, stood as a silent witness to the sacrifices made in the name of sealing the ancient darkness within its spectral corridors.

However, the calm was deceptive, for a greater malevolence seemed to seep through the very walls of the old house. The air, heavy with the essence of the supernatural, carried an ominous energy that hinted at the lingering darkness within. Sheila and Rob, their senses heightened by the aftermath of the sacrifice, exchanged wary glances as they navigated the dimly lit corridors.

Unbeknownst to them, the sacrifice had unleashed unforeseen consequences—unsettling manifestations that defied rational explanation. Shadows danced on the walls, and whispers, now a dissonant symphony, seemed to echo through the haunted dwelling, conveying a spectral

unrest that transcended the mortal realm. The old house, though momentarily quelled, stood as a battleground where the forces of the living and the supernatural clashed in an otherworldly dance.

As night fell over the old house, the spectral disturbances intensified. Objects moved mysteriously, and the air vibrated with a spectral resonance that hinted at a malevolent force lingering within the haunted dwelling. The whispers, now a relentless drone, guided Sheila and Rob toward the heart of the spectral storm—an impending confrontation with the consequences of the sacrifice.

In the dim light, Sheila and Rob felt an otherworldly presence—an entity that seemed to feed on the residual energies of the sacrificed blood. The whispers, now a haunting lament, spoke of a darkness that sought communion with the living, defying the constraints of the ritual. The haunted dwelling, its spectral foundations shaken by the consequences of the sacrifice, stood as a conduit for the malevolent forces that sought release.

As they explored the old house, Sheila and Rob discovered cryptic symbols appearing on the walls—a manifestation of the supernatural disturbances that had been unleashed. The whispers, now a spectral symphony, guided them through the haunted corridors, conveying the urgency of a greater darkness that loomed on the horizon. The air, charged with an otherworldly energy, carried a spectral resonance that hinted at the impending confrontation with the malevolent entity.

Sheila and Rob sought the guidance of the psychic medium who had assisted them in the cleansing ritual. The whispers, now a haunting melody, seemed to echo through the secluded residence of the medium, conveying the urgency of the situation. The air, thick with the residual energies of the supernatural encounter, guided them toward a revelation that defied comprehension.

The psychic medium, aware of the consequences of the sacrifice, spoke of a greater malevolence that had been awakened—an entity that defied the boundaries of the ritual. The whispers, now a relentless drone, urged Sheila and Rob to confront the looming darkness before

it consumed the haunted dwelling. The air, heavy with the essence of the supernatural, carried a spectral resonance that transcended the mortal realm.

Determined to face the consequences of their actions, Sheila and Rob returned to the old house, armed with newfound knowledge. The whispers, now a spectral chorus, seemed to align with their resolve as they ventured into the dimly lit halls. The haunted dwelling, though momentarily quelled, awaited the final confrontation with the malevolent entity that lingered within its spectral depths.

As night settled over the old house, Sheila and Rob felt the temperature drop—a chilling sign of the entity's presence. Shadows danced on the walls, and the air vibrated with a spectral resonance that hinted at the impending confrontation. The whispers, now a haunting lament, guided them toward the heart of the spectral storm—an epicenter where the forces of the living and the supernatural converged.

In the dim light, Sheila and Rob glimpsed fleeting apparitions—manifestations of the greater darkness that had been unleashed. The whispers, now a dissonant symphony, seemed to speak of a malevolence that sought communion with the living, defying the constraints of the ritual. The haunted dwelling, its spectral foundations saturated with the essence of the supernatural, stood as a battleground where the consequences of the sacrifice unfolded in a terrifying crescendo.

Suddenly, the room quivered with unseen energies, and the temperature plummeted. The whispers, now a spectral chorus, guided Sheila and Rob toward the epicenter of the supernatural disturbance. The air, charged with an otherworldly energy, carried a spectral resonance that hinted at the imminent confrontation with the malevolent entity.

As they approached the heart of the spectral storm, Sheila and Rob felt an oppressive force—a darkness that seemed to envelop them. The whispers, now a relentless drone, seemed to echo through the haunted dwelling, urging them to confront the malevolent entity that lurked within the shadows. The old house, though momentarily quelled, stood

as a stage for the final showdown between the forces of the living and the supernatural.

In the dimly lit chamber, Sheila and Rob confronted the malevolent entity. The whispers, now a haunting melody, guided them through the spectral encounter—a dance between the living and the abyss. The haunted dwelling, its spectral foundations shaken by the consequences of the sacrifice, became a crucible where the boundaries between reality and the supernatural blurred.

The entity, a manifestation of the ancient darkness that had been awakened, spoke through the spectral symphony. The whispers, now a dissonant chorus, conveyed the grievances and malevolence of the malevolent force that sought communion with the living. The haunted dwelling, a conduit for the supernatural forces, bore silent witness to the final showdown that unfolded within its spectral corridors.

Sheila and Rob, their senses heightened by the supernatural onslaught, faced a choice—succumb to the malevolent forces or confront the entity head-on. The whispers, now a relentless drone, urged them toward a revelation that defied comprehension. The haunted dwelling, its spectral foundations saturated with the essence of the living, stood as a battleground where the forces of the living and the supernatural clashed in a terrifying crescendo.

In the dim light, Sheila and Rob glimpsed shadowy figures—apparitions of the past that materialized in the spectral realm. The whispers, now a haunting lament, spoke of the tormented souls that lingered within the haunted dwelling. The air, charged with an otherworldly energy, guided them toward the epicenter of the spectral storm—an impending confrontation with the malevolent entity.

As the entity recoiled, the whispers, now a spectral chorus, intensified. Sheila and Rob, their resolve tested by the supernatural onslaught, faced the malevolent force with determination. The haunted dwelling, its spectral foundations shaken by the consequences of the sacrifice, became a silent witness to the final confrontation between the living and the supernatural.

With an otherworldly surge of energy, Sheila and Rob confronted the entity head-on. The whispers, now a relentless drone, seemed to align with the living as the spectral encounter reached its zenith. The haunted dwelling, its foundations saturated with the essence of the supernatural, stood as a crucible where the forces of light and darkness clashed in a terrifying crescendo.

Unexpectedly, the entity recoiled—a spectral manifestation weakened by the determination of the living. The whispers, now a fading memory, left an eerie stillness in their wake. Sheila and Rob, their senses overwhelmed by the supernatural encounter, stood amidst the remnants of the spectral storm. The haunted dwelling, though momentarily quelled, seemed to sigh with a spectral resignation as if acknowledging the fleeting victory over the malevolent forces.

As Sheila and Rob emerged from the confrontation, a sense of cautious hope lingered in the air. The whispers, now a distant murmur, guided them through the dimly lit halls of the old house—the battleground where the forces of the living had triumphed over the malevolent entity. The haunted dwelling, though forever scarred by the supernatural encounter, stood as a testament to the resilience of those who dared to confront the ancient darkness that lurked within its spectral confines.

Little did Sheila and Rob know that the true horror, a revelation that would redefine their very existence, awaited in the shadows of the haunted dwelling. The whispers, now a fading memory, left the door ajar for the looming terror that awaited in the aftermath of the supernatural sacrifice. Sheila and Rob, bound by the malevolent forces that lingered within, faced an uncertain future where the horrors of the past cast a long, lingering shadow over their fragile grasp on reality.

Chapter 17: The Confrontation

In the aftermath of the supernatural encounter, Sheila and Rob found themselves standing amidst the remnants of the spectral storm that had gripped the old house. The air, heavy with the essence of the supernatural, carried a spectral resonance that hinted at the lingering

forces within the haunted dwelling. The whispers, now a distant murmur, guided them through the dimly lit halls as they grappled with the aftermath of the harrowing confrontation.

As they explored the old house, Sheila and Rob felt a palpable tension—an unsettling energy that seemed to emanate from the very walls. Shadows danced on the walls, and the air vibrated with a spectral resonance that hinted at a lingering malevolence. The whispers, now a haunting lament, guided them toward the heart of the spectral disturbance—an impending confrontation with the consequences of the sacrifice.

Unbeknownst to them, the malevolent entity, though weakened, lingered within the haunted dwelling, seeking revenge for the disruption of its spectral communion. The air, thick with the essence of the supernatural, carried an ominous energy that hinted at the impending clash between the living and the lingering darkness. Sheila and Rob, their nerves on edge, exchanged wary glances as they ventured into the dimly lit corridors.

As night fell over the old house, the spectral disturbances intensified. Objects moved mysteriously, and the whispers, now a relentless drone, seemed to echo through the haunted dwelling. The air, charged with an otherworldly energy, guided Sheila and Rob toward the epicenter of the spectral storm—a confrontation with the malevolent forces that sought release.

In the dim light, Sheila and Rob discovered cryptic symbols appearing on the walls—a manifestation of the supernatural disturbances that had been unleashed. The whispers, now a spectral symphony, intensified as they delved into the haunted corridors, conveying the urgency of a greater darkness that loomed on the horizon. The old house, though momentarily quelled, stood as a battleground where the forces of the living and the supernatural clashed in an otherworldly dance.

Sheila and Rob sought the guidance of the psychic medium who had assisted them in the cleansing ritual. The whispers, now a haunting melody, seemed to echo through the secluded residence of the medium,

conveying the urgency of the situation. The air, thick with the residual energies of the supernatural encounter, guided them toward a revelation that defied comprehension.

The psychic medium, aware of the lingering malevolence, spoke of the entity's resilience—a force that defied the boundaries of the ritual. The whispers, now a relentless drone, urged Sheila and Rob to confront the looming darkness before it consumed the haunted dwelling. The air, heavy with the essence of the supernatural, carried a spectral resonance that transcended the mortal realm.

Determined to face the consequences of their actions, Sheila and Rob returned to the old house, armed with newfound knowledge. The whispers, now a spectral chorus, seemed to align with their resolve as they ventured into the dimly lit halls. The haunted dwelling, though momentarily quelled, awaited the final confrontation with the malevolent entity that lingered within its spectral depths.

As night settled over the old house, Sheila and Rob felt the temperature drop—a chilling sign of the entity's presence. Shadows danced on the walls, and the air vibrated with a spectral resonance that hinted at the impending confrontation. The whispers, now a haunting lament, guided them toward the heart of the spectral storm—an epicenter where the forces of the living and the supernatural converged.

In the dim light, Sheila and Rob glimpsed fleeting apparitions—manifestations of the greater darkness that had been unleashed. The whispers, now a dissonant symphony, seemed to speak of a malevolence that sought communion with the living, defying the constraints of the ritual. The haunted dwelling, its spectral foundations saturated with the essence of the supernatural, stood as a battleground where the consequences of the sacrifice unfolded in a terrifying crescendo.

Suddenly, the room quivered with unseen energies, and the temperature plummeted. The whispers, now a spectral chorus, guided Sheila and Rob toward the epicenter of the supernatural disturbance. The air, charged with an otherworldly energy, carried a spectral resonance that hinted at the imminent confrontation with the malevolent entity.

As they approached the heart of the spectral storm, Sheila and Rob felt an oppressive force—a darkness that seemed to envelop them. The whispers, now a relentless drone, seemed to echo through the haunted dwelling, urging them to confront the malevolent entity that lurked within the shadows. The old house, though momentarily quelled, stood as a stage for the final showdown between the forces of the living and the supernatural.

In the dimly lit chamber, Sheila and Rob confronted the malevolent entity. The whispers, now a haunting melody, guided them through the spectral encounter—a dance between the living and the abyss. The haunted dwelling, its spectral foundations shaken by the consequences of the sacrifice, became a crucible where the boundaries between reality and the supernatural blurred.

The entity, a manifestation of the ancient darkness that had been awakened, spoke through the spectral symphony. The whispers, now a dissonant chorus, conveyed the grievances and malevolence of the malevolent force that sought communion with the living. The haunted dwelling, a conduit for the supernatural forces, bore silent witness to the final showdown that unfolded within its spectral corridors.

Sheila and Rob, their senses heightened by the supernatural on-slaught, faced a choice—succumb to the malevolent forces or confront the entity head-on. The whispers, now a relentless drone, urged them toward a revelation that defied comprehension. The haunted dwelling, its spectral foundations saturated with the essence of the living, stood as a battleground where the forces of the living and the supernatural clashed in a terrifying crescendo.

In the dim light, Sheila and Rob glimpsed shadowy figures—apparitions of the past that materialized in the spectral realm. The whispers, now a haunting lament, spoke of the tormented souls that lingered within the haunted dwelling. The air, charged with an otherworldly energy, guided them toward the epicenter of the spectral storm—an impending confrontation with the malevolent entity.

As the entity recoiled, the whispers, now a spectral chorus, intensified. Sheila and Rob, their resolve tested by the supernatural onslaught, faced the malevolent force with determination. The haunted dwelling, its spectral foundations saturated with the essence of the supernatural, stood as a crucible where the forces of light and darkness clashed in a terrifying crescendo.

Unexpectedly, the entity recoiled—a spectral manifestation weakened by the determination of the living. The whispers, now a fading memory, left an eerie stillness in their wake. Sheila and Rob, their senses overwhelmed by the supernatural encounter, stood amidst the remnants of the spectral storm. The haunted dwelling, though momentarily quelled, seemed to sigh with a spectral resignation as if acknowledging the fleeting victory over the malevolent forces.

As Sheila and Rob emerged from the confrontation, a sense of cautious hope lingered in the air. The whispers, now a distant murmur, guided them through the dimly lit halls of the old house—the battleground where the forces of the living had triumphed over the malevolent entity. The haunted dwelling, though forever scarred by the supernatural encounter, stood as a testament to the resilience of those who dared to confront the ancient darkness that lurked within its spectral confines.

Little did Sheila and Rob know that the true horror, a revelation that would redefine their very existence, awaited in the shadows of the haunted dwelling. The whispers, now a fading memory, left the door ajar for the looming terror that awaited in the aftermath of the supernatural sacrifice. Sheila and Rob, bound by the malevolent forces that lingered within, faced an uncertain future where the horrors of the past cast a long, lingering shadow over their fragile grasp on reality.

Chapter 18: The Resolution

The aftermath of the confrontation left Sheila and Rob in a state of emotional turmoil. The air, thick with the remnants of the supernatural encounter, carried a spectral resonance that seemed to linger within the haunted dwelling. The whispers, now a distant murmur, guided

them through the dimly lit halls as they grappled with the irreversible consequences of the sacrifice and the lingering darkness that clung to the old house.

As they explored the haunted corridors, Sheila and Rob discovered that the malevolent entity, though weakened, had left an indelible mark on the spectral fabric of the old house. Shadows danced on the walls, and the air vibrated with a spectral resonance that hinted at the lingering malevolence. The whispers, now a haunting lament, guided them toward the heart of the spectral disturbance—an exploration of the haunted dwelling's newfound reality.

Unbeknownst to them, the sacrifice had not only sealed the ancient evil but had woven the malevolent forces into the very fabric of the haunted dwelling. The air, heavy with the essence of the supernatural, carried an ominous energy that hinted at the spectral unrest within. Sheila and Rob, their senses heightened by the aftermath of the confrontation, exchanged wary glances as they ventured into the dimly lit corridors.

As night fell over the old house, the spectral disturbances intensified. Objects moved mysteriously, and the whispers, now a relentless drone, seemed to echo through the haunted dwelling. The air, charged with an otherworldly energy, guided Sheila and Rob toward the epicenter of the spectral storm—a realization that the malevolent forces were not entirely quelled.

In the dim light, Sheila and Rob glimpsed cryptic symbols appearing on the walls—a manifestation of the supernatural disturbances that had been woven into the spectral fabric of the old house. The whispers, now a spectral symphony, intensified as they delved into the haunted corridors, conveying the urgency of a greater darkness that loomed on the horizon. The haunted dwelling, though momentarily quelled, stood as a battleground where the forces of the living and the supernatural clashed in an otherworldly dance.

Sheila and Rob sought the guidance of the psychic medium who had assisted them in the cleansing ritual. The whispers, now a haunting

melody, seemed to echo through the secluded residence of the medium, conveying the urgency of the situation. The air, thick with the residual energies of the supernatural encounter, guided them toward a revelation that defied comprehension.

The psychic medium, aware of the lingering malevolence, spoke of the residual energies that had become entwined with the old house's spectral fabric. The whispers, now a relentless drone, urged Sheila and Rob to confront the lingering darkness before it consumed the haunted dwelling. The air, heavy with the essence of the supernatural, carried a spectral resonance that transcended the mortal realm.

Determined to face the consequences of their actions, Sheila and Rob returned to the old house, armed with newfound knowledge. The whispers, now a spectral chorus, seemed to align with their resolve as they ventured into the dimly lit halls. The haunted dwelling, though momentarily quelled, awaited the final confrontation with the residual malevolent forces that lingered within its spectral depths.

As night settled over the old house, Sheila and Rob felt the temperature drop—a chilling sign of the residual entity's presence. Shadows danced on the walls, and the air vibrated with a spectral resonance that hinted at the impending confrontation. The whispers, now a haunting lament, guided them toward the heart of the spectral storm—an epicenter where the forces of the living and the supernatural converged.

In the dim light, Sheila and Rob glimpsed fleeting apparitions—manifestations of the residual darkness that clung to the haunted dwelling. The whispers, now a dissonant symphony, seemed to speak of a malevolence that sought communion with the living, defying the constraints of the ritual. The old house, though momentarily quelled, stood as a battleground where the consequences of the sacrifice unfolded in a terrifying crescendo.

Suddenly, the room quivered with unseen energies, and the temperature plummeted. The whispers, now a spectral chorus, guided Sheila and Rob toward the epicenter of the supernatural disturbance. The air, charged with an otherworldly energy, carried a spectral resonance

that hinted at the imminent confrontation with the residual malevolent forces.

As they approached the heart of the spectral storm, Sheila and Rob felt an oppressive force—a darkness that seemed to envelop them. The whispers, now a relentless drone, seemed to echo through the haunted dwelling, urging them to confront the lingering malevolent forces that lurked within the shadows. The old house, though momentarily quelled, stood as a stage for the final showdown between the forces of the living and the residual supernatural darkness.

In the dimly lit chamber, Sheila and Rob confronted the residual malevolent forces. The whispers, now a haunting melody, guided them through the spectral encounter—a dance between the living and the lingering abyss. The haunted dwelling, its spectral foundations shaken by the consequences of the sacrifice, became a crucible where the boundaries between reality and the residual supernatural blurred.

The residual entity, a manifestation of the ancient darkness that had been entwined with the spectral fabric, spoke through the dissonant chorus. The whispers, now a relentless drone, conveyed the grievances and malevolence of the lingering force that sought communion with the living. The haunted dwelling, a conduit for the residual supernatural forces, bore silent witness to the final showdown that unfolded within its spectral corridors.

Sheila and Rob, their senses heightened by the supernatural on-slaught, faced a choice—succumb to the lingering malevolent forces or confront the residual entity head-on. The whispers, now a relentless drone, urged them toward a revelation that defied comprehension. The haunted dwelling, its spectral foundations saturated with the essence of the living, stood as a battleground where the forces of the living and the residual supernatural clashed in a terrifying crescendo.

In the dim light, Sheila and Rob glimpsed shadowy figures—appa-ritions of the past that materialized in the spectral realm. The whispers, now a haunting lament, spoke of the tormented souls that lingered within the haunted dwelling. The air, charged with an otherworldly

energy, guided them toward the epicenter of the spectral storm—an impending confrontation with the residual malevolent entity.

As the entity recoiled, the whispers, now a spectral chorus, intensified. Sheila and Rob, their resolve tested by the supernatural onslaught, faced the residual malevolent force with determination. The haunted dwelling, its spectral foundations saturated with the essence of the supernatural, stood as a crucible where the forces of light and darkness clashed in a terrifying crescendo.

Unexpectedly, the residual entity recoiled—a spectral manifestation weakened by the determination of the living. The whispers, now a fading memory, left an eerie stillness in their wake. Sheila and Rob, their senses overwhelmed by the supernatural encounter, stood amidst the remnants of the residual spectral storm. The haunted dwelling, though momentarily quelled, seemed to sigh with a spectral resignation as if acknowledging the fleeting victory over the lingering malevolent forces.

As Sheila and Rob emerged from the confrontation, a sense of cautious hope lingered in the air. The whispers, now a distant murmur, guided them through the dimly lit halls of the old house—the battleground where the forces of the living had once again triumphed over the residual malevolent entity. The haunted dwelling, though forever scarred by the supernatural encounter, stood as a testament to the resilience of those who dared to confront the ancient darkness that lingered within its spectral confines.

Little did Sheila and Rob know that the true horror, a revelation that would redefine their very existence, awaited in the shadows of the haunted dwelling. The whispers, now a fading memory, left the door ajar for the looming terror that awaited in the aftermath of the supernatural sacrifice. Sheila and Rob, bound by the lingering forces that clung within, faced an uncertain future where the horrors of the past cast a long, lingering shadow over their fragile grasp on reality.

Chapter 19: The Awakening

As Sheila and Rob emerged from the lingering shadows of the haunted dwelling, a fragile sense of hope clung to the air. The whispers,

now a distant murmur, guided them through the dimly lit halls—the haunted battleground where they had confronted the malevolent forces and the residual darkness. However, the old house, forever scarred by the supernatural encounter, bore the weight of a haunting legacy that transcended the physical realm.

In the aftermath of the confrontation, Sheila and Rob felt a disquieting calm settle over the old house. The air, heavy with the essence of the supernatural, carried a spectral resonance that hinted at the lingering forces within the haunted dwelling. Shadows danced on the walls, and the whispers, now a fading memory, seemed to echo through the spectral corridors—an eerie reminder of the harrowing journey that had unfolded within the confines of the ancient dwelling.

Unbeknownst to them, the supernatural encounter had left an indelible mark on Sheila's soul. As night fell over the old house, a subtle shift occurred within Sheila—an awakening to a new reality that transcended the boundaries of the living. The whispers, now a distant melody, guided her through the haunted corridors, leading her toward a revelation that defied comprehension.

As they explored the old house, Sheila and Rob discovered that the residual energies had imprinted themselves onto the very fabric of Sheila's being. Shadows, now a spectral dance, seemed to weave through her existence, blurring the boundaries between the living and the supernatural. The whispers, now a haunting lament, echoed through her consciousness—an unsettling reminder that the spectral legacy lingered within.

In the dim light, Sheila and Rob witnessed cryptic symbols appearing on Sheila's skin—a manifestation of the supernatural imprint left by the ancient darkness. The whispers, now a spectral symphony, intensified as they delved into the haunted corridors, conveying the urgency of a greater awakening that loomed on the horizon. The old house, though momentarily quelled, stood as a conduit for Sheila's transformation—an evolution that defied the constraints of the mortal realm.

Sheila, grappling with the newfound reality, sought the guidance of the psychic medium who had assisted them in the cleansing ritual. The whispers, now a haunting melody, seemed to echo through the secluded residence of the medium, conveying the urgency of Sheila's awakening. The air, thick with the residual energies of the supernatural encounter, guided them toward a revelation that went beyond the haunted dwelling's spectral confines.

The psychic medium, attuned to the supernatural currents, spoke of Sheila's connection to the ancient darkness—an awakening that defied the boundaries of the ritual. The whispers, now a relentless drone, urged Sheila to embrace the spectral legacy within her. The air, heavy with the essence of the supernatural, carried a spectral resonance that transcended the mortal realm.

Determined to understand the extent of her transformation, Sheila returned to the old house, her senses heightened by the lingering supernatural energies. The whispers, now a spectral chorus, seemed to align with her evolving awareness as she ventured into the dimly lit halls. The haunted dwelling, though scarred by the supernatural encounter, awaited the next chapter in Sheila's journey—an odyssey that would redefine her very existence.

As night settled over the old house, Sheila felt the temperature drop—a chilling sign of her newfound connection to the lingering forces. Shadows danced on the walls, and the air vibrated with a spectral resonance that hinted at the awakening within her. The whispers, now a haunting lament, guided her toward the heart of the spectral storm—an epicenter where the forces of the living and the supernatural converged within her being.

In the dim light, Sheila glimpsed fleeting apparitions—manifestations of the ancient darkness that had become intertwined with her soul. The whispers, now a dissonant symphony, seemed to speak of a malevolence seeking communion with her, defying the constraints of the ritual. The old house, though momentarily quelled, stood as a

witness to Sheila's metamorphosis—an evolution that transcended the boundaries of the living.

Suddenly, the room quivered with unseen energies, and the temperature plummeted. The whispers, now a spectral chorus, intensified as Sheila confronted the epicenter of the supernatural disturbance within herself. The air, charged with an otherworldly energy, carried a spectral resonance that hinted at the imminent confrontation with the ancient darkness that had become a part of her very essence.

As Sheila approached the heart of the spectral storm within her, she felt an oppressive force—an awakening darkness that seemed to envelop her being. The whispers, now a relentless drone, echoed through her consciousness, urging her to confront the malevolent forces that lingered within the depths of her soul. Sheila, standing at the threshold of her own transformation, faced the haunting legacy that had become an integral part of her existence.

In the dimly lit chamber of her consciousness, Sheila confronted the residual malevolent forces that lingered within her. The whispers, now a haunting melody, guided her through the spectral encounter—a dance between her awakened self and the lingering abyss. The haunted dwelling, its spectral foundations shaken by the consequences of the sacrifice, became a crucible where the boundaries between Sheila's reality and the supernatural blurred.

The residual entity within Sheila, a manifestation of the ancient darkness, spoke through the spectral symphony within her soul. The whispers, now a dissonant chorus, conveyed the grievances and malevolence of the lingering force that sought communion with her. Sheila, in a surreal confrontation with her own awakening, faced the ancient darkness that had become intertwined with her very essence. The haunted dwelling, a conduit for the residual supernatural forces, bore silent witness to the final showdown within the depths of Sheila's consciousness.

As Sheila grappled with the malevolent forces within her, the whispers, now a relentless drone, urged her toward a revelation that defied comprehension. The haunted dwelling, its spectral foundations

saturated with the essence of Sheila's transformation, stood as a battleground where the forces of light and darkness clashed in a terrifying crescendo within the depths of her soul.

In the dim light, Sheila glimpsed shadowy figures—apparitions of the past that materialized in the spectral realm within her consciousness. The whispers, now a haunting lament, spoke of the tormented souls that lingered within her awakened self. The air, charged with an otherworldly energy, guided her toward the epicenter of the spectral storm—an impending confrontation with the malevolent entity that had become an integral part of her very existence.

As Sheila confronted the entity within, the whispers, now a spectral chorus, intensified. Her resolve tested by the supernatural onslaught, she faced the residual malevolent force with determination. The haunted dwelling, its spectral foundations saturated with the essence of the supernatural, stood as a crucible where the forces of light and darkness clashed in a terrifying crescendo within the depths of Sheila's soul.

Unexpectedly, the residual entity within Sheila recoiled—a spectral manifestation weakened by her determination to overcome the malevolent forces. The whispers, now a fading memory, left an eerie stillness in the chambers of her consciousness. Sheila, her senses overwhelmed by the supernatural encounter within, stood amidst the remnants of the spectral storm that had unfolded within her soul. The haunted dwelling, though momentarily quelled, seemed to sigh with a spectral resignation as if acknowledging the fleeting victory over the lingering malevolent forces.

As Sheila emerged from the depths of her own awakening, a sense of cautious hope lingered in the air. The whispers, now a distant murmur, guided her through the dimly lit halls of her own consciousness—the battleground where she had triumphed over the malevolent forces within. The haunted dwelling, forever scarred by the supernatural encounter, stood as a testament to the resilience of the human spirit and the capacity to confront the ancient darkness that lurked within one's own soul.

Little did Sheila know that her journey was far from over. The whispers, now a fading memory, left the door ajar for the looming terror that awaited in the aftermath of her awakening. Sheila, forever changed by the harrowing ordeal within herself, faced an uncertain future where the horrors of her own past cast a long, lingering shadow over her fragile grasp on reality. The haunted dwelling, a reflection of her awakened soul, awaited the next chapter in Sheila's journey—a journey that would redefine the very fabric of her existence.

Chapter 20: The Return

In the aftermath of Sheila's awakening, a deceptive calm settled over the old house. The air, thick with the remnants of the supernatural encounter within her soul, carried an unsettling resonance that hinted at the depths of her transformation. The whispers, now a distant murmur, guided Sheila through the dimly lit halls—a haunting reminder of the malevolent forces that lingered within her awakened self.

As night fell over the old house, Sheila's senses heightened, attuned to the subtle shifts in the spectral currents that surrounded her. Shadows danced on the walls, and the air vibrated with a spectral resonance that hinted at the lingering darkness within her. The whispers, now a fading memory, seemed to echo through the haunted corridors—an ominous prelude to the return of the malevolent forces that had become entwined with her very essence.

Unbeknownst to Sheila, her awakening had not only transformed her soul but had left an indelible mark on the haunted dwelling itself. The air, heavy with the essence of the supernatural, carried an ominous energy that hinted at a spectral unrest within the old house. The whispers, now a haunting lament, guided her toward the epicenter of the spectral storm—an awareness that the malevolent forces were not confined to her consciousness alone.

In the dim light, Sheila and Rob witnessed cryptic symbols reappearing on the walls—a manifestation of the malevolent forces that had returned to the spectral fabric of the old house. The whispers, now a spectral symphony, intensified as they delved into the haunted

corridors, conveying the urgency of a greater darkness that loomed on the horizon. The old house, though scarred by the supernatural encounter, stood as a stage for the malevolent forces' return—an encore that defied the constraints of the ritual.

Sheila, grappling with the resurgence of the malevolent forces, sought the guidance of the psychic medium who had assisted them in the cleansing ritual. The whispers, now a haunting melody, seemed to echo through the secluded residence of the medium, conveying the urgency of the situation. The air, thick with the residual energies of the supernatural encounter, guided them toward a revelation that went beyond the haunted dwelling's spectral confines.

The psychic medium, aware of the lingering malevolence, spoke of the malevolent forces' return—an awakening that defied the boundaries of the ritual. The whispers, now a relentless drone, urged Sheila and Rob to confront the looming darkness before it consumed the haunted dwelling. The air, heavy with the essence of the supernatural, carried a spectral resonance that transcended the mortal realm.

Determined to face the consequences of her awakening, Sheila returned to the old house, her senses heightened by the lingering supernatural energies. The whispers, now a spectral chorus, seemed to align with her evolving awareness as she ventured into the dimly lit halls. The haunted dwelling, though scarred by the supernatural encounter, awaited the next chapter in Sheila's journey—an odyssey that would test the limits of her newfound connection to the malevolent forces.

As night settled over the old house, Sheila felt the temperature drop—a chilling sign of the malevolent forces' return. Shadows danced on the walls, and the air vibrated with a spectral resonance that hinted at the impending confrontation. The whispers, now a haunting lament, guided her toward the heart of the spectral storm—an epicenter where the forces of the living and the supernatural converged within her being.

In the dim light, Sheila glimpsed fleeting apparitions—manifestations of the malevolent forces that had returned to the haunted dwelling. The whispers, now a dissonant symphony, seemed to speak of a

malevolence seeking communion with her, defying the constraints of the ritual. The old house, though momentarily quelled, stood as a witness to Sheila's confrontation with the return of the malevolent forces —an encore that echoed through the spectral corridors.

Suddenly, the room quivered with unseen energies, and the temperature plummeted. The whispers, now a spectral chorus, intensified as Sheila confronted the epicenter of the supernatural disturbance within herself. The air, charged with an otherworldly energy, carried a spectral resonance that hinted at the imminent confrontation with the malevolent forces that had returned to the old house.

As Sheila approached the heart of the spectral storm within her, she felt an oppressive force—an awakening darkness that seemed to envelop her being. The whispers, now a relentless drone, echoed through her consciousness, urging her to confront the malevolent forces that lingered within the depths of her soul. Sheila, standing at the threshold of her own transformation, faced the haunting encore that had become an integral part of her existence.

In the dimly lit chamber of her consciousness, Sheila confronted the return of the malevolent forces that lingered within her. The whispers, now a haunting melody, guided her through the spectral encounter—a dance between her awakened self and the lingering abyss. The haunted dwelling, its spectral foundations shaken by the consequences of the sacrifice, became a crucible where the boundaries between Sheila's reality and the return of the malevolent forces blurred.

The malevolent forces within Sheila, a manifestation of the ancient darkness, spoke through the spectral symphony within her soul. The whispers, now a dissonant chorus, conveyed the grievances and malevolence of the lingering force that sought communion with her. Sheila, in a surreal confrontation with the return of the malevolent forces, faced the ancient darkness that had become intertwined with her very essence. The haunted dwelling, a conduit for the malevolent supernatural forces, bore silent witness to the encore within the depths of Sheila's consciousness.

As Sheila grappled with the malevolent forces within her, the whispers, now a relentless drone, urged her toward a revelation that defied comprehension. The haunted dwelling, its spectral foundations saturated with the essence of Sheila's confrontation, stood as a battleground where the forces of light and darkness clashed in a terrifying encore within the depths of her soul.

In the dim light, Sheila glimpsed shadowy figures—apparitions of the past that materialized in the spectral realm within her consciousness. The whispers, now a haunting lament, spoke of the tormented souls that lingered within her awakened self. The air, charged with an otherworldly energy, guided her toward the epicenter of the spectral storm— an impending encore with the malevolent entity that had become an integral part of her very existence.

As Sheila confronted the entity within, the whispers, now a spectral chorus, intensified. Her resolve tested by the supernatural encore, she faced the return of the malevolent force with determination. The haunted dwelling, its spectral foundations saturated with the essence of the supernatural, stood as a crucible where the forces of light and darkness clashed in a terrifying encore within the depths of Sheila's soul.

Unexpectedly, the return of the malevolent forces within Sheila recoiled—a spectral manifestation weakened by her determination to overcome the malevolent encore. The whispers, now a fading memory, left an eerie stillness in the chambers of her consciousness. Sheila, her senses overwhelmed by the supernatural encore within, stood amidst the remnants of the spectral storm that had unfolded within her soul. The haunted dwelling, though momentarily quelled, seemed to sigh with a spectral resignation as if acknowledging the fleeting victory over the lingering malevolent forces.

As Sheila emerged from the depths of her own confrontation, a sense of cautious hope lingered in the air. The whispers, now a distant murmur, guided her through the dimly lit halls of her own consciousness—the battleground where she had triumphed over the malevolent forces within. The haunted dwelling, forever scarred by the supernatural

encore, stood as a testament to the resilience of the human spirit and the capacity to confront the ancient darkness that lurked within one's own soul.

Little did Sheila know that the return of the malevolent forces signaled a new chapter in her journey. The whispers, now a fading memory, left the door ajar for the looming terror that awaited in the aftermath of the supernatural encore. Sheila, forever changed by the harrowing ordeal within herself, faced an uncertain future where the horrors of her own past cast a long, lingering shadow over her fragile grasp on reality. The haunted dwelling, a reflection of her awakened soul, awaited the next chapter in Sheila's journey—a journey that would redefine the very fabric of her existence.

Chapter 21: The Revelation

In the wake of the malevolent forces' return, the old house stood as a silent witness to the unfolding nightmare that awaited Sheila. The air, thick with the supernatural energies that clung to her awakened soul, carried an oppressive weight that seemed to permeate every corner of the haunted dwelling. The whispers, now a distant murmur, guided Sheila through the dimly lit halls—a foreboding prelude to the revelation that awaited in the shadows.

As night fell over the old house, Sheila's senses remained on edge, attuned to the subtle shifts in the spectral currents that surrounded her. Shadows danced on the walls, and the air vibrated with a spectral resonance that hinted at the impending revelation. The whispers, now a fading memory, seemed to echo through the haunted corridors—an eerie reminder of the malevolent forces that lurked within the depths of her awakened self.

Unbeknownst to Sheila, the return of the malevolent forces had not only marked the old house but had woven a dark tapestry that transcended the physical realm. The air, heavy with the essence of the supernatural encore, carried an ominous energy that hinted at a spectral unrest within the very fabric of the haunted dwelling. The whispers, now a haunting lament, guided her toward the epicenter of

the spectral storm—an awareness that the malevolent forces sought not only communion with her soul but also a greater revelation that defied comprehension.

In the dim light, Sheila and Rob witnessed cryptic symbols reappearing on the walls—a manifestation of the malevolent forces that had returned to the spectral fabric of the old house. The whispers, now a spectral symphony, intensified as they delved into the haunted corridors, conveying the urgency of a revelation that went beyond the boundaries of the living. The old house, though momentarily quelled, stood as a stage for the malevolent forces' revelation—an unveiling that defied the constraints of the mortal realm.

Sheila, grappling with the ominous energies that clung to her awakened soul, sought the guidance of the psychic medium who had assisted them in the cleansing ritual. The whispers, now a haunting melody, seemed to echo through the secluded residence of the medium, conveying the urgency of the situation. The air, thick with the residual energies of the supernatural encore, guided them toward a revelation that transcended the haunted dwelling's spectral confines.

The psychic medium, attuned to the supernatural currents, spoke of a revelation that went beyond the malevolent forces' return—an awakening that defied the boundaries of the ritual. The whispers, now a relentless drone, urged Sheila and Rob to confront the looming darkness before it consumed not only their souls but also the very fabric of reality. The air, heavy with the essence of the supernatural, carried a spectral resonance that transcended the mortal realm.

Determined to face the consequences of the revelation, Sheila returned to the old house, her senses heightened by the lingering supernatural energies. The whispers, now a spectral chorus, seemed to align with her evolving awareness as she ventured into the dimly lit halls. The haunted dwelling, scarred by the supernatural encounter and the malevolent encore, awaited the next chapter in Sheila's journey—an odyssey that would test the limits of her newfound connection to the malevolent forces and the revelation that awaited in the shadows.

As night settled over the old house, Sheila felt the temperature drop—a chilling sign of the revelation that loomed on the horizon. Shadows danced on the walls, and the air vibrated with a spectral resonance that hinted at the impending unveiling. The whispers, now a haunting lament, guided her toward the heart of the spectral storm—an epicenter where the forces of the living and the supernatural converged within her being.

In the dim light, Sheila glimpsed fleeting apparitions—manifestations of the malevolent forces that had returned to the haunted dwelling. The whispers, now a dissonant symphony, seemed to speak of a malevolence seeking communion with her, defying the constraints of the ritual. The old house, though momentarily quelled, stood as a witness to Sheila's confrontation with the revelation—an unveiling that echoed through the spectral corridors.

Suddenly, the room quivered with unseen energies, and the temperature plummeted. The whispers, now a spectral chorus, intensified as Sheila confronted the epicenter of the supernatural disturbance within herself. The air, charged with an otherworldly energy, carried a spectral resonance that hinted at the imminent confrontation with the revelation that had become intertwined with her very essence.

As Sheila approached the heart of the spectral storm within her, she felt an oppressive force—an awakening darkness that seemed to envelop her being. The whispers, now a relentless drone, echoed through her consciousness, urging her to confront the malevolent forces and the revelation that lingered within the depths of her soul. Sheila, standing at the threshold of her own transformation, faced the haunting unveiling that had become an integral part of her existence.

In the dimly lit chamber of her consciousness, Sheila confronted the revelation that unfolded within her soul. The whispers, now a haunting melody, guided her through the spectral encounter—a dance between her awakened self and the lingering abyss. The haunted dwelling, its spectral foundations shaken by the consequences of the sacrifice and the

malevolent encore, became a crucible where the boundaries between Sheila's reality and the revelation blurred.

The revelation within Sheila, a manifestation of the ancient darkness, spoke through the spectral symphony within her soul. The whispers, now a dissonant chorus, conveyed the grievances and malevolence of the lingering force that sought communion with her. Sheila, in a surreal confrontation with the revelation, faced the ancient darkness that had become intertwined with her very essence. The haunted dwelling, a conduit for the malevolent supernatural forces and the revelation, bore silent witness to the final unveiling within the depths of Sheila's consciousness.

As Sheila grappled with the malevolent forces and the revelation within her, the whispers, now a relentless drone, urged her toward a revelation that defied comprehension. The haunted dwelling, its spectral foundations saturated with the essence of Sheila's confrontation and the revelation, stood as a battleground where the forces of light and darkness clashed in a terrifying crescendo within the depths of her soul.

In the dim light, Sheila glimpsed shadowy figures—apparitions of the past that materialized in the spectral realm within her consciousness. The whispers, now a haunting lament, spoke of the tormented souls that lingered within her awakened self. The air, charged with an otherworldly energy, guided her toward the epicenter of the spectral storm— an impending revelation with the malevolent entity that had become an integral part of her very existence.

As Sheila confronted the entity within, the whispers, now a spectral chorus, intensified. Her resolve tested by the supernatural onslaught, she faced the revelation and the return of the malevolent force with determination. The haunted dwelling, its spectral foundations saturated with the essence of the supernatural, stood as a crucible where the forces of light and darkness clashed in a terrifying crescendo within the depths of Sheila's soul.

Unexpectedly, the revelation within Sheila recoiled—a spectral manifestation weakened by her determination to overcome the malevolent

forces. The whispers, now a fading memory, left an eerie stillness in the chambers of her consciousness. Sheila, her senses overwhelmed by the supernatural encounter within and the revelation, stood amidst the remnants of the spectral storm that had unfolded within her soul. The haunted dwelling, though momentarily quelled, seemed to sigh with a spectral resignation as if acknowledging the fleeting victory over the lingering malevolent forces and the revelation.

As Sheila emerged from the depths of her own confrontation and the revelation, a sense of cautious hope lingered in the air. The whispers, now a distant murmur, guided her through the dimly lit halls of her own consciousness—the battleground where she had triumphed over the malevolent forces and the revelation within. The haunted dwelling, forever scarred by the supernatural encounter, the malevolent encore, and the revelation, stood as a testament to the resilience of the human spirit and the capacity to confront the ancient darkness that lurked within one's own soul.

Little did Sheila know that the revelation signaled a new chapter in her journey. The whispers, now a fading memory, left the door ajar for the looming terror that awaited in the aftermath of the supernatural encounter, the malevolent encore, and the revelation. Sheila, forever changed by the harrowing ordeal within herself, faced an uncertain future where the horrors of her own past cast a long, lingering shadow over her fragile grasp on reality. The haunted dwelling, a reflection of her awakened soul, awaited the next chapter in Sheila's journey—a journey that would redefine the very fabric of her existence.

Chapter 22: The Sacrifice

As Sheila emerged from the depths of the haunting revelation, an uneasy calm settled over the old house. The air, thick with the remnants of the supernatural encounter, the malevolent encore, and the revelation within her soul, carried a weight that seemed to hang in the dimly lit halls. The whispers, now a distant murmur, guided Sheila through the spectral corridors—an ominous reminder of the malevolent forces and the revelation that lingered within the shadows.

The old house, scarred by the supernatural events that had unfolded within its walls, stood as a testament to the harrowing journey Sheila had traversed. Shadows danced on the walls, and the air vibrated with a spectral resonance that hinted at the lingering darkness within her. The whispers, now a fading memory, seemed to echo through the haunted dwelling—an eerie prelude to the final chapter that awaited Sheila.

Unbeknownst to her, the malevolent forces, the revelation, and the haunting encore had left an indelible mark not only on her soul but also on the spectral fabric of the old house. The air, heavy with the essence of the supernatural, carried an ominous energy that hinted at a lingering presence—a spectral force that awaited the culmination of Sheila's journey. The whispers, now a haunting lament, guided her toward the epicenter of the spectral storm—an awareness that the malevolent forces and the revelation were not mere echoes of the past but a looming threat that sought a resolution.

In the dim light, Sheila and Rob observed cryptic symbols etching themselves onto the walls—a manifestation of the malevolent forces, the revelation, and the encore that had become intertwined with the haunted dwelling. The whispers, now a spectral symphony, intensified as they delved into the haunted corridors, conveying the urgency of a greater darkness that loomed on the horizon. The old house, though momentarily quelled, stood as a stage for the malevolent forces' final act—an act that defied the constraints of the ritual and hinted at a resolution that transcended the boundaries of the living.

Sheila, grappling with the weight of the revelation, sought the guidance of the psychic medium who had assisted them in the cleansing ritual. The whispers, now a haunting melody, seemed to echo through the secluded residence of the medium, conveying the urgency of the situation. The air, thick with the residual energies of the supernatural encounter, the malevolent encore, and the revelation, guided them toward a resolution that went beyond the haunted dwelling's spectral confines.

The psychic medium, aware of the lingering malevolence, spoke of a resolution that defied the boundaries of the ritual. The whispers, now a relentless drone, urged Sheila and Rob to confront the looming darkness before it consumed not only their souls but also the very fabric of reality. The air, heavy with the essence of the supernatural, carried a spectral resonance that transcended the mortal realm.

Determined to face the consequences of the supernatural events, Sheila returned to the old house, her senses heightened by the lingering energies. The whispers, now a spectral chorus, seemed to align with her evolving awareness as she ventured into the dimly lit halls. The haunted dwelling, scarred by the supernatural events and the revelation, awaited the next chapter in Sheila's journey—an odyssey that would test the limits of her newfound connection to the malevolent forces.

As night settled over the old house, Sheila felt the temperature drop—a chilling sign of the impending resolution. Shadows danced on the walls, and the air vibrated with a spectral resonance that hinted at the imminent confrontation. The whispers, now a haunting lament, guided her toward the heart of the spectral storm—an epicenter where the forces of the living and the supernatural converged within her being.

In the dim light, Sheila glimpsed fleeting apparitions—manifestations of the malevolent forces that had returned to the haunted dwelling. The whispers, now a dissonant symphony, seemed to speak of a malevolence seeking communion with her, defying the constraints of the ritual. The old house, though momentarily quelled, stood as a witness to Sheila's confrontation with the resolution—an act that echoed through the spectral corridors.

Suddenly, the room quivered with unseen energies, and the temperature plummeted. The whispers, now a spectral chorus, intensified as Sheila confronted the epicenter of the supernatural disturbance within herself. The air, charged with an otherworldly energy, carried a spectral resonance that hinted at the imminent confrontation with the resolution that had become intertwined with her very essence.

As Sheila approached the heart of the spectral storm within her, she felt an oppressive force—an awakening darkness that seemed to envelop her being. The whispers, now a relentless drone, echoed through her consciousness, urging her to confront the malevolent forces and the resolution that lingered within the depths of her soul. Sheila, standing at the threshold of her own transformation, faced the haunting resolution that had become an integral part of her existence.

In the dimly lit chamber of her consciousness, Sheila confronted the resolution that unfolded within her soul. The whispers, now a haunting melody, guided her through the spectral encounter—a dance between her awakened self and the lingering abyss. The haunted dwelling, its spectral foundations shaken by the consequences of the sacrifice, the malevolent encore, and the revelation, became a crucible where the boundaries between Sheila's reality and the resolution blurred.

The resolution within Sheila, a manifestation of the ancient darkness, spoke through the spectral symphony within her soul. The whispers, now a dissonant chorus, conveyed the grievances and malevolence of the lingering force that sought communion with her. Sheila, in a surreal confrontation with the resolution, faced the ancient darkness that had become intertwined with her very essence. The haunted dwelling, a conduit for the malevolent supernatural forces and the resolution, bore silent witness to the final act within the depths of Sheila's consciousness.

As Sheila grappled with the malevolent forces and the resolution within her, the whispers, now a relentless drone, urged her toward a resolution that defied comprehension. The haunted dwelling, its spectral foundations saturated with the essence of Sheila's confrontation, the malevolent encore, and the revelation, stood as a battleground where the forces of light and darkness clashed in a terrifying crescendo within the depths of her soul.

In the dim light, Sheila glimpsed shadowy figures—apparitions of the past that materialized in the spectral realm within her consciousness. The whispers, now a haunting lament, spoke of the tormented souls

that lingered within her awakened self. The air, charged with an other-worldly energy, guided her toward the epicenter of the spectral storm—an impending resolution with the malevolent entity that had become an integral part of her very existence.

As Sheila confronted the entity within, the whispers, now a spectral chorus, intensified. Her resolve tested by the supernatural onslaught, she faced the resolution and the return of the malevolent force with determination. The haunted dwelling, its spectral foundations saturated with the essence of the supernatural, stood as a crucible where the forces of light and darkness clashed in a terrifying crescendo within the depths of Sheila's soul.

Unexpectedly, the resolution within Sheila recoiled—a spectral manifestation weakened by her determination to overcome the malevolent forces. The whispers, now a fading memory, left an eerie stillness in the chambers of her consciousness. Sheila, her senses overwhelmed by the supernatural encounter, the malevolent encore, and the resolution, stood amidst the remnants of the spectral storm that had unfolded within her soul. The haunted dwelling, though momentarily quelled, seemed to sigh with a spectral resignation as if acknowledging the fleeting victory over the lingering malevolent forces and the resolution.

As Sheila emerged from the depths of her own confrontation and the resolution, a sense of cautious hope lingered in the air. The whispers, now a distant murmur, guided her through the dimly lit halls of her own consciousness—the battleground where she had triumphed over the malevolent forces, the revelation, and the resolution within. The haunted dwelling, forever scarred by the supernatural encounter, stood as a testament to the resilience of the human spirit and the capacity to confront the ancient darkness that lurked within one's own soul.

Little did Sheila know that the resolution marked the final chapter in her journey. The whispers, now a fading memory, left the door ajar for the looming terror that awaited in the aftermath of the supernatural encounter, the malevolent encore, and the revelation. Sheila, forever changed by the harrowing ordeal within herself, faced an uncertain

future where the horrors of her own past cast a long, lingering shadow over her fragile grasp on reality. The haunted dwelling, a reflection of her awakened soul, awaited the next chapter in Sheila's journey—a journey that would redefine the very fabric of her existence.

**The Horror Inside
The House Awaits
By
Doug Hensley
Table Of Contents**

Chapter 1: The New House - Sheila moves into a beautiful but eerie old house, noticing strange noises and feeling uneasy.

Chapter 2: The Whispers - Sheila hears faint voices whispering when alone at night, making her question her sanity.

Chapter 3: The Dark History - Sheila researches the house's past, finding a dark tale of murder and suicide. Chapter 4: The Warning - An elderly neighbor tells Sheila she must leave the house before it's too late. Sheila refuses.

Chapter 5: The Apparition - Sheila sees a ghostly figure staring at her from the hall, but it disappears before she can investigate.

Chapter 6: The Visitor - Sheila's childhood friend Rob stays the night, also experiencing unsettling events in the house.

Chapter 7: The Presence - Doors open on their own, objects move mysteriously, and Sheila feels someone watching, though Rob remains oblivious.

Chapter 8: The Message - Cryptic words are scrawled on the bathroom mirror when Sheila and Rob wake up, leaving them shaken.

Chapter 9: The History Revealed - Sheila finds an old diary explaining gruesome rituals once held in the house's basement.

Chapter 10: The Basement - Sheila and Rob find a secret door leading down to a dark basement. Going down, they trigger a cave-in, trapping them inside.

Chapter 11: The Escape - After finding ritual items in the basement, Sheila and Rob escape and block the basement door, believing the nightmare is over.

Chapter 12: The Attacks - Paranormal attacks on Sheila grow violent. Desperate, she considers holding a seance.

Chapter 13: The Seance - The seance summons malevolent spirits. One possesses Rob, forcing Sheila to take drastic measures.

Chapter 14: The Cleansing - Sheila enlists a psychic medium to cleanse the home. The process seems successful until things escalate again. Chapter 15: The Truth - Research reveals the house was built for occult rituals, with a dark energy woven into the walls. There is only one way to stop it.

Chapter 16: The Sacrifice - Sheila learns she must offer a blood sacrifice in the house to seal the evil presence. She prepares for the ritual.

Chapter 17: The Confrontation - Unexpected twists force Sheila into a final showdown with the sinister forces in the house. All seems lost until she embraces her destiny. Chapter 18: The Resolution - Sheila defeats the evil forces at great personal cost. The house is finally at peace, but so much has changed. Chapter 19: The Awakening - Sheila slowly recovers, adjusting to a new normal. For the first time in years, she feels hope.

Chapter 20: The Return - Strange events make Sheila question if the evil presence was truly eradicated. Ominous signs suggest a greater darkness.

Chapter 21: The Revelation - Sheila discovers the house's evil has corrupted her soul. She must act quickly if she hopes to save herself. Chapter 22: The Sacrifice - Sheila makes one final sacrifice, for her own sake rather than the house's. Her journey ends, for better or worse.

Chapter 1: The New House

Sheila, a young woman seeking a fresh start, moves into a beautiful yet eerie old house. Almost immediately, strange noises and an overwhelming feeling of unease settle in, setting the stage for the supernatural events that will unfold.

Chapter 2: The Whispers As Sheila settles into her new home, she begins hearing faint voices whispering to her when she's alone at night. The mysterious whispers cast doubt on her sanity and create an atmosphere of increasing tension.

Chapter 3: The Dark History Driven by curiosity and a growing sense of dread, Sheila delves into the house's past. Her research reveals a dark tale of murder and suicide, hinting at the malevolent forces that may be at play.

Chapter 4: The Warning An elderly neighbor warns Sheila of impending danger and urges her to leave the house before it's too late. Despite the ominous warning, Sheila stubbornly refuses to abandon her new home.

Chapter 5: The Apparition Sheila's fears intensify when she catches a glimpse of a ghostly figure staring at her from the hall. However, the apparition vanishes before she can investigate further, leaving her to grapple with the supernatural occurrences.

Chapter 6: The Visitor In an attempt to find solace, Sheila invites her childhood friend Rob to stay the night. Rob, too, experiences unsettling events in the house, heightening the sense of foreboding.

Chapter 7: The Presence Doors open on their own, objects move mysteriously, and Sheila senses an unseen presence watching her. Despite the escalating paranormal activity, Rob remains oblivious to the unfolding horror.

Chapter 8: The Message Sheila and Rob wake up to cryptic words scrawled on the bathroom mirror, further deepening the mystery and leaving them shaken. The supernatural forces in the house are making their presence known in unsettling ways.

Chapter 9: The History Revealed Sheila discovers an old diary in the house, unveiling the gruesome rituals that were once held in its dark

basement. The revelation adds a layer of horror to the already chilling atmosphere.

Chapter 10: The Basement Driven by the need to unravel the mysteries surrounding the house, Sheila and Rob find a secret door leading to a dark basement. Their exploration triggers a cave-in, trapping them inside and marking a point of no return.

Chapter 11: The Escape Believing the nightmare is over, Sheila and Rob manage to escape the basement and block the door, thinking they have successfully sealed away the malevolent forces. However, the worst is yet to come.

Chapter 12: The Attacks Paranormal attacks on Sheila escalate, growing increasingly violent. Desperate for answers, she contemplates holding a seance to communicate with the otherworldly entities.

Chapter 13: The Seance The seance takes a dark turn as malevolent spirits are summoned, with one possessing Rob. Sheila is forced to take drastic measures to confront the supernatural threat.

Chapter 14: The Cleansing Sheila enlists the help of a psychic medium to cleanse the home. Initially, the process appears successful, providing a false sense of security. However, the calm is short-lived as the haunting experiences resume.

Chapter 15: The Truth Through extensive research, Sheila uncovers that the house was purposefully built for occult rituals, with a dark energy woven into its very walls. The revelation leaves her with the chilling realization that only one method can put an end to the terror.

Chapter 16: The Sacrifice Sheila learns that she must make a blood sacrifice within the house to seal the evil presence once and for all. As she prepares for the ritual, the gravity of the situation weighs heavily on her.

Chapter 17: The Confrontation Unexpected twists and turns force Sheila into a final showdown with the sinister forces in the house. All seems lost until she embraces her destiny, revealing a strength she never knew she possessed.

Chapter 18: The Resolution At great personal cost, Sheila successfully defeats the evil forces within the house. While the dwelling is finally at peace, the toll on Sheila is profound, leaving her forever changed.

Chapter 19: The Awakening As Sheila slowly recovers, she must adjust to a new normal. For the first time in years, she feels a glimmer of hope, but the scars of the harrowing ordeal run deep.

Chapter 20: The Return Strange events begin to unfold, making Sheila question if the evil presence was truly eradicated. Ominous signs suggest a greater darkness that may linger, threatening to undo everything she thought she had achieved.

Chapter 21: The Revelation In a shocking discovery, Sheila realizes that the house's evil has corrupted her soul. With time running out, she must act swiftly to save herself from the malevolent forces that have taken root within her.

Chapter 22: The Sacrifice In a final, desperate act, Sheila makes one last sacrifice—this time for her own sake rather than the house's. Her journey comes to an end, leaving readers to wonder if the darkness truly dissipates or if it merely finds a new host.

Chapter 1: The New House

The creaking floorboards echoed through the empty rooms as Sheila cautiously stepped into her new home. The air felt heavy, laden with an unspoken history that sent shivers down her spine. The walls, adorned with faded wallpaper, seemed to hold secrets, and the windows allowed only a dim, feeble light to penetrate the gloom.

Sheila's belongings were scattered in disarray, yet the beauty of the old house couldn't be denied. As the sun dipped below the horizon, casting long, eerie shadows across the wooden floors, Sheila couldn't shake the feeling that she was not alone.

Night descended with a whispering chill, and Sheila settled into her bed. But as the clock struck midnight, the house came alive with strange noises. Whispers, soft and elusive, slithered through the silence, causing her heart to race. She strained her ears, catching fragmented words that left her questioning her sanity.

In the dimness, Sheila felt the presence of something unseen. It was as if the very walls held a malevolent secret, a history buried deep within the foundation. Her unease intensified as the whispers grew into an indistinct murmur that seemed to resonate with the pulse of the house.

The next day, Sheila decided to uncover the mysteries surrounding her new abode. Armed with curiosity and a sense of foreboding, she delved into the house's past. Dusty old books and faded photographs revealed a dark tale of murder and suicide that had stained the very essence of the building.

As Sheila immersed herself in the grim accounts of the past, the atmosphere in the house seemed to shift. Shadows danced along the walls, and the temperature dropped, making her breath visible in the cold air. The weight of the house's history pressed upon her, like an invisible hand tightening around her throat.

A knock on the door interrupted Sheila's unsettling discoveries. An elderly neighbor, eyes clouded with concern, warned her of the impending danger that lurked within the house. "Leave, child, before it devours your soul," the old woman pleaded, but Sheila, fueled by stubborn determination, dismissed the ominous advice.

Nightfall brought with it a ghastly apparition. Sheila, bathed in the pale glow of the moonlight, glimpsed a ghostly figure in the hallway. It stared at her with hollow eyes, sending a chill through her veins. Before she could react, the apparition dissolved into the shadows, leaving Sheila trembling in the oppressive silence.

Desperate for solace, Sheila invited her childhood friend Rob to stay the night. As the hours passed, the house unleashed its malevolent grip on them both. Objects moved of their own accord, doors swung open with an otherworldly force, and a pervasive feeling of being watched hung in the air. Yet, Rob remained oblivious to the supernatural dance unfolding around them.

Cryptic messages appeared on the bathroom mirror the following morning. Scrawled in an otherworldly hand, the words sent shivers

down Sheila's spine. The house was communicating with them, leaving an indelible mark on their reality.

With each passing day, the house's dark history unveiled itself in more sinister ways. Sheila discovered an old diary tucked away in a forgotten corner, detailing gruesome rituals held in the very basement she had yet to explore.

Determined to confront the source of the malevolence, Sheila and Rob discovered a hidden door leading to the ominous depths of the basement. The air grew thick with anticipation as they descended, unaware that they were stepping into a trap set by forces beyond their comprehension.

A sudden and violent cave-in trapped Sheila and Rob in the lightless abyss. Panic set in as the walls seemed to close in around them. Shadows danced in the dim illumination of their flashlights, and the oppressive darkness whispered promises of doom.

Hours passed before they managed to escape, their faces etched with fear. Convinced that sealing the basement door had ended the nightmare, Sheila dared to hope for a return to normalcy. Little did she know, the true horror had only just begun.

Paranormal attacks on Sheila intensified, the unseen forces growing bolder and more malevolent. Objects hurled across rooms, chilling whispers turned into guttural growls, and a sinister presence loomed over her every move.

Desperation led Sheila to consider a seance, a desperate attempt to communicate with the entities plaguing her. The air crackled with tension as she and Rob sat in a circle, hands trembling as they called out to the unknown. But the seance took a dark turn, as malevolent spirits seized the opportunity to manifest their malevolence.

Rob, overcome by an unseen force, became a vessel for the malevolent entities. Sheila, faced with a friend turned foe, had no choice but to take drastic measures. The once comforting bonds of friendship now strained under the weight of supernatural possession.

In her quest for salvation, Sheila sought the help of a psychic medium to cleanse the home. The air thickened with anticipation as the medium performed rituals to banish the malevolent entities. For a fleeting moment, the house seemed at peace, and Sheila allowed herself a breath of relief.

However, the calm proved short-lived. The house, it seemed, had only been biding its time. The cleansing had only served to agitate the dormant evil that lingered within the very fabric of the walls.

Driven by an insatiable need for the truth, Sheila's research revealed that the house was purposefully constructed for occult rituals. A dark energy, woven into the very foundation, defied any attempts to eradicate it conventionally. The realization struck her like a physical blow, and the oppressive weight of the house's malevolence pressed down on her soul.

Sheila learned of a chilling solution—one that required a blood sacrifice to seal the evil presence. The revelation sent shivers down her spine, but with unwavering resolve, she prepared for the ritual. The air in the house crackled with a palpable tension as Sheila steeled herself for the harrowing task that lay ahead.

As the appointed hour arrived, Sheila embarked on the ritual, guided by the cryptic instructions she had unearthed. The air thickened with an otherworldly energy as she treaded the fine line between the living and the supernatural. The house seemed to breathe, its walls pulsating with an unholy heartbeat.

Unexpected twists and turns forced Sheila into a final confrontation with the sinister forces that had tormented her. The battle unfolded in a crescendo of terror, with each moment pushing her to the brink of despair. All seemed lost until Sheila, drawing upon a strength she never knew she possessed, embraced her destiny and faced the malevolent entities head-on.

At great personal cost, Sheila emerged victorious. The malevolent forces were banished, and the house fell silent. But victory came at a price—Sheila was forever changed, scarred by the ordeal that had tested her sanity and resilience.

As Sheila grappled with the aftermath of the climactic events, she found herself in a house that bore the marks of the supernatural battle. The once-elegant rooms, now tinged with an otherworldly aura, stood as a testament to the horrors that had unfolded within their walls.

The awakening came slowly for Sheila. She found herself in a surreal new normal, haunted by memories of the malevolence that had once claimed her every waking moment. Yet, for the first time in years, a flicker of hope ignited within her.

But the return to normalcy proved elusive. Strange events unfolded around Sheila, casting doubt on whether the evil presence had truly been eradicated. Ominous signs, subtle yet undeniable, hinted at a darkness that lingered, threatening to unravel everything she had fought so hard to achieve.

In a shocking revelation, Sheila discovered that the house's evil had not only touched the walls but had also corrupted her very soul. Time was of the essence as she grappled with the realization that salvation required swift and decisive action.

The final sacrifice loomed before Sheila—a desperate act to save herself from the malevolent forces that sought to claim her. Her journey reached its conclusion, leaving her standing at the precipice of the unknown. Whether the darkness dissipated or found a new host remained a lingering question, echoing in the silence of the house that had become a battleground between the living and the supernatural.

Chapter 2: The Whispers

As the haunting echoes of the previous night lingered, Sheila awoke to a house cloaked in shadows. The morning light struggled to penetrate the heavy curtains, casting an eerie glow across the room. The unsettling events of the night before weighed on her mind, and a sense of trepidation settled in her chest.

Dragging herself out of bed, Sheila couldn't shake the feeling that the walls were watching her every move. The air seemed to hum with an unnatural energy, and she wondered if the house itself held memories of the whispers that had invaded her sleep.

As dusk settled once again, the atmosphere in the house shifted. The creaking floorboards beneath Sheila's tentative steps seemed to resonate with a spectral rhythm. The shadows danced in a macabre ballet, and the air took on a frigid chill that seeped into her bones.

Alone in the dimly lit living room, Sheila felt a subtle change in the air—a whispering murmur that curled around her consciousness like tendrils of smoke. A strange sensation crawled up her spine, and she strained to catch the fragmented words carried by the unseen voices.

The whispers, soft and elusive, wrapped around her mind like a ghostly embrace. Sheila couldn't discern the origin of the ethereal voices, and a growing unease settled in the pit of her stomach. The words, a dissonant symphony of indistinct muttering, seemed to weave tales of forgotten sorrows and ancient malevolence.

Torn between fear and curiosity, Sheila followed the whispers as they led her through the labyrinthine corridors of the old house. The air grew heavier, and the oppressive darkness seemed to amplify the haunting voices that echoed through the halls.

The night unfolded in a surreal dance of shadows and secrets. Sheila, guided by the mysterious whispers, wandered deeper into the heart of the house. Each step felt like a descent into a realm where reality and the supernatural coexisted in a fragile balance.

In the heart of the house, Sheila found herself standing before a weathered door. The whispers, now a cacophony of urgent voices, beckoned her to open it. Hesitant but driven by an unexplainable force, she turned the rusted doorknob.

The room beyond was shrouded in an impenetrable darkness. The air felt charged with an otherworldly energy, and the whispers reached a fevered pitch. As Sheila stepped into the room, a chilling wind swept through, extinguishing the feeble candlelight that flickered in the corners.

In the profound darkness, shapes and shadows materialized, dancing on the periphery of Sheila's vision. The whispers coalesced into a haunting chorus, a symphony of forgotten souls yearning to be heard.

Goosebumps erupted on Sheila's skin as she realized that she was not alone in the spectral gathering.

The room seemed to pulse with an unseen heartbeat, and Sheila felt a cold breath on the nape of her neck. The whispers, now mere inches away, spoke directly into her mind. Words, ancient and cryptic, intertwined with her thoughts, creating a disorienting fusion of reality and the supernatural.

Sheila, paralyzed by the ghostly communion, struggled to comprehend the weight of the revelations. The whispers spoke of long-buried secrets, of a history stained with sorrow and malevolence. The house, it seemed, held memories that transcended the boundaries of time.

In a crescendo of spectral intensity, the whispers began to echo the names of the departed, their voices rising and falling like a spectral tide. Sheila felt an overwhelming sadness wash over her as she became a vessel for the collective lament of the forgotten souls trapped within the walls.

As the spectral symphony reached its zenith, Sheila's surroundings blurred into a phantasmagoric dreamscape. Shadows danced in a macabre ballet, and ghostly apparitions materialized before her. The faces of the departed stared into her soul, their eyes reflecting an eternity of suffering.

In a sudden, jarring silence, the room plunged into darkness once more. Sheila stood alone, her breath ragged and heart pounding. The weight of the revelations pressed down on her shoulders, and the whispers, now a mere echo in the recesses of her mind, faded into the obscurity of the old house.

Sheila stumbled back into the dimly lit corridor, disoriented and shaken. The whispers, though momentarily silenced, lingered in the air like an unseen specter. The house, now charged with an unsettling energy, seemed to watch her with an intensity that transcended the physical realm.

Haunted by the night's spectral communion, Sheila retreated to the safety of her room. The whispers, though subdued, continued to echo in the corners of her mind. Sleep, an elusive sanctuary, offered no respite

as the haunting voices seeped into her dreams, intertwining reality and nightmare in a disconcerting tapestry.

Morning brought little solace as Sheila grappled with the aftermath of the spectral encounter. The once-charming house now bore the weight of its own history, and every creak and groan seemed to carry the echoes of the departed. The whispers, now a constant companion, followed her every move, leaving her sanity teetering on the edge of an abyss.

As Sheila navigated the mundane tasks of daily life, the spectral voices whispered secrets that tore at the fabric of her understanding. The house, it seemed, held a malevolent legacy that transcended the passage of time, and Sheila found herself entangled in a web of forgotten sorrows and ancient grievances.

The days blurred into a disorienting haze as Sheila, haunted by the whispers, grappled with a reality that seemed to unravel at the seams. The walls, once silent witnesses to the passage of time, now pulsed with an otherworldly energy that defied rational explanation.

In the suffocating embrace of the old house, Sheila faced a choice—succumb to the spectral whispers that threatened to unravel her sanity or confront the malevolent forces that lurked in the shadows. Little did she know that the true horror, like a dormant beast, awaited its awakening in the depths of the house's dark history. The whispers, a prelude to the malevolence that lay ahead, continued to echo through the corridors, weaving a sinister tale that intertwined with Sheila's very existence. The house, a malevolent entity in its own right, had claimed her as its unwilling conduit, a vessel through which the forgotten voices sought to rewrite the narrative of their tragic past. As night fell once again, Sheila stood at the precipice of a nightmare, the echoes of the whispers lingering like a ghostly requiem. The darkness, pregnant with unspoken horrors, awaited its chance to consume her soul. Little did Sheila know that the true terror, the culmination of the spectral whispers, loomed on the horizon, threatening to plunge her into a darkness from which there might be no escape. The whispers, a harbinger of an

ancient malevolence, echoed through the haunted corridors, signaling the beginning of a descent into the heart of terror.

Chapter 3: The Dark History

The day unfolded with a sense of oppressive anticipation as Sheila, haunted by the lingering whispers, delved into the dark history of the house. Dust-covered books, their pages brittle with age, beckoned to her from the shelves, revealing tales of sorrow and malevolence that clung to the very essence of the dwelling.

Sheila's fingers traced the words on the yellowed pages, each revelation a cold breath against her skin. The house, it seemed, bore witness to a tapestry of tragedies—a canvas painted with the blood of those long forgotten. Murmurs of untold horrors seemed to emanate from the pages, seeping into her consciousness like an insidious poison.

The sun dipped below the horizon, casting elongated shadows that danced along the walls. Sheila, now immersed in the chilling accounts of the past, couldn't escape the feeling that the very air she breathed carried the weight of the malevolent history woven into the fabric of the house.

As darkness claimed the landscape outside, Sheila's mind echoed with the stories of those who had once called the house their home. A family torn asunder by betrayal, a forbidden love that led to tragedy, and the anguished cries of lost souls echoed through the corridors, merging with the persistent whispers that lingered like a ghostly chorus.

Driven by a compulsion she couldn't fully comprehend, Sheila unearthed old photographs from a dusty box hidden in the attic. Faces frozen in time stared back at her, their eyes holding the secrets of a bygone era. She felt an inexplicable connection to these spectral visages, as if their silent pleas for remembrance echoed in the recesses of her mind.

The photographs revealed a family whose smiles hid a darker truth—a truth that the house guarded with a possessive malevolence. In one faded picture, a child's eyes seemed to bore into Sheila's soul, a silent plea etched in their depths. The whispers intensified, an unseen

hand guiding her through the labyrinth of familial tragedies that stained the house with a legacy of sorrow.

In her search for understanding, Sheila stumbled upon a hidden compartment in the attic. Within its confines lay a collection of letters, brittle with age and tinged with the desperation of the departed. The correspondence spoke of forbidden rituals and a pact sealed in blood—a pact that bound the souls of the house to an otherworldly realm.

The revelation sent shivers down Sheila's spine as the echoes of the past reverberated in the dimly lit room. The house, it seemed, was a vessel for dark forces that defied the boundaries between the living and the dead. Sheila, now an unwitting participant in the spectral drama, grappled with the weight of the malevolent history that clung to her like a suffocating shroud.

Night descended, and Sheila found herself standing before the door that led to the basement—the epicenter of the house's darkest secrets. The whispers, now a cacophony of spectral voices, urged her to descend into the abyss and confront the malevolence that lurked in the hidden recesses.

The creaking stairs groaned under her weight as Sheila descended into the subterranean realm. The air grew colder with each step, and the oppressive darkness seemed to swallow the feeble light of her flashlight. Shadows clung to the walls like spectral tendrils, and the whispers reached a fevered pitch, guiding her deeper into the heart of the supernatural abyss.

As Sheila entered the basement, a chill crawled up her spine. The room, bathed in an otherworldly gloom, revealed the remnants of forgotten rituals—a sacrificial altar, cryptic symbols etched into the walls, and a palpable malevolence that seemed to pulse with a life of its own.

Sheila's breath caught as she uncovered an old diary amidst the dust-covered artifacts. Its pages, stained with the ink of a tormented soul, detailed the ghastly rituals conducted in the name of an otherworldly entity. The diary spoke of a darkness that hungered for innocent souls, a darkness that had claimed the very foundations of the house.

With trembling hands, Sheila read aloud the incantations that had once reverberated within the cold stone walls. The air thickened with an unseen presence as the words echoed through the basement, awakening the dormant malevolence that lingered like a dormant beast.

A sudden gust of wind extinguished the feeble light, plunging Sheila into a darkness that seemed to consume her very essence. Whispers surrounded her, their voices intertwining with the oppressive silence. Shadows danced in the obscurity, and Sheila felt a spectral presence closing in around her.

As she fumbled to relight her flashlight, Sheila caught a glimpse of ghostly figures that materialized in the shadows. Eyes devoid of life stared at her, their hollow gazes filled with an insatiable hunger. The apparitions seemed to reach out from the shadows, their fingers brushing against her skin like the breath of a long-forgotten nightmare.

In the suffocating darkness, Sheila stumbled backward, her heart pounding in her chest. The whispers, now an anguished wail, reverberated through the basement, creating a dissonant symphony of horror. The malevolent forces that had slumbered within the house were now awake, hungry for the essence of the living.

In a desperate attempt to escape the spectral onslaught, Sheila retraced her steps through the labyrinthine corridors of the basement. The walls seemed to close in around her, and the air pulsed with an otherworldly energy that clung to her like a suffocating fog.

As she reached the basement stairs, a cold hand brushed against the nape of her neck. Sheila recoiled, her senses overwhelmed by the touch of unseen fingers. The whispers, now a maddening cacophony, echoed in her ears like a chorus of the damned.

With every step she climbed, the malevolence pursued her like a relentless shadow. The basement seemed to resist her escape, its unseen tendrils reaching out to claim her soul. Sheila emerged into the dimly lit corridor, gasping for breath as the weight of the supernatural encounter pressed down on her chest.

The house, now a malevolent entity awakened from its slumber, seemed to watch Sheila with an insatiable hunger. The whispers, though momentarily subdued, lingered in the air like a haunting refrain. The basement, a portal to an otherworldly realm, had unleashed a darkness that threatened to consume everything in its path.

Sheila, shaken to her core, stumbled into her room and barricaded the door as if shielding herself from the unseen forces that lurked outside. The whispers, now a persistent hum in the background, continued to echo through the walls, their spectral voices weaving a tapestry of horror that seemed to stretch across time and space.

Sleep, elusive and treacherous, offered no refuge as Sheila found herself trapped in a nightmare that transcended the boundaries of the waking world. Shadows danced on the edges of her consciousness, and ghostly apparitions lurked in the recesses of her dreams.

Morning brought little solace as Sheila awoke to a house shrouded in an oppressive silence. The whispers, though momentarily silenced, lingered like a malevolent residue. The basement, now a forbidden chasm that bridged the realms of the living and the dead, beckoned to her with an unseen gravity.

The day unfolded with a palpable tension as Sheila, now a reluctant participant in a supernatural drama, grappled with the malevolence that had been unleashed. The dark history of the house, etched into its very foundations, loomed like a specter over every room, every corridor.

The house, now a living entity that hungered for the essence of the living, seemed to watch Sheila with an insatiable appetite. The whispers, a relentless chorus that echoed through the haunted halls, hinted at a darkness that transcended the limits of her understanding.

As night descended once again, Sheila stood at the crossroads of horror, the echoes of the dark history pulsating through the very walls. The malevolent forces, awakened from their slumber, awaited their next move in a macabre dance that threatened to consume Sheila's very soul. The house, a conduit for ancient malevolence, seemed to pulse with a malevolent energy that defied all attempts at rational explanation. Little

did Sheila know that the true terror, a malevolent force that transcended the boundaries of the supernatural, awaited its moment to strike in the chilling depths of the haunted dwelling.

Chapter 4: The Warning

The oppressive weight of the malevolent history lingered in the air as Sheila, haunted by the nightmarish events in the basement, found herself thrust deeper into the clutches of the old house. The whispers, though momentarily subdued, continued to echo through the corridors like an unseen presence that refused to be silenced.

As the sun dipped below the horizon, casting long shadows that stretched like spectral fingers, Sheila roamed the dimly lit rooms in a daze. The walls, adorned with faded wallpaper, seemed to close in around her like a suffocating embrace. Every creak and groan of the aging structure resonated with the echoes of the dark history that clung to the very fabric of the dwelling.

In a feeble attempt to regain a semblance of control, Sheila decided to venture outside. The night air, cool and crisp, offered a brief respite from the oppressive atmosphere within the house. As she stepped onto the porch, the world beyond seemed to hold its breath, as if aware of the supernatural forces that pulsed within the walls.

The neighboring houses stood in stoic silence, their windows gazing like empty eyes into the night. A distant streetlamp flickered intermittently, casting eerie shadows that danced on the pavement. Sheila, shivering in the cold, felt an inexplicable sense of being watched—an unseen gaze that followed her every move.

A sudden gust of wind carried with it a spectral whisper that sent a chill down Sheila's spine. The voice, laden with urgency, seemed to carry a warning—an ethereal plea that resonated with the very core of her being. Unsettled, she turned toward the source of the whisper, but the darkness offered no clues, concealing its secrets within its velvety embrace.

Returning to the house, Sheila couldn't escape the feeling that the very air held a sense of foreboding. The whispers, now a constant

companion, seemed to guide her toward the heart of the malevolence that lurked within. As she ascended the creaking stairs, the old house seemed to creak and groan in protest, as if resisting her attempts to uncover its darkest secrets.

The attic, a repository of forgotten artifacts, drew Sheila with an irresistible gravity. The air grew thick with an otherworldly energy as she approached the door leading to the mysterious space. As she turned the doorknob, a fleeting vision of ghostly figures danced on the periphery of her vision, vanishing as quickly as they appeared.

The attic, bathed in the feeble glow of a single bulb, revealed a myriad of forgotten relics—a dusty collection of forgotten memories. Sheila's flashlight illuminated old trunks, moth-eaten clothing, and a peculiar assortment of items that seemed frozen in time. Each artifact, a silent witness to the house's twisted history, exuded an otherworldly aura that seemed to tug at the edges of Sheila's sanity.

Among the forgotten relics, Sheila discovered an old photograph album. Its pages, yellowed with age, unveiled the lives of those who had once called the house their home. Family gatherings frozen in time, celebrations tainted by an unseen darkness, and the eyes of children who seemed to peer through the veil of the past—all spoke of a history steeped in sorrow.

As Sheila flipped through the photographs, a sudden chill settled in the room. Shadows danced along the walls, and the whispers intensified, their urgency now laced with an unspoken dread. The album, like a portal to the past, beckoned her to uncover the secrets that lingered within its pages.

The images told a tale of a family whose smiles concealed a tragic fate. A mother, her eyes reflecting a haunting sadness, held her children close in a sepia-toned embrace. The father, a stern figure with a haunted gaze, seemed to carry the weight of a malevolence that transcended the boundaries of the photograph.

In one particularly unsettling image, Sheila noticed a figure standing in the background—a silhouette that seemed to merge with the

shadows, its eyes staring into the depths of her soul. The whispers, now a dissonant chorus, echoed the name of the figure—an entity known only as "The Watcher."

A sudden realization gripped Sheila—the warnings she had received, the spectral figures in the attic, and the ever-present whispers—all converged on the ominous presence of The Watcher. As she traced the figure's silhouette with her trembling finger, the air thickened with an oppressive energy that seemed to bear the weight of the malevolent entity.

Driven by a desperate need to understand, Sheila decided to consult the elderly neighbor who had issued the initial warning. With the photograph album in hand, she ventured outside once again, the night air carrying with it a sense of impending doom.

The neighbor's house, a weathered structure bathed in the glow of a flickering porch light, seemed to emanate a warmth that stood in stark contrast to the cold atmosphere within Sheila's own dwelling. The old woman, with eyes clouded by the passage of time, opened the door with a knowing look that hinted at a lifetime of secrets.

As Sheila explained the events that had transpired—the whispers, the spectral figures, and the ominous presence of The Watcher—the elderly neighbor listened in solemn silence. When Sheila showed her the photograph album, the neighbor's eyes widened in recognition, and a shiver ran down her spine.

"You've unearthed a dark legacy," the old woman murmured, her voice a hushed whisper that seemed to carry the weight of untold secrets. She invited Sheila inside, where the walls seemed to resonate with a history that had long been buried.

Seated in a dimly lit room adorned with faded tapestries, the neighbor began to weave a tale that sent shivers down Sheila's spine. The house, it seemed, had once been a haven for a family whose lives had become entwined with an otherworldly force—a force that had claimed them in a twisted dance of tragedy.

The elderly neighbor spoke of The Watcher, an entity born from forbidden rituals conducted in the very heart of the house. Its malevolence, fueled by the suffering of the past, lingered like a vengeful specter, a guardian of dark secrets that defied the boundaries between the living and the dead.

The family in the photographs, the whispers, and the spectral figures —all were linked to The Watcher's insatiable hunger for the souls of the living. The old woman's words painted a harrowing picture of a malevolent force that sought to reclaim what had been lost—an entity that fed on the essence of the unsuspecting inhabitants.

As the elderly neighbor spoke, Sheila felt the weight of The Watcher's gaze upon her. The air in the room grew dense with an unseen presence, and the whispers, now a mournful lament, echoed through the walls like a requiem for the damned.

"You must leave this place," the old woman implored, her eyes reflecting a depth of sorrow that seemed to transcend the confines of the room. "The Watcher is awakened, and its hunger knows no bounds. Your very soul is in peril."

Fear gripped Sheila's heart as the magnitude of the malevolence became apparent. The warnings, the whispers, and the dark history of the house all converged on a chilling reality—a reality in which Sheila stood on the precipice of a supernatural abyss.

Determined to confront The Watcher and unravel the malevolent forces that held the house in their clutches, Sheila returned to her home with a sense of grim resolve. The night, now heavy with the weight of unseen eyes, seemed to pulse with an otherworldly energy that hinted at the imminent confrontation.

The house, a silent witness to the unfolding horror, awaited its fate in the embrace of darkness. Sheila, armed with the knowledge of the malevolent history and the warnings of The Watcher's insatiable hunger, steeled herself for a battle that would transcend the boundaries of the living and the dead. The whispers, now a chorus of spectral voices, guided her toward the heart of the supernatural storm that awaited in

the haunted corridors of the old dwelling. Little did she know that the true terror, a confrontation with The Watcher that would redefine the very fabric of reality, loomed on the horizon, threatening to plunge her into a darkness from which there might be no escape. The night, pregnant with the weight of unspoken horrors, unfolded with a spectral symphony that echoed the malevolent legacy of The Watcher—a force that hungered for the essence of the living, a force that would stop at nothing to reclaim what had been lost in the shadows of the past.

Chapter 5: The Apparition

As Sheila braced herself for the impending confrontation with The Watcher, the house seemed to hold its breath in a malevolent silence. The air, thick with the weight of unseen eyes, pressed against her skin like a suffocating shroud. Every step she took echoed in the dimly lit corridors, the whispers guiding her toward the heart of the supernatural storm.

The attic, a spectral realm illuminated by a feeble bulb, awaited her return. The artifacts, relics of a twisted history, seemed to resonate with an otherworldly energy as Sheila ascended the creaking stairs. The photograph album, now a key to the malevolent secrets that lurked within, clutched in her trembling hands, felt like a talisman against the encroaching darkness.

The whispers, now a relentless chorus that echoed through the haunted halls, intensified as Sheila reached the attic. The air pulsed with an unseen presence, and the shadows danced on the walls in a macabre ballet. The photograph album, when opened, revealed spectral figures that seemed to move within the confines of the images—a silent procession of lost souls tethered to The Watcher's insatiable hunger.

With a heavy heart, Sheila placed the photograph album on a dusty table in the center of the attic. The air seemed to vibrate with an unseen energy, and the whispers reached a fevered pitch. A sudden gust of wind extinguished the feeble bulb, plunging the attic into darkness.

In the obscurity, Sheila felt a spectral presence closing in around her. The whispers, now an anguished wail, surrounded her like a ghostly

chorus. The air seemed charged with an otherworldly force as The Watcher's malevolence manifested in the shadows.

A cold breath brushed against Sheila's neck, and she sensed the gaze of unseen eyes upon her. The spectral figures from the photographs materialized in the darkness, their eyes reflecting a hunger that transcended the boundaries of the living and the dead.

In the suffocating darkness, Sheila felt a touch—a caress of unseen fingers that traced the contours of her face. The whispers, now a maddening cacophony, echoed through the attic, creating a dissonant symphony of horror. The Watcher, a malevolent force that defied explanation, sought to claim her soul in a spectral dance of damnation.

Desperation gripped Sheila as she fumbled for her flashlight, the feeble beam cutting through the obscurity like a beacon of fragile hope. The spectral figures, their faces twisted in silent anguish, retreated into the shadows as the light pierced the darkness.

With trembling hands, Sheila retrieved the photograph album. The images, though now devoid of spectral movement, seemed to carry the weight of the malevolent history that clung to the house. The Watcher, its presence still palpable in the obscurity, awaited its chance to strike once again.

The whispers, now a haunting melody, guided Sheila back through the labyrinthine corridors. The old house, a spectral battleground, seemed to pulse with an otherworldly energy that defied rational explanation. As she descended the creaking stairs, the weight of The Watcher's malevolence bore down on her shoulders like an unseen burden.

In the dimly lit living room, Sheila's flashlight revealed a ghostly figure standing in the hall—a silhouette that seemed to merge with the shadows. The Watcher, its form obscured by the darkness, stared at her with eyes that held the emptiness of eternity.

Fear clawed at Sheila's chest as she confronted the spectral entity that lurked within the old house. The whispers, now a mournful lament, echoed through the corridors, intertwining with the malevolent

presence that encircled her. The time for understanding was over; the time for confrontation had arrived.

Sheila, driven by a grim resolve, approached The Watcher. The air seemed to ripple with an unseen force, and the whispers reached a crescendo as she stood face to face with the malevolent entity. The Watcher, a manifestation of forgotten sorrows and ancient grievances, exuded an otherworldly aura that seemed to defy the very laws of nature.

In the spectral confrontation, Sheila felt a cold hand brush against her cheek—a touch that carried the weight of a thousand lost souls. The whispers, now an ethereal chorus, spoke words that resonated with the depths of her consciousness. The Watcher sought communion, a merging of the living and the dead in a twisted dance of supernatural entanglement.

With a surge of determination, Sheila raised the photograph album. The images, now illuminated by the feeble glow of her flashlight, held a spectral resonance that seemed to repel The Watcher. The entity recoiled, its form dissipating like mist in the face of an unseen force.

In the haunting confrontation, Sheila felt a surge of power—the power of the forgotten souls that lingered within the photographs. The whispers, now a triumphant hymn, reverberated through the haunted halls as The Watcher retreated into the shadows. The malevolent force, thwarted by the spectral energy of the past, seemed to dissipate like a fading nightmare.

The old house, once a battleground between the living and the dead, fell silent. The whispers, now a fading echo, lingered in the air like a melancholic melody. Sheila, exhausted and shaken, stood amidst the remnants of the spectral encounter, the photograph album clutched in her trembling hands.

As the oppressive atmosphere lifted, Sheila felt a profound change in the house—a sense of peace that transcended the malevolent legacy of The Watcher. The whispers, though subdued, carried a lingering gratitude, as if the forgotten souls had found solace in the spectral confrontation.

With a heavy heart, Sheila descended into the basement—the very heart of the house's dark history. The air, once thick with malevolence, now held a somber tranquility. The relics of forgotten rituals seemed frozen in time, their significance transformed by the spectral encounter.

In the dim light, Sheila uncovered the old diary—the key to the understanding of the house's twisted past. The pages, though stained with the ink of tormented souls, now bore a sense of closure. The Watcher, defeated by the power of the forgotten, had relinquished its hold on the old dwelling.

As Sheila emerged from the basement, the morning sun began to cast its gentle rays on the once-foreboding structure. The old house, no longer a haven for malevolent forces, seemed to stand in quiet reverence to the spectral encounter that had unfolded within its walls.

The whispers, now a distant echo, guided Sheila to the attic—the epicenter of the supernatural storm. The photograph album, placed back in its dusty corner, exuded a spectral resonance that seemed to linger in the air. The spectral figures within the images, their faces now frozen in peace, bore silent witness to the resolution of a malevolent legacy.

Sheila, now forever changed by the harrowing ordeal, stepped outside into the cool morning air. The neighborhood, once draped in a veil of darkness, now basked in the warmth of the rising sun. The whispers, though a mere memory, carried a final message—a farewell from the forgotten souls who had found redemption in the face of supernatural turmoil.

As Sheila walked away from the old house, the sense of normalcy slowly returned. The neighborhood, once tainted by the malevolent force that had claimed the dwelling, now stood as a testament to the triumph of the living over the specters of the past.

Little did Sheila know that the true horror, a final revelation that would redefine the very fabric of her existence, awaited in the shadows of her newfound peace. The old house, though freed from the clutches of The Watcher, held a secret that would unveil itself in a chilling twist

of fate—one that would test the limits of Sheila's resilience and plunge her into a darkness from which there might be no escape.

The whispers, now a distant memory, left the door open for the looming terror that awaited in the aftermath of the supernatural storm. The haunting melody of the forgotten lingered in the air as Sheila ventured into the uncertain future—a future where the boundaries between the living and the dead remained blurred, and the horrors of the past cast a long, lingering shadow over the new normal that awaited her.

Chapter 6: The Visitor

In the wake of the harrowing confrontation with The Watcher, Sheila grappled with the aftermath of the supernatural storm that had engulfed the old house. The whispers, now a distant echo, left an eerie silence in their wake—a silence that seemed to stretch across the haunted halls like a spectral tapestry.

As Sheila navigated the dimly lit rooms, the old house felt different. The air, once thick with malevolence, now carried a palpable tranquility. The remnants of forgotten rituals in the basement seemed frozen in time, their significance transformed by the spectral encounter. The photograph album, placed back in its dusty corner in the attic, exuded a spectral resonance that lingered like a fading memory.

Despite the apparent peace that settled over the dwelling, Sheila couldn't shake the feeling that the old house held secrets yet to be unveiled. The neighborhood, seemingly untouched by the supernatural turmoil, continued its daily rhythm. Sheila's neighbors, unaware of the malevolent force that had gripped their midst, carried on with their lives in blissful ignorance.

The morning sun cast a warm glow on the neighborhood, and Sheila decided to take a stroll outside. The fresh air, tinged with the scent of dew-kissed grass, offered a reprieve from the suffocating atmosphere within the old house. As she walked down the quiet streets, the whispers, though faint, seemed to guide her steps toward a sense of normalcy.

In the midst of the peaceful neighborhood, Sheila encountered a figure from her past—Rob, her childhood friend who had experienced the unsettling events in the house. Rob, unaware of the supernatural horrors that had transpired, greeted Sheila with a warm smile.

As they exchanged pleasantries, Sheila hesitated to divulge the haunting experiences she had faced. The whispers, now a gentle hum in the background, seemed to caution her against revealing the spectral truth that lingered within the old house. Instead, she chose to enjoy the fleeting moments of normalcy with Rob, hoping to leave the malevolent past behind.

The day unfolded with a semblance of serenity as Sheila and Rob reminisced about their shared childhood memories. Laughter echoed through the air, temporarily drowning out the lingering echoes of the supernatural encounter. The old house, its haunted corridors temporarily silenced, stood as a mere backdrop to the facade of normalcy that enveloped the neighborhood.

As night descended, Sheila invited Rob to stay the night—a decision that would unwittingly drag him into the lingering shadows of the malevolent past. The whispers, though muted, seemed to intensify as darkness cloaked the old house in an otherworldly stillness.

In the dimly lit living room, Sheila and Rob shared stories from their past, seeking refuge in the familiarity of friendship. The air, though seemingly calm, held a sense of foreboding as the whispers, now a spectral melody, intertwined with the gentle hum of the night.

As they settled in for the night, Sheila couldn't escape the feeling that The Watcher's malevolence lingered in the shadows. The spectral figures from the photographs, now etched in her memory, seemed to cast ghostly shadows on the walls. The old house, once a haven for dark forces, bore silent witness to the unsuspecting visitors who dared to cross its threshold.

The night progressed in a semblance of tranquility, the whispers fading into the background. Yet, as the clock ticked towards midnight, an unspoken tension enveloped the dwelling. Sheila, restless and haunted

by the memories of the supernatural storm, found herself drawn to the attic—the epicenter of the spectral encounter.

In the attic, the photograph album lay in its dusty corner, seemingly untouched by the passage of time. The whispers, though muted, urged Sheila to revisit the malevolent history that clung to the old house. With a heavy heart, she opened the album, its pages revealing the spectral figures that had once danced within its confines.

As Sheila traced the images with her trembling finger, a sudden gust of wind extinguished the feeble bulb, plunging the attic into darkness. The whispers, now a mournful lament, echoed through the spectral realm as the photographs seemed to come to life once again.

In the obscurity, Sheila felt a spectral presence closing in around her. The whispers, now a dissonant chorus, spoke words that seemed to reverberate with the anguished cries of the forgotten. The Watcher, its malevolence not fully vanquished, sought communion with the living in a macabre dance of supernatural entanglement.

Rob, stirred from his sleep by the eerie atmosphere, joined Sheila in the attic. The air seemed to vibrate with an unseen force as the whispers guided them toward the heart of the spectral storm. The photograph album, now a conduit to the malevolent past, exuded an otherworldly energy that drew them deeper into the supernatural abyss.

As they stood in the darkness, the spectral figures from the photographs materialized around them. Eyes devoid of life stared at Sheila and Rob, their hollow gazes filled with an insatiable hunger. The whispers, now a haunting melody, spoke of unresolved sorrows that lingered within the old house.

In the spectral confrontation, Sheila and Rob felt the weight of unseen eyes upon them. The Watcher, though seemingly thwarted, manifested in the shadows with a renewed malevolence. The whispers, now a spectral symphony, hinted at a darkness that defied the boundaries of the living and the dead.

Desperation gripped Sheila as she clutched the photograph album. The images, now illuminated by the feeble glow of Rob's flashlight,

held a spectral resonance that seemed to repel The Watcher. The entity recoiled, its form dissipating like mist in the face of an unseen force.

In the haunting confrontation, Sheila and Rob felt a surge of power—the power of the forgotten souls that lingered within the photographs. The whispers, now a triumphant hymn, reverberated through the haunted attic as The Watcher retreated into the shadows. The malevolent force, though temporarily thwarted, lingered like a specter in the lingering darkness.

The attic, once a battleground between the living and the dead, fell silent. The whispers, now a fading echo, left an eerie stillness in their wake. Sheila and Rob, exhausted and shaken, stood amidst the remnants of the spectral encounter, the photograph album a testament to the unresolved sorrows that clung to the old house.

As they descended from the attic, the old house seemed to sigh with a spectral resignation. The whispers, though subdued, lingered in the air like a melancholic melody. The night, pregnant with the weight of unspoken horrors, unfolded with a sense of uncertainty—a future where the boundaries between the living and the dead remained blurred.

Sheila and Rob, now forever entwined in the malevolent legacy of the old house, sought refuge in the dimly lit living room. The whispers, though muted, hinted at a lingering terror that awaited in the shadows. Little did they know that the true horror, a revelation that would redefine the very fabric of their existence, loomed on the horizon—a revelation that would test the limits of their resilience and plunge them into a darkness from which there might be no escape.

The whispers, now a distant murmur, left the door ajar for the looming terror that awaited in the aftermath of the spectral storm. The old house, its haunted corridors pulsating with unresolved sorrows, stood as a gateway to a supernatural abyss. Sheila and Rob, bound by the malevolent forces that lingered within, faced an uncertain future where the horrors of the past cast a long, lingering shadow over their fragile grasp on reality.

Chapter 7: The Presence

The night, once a harbinger of supernatural turmoil, descended upon the old house with an unsettling stillness. Sheila and Rob, shaken by the spectral encounter in the attic, sought solace in the dimly lit living room. The air, though seemingly calm, carried an unspoken tension—a tension that seemed to thicken with every passing moment.

As they sat in the silence, the whispers, now a muted hum, seemed to guide Sheila's attention toward the shadows that lurked in the corners of the room. The old house, a silent witness to the malevolent forces that had unfolded within its walls, exuded an otherworldly energy that defied the confines of the living and the dead.

A subtle chill crept through the air as the temperature in the room dropped. The whispers, though faint, took on a dissonant tone—a spectral melody that hinted at the lingering presence of The Watcher. Sheila and Rob, their senses heightened by the supernatural ordeal, felt an unseen gaze upon them.

In the dim light, objects in the room seemed to shift mysteriously. A picture frame trembled on the wall, and the flickering flame of a candle cast dancing shadows that defied the laws of physics. The old house, now a conduit for the residual malevolence, pulsed with an unseen force that sought communion with the living.

Unease settled over Sheila and Rob as they exchanged wary glances. The whispers, now a spectral chorus, seemed to speak of a malevolent force that had not been fully vanquished—a force that lingered in the shadows, biding its time for a resurgence. The old house, once a haven for dark rituals, held its secrets close, and the unsuspecting inhabitants stood at the mercy of the supernatural storm that raged within its walls.

In an attempt to dispel the ominous atmosphere, Sheila suggested a distraction—turning on the television to drown out the spectral whispers. As they sat on the worn-out couch, the flickering images on the screen seemed to offer a brief respite from the encroaching darkness. However, the shadows that danced in the periphery of their vision hinted at a malevolence that refused to be ignored.

The night unfolded with a deceptive calmness, the television casting a pale glow that struggled against the encroaching darkness. Sheila and Rob, though attempting to maintain a façade of normalcy, couldn't shake the feeling that The Watcher's presence lingered like a spectral specter in the room.

As the clock struck midnight, a sudden drop in temperature sent shivers down their spines. The whispers, now a mournful wail, echoed through the haunted halls, creating an ethereal symphony of dread. Sheila and Rob, bound by the malevolent legacy of the old house, felt an unseen force closing in around them.

In the dim light, a shadowy figure materialized in the hall—a silhouette that seemed to defy the laws of the physical world. The Watcher, its malevolence not fully quelled, stood as a spectral guardian in the shadows. The whispers, now a dissonant chorus, spoke of an unresolved darkness that sought to reclaim the living.

Fear gripped Sheila and Rob as The Watcher's presence manifested in the room. The air seemed charged with an otherworldly energy as the entity, now a tangible force, cast a haunting gaze upon the unsuspecting visitors. The whispers, though muted, carried a warning—an anguished plea to leave the old house before it succumbed to the malevolent forces that clung to its very foundations.

In a desperate attempt to defy the encroaching darkness, Sheila and Rob decided to leave the living room and venture into the seemingly unaffected parts of the house. The whispers, now a relentless drone, seemed to guide them toward the heart of the supernatural storm.

As they ascended the creaking stairs, the oppressive atmosphere intensified. The walls, adorned with faded wallpaper, seemed to close in around them like a suffocating embrace. The Watcher's presence, a spectral entity that defied rational explanation, pulsed with an unseen force that sought to ensnare their very souls.

In the upstairs hallway, a door creaked open on its own—a manifestation of the lingering malevolence that gripped the old house. The whispers, now a haunting lament, guided Sheila and Rob toward the

threshold of the mysteriously opened door. The room beyond, bathed in an unnatural darkness, beckoned them to confront the unresolved sorrows that lingered within.

As they entered the room, the air thickened with an oppressive energy. The temperature dropped, and the whispers reached a fevered pitch. The Watcher's presence, now an undeniable force, seemed to co-alesce in the shadows—a spectral guardian that stood between the living and the abyss.

In the dim light, Sheila and Rob discovered an old mirror—a relic that seemed to hold the key to the malevolent forces that plagued the old house. The whispers, now a cacophony of spectral voices, spoke of a dark energy woven into the very fabric of the reflection.

As they stared into the mirror, their reflections seemed distorted—a ghastly image that hinted at the malevolent entity that lurked within the haunted dwelling. The Watcher, its form now a nightmarish ap-parition in the reflective surface, bore silent witness to the unfolding confrontation.

A sudden realization gripped Sheila—the mirror, a conduit for The Watcher's malevolence, held the key to the unresolved darkness that clung to the old house. The whispers, though chaotic, seemed to guide her toward a revelation that would redefine the boundaries between the living and the dead.

Driven by a grim resolve, Sheila and Rob decided to confront The Watcher through the mirror—a ritual that promised to unveil the malevolent forces that lurked within. The room, now bathed in an otherworldly glow, felt like a spectral battleground where the living and the dead converged in a macabre dance of supernatural entanglement.

As they stood before the mirror, the whispers reached a crescendo. The Watcher's apparition, now a nightmarish entity that defied descrip-tion, materialized in the reflective surface. The air seemed to vibrate with an unseen force as Sheila and Rob prepared to confront the malevolent force that had haunted them.

The room, now a spectral realm suspended between the living and the dead, bore witness to the spectral encounter. The Watcher, its malevolence intensified by the confrontation, sought communion with the living in a ghastly manifestation that defied the laws of nature.

In the mirror's reflection, Sheila and Rob felt the weight of unseen eyes upon them. The Watcher's gaze, a haunting stare that held the emptiness of eternity, sought to penetrate the very depths of their souls. The whispers, now a mournful hymn, intertwined with the oppressive energy as the supernatural battle unfolded.

With a surge of spectral power, Sheila and Rob confronted The Watcher through the mirror. The whispers, though chaotic, seemed to align with the living, creating a dissonant symphony that echoed through the spectral realm. The Watcher, now faced with the combined resilience of the living, recoiled in the face of an unseen force.

In the haunting confrontation, the mirror shattered—an explosion of glass that seemed to reverberate through the haunted halls. The Watcher's malevolence, now fractured and dispersed, retreated into the shadows like a fading nightmare. The room, once a battleground between the living and the abyss, fell silent.

Sheila and Rob, exhausted and shaken, stood amidst the shards of the shattered mirror. The whispers, now a distant echo, carried a sense of fleeting victory. The old house, though still haunted by the malevolent forces that clung to its foundations, seemed to sigh with a spectral resignation.

The night, now heavy with the weight of supernatural turmoil, unfolded with an unsettling stillness. Sheila and Rob, their resolve tested by the spectral encounter, descended from the upstairs realm and returned to the living room. The air, though laden with the remnants of the supernatural battle, felt lighter as if a temporary reprieve had been granted.

Little did they know that the true horror, a revelation that would redefine the very fabric of their existence, awaited in the shadows of their newfound victory. The old house, though temporarily quelled, held

secrets that would unveil themselves in a chilling twist of fate—one that would test the limits of Sheila and Rob's resilience and plunge them into a darkness from which there might be no escape.

The whispers, now a fading memory, left the door ajar for the looming terror that awaited in the aftermath of the spectral storm. The old house, its haunted corridors pulsating with unresolved sorrows, stood as a gateway to a supernatural abyss. Sheila and Rob, bound by the malevolent forces that lingered within, faced an uncertain future where the horrors of the past cast a long, lingering shadow over their fragile grasp on reality.

Chapter 8: The Message

The night, now heavy with the echoes of the spectral confrontation, unfolded with an eerie stillness in the old house. Sheila and Rob, their nerves still on edge from the encounter in the haunted room, sought refuge in the dimly lit living room. The air, though seemingly calm, carried the residual tension of the supernatural battle that had unfolded within the haunted dwelling.

As they settled on the worn-out couch, the whispers, though subdued, lingered in the air like a spectral melody. The old house, once a haven for dark rituals and spectral forces, seemed to hold its breath in the aftermath of the shattered mirror. Sheila and Rob, their senses heightened by the otherworldly encounter, exchanged wary glances as they awaited the next manifestation of The Watcher's malevolence.

The television, now a mere flickering glow in the dim room, offered a semblance of normalcy. Sheila, attempting to distract herself from the lingering horrors, suggested turning on the lights to dispel the encroaching darkness. As she reached for the switch, a sudden power outage plunged the old house into complete darkness.

In the pitch-black silence, the whispers intensified. The air seemed charged with an otherworldly energy, and a sense of dread settled over Sheila and Rob like a suffocating shroud. The old house, now devoid of any artificial illumination, became a spectral realm where the living and the dead coexisted in an uneasy truce.

Amidst the darkness, an ominous presence loomed—a manifestation of The Watcher's lingering malevolence. The whispers, now a dissonant chorus, guided Sheila and Rob toward the heart of the supernatural storm. The basement, a place fraught with the echoes of forgotten rituals, beckoned them to confront the unresolved darkness that clung to the old house.

With flashlights in hand, Sheila and Rob descended into the dimly lit basement. The air, thick with the weight of unseen eyes, seemed to pulse with a spectral energy that transcended the boundaries of the living and the dead. The whispers, now a haunting murmur, guided them toward a message—a cryptic revelation that awaited in the subterranean depths.

In the basement, amidst the relics of forgotten rituals, Sheila discovered an old Ouija board—an artifact that seemed to carry the spectral residue of past seances. The whispers, now a relentless drone, urged them to communicate with the other side in a desperate attempt to unravel the malevolent mysteries that clung to the old house.

With hesitant resolve, Sheila and Rob placed their trembling hands on the planchette. The Ouija board, now a conduit for the spectral forces, seemed to come alive with an otherworldly energy. The whispers, though chaotic, aligned with the planchette's movements, guiding them through a spectral conversation with the entities that lingered in the shadows.

As they sought answers from the other side, the planchette spelled out cryptic words on the Ouija board. The whispers, now a spectral symphony, intensified as the message unfolded. "He watches," the planchette spelled out, the words etched in an otherworldly script that seemed to defy rational explanation.

A chill ran down Sheila's spine as the whispers spoke of The Watcher's insatiable hunger—an entity that observed the living with an unrelenting gaze. The message, though cryptic, hinted at a darkness that transcended the boundaries of the living and the dead. The old house,

a silent witness to the supernatural turmoil, bore witness to a revelation that would redefine the very fabric of reality.

In the dim light of the basement, Sheila and Rob felt an unseen force closing in around them. The whispers, now a haunting melody, intertwined with the spectral energy that permeated the air. The Ouija board, a conduit for the malevolent forces, seemed to carry a message from beyond—a message that foretold a greater darkness that awaited in the shadows.

With a sense of trepidation, Sheila and Rob decided to delve deeper into the basement—a place where the old house's dark history unfolded in the form of forgotten rituals and malevolent entities. The whispers, though chaotic, seemed to guide them toward an altar—a focal point of the supernatural energies that pulsed through the subterranean depths.

As they reached the heart of the basement, a cold wind swept through the air—a spectral breeze that carried with it the echoes of forgotten incantations. The whispers, now a mournful lament, spoke of a ritual that could potentially unveil the true nature of The Watcher's malevolence.

On the altar, Sheila found an ancient book—an occult tome that detailed the dark history woven into the very foundations of the old house. The whispers, though fragmented, urged her to decipher the cryptic symbols and incantations that adorned the pages. The malevolent legacy, now laid bare in the pages of the ancient book, hinted at a supernatural force that defied comprehension.

With a heavy heart, Sheila began to read aloud the incantations—a desperate attempt to commune with the entities that lingered in the shadows. The whispers, now a spectral chorus, seemed to align with the words of the ritual, creating a dissonant symphony that reverberated through the basement.

As the incantations reached a fevered pitch, the air in the basement seemed to warp and twist. Shadows danced on the walls, and the whispers, now a cacophony of spectral voices, spoke of a portal—a gateway between the living and the abyss. The old house, its spectral foundations

shaken by the unfolding ritual, became a conduit for the malevolent forces that sought communion with the living.

In the dim light, the basement transformed into a spectral realm—a place suspended between the living and the dead. The whispers, now an anguished wail, guided Sheila and Rob toward the heart of the supernatural storm. The ritual, though wrought with danger, promised to unveil the true nature of The Watcher's malevolence.

As they stood at the precipice of the ritual's culmination, a sudden gust of wind extinguished their flashlights. Darkness enveloped them, and the whispers, now a relentless drone, seemed to merge with the shadows that danced in the spectral realm. The Ouija board, the ancient book, and the altar became mere silhouettes in the obscurity—a spectral tableau that hinted at the imminent confrontation with the unknown.

In the darkness, Sheila and Rob felt a surge of supernatural energy— the very fabric of reality seemed to warp and bend. The whispers, now a spectral symphony, reached a crescendo as the ritual reached its zenith. The portal, a shimmering gateway between the living and the abyss, beckoned them to confront the malevolent forces that awaited on the other side.

With a hesitant step, Sheila and Rob crossed the threshold of the portal. The whispers, now a haunting melody, surrounded them like a ghostly chorus. The old house, its foundations shaken by the unfolding ritual, bore silent witness to the spectral encounter that transcended the boundaries of the living and the dead.

As they entered the other side, the supernatural realm unfolded with an eerie beauty. Ethereal

Chapter 9: The History Revealed

In the supernatural realm beyond the portal, Sheila and Rob found themselves surrounded by a surreal landscape. Ghostly echoes of forgotten rituals and spectral entities painted the ethereal canvas. The whispers, now a haunting melody, guided them deeper into the spectral abyss—a place where the dark history of the old house unraveled in a dissonant symphony of the supernatural.

As they ventured through the ghostly landscape, Sheila and Rob discovered fragments of the past—a spectral montage that revealed the horrors once held within the old house's walls. The whispers, though fragmented, spoke of gruesome rituals and malevolent entities that had left an indelible mark on the haunted dwelling.

Images of hooded figures engaged in forbidden ceremonies danced before their eyes. The air, thick with the scent of incense and spectral energy, carried the echoes of tormented souls who had fallen victim to the malevolent forces that once reigned in the old house. The whispers, now a mournful lament, spoke of an occult legacy woven into the very fabric of the supernatural realm.

In their spectral journey, Sheila and Rob stumbled upon an ancient diary—an artifact that seemed to hold the key to the malevolent history that plagued the old house. The diary, its pages yellowed with age, detailed the dark rituals that had once unfolded in the basement. The whispers, now a spectral chorus, urged them to read the words that revealed the origin of The Watcher's malevolence.

As Sheila deciphered the cryptic entries, the images of hooded figures engaging in occult ceremonies became vivid in her mind. The diary spoke of a cult that had once thrived within the old house, conducting rituals that sought communion with otherworldly entities. The whispers, though haunting, hinted at a darkness that transcended the boundaries of the living and the dead.

In the spectral realm, Sheila and Rob felt the weight of the forgotten souls that had fallen victim to the cult's malevolence. The air, charged with an otherworldly energy, seemed to vibrate with the echoes of tormented cries. The old house, once a haven for dark forces, bore witness to the anguished spirits that lingered within the supernatural tapestry.

As they delved deeper into the spectral landscape, the whispers guided them toward a hidden chamber—a place where the cult's rituals had reached their zenith. The air in the chamber felt oppressive, and the whispers, now a relentless drone, seemed to speak of a malevolent energy woven into the very walls of the old house.

In the chamber, Sheila and Rob discovered an altar—an ancient stone slab adorned with cryptic symbols. The whispers, now a cacophony of spectral voices, spoke of blood sacrifices and forbidden rites that had stained the altar with the anguish of the forgotten. The old house, its spectral foundations steeped in the malevolent legacy, became a witness to the horrors that had transpired within its confines.

The images in the spectral landscape became more vivid—a macabre display of hooded figures performing dark rituals in the dimly lit chamber. The whispers, now a mournful hymn, conveyed the desperation of the tormented souls who had once walked the halls of the old house. Sheila and Rob, entwined in the spectral tapestry, felt the weight of the dark history that clung to their very beings.

As they reached the climax of the spectral journey, the whispers guided them toward a hidden passage in the chamber. A secret door, concealed by centuries-old dust, beckoned them to confront the source of The Watcher's malevolence. The old house, its spectral corridors pulsating with the echoes of the past, stood as a gateway to a deeper darkness that awaited in the shadows.

With trepidation, Sheila and Rob opened the secret door, revealing a staircase that descended into the depths of the supernatural realm. The air, now thick with the energy of the forgotten, guided them toward an underground cavern—a place where the cult's rituals had once reached their zenith.

In the cavern, the whispers reached a fevered pitch. The air seemed charged with an unseen force as Sheila and Rob navigated through the dimly lit passages. The walls, adorned with ancient symbols, spoke of a dark energy that permeated the very foundations of the old house.

As they reached the heart of the cavern, a revelation unfolded—a sacrificial chamber adorned with an altar bathed in an otherworldly glow. The whispers, now a dissonant symphony, spoke of the need for a blood sacrifice to seal the malevolent forces that lingered within the old house. Sheila and Rob, bound by the supernatural forces that guided

their journey, faced an unimaginable choice that would redefine the very fabric of their existence.

The images in the cavern came to life—a spectral replay of the cult's rituals and the sacrifices that had stained the altar with the blood of the innocent. The whispers, now a haunting melody, spoke of The Watcher's insatiable hunger and the need for a final sacrifice to quell the malevolent forces.

In the cavern's depths, Sheila and Rob confronted the truth—the old house, built for occult rituals, held a dark energy woven into its very walls. The whispers, though chaotic, conveyed a revelation that transcended the boundaries of the living and the dead. The sacrificial chamber, a place where the malevolent legacy reached its zenith, became a battleground between the supernatural and the mortal.

With a heavy heart, Sheila and Rob realized the only way to seal the malevolent forces was through a blood sacrifice. The whispers, now a mournful lament, spoke of the necessity to offer a part of themselves to quell the insatiable hunger of The Watcher. The old house, its spectral foundations shaken by the revelation, stood as a testament to the price that must be paid to vanquish the malevolent legacy.

In the dim light of the sacrificial chamber, Sheila and Rob prepared for the ritual—a desperate attempt to seal the malevolent forces that clung to the old house. The whispers, now a spectral symphony, guided them through the ancient rites that had once unleashed the supernatural storm within the haunted dwelling.

As the ritual reached its climax, Sheila and Rob felt an otherworldly energy enveloping them. The air pulsed with the echoes of forgotten incantations, and the sacrificial chamber seemed to vibrate with a spectral resonance. The whispers, though haunting, guided them toward a destiny entwined with the malevolent forces that sought communion with the living.

With a surge of supernatural power, Sheila and Rob offered a part of themselves to the sacrificial chamber. The whispers, now a triumphant hymn, echoed through the cavern as their sacrifice became a beacon of

light in the spectral darkness. The old house, its foundations saturated with the essence of the living, stood at the precipice of a resolution that transcended the boundaries of the mortal realm.

In the aftermath of the ritual, the cavern fell silent. The whispers, though fading, left an eerie stillness in their wake. Sheila and Rob, exhausted and shaken, stood amidst the spectral remnants of the sacrificial chamber. The old house, though still haunted by the echoes of the past, seemed to sigh with a spectral resignation.

The supernatural realm, now devoid of the malevolent forces that once tormented the haunted dwelling, unfolded with an unsettling stillness. Sheila and Rob, their journey through the spectral abyss complete, ascended from the underground cavern and returned to the haunted halls of the old house.

As they emerged into the dim light of the old house, a sense of eerie calm settled over them. The whispers, now a distant echo, carried a semblance of victory—a fleeting reprieve from the encroaching darkness. Little did they know that the true challenge awaited in the aftermath of the ritual—a revelation that would test the limits of their resilience and plunge them into a darkness from which there might be no escape.

The old house, though temporarily quelled, bore witness to the sacrifices made to seal the malevolent forces within its spectral confines. Sheila and Rob, forever changed by the ritual, faced an uncertain future where the echoes of the past lingered like a spectral shadow. The whispers, now a fading memory, left the door ajar for the looming terror that awaited in the aftermath of the spectral storm.

In the dim light of the old house, Sheila and Rob, their spirits weighed down by the sacrifice, descended from the underground cavern and returned to the living room. The air, though laden with the remnants of the supernatural battle, felt lighter as if a temporary reprieve had been granted.

As they navigated the haunted halls, a realization gripped Sheila and Rob—the old house, though temporarily quelled, held secrets that would unveil themselves in a chilling twist of fate. The whispers, now

a fading memory, left the door ajar for the looming terror that awaited in the aftermath of the spectral storm. The old house, its foundations saturated with the essence of the living, stood as a gateway to a supernatural abyss. Sheila and Rob, bound by the malevolent forces that lingered within, faced an uncertain future where the horrors of the past cast a long, lingering shadow over their fragile grasp on reality.

Chapter 10: The Basement

After sealing the malevolent forces within the old house through the sacrificial ritual, Sheila and Rob found themselves back in the dimly lit living room. The air, though tinged with an unsettling calm, carried the echoes of the supernatural journey they had undertaken. The whispers, now a distant memory, left a spectral resonance in the haunted dwelling.

As Sheila and Rob attempted to regain their bearings, a foreboding sensation lingered in the air. The old house, once a haven for dark rituals, stood as a testament to the sacrifices made to quell the malevolent forces. Little did they know that the true test awaited in the aftermath of the ritual—a revelation that would redefine the very fabric of their existence.

In the eerie quiet, Sheila's gaze was drawn to the basement door—the same door that had led them to the depths of the supernatural realm. The whispers, though muted, seemed to guide her attention toward the subterranean depths where forgotten rituals had once unfolded. A sense of trepidation settled over her as the basement became a focal point of the encroaching darkness.

Rob, too, felt an unspoken unease as he followed Sheila's gaze toward the basement door. The air, though seemingly calm, carried a spectral energy that hinted at the unresolved mysteries lurking within the subterranean depths. The old house, though momentarily at peace, seemed to hold secrets that demanded further exploration.

Driven by an unspoken compulsion, Sheila and Rob approached the basement door. The whispers, now a faint murmur, seemed to beckon them to descend once more into the depths of the haunted dwelling. The wooden stairs creaked under their weight as they descended into

the dimly lit basement—a place where the supernatural energies still lingered, weaving a spectral tapestry of the past.

In the basement, the air felt charged with an otherworldly energy. The whispers, though subdued, guided Sheila and Rob toward the heart of the supernatural storm. The old house, its foundations saturated with the essence of the living, seemed to pulse with an unseen force that transcended the boundaries of the mortal realm.

As they ventured deeper into the basement, Sheila's flashlight revealed forgotten artifacts—relics of the occult rituals that had once held sway within the haunted dwelling. The whispers, though fragmented, spoke of a lingering malevolence that refused to be fully contained. The old house, its spectral corridors echoing with the whispers of the past, became a gateway to a darkness that awaited in the shadows.

A sudden drop in temperature signaled a change in the atmosphere. The whispers, now a haunting lament, guided Sheila and Rob toward a hidden corner of the basement. There, obscured by shadows, they discovered a mysterious door—an entrance to a forgotten chamber that had eluded their previous exploration.

With trepidation, Sheila and Rob opened the door, revealing a chamber bathed in an unnatural darkness. The air, thick with the scent of ancient incense, seemed to vibrate with the echoes of spectral energy. The whispers, now a dissonant symphony, spoke of a deeper layer of malevolence that awaited discovery.

As they entered the hidden chamber, Sheila's flashlight revealed cryptic symbols etched into the walls—a language of the occult that spoke of forbidden knowledge and ancient rites. The whispers, though chaotic, seemed to convey a message—a revelation that transcended the boundaries of the living and the dead. The old house, now a conduit for the supernatural, bore witness to the unfolding mysteries that awaited in the hidden chamber.

In the dim light, Sheila and Rob stumbled upon an ancient tome— an occult grimoire that held the secrets of the forgotten rituals. The whispers, now a spectral chorus, urged Sheila to decipher the cryptic

symbols that adorned the pages. The malevolent legacy, though temporarily quelled, seemed to find its voice in the ancient words that unfolded in the flickering light.

As Sheila read aloud the incantations, the chamber seemed to come alive with an otherworldly energy. Shadows danced on the walls, and the whispers, now a cacophony of spectral voices, spoke of a deeper darkness that had yet to be unveiled. The old house, a witness to the unfolding ritual, became a gateway to the unknown—a place where the living and the dead converged in a macabre dance.

In the spectral glow, the hidden chamber transformed into a supernatural realm—a place suspended between the living and the abyss. The whispers, now a mournful wail, guided Sheila and Rob toward a revelation that would test the limits of their resilience. The old house, its foundations shaken by the unfolding ritual, became a battleground where the supernatural and the mortal collided.

As they delved deeper into the hidden chamber, the symbols on the walls seemed to shift—a spectral language that defied comprehension. The whispers, though haunting, spoke of an ancient evil that had been awakened by their presence. Sheila and Rob, bound by the malevolent forces that lingered within the old house, faced an unforeseen challenge that awaited in the shadows.

A sudden gust of wind extinguished their flashlights, plunging the hidden chamber into complete darkness. The whispers, now a relentless drone, seemed to merge with the shadows that danced in the spectral realm. The old house, its spectral foundations saturated with the essence of the living, stood at the precipice of a new, malevolent revelation.

In the darkness, Sheila and Rob felt an unseen force closing in around them. The whispers, now a spectral symphony, guided them toward a spectral entity that awaited in the hidden corners of the chamber. The old house, a silent witness to the unfolding darkness, seemed to sigh with a spectral resignation.

With a sense of urgency, Sheila and Rob fumbled for their flashlights, attempting to pierce the veil of darkness that surrounded them.

The whispers, though chaotic, spoke of an ancient evil that sought communion with the living. The hidden chamber, now a battleground between the mortal and the supernatural, became a place where the boundaries between reality and the abyss blurred.

As their flashlights flickered to life, Sheila and Rob beheld a chilling sight—a spectral entity, its form indistinct in the shadows, stood before them. The whispers, now a haunting melody, spoke of an ancient evil that had been awakened by their presence. The old house, a conduit for the malevolent forces, bore silent witness to the spectral encounter that unfolded in the hidden chamber.

The entity, a manifestation of the ancient evil that had lingered within the old house, seemed to reach out from the shadows. The whispers, now a dissonant chorus, urged Sheila and Rob to confront the malevolent force that awaited in the spectral realm. The old house, though temporarily quelled, stood as a gateway to a darkness that defied rational explanation.

With a surge of supernatural power, the entity confronted Sheila and Rob. The whispers, now a mournful hymn, seemed to align with the malevolent force as the spectral encounter reached its zenith. The old house, its foundations saturated with the essence of the living, became a battleground where the living and the dead converged in a macabre dance of supernatural entanglement.

Sheila and Rob, entwined in the spectral tapestry, felt the weight of unseen eyes upon them. The whispers, now a relentless drone, seemed to echo through the hidden chamber—a spectral symphony that reverberated through the haunted dwelling. The old house, its spectral foundations shaken by the malevolent revelation, stood at the precipice of a new, horrifying chapter in its dark history.

As the entity reached out with spectral tendrils, Sheila and Rob, driven by an unspoken determination, faced the malevolent force with a courage born of desperation. The whispers, though chaotic, guided them through the spectral encounter—a dance between the living and the abyss. The old house, a silent witness to the unfolding darkness,

stood as a battleground where the forces of the supernatural and the mortal clashed in a terrifying crescendo.

In the dim light of the hidden chamber, a struggle unfolded—a battle between the living and the spectral entity that sought communion with the living. The whispers, now a spectral symphony, intensified as Sheila and Rob confronted the ancient evil that had been awakened by their presence. The old house, its foundations saturated with the essence of the living, became a crucible where the boundaries between reality and the abyss blurred.

With a surge of supernatural energy, Sheila and Rob channeled the remnants of the sacrificial ritual into a desperate confrontation with the entity. The whispers, now a haunting melody, seemed to align with the living as the spectral encounter reached its climax. The old house, a silent witness to the unfolding darkness, stood as a testament to the resilience of those who dared to confront the malevolent forces that lurked within its haunted halls.

As the spectral entity recoiled, the whispers, now a fading memory, left an eerie stillness in their wake. Sheila and Rob, exhausted and shaken, stood amidst the spectral remnants of the hidden chamber. The old house, though still haunted by the echoes of the past, seemed to sigh with a spectral resignation.

The supernatural realm, now devoid of the malevolent entity that had sought communion with the living, unfolded with an unsettling stillness. Sheila and Rob, their courage tested by the spectral encounter, ascended from the hidden chamber and returned to the haunted halls of the old house. The air, though laden with the remnants of the supernatural battle, felt lighter as if a temporary reprieve had been granted.

Little did they know that the true horror, a revelation that would redefine the very fabric of their existence, awaited in the shadows of their newfound victory. The old house, though temporarily quelled, held secrets that would unveil themselves in a chilling twist of fate—one that would test the limits of Sheila and Rob's resilience and plunge them into a darkness from which there might be no escape.

The whispers, now a fading memory, left the door ajar for the looming terror that awaited in the aftermath of the spectral storm. The old house, its haunted corridors pulsating with unresolved sorrows, stood as a gateway to a supernatural abyss. Sheila and Rob, bound by the malevolent forces that lingered within, faced an uncertain future where the horrors of the past cast a long, lingering shadow over their fragile grasp on reality.

Chapter 11: The Escape

Having confronted the malevolent forces in the hidden chamber, Sheila and Rob ascended from the basement, their nerves on edge from the spectral encounter. The air in the old house, though momentarily relieved of the oppressive darkness, still held a spectral tension—a silent reminder of the horrors that lurked within its haunted halls. Unbeknownst to them, a new chapter of terror awaited as the old house seemed to cling to the malevolence that had taken root in its very foundations.

As they emerged into the dim light of the living room, Sheila and Rob exchanged glances laden with unspoken fear. The whispers, though muted, seemed to linger in the air like a haunting refrain. The old house, its spectral corridors echoing with the echoes of the past, stood as a silent witness to the unfolding nightmare that awaited the unwitting inhabitants.

A sense of urgency gripped Sheila as her gaze once again fell upon the basement door—the same door that had led them to the depths of the supernatural realm. The whispers, though subdued, seemed to guide her attention toward the subterranean depths where forgotten rituals had once unfolded. The basement, now a nexus of malevolence, beckoned them to confront the unresolved mysteries that lingered within.

Rob, his nerves still raw from the spectral encounter, hesitated as Sheila approached the basement door. The air, though seemingly calm, carried a spectral resonance that hinted at the lingering darkness within the haunted dwelling. The old house, a silent observer to the unfolding

terror, seemed to pulse with an unseen force that transcended the boundaries of the living and the dead.

With a sense of trepidation, Sheila opened the basement door, revealing the wooden stairs that led to the subterranean depths. The whispers, now a faint murmur, seemed to echo through the haunted halls, guiding them toward the heart of the encroaching darkness. The old house, though momentarily quelled, held secrets that demanded further exploration—a revelation that would test the limits of Sheila and Rob's resilience.

As they descended into the dimly lit basement, the air felt heavy with an otherworldly energy. The whispers, though muted, seemed to guide Sheila and Rob toward the epicenter of the supernatural storm. The old house, its spectral foundations saturated with the essence of the living, became a conduit for the malevolent forces that sought communion with the unwitting inhabitants.

In the basement, the artifacts of forgotten rituals lay in shadowed corners, silent witnesses to the malevolence that had once thrived within the haunted dwelling. The whispers, though fragmented, spoke of a lingering darkness that refused to be fully contained. The old house, a spectral battleground, seemed to pulse with an unseen force that beckoned Sheila and Rob to delve deeper into the abyss.

As they ventured into the basement's depths, Sheila's flashlight revealed a hidden passage—a secret corridor that led to unexplored realms within the haunted dwelling. The whispers, though haunting, guided them toward a revelation that transcended the boundaries of the living and the dead. The old house, now a labyrinth of malevolence, became a spectral tapestry where the living and the abyss converged in an eerie dance.

A sudden drop in temperature signaled a shift in the atmosphere. The whispers, now a haunting lament, guided Sheila and Rob toward an ancient doorway—an entrance to a forgotten chamber that had eluded their previous exploration. The old house, though momentarily

quelled, seemed to cling to the malevolent forces that lurked within its spectral depths.

With trepidation, Sheila and Rob opened the ancient doorway, revealing a chamber bathed in an unnatural darkness. The air, thick with the scent of ancient incense, seemed to vibrate with the echoes of spectral energy. The whispers, now a dissonant symphony, spoke of a deeper layer of malevolence that awaited discovery.

In the dim light, Sheila and Rob stumbled upon an ancient altar—an occult relic that held the secrets of forbidden rituals. The whispers, though chaotic, urged Sheila to decipher the cryptic symbols that adorned the altar. The malevolent legacy, though temporarily quelled, seemed to find its voice in the ancient rites that unfolded in the flickering light.

As Sheila and Rob examined the altar, a sudden gust of wind extinguished their flashlights, plunging the chamber into complete darkness. The whispers, now a relentless drone, merged with the shadows that danced in the spectral realm. The old house, its spectral foundations saturated with the essence of the living, stood at the precipice of a new, malevolent revelation.

In the darkness, Sheila and Rob felt an unseen force closing in around them. The whispers, now a spectral symphony, guided them toward a spectral entity that awaited in the hidden corners of the chamber. The old house, a silent witness to the unfolding darkness, seemed to sigh with a spectral resignation.

With a sense of urgency, Sheila and Rob fumbled for their flashlights, attempting to pierce the veil of darkness that surrounded them. The whispers, though chaotic, spoke of an ancient evil that sought communion with the living. The hidden chamber, now a battleground between the mortal and the supernatural, became a place where the boundaries between reality and the abyss blurred.

As their flashlights flickered to life, Sheila and Rob beheld a chilling sight—a spectral entity, its form indistinct in the shadows, stood before them. The whispers, now a haunting melody, spoke of an ancient evil

that had been awakened by their presence. The old house, a conduit for the malevolent forces, bore silent witness to the spectral encounter that unfolded in the hidden chamber.

The entity, a manifestation of the ancient evil that had lingered within the old house, seemed to reach out from the shadows. The whispers, now a dissonant chorus, urged Sheila and Rob to confront the malevolent force that awaited in the spectral realm. The old house, though temporarily quelled, stood as a gateway to a darkness that defied rational explanation.

With a surge of supernatural power, the entity confronted Sheila and Rob. The whispers, now a mournful hymn, seemed to align with the malevolent force as the spectral encounter reached its zenith. The old house, its foundations saturated with the essence of the living, became a battleground where the living and the dead converged in a macabre dance.

Sheila and Rob, entwined in the spectral tapestry, felt the weight of unseen eyes upon them. The whispers, now a relentless drone, seemed to echo through the hidden chamber—a spectral symphony that reverberated through the haunted dwelling. The old house, its spectral foundations shaken by the malevolent revelation, stood at the precipice of a new, horrifying chapter in its dark history.

As the entity reached out with spectral tendrils, Sheila and Rob, driven by an unspoken determination, faced the malevolent force with a courage born of desperation. The whispers, though chaotic, guided them through the spectral encounter—a dance between the living and the abyss. The old house, a silent witness to the unfolding darkness, stood as a battleground where the forces of the supernatural and the mortal clashed in a terrifying crescendo.

In the dim light of the hidden chamber, a struggle unfolded—a battle between the living and the spectral entity that sought communion with the living. The whispers, now a spectral symphony, intensified as Sheila and Rob confronted the ancient evil that had been awakened by their presence. The old house, its foundations saturated with the essence of

the living, became a crucible where the boundaries between reality and the abyss blurred.

With a surge of supernatural energy, Sheila and Rob channeled the remnants of the sacrificial ritual into a desperate confrontation with the entity. The whispers, now a haunting melody, seemed to align with the living as the spectral encounter reached its climax. The old house, a silent witness to the unfolding darkness, stood as a testament to the resilience of those who dared to confront the malevolent forces that lurked within its haunted halls.

As the spectral entity recoiled, the whispers, now a fading memory, left an eerie stillness in their wake. Sheila and Rob, exhausted and shaken, stood amidst the spectral remnants of the hidden chamber. The old house, though still haunted by the echoes of the past, seemed to sigh with a spectral resignation.

The supernatural realm, now devoid of the malevolent entity that had sought communion with the living, unfolded with an unsettling stillness. Sheila and Rob, their courage tested by the spectral encounter, ascended from the hidden chamber and returned to the haunted halls of the old house. The air, though laden with the remnants of the supernatural battle, felt lighter as if a temporary reprieve had been granted.

Little did they know that the true horror, a revelation that would redefine the very fabric of their existence, awaited in the shadows of their newfound victory. The old house, though temporarily quelled, held secrets that would unveil themselves in a chilling twist of fate—one that would test the limits of Sheila and Rob's resilience and plunge them into a darkness from which there might be no escape.

The whispers, now a fading memory, left the door ajar for the looming terror that awaited in the aftermath of the spectral storm. The old house, its haunted corridors pulsating with unresolved sorrows, stood as a gateway to a supernatural abyss. Sheila and Rob, bound by the malevolent forces that lingered within, faced an uncertain future where the horrors of the past cast a long, lingering shadow over their fragile grasp on reality.

Chapter 12: The Attacks

As Sheila and Rob emerged from the hidden chamber, a sense of unease lingered in the air. The old house, though temporarily quelled by their confrontation with the spectral entity, exuded an eerie calm that belied the malevolence buried within its haunted corridors. Unbeknownst to the shaken inhabitants, the aftermath of the ritual had set into motion a series of paranormal attacks that would test the limits of their courage and resilience.

The whispers, though muted, seemed to carry a warning—a spectral echo of the malevolent forces that still clung to the very fabric of the old house. Sheila and Rob, their nerves raw from the supernatural encounter, exchanged wary glances as they navigated the dimly lit halls. The air, laden with the remnants of the spectral battle, became a spectral tapestry where the living and the dead converged in an unsettling dance.

As night fell over the old house, Sheila found herself alone in the living room. The whispers, now a distant murmur, seemed to beckon her toward the spectral energies that lingered within the haunted dwelling. The old house, a silent witness to the unfolding nightmare, held secrets that awaited discovery—a revelation that would thrust Sheila into a harrowing series of paranormal attacks.

The attacks began subtly—a flickering of lights, objects moving mysteriously, and an unshakable feeling of being watched. Sheila, though initially dismissive, couldn't ignore the mounting sense of dread that accompanied these strange occurrences. The whispers, now a haunting melody, seemed to intensify as if heralding the approach of an unseen malevolence.

One night, as Sheila lay in bed, the attacks escalated. Shadows danced on the walls, and an otherworldly chill permeated the room. The whispers, now a dissonant chorus, filled the air with a spectral energy that seemed to converge around her. The old house, its foundations saturated with the essence of the living, became a battleground where the forces of the supernatural sought communion with the unsuspecting inhabitants.

Sheila, gripped by a growing terror, sought solace in the presence of Rob. Together, they confronted the escalating attacks, attempting to rationalize the paranormal occurrences that defied logical explanation. The old house, though momentarily quelled, seemed to pulse with an unseen force that defied the boundaries of the mortal realm.

The attacks took a violent turn, as unseen forces hurled objects across the room and ominous shadows seemed to reach out from the spectral realm. Sheila and Rob, their nerves stretched to the breaking point, struggled to maintain their grasp on reality. The whispers, now a relentless drone, echoed through the haunted halls, guiding the malevolent forces in their torment of the unsuspecting inhabitants.

Desperate for answers, Sheila delved into her research, revisiting the ancient tome and the diary that chronicled the house's dark history. The whispers, though fragmented, seemed to offer cryptic clues that hinted at a malevolent presence seeking revenge. The old house, its haunted corridors echoing with the sorrows of the past, held the key to understanding the origins of the supernatural attacks.

In their quest for answers, Sheila and Rob enlisted the help of a local paranormal investigator. The whispers, now a spectral symphony, seemed to intensify as the investigator delved into the history of the old house. The malevolent forces, though temporarily restrained, resisted the intrusion, escalating the attacks in retaliation.

The investigator, a skeptic turned believer, witnessed the paranormal onslaught firsthand. Doors slammed shut, eerie whispers reverberated through the halls, and unseen hands seemed to grab at those who dared to venture into the haunted dwelling. The old house, now a battleground for the living and the supernatural, exuded a malevolence that defied rational explanation.

In a desperate attempt to quell the attacks, Sheila and Rob decided to hold a seance—an act that would either provide answers or further provoke the wrath of the malevolent forces. The whispers, now a haunting lament, seemed to guide them toward the living room where the seance would take place. The old house, its spectral foundations

shaken by the paranormal onslaught, awaited the unfolding ritual with a spectral resignation.

As the seance began, the air in the living room became charged with an otherworldly energy. The whispers, now a cacophony of spectral voices, spoke of the ancient evil that sought communion with the living. The old house, its haunted halls bearing witness to the unfolding ritual, seemed to sigh with a spectral anticipation.

Suddenly, the room plunged into darkness, and a chilling wind swept through the living room. The whispers, now a spectral chorus, guided Sheila and Rob toward a revelation that transcended the boundaries of the living and the dead. The old house, its foundations saturated with the essence of the living, became a conduit for the malevolent forces that sought release through the seance.

In the darkness, Sheila felt an unseen presence—the very embodiment of the malevolence that had plagued the old house. The whispers, now a mournful hymn, seemed to echo through the spectral realm as the ancient evil made itself known. The old house, a witness to the unfolding ritual, stood at the precipice of a terrifying revelation.

The entity, a manifestation of the supernatural forces, spoke through the seance—a voice that sent shivers down the spines of those present. The whispers, now a spectral symphony, conveyed the entity's grievances and the reasons behind the relentless attacks. The old house, its spectral foundations saturated with the essence of the living, became a stage for the malevolent forces to voice their unholy intentions.

As the seance reached its climax, Sheila and Rob faced a choice—succumb to the malevolent forces or confront the entity head-on. The whispers, now a haunting melody, seemed to offer a glimmer of hope amidst the overwhelming darkness. The old house, its haunted corridors pulsating with the echoes of the past, awaited the resolution of the supernatural conflict that unfolded within its spectral confines.

With determination born of desperation, Sheila and Rob confronted the entity. The whispers, now a spectral chorus, guided them through the confrontation—a dance between the living and the abyss. The old

house, a silent witness to the unfolding darkness, stood as a battleground where the forces of the supernatural and the mortal clashed in a terrifying crescendo.

As Sheila and Rob faced the entity, a surge of supernatural energy filled the room. The whispers, now a relentless drone, seemed to align with the living as the spectral encounter reached its zenith. The old house, its foundations saturated with the essence of the living, became a crucible where the boundaries between reality and the abyss blurred.

In the dim light of the living room, a struggle unfolded—a battle between the living and the malevolent entity that sought communion with the living. The whispers, now a spectral symphony, intensified as Sheila and Rob confronted the ancient evil that had been awakened by their presence. The old house, its haunted foundations shaken by the paranormal conflict, stood as a testament to the resilience of those who dared to confront the malevolent forces that lurked within its spectral halls.

As the entity recoiled, the whispers, now a fading memory, left an eerie stillness in their wake. Sheila and Rob, exhausted and shaken, stood amidst the spectral remnants of the seance. The old house, though still haunted by the echoes of the past, seemed to sigh with a spectral resignation.

The supernatural realm, now devoid of the entity that had sought communion with the living, unfolded with an unsettling stillness. Sheila and Rob, their courage tested by the spectral encounter, navigated the haunted halls of the old house. The air, though laden with the remnants of the paranormal conflict, felt lighter as if a temporary reprieve had been granted.

Little did they know that the true horror, a revelation that would redefine the very fabric of their existence, awaited in the shadows of their newfound victory. The old house, though temporarily quelled, held secrets that would unveil themselves in a chilling twist of fate—one that would test the limits of Sheila and Rob's resilience and plunge them into a darkness from which there might be no escape.

The whispers, now a fading memory, left the door ajar for the looming terror that awaited in the aftermath of the supernatural onslaught. The old house, its haunted corridors pulsating with unresolved sorrows, stood as a gateway to a supernatural abyss. Sheila and Rob, bound by the malevolent forces that lingered within, faced an uncertain future where the horrors of the past cast a long, lingering shadow over their fragile grasp on reality.

Chapter 13: The Seance

As the aftermath of the paranormal attacks lingered in the old house, Sheila and Rob, driven by a desperate need for answers, decided to delve deeper into the supernatural realm. The whispers, though diminished, seemed to guide them toward a fateful decision—the summoning of forces beyond their understanding through a seance. The old house, its haunted corridors pulsating with unresolved sorrows, awaited the unfolding ritual with a spectral anticipation.

Sheila and Rob gathered in the living room, surrounded by flickering candles and the musty scent of ancient incense. The whispers, now a distant murmur, seemed to converge around them as they prepared for the seance. The air in the room became charged with an otherworldly energy, and the old house, a silent witness to the unfolding ritual, stood at the precipice of a new, unsettling chapter.

The seance began with the chanting of incantations from an ancient tome Sheila had found in her research. The whispers, now a haunting lament, filled the room with a spectral resonance that transcended the boundaries of the living and the dead. The old house, its spectral foundations saturated with the essence of the living, became a conduit for the malevolent forces that awaited release through the ritual.

As the incantations echoed through the room, a sudden drop in temperature signaled the arrival of unseen entities. The whispers, now a spectral symphony, seemed to guide Sheila and Rob toward a revelation that defied rational explanation. The old house, its haunted halls bearing witness to the unfolding ritual, exuded a spectral energy that reached beyond the mortal realm.

In the dim light, Sheila and Rob felt an otherworldly presence—the very embodiment of the malevolence that had plagued the old house. The whispers, now a dissonant chorus, urged them to maintain their focus as the spectral entities made themselves known. The old house, a stage for the supernatural forces, stood as a gateway to a darkness that defied comprehension.

As the seance continued, the room filled with eerie whispers, shadows danced on the walls, and an unseen force seemed to grip those present. Sheila and Rob, their senses heightened by the supernatural energies, felt the weight of unseen eyes upon them. The old house, its spectral foundations shaken by the unfolding ritual, became a battleground where the living and the abyss converged in an unsettling dance.

Suddenly, the room plunged into darkness, and an otherworldly wind swept through the living room. The whispers, now a relentless drone, guided Sheila and Rob toward the epicenter of the spectral storm. The old house, though momentarily quelled, seemed to pulse with an unseen force that defied the boundaries of the mortal realm.

In the darkness, Sheila and Rob glimpsed shadowy figures—apparitions of the past that materialized in the spectral realm. The whispers, now a spectral chorus, spoke of the tormented souls that lingered within the haunted dwelling. The old house, its haunted corridors echoing with the sorrows of the past, became a tapestry of spectral entities seeking release through the seance.

As the apparitions manifested, the room resonated with their ethereal presence. The whispers, now a haunting melody, conveyed the grievances of the tormented souls that sought communion with the living. The old house, a conduit for the spectral forces, bore witness to the unfolding drama between the mortal and the supernatural.

Amidst the spectral symphony, Sheila and Rob felt a sudden shift—a malevolent entity seizing the opportunity to make its presence known. The whispers, now a dissonant chorus, guided them toward a revelation that sent shivers down their spines. The old house, its spectral

foundations saturated with the essence of the living, stood as a stage for the malevolent force that awaited confrontation.

The entity, a manifestation of the ancient evil that lingered within the old house, spoke through the seance—a voice that echoed with a chilling resonance. The whispers, now a mournful hymn, conveyed the entity's grievances and the reasons behind the relentless attacks. The old house, its haunted halls bearing witness to the unfolding ritual, seemed to sigh with a spectral anticipation.

Sheila and Rob, their senses overwhelmed by the supernatural on-slaught, faced a choice—succumb to the malevolent forces or confront the entity head-on. The whispers, now a haunting melody, seemed to offer a glimmer of hope amidst the overwhelming darkness. The old house, its haunted corridors pulsating with the echoes of the past, awaited the resolution of the supernatural conflict that unfolded within its spectral confines.

With determination born of desperation, Sheila and Rob confronted the entity. The whispers, now a spectral chorus, guided them through the confrontation—a dance between the living and the abyss. The old house, a silent witness to the unfolding darkness, stood as a battle-ground where the forces of the supernatural and the mortal clashed in a terrifying crescendo.

As Sheila and Rob faced the entity, a surge of supernatural energy filled the room. The whispers, now a relentless drone, seemed to align with the living as the spectral encounter reached its zenith. The old house, its foundations saturated with the essence of the living, became a crucible where the boundaries between reality and the abyss blurred.

In the dim light of the living room, a struggle unfolded—a battle between the living and the malevolent entity that sought communion with the living. The whispers, now a spectral symphony, intensified as Sheila and Rob confronted the ancient evil that had been awakened by their presence. The old house, its haunted foundations shaken by the paranormal conflict, stood as a testament to the resilience of those

who dared to confront the malevolent forces that lurked within its spectral halls.

As the entity recoiled, the whispers, now a fading memory, left an eerie stillness in their wake. Sheila and Rob, exhausted and shaken, stood amidst the spectral remnants of the seance. The old house, though still haunted by the echoes of the past, seemed to sigh with a spectral resignation.

The supernatural realm, now devoid of the entity that had sought communion with the living, unfolded with an unsettling stillness. Sheila and Rob, their courage tested by the spectral encounter, navigated the haunted halls of the old house. The air, though laden with the remnants of the paranormal conflict, felt lighter as if a temporary reprieve had been granted.

Little did they know that the true horror, a revelation that would redefine the very fabric of their existence, awaited in the shadows of their newfound victory. The old house, though temporarily quelled, held secrets that would unveil themselves in a chilling twist of fate—one that would test the limits of Sheila and Rob's resilience and plunge them into a darkness from which there might be no escape.

The whispers, now a fading memory, left the door ajar for the looming terror that awaited in the aftermath of the supernatural onslaught. The old house, its haunted corridors pulsating with unresolved sorrows, stood as a gateway to a supernatural abyss. Sheila and Rob, bound by the malevolent forces that lingered within, faced an uncertain future where the horrors of the past cast a long, lingering shadow over their fragile grasp on reality.

Chapter 14: The Cleansing

In the wake of the seance, Sheila and Rob, still reeling from the otherworldly encounter, found themselves at a crossroads. The old house, though momentarily relieved of the malevolent entity's presence, exuded an eerie calm that hinted at the lingering supernatural forces within its haunted walls. Determined to put an end to the paranormal onslaught, Sheila sought the guidance of a psychic medium—an expert

in the arcane arts who might hold the key to cleansing the ancient dwelling.

The whispers, now a faint echo of the malevolence that had permeated the old house, guided Sheila and Rob toward the psychic medium's secluded residence. The air, heavy with the remnants of the spectral storm, carried a spectral resonance that seemed to converge around them. The old house, its spectral foundations saturated with the essence of the living, became a distant backdrop to the unfolding quest for purification.

The psychic medium, a mysterious figure with a demeanor that mirrored the enigmatic forces surrounding the old house, welcomed Sheila and Rob into a dimly lit room adorned with mystical artifacts. The whispers, now a haunting melody, seemed to intensify in the presence of the psychic medium. The air became charged with an otherworldly energy as the cleansing ritual began.

As the psychic medium delved into the spiritual realm, Sheila and Rob felt a shift in the atmosphere. The whispers, now a spectral symphony, guided the medium's hands as they moved through intricate gestures, channeling supernatural forces to cleanse the old house of its malevolent energies. The haunted dwelling, a silent witness to the unfolding ritual, awaited the purifying touch of the arcane.

Suddenly, the room quivered with unseen energies. Shadows danced on the walls, and the air vibrated with a spectral resonance. The whispers, now a dissonant chorus, echoed through the room, carrying the remnants of the malevolent entity's presence. The old house, though momentarily quelled, seemed to resist the cleansing as if clinging to the dark energies that had taken root within its spectral depths.

As the cleansing ritual continued, Sheila and Rob witnessed a manifestation of spectral mists swirling through the room. The whispers, now a relentless drone, seemed to speak of the ancient sorrows that clung to the old house like a malevolent shroud. The psychic medium, undeterred by the supernatural turbulence, pressed on with the purifying incantations.

In the dim light, Sheila and Rob glimpsed fleeting apparitions—the tormented souls that lingered within the old house. The whispers, now a haunting lament, carried the voices of the restless spirits seeking release through the cleansing ritual. The haunted dwelling, its spectral foundations shaken by the purifying energies, became a nexus where the living and the dead converged in an otherworldly dance.

Unexpectedly, the psychic medium's eyes glazed over, and her voice took on an otherworldly resonance. The whispers, now a mournful hymn, spoke through the medium, conveying the grievances of the ancient spirits that had been disturbed by the malevolent entity. The old house, a conduit for the spectral forces, bore silent witness to the spectral communion that unfolded in the purifying ritual.

As the psychic medium channeled the spirits, Sheila and Rob felt a surge of supernatural energy coursing through the room. The whispers, now a spectral chorus, guided them toward a revelation that transcended the boundaries of the living and the dead. The old house, though momentarily quelled, seemed to sigh with a spectral resignation as the purifying energies sought to dispel the malevolent forces that clung to its haunted corridors.

The psychic medium, still in the grip of the supernatural trance, uttered cryptic words that seemed to unlock the secrets of the old house's dark history. The whispers, now a dissonant symphony, guided Sheila and Rob toward a hidden chamber—an ancient sanctum where forgotten rituals had once unfolded. The haunted dwelling, its spectral foundations saturated with the essence of the living, became a battleground for the living and the supernatural.

As the purifying ritual reached its climax, Sheila and Rob, entranced by the spectral energies, witnessed a spectral convergence. The whispers, now a spectral melody, spoke of the ancient rituals that had bound the malevolent forces to the old house. The psychic medium, still in communion with the spirits, channeled the supernatural energies toward the heart of the spectral storm.

A sudden burst of light illuminated the room as the cleansing energies reached their zenith. The whispers, now a fading memory, left an eerie stillness in their wake. Sheila and Rob, their senses overwhelmed by the spectral convergence, stood amidst the remnants of the purifying ritual. The old house, though still haunted by the echoes of the past, seemed to sigh with a spectral resignation as if acknowledging the fleeting victory over the malevolent forces.

The psychic medium, released from the supernatural trance, conveyed the success of the cleansing ritual. The whispers, now a distant murmur, hinted at a temporary reprieve from the paranormal onslaught. The old house, its spectral foundations shaken by the purifying energies, awaited the aftermath of the cleansing—a revelation that would test the limits of Sheila and Rob's resilience and unravel the mysteries hidden within its haunted corridors.

As Sheila and Rob left the psychic medium's residence, a sense of cautious hope lingered in the air. The whispers, now a faint echo of the supernatural forces, guided them back to the old house—the battleground where the forces of the living and the dead had clashed in a spectral dance. The haunted dwelling, though momentarily relieved of the malevolent entity's presence, held secrets that awaited unraveling as the aftermath of the cleansing ritual cast a spectral light on the mysteries that lay hidden within its spectral confines.

Chapter 15: The Truth

With the cleansing ritual behind them, Sheila and Rob returned to the old house, hoping for a respite from the malevolent forces that had plagued them. The whispers, now a mere whisper of the supernatural energies that once gripped the haunted dwelling, guided them through the dimly lit halls. The air, heavy with the aftermath of the purifying ritual, carried a spectral resonance that hinted at the revelations awaiting them.

As Sheila and Rob explored the old house, a sense of cautious optimism settled over them. The whispers, though diminished, seemed to convey a temporary peace—a fragile equilibrium between the living

and the supernatural. The haunted dwelling, a silent witness to the unfolding events, exuded an eerie calm that belied the mysteries hidden within its spectral depths.

However, as night fell over the old house, an unsettling energy permeated the air. The whispers, now a distant murmur, hinted at a resurgence of the malevolent forces. Sheila and Rob, their nerves on edge, exchanged wary glances as they navigated the dimly lit corridors. The haunted dwelling, though momentarily quelled, held secrets that awaited revelation in the spectral silence of the night.

A series of cryptic symbols appeared on the walls—manifestations of the supernatural energies that lingered within the old house. The whispers, now a haunting melody, seemed to speak through the spectral symbols, conveying a message that defied rational explanation. The air, charged with an otherworldly energy, guided Sheila and Rob toward the heart of the spectral disturbance.

In the dim light, they discovered a hidden chamber—a forgotten sanctum where the malevolent rituals of the past had unfolded. The whispers, now a spectral symphony, intensified as Sheila and Rob delved into the secrets concealed within the ancient chamber. The haunted dwelling, its spectral foundations saturated with the essence of the living, became a tapestry where the past and present converged in an unsettling dance.

As they explored the hidden chamber, Sheila uncovered an old diary that chronicled the house's dark history. The whispers, now a dissonant chorus, guided her through the cryptic entries that spoke of occult rituals and malevolent forces bound to the old house. The air, thick with the residual energies of the past, carried a spectral resonance that transcended the boundaries of time.

The diary revealed a gruesome truth—the old house had been built for occult rituals, with a dark energy woven into its very walls. The whispers, now a relentless drone, conveyed the malevolent forces that had been awakened by the unwitting presence of Sheila and Rob. The haunted dwelling, a silent witness to the unfolding revelations, stood

as a testament to the ancient darkness that sought communion with the living.

As Sheila and Rob grappled with the horrifying truth, the whispers guided them toward a chilling realization—there was only one way to stop the malevolent forces that had been unleashed. The haunted dwelling, though momentarily quelled by the cleansing ritual, demanded a final sacrifice to seal the ancient evil that lurked within its spectral depths.

The revelation weighed heavily on Sheila's shoulders as she contemplated the harrowing decision that awaited her. The whispers, now a haunting lament, seemed to offer guidance through the darkness that enveloped the old house. The air, heavy with the echoes of the past, carried a spectral energy that transcended the mortal realm.

Determined to confront the malevolent forces head-on, Sheila and Rob sought counsel from the psychic medium who had guided them through the cleansing ritual. The whispers, now a spectral chorus, guided them to the medium's secluded residence, where the air buzzed with the residual energies of the supernatural encounter. The haunted dwelling, a distant backdrop to the unfolding quest, awaited the resolution of the spectral conflict that had gripped its haunted halls.

The psychic medium, aware of the lingering malevolence, spoke of the ancient ritual that could seal the evil presence within the old house. The whispers, now a spectral melody, seemed to convey the urgency of the impending sacrifice. The air, thick with the spectral energies, guided Sheila and Rob toward a path that would test the limits of their courage and resilience.

Sheila, faced with an unimaginable choice, grappled with the weight of the revelation. The whispers, now a dissonant symphony, urged her to confront the malevolent forces head-on. The haunted dwelling, its spectral foundations shaken by the impending decision, stood as a crucible where the boundaries between the living and the supernatural blurred.

As night fell over the old house, Sheila prepared for the ritual—a blood sacrifice that would bind the malevolent forces and seal the ancient evil within the spectral confines. The whispers, now a relentless drone, echoed through the haunted dwelling, guiding her toward the heart of the spectral storm. The air, heavy with the essence of the supernatural, carried a spectral resonance that transcended the mortal realm.

Rob, torn between loyalty and the impending sacrifice, stood by Sheila's side as she embraced her destiny. The whispers, now a haunting lament, seemed to offer solace in the face of the inevitable. The haunted dwelling, a silent witness to the unfolding ritual, exuded an eerie calm that belied the impending darkness.

In the dimly lit chamber, Sheila performed the ritual with a heavy heart. The whispers, now a spectral symphony, guided her through the ancient incantations that would bind the malevolent forces to the old house. The air, charged with an otherworldly energy, carried the weight of the sacrifice that would determine the fate of the haunted dwelling.

As Sheila completed the ritual, a surge of supernatural energy filled the room. The whispers, now a fading memory, left an eerie stillness in their wake. The haunted dwelling, though temporarily quelled, seemed to sigh with a spectral resignation. The air, thick with the remnants of the ritual, carried a spectral resonance that lingered in the haunted corridors.

In the aftermath of the sacrifice, Sheila and Rob, exhausted and shaken, emerged from the hidden chamber. The whispers, now a distant murmur, guided them through the dimly lit halls of the old house. The haunted dwelling, though momentarily relieved of the malevolent entity's presence, held secrets that awaited unraveling in the aftermath of the ritual.

As Sheila and Rob faced the uncertain aftermath, a chilling realization dawned upon them—the sacrifice, though sealing the ancient evil, had forever changed the fabric of their existence. The whispers, now a spectral chorus, seemed to convey the irreversible consequences of the harrowing ordeal. The haunted dwelling, a silent witness to the

unfolding aftermath, stood as a testament to the sacrifices made in the name of sealing the ancient darkness within its spectral confines.

Little did they know that the true horror, a revelation that would redefine their very existence, awaited in the shadows of the haunted dwelling. The whispers, now a fading memory, left the door ajar for the looming terror that awaited in the aftermath of the supernatural sacrifice. Sheila and Rob, bound by the malevolent forces that lingered within, faced an uncertain future where the horrors of the past cast a long, lingering shadow over their fragile grasp on reality.

Chapter 16: The Sacrifice

With the echoes of the ritual still reverberating through the old house, Sheila and Rob grappled with the aftermath of the harrowing sacrifice. The air, thick with the remnants of supernatural energies, carried a spectral resonance that seemed to linger in the haunted dwelling. The whispers, now a distant murmur, guided them through the dimly lit halls as they confronted the irreversible consequences of sealing the ancient evil within the spectral confines.

As Sheila and Rob emerged from the hidden chamber, an unsettling stillness enveloped the old house. The whispers, now a fading memory, left an eerie calm in their wake. The haunted dwelling, though momentarily relieved of the malevolent entity's presence, stood as a silent witness to the sacrifices made in the name of sealing the ancient darkness within its spectral corridors.

However, the calm was deceptive, for a greater malevolence seemed to seep through the very walls of the old house. The air, heavy with the essence of the supernatural, carried an ominous energy that hinted at the lingering darkness within. Sheila and Rob, their senses heightened by the aftermath of the sacrifice, exchanged wary glances as they navigated the dimly lit corridors.

Unbeknownst to them, the sacrifice had unleashed unforeseen consequences—unsettling manifestations that defied rational explanation. Shadows danced on the walls, and whispers, now a dissonant symphony, seemed to echo through the haunted dwelling, conveying a spectral

unrest that transcended the mortal realm. The old house, though momentarily quelled, stood as a battleground where the forces of the living and the supernatural clashed in an otherworldly dance.

As night fell over the old house, the spectral disturbances intensified. Objects moved mysteriously, and the air vibrated with a spectral resonance that hinted at a malevolent force lingering within the haunted dwelling. The whispers, now a relentless drone, guided Sheila and Rob toward the heart of the spectral storm—an impending confrontation with the consequences of the sacrifice.

In the dim light, Sheila and Rob felt an otherworldly presence—an entity that seemed to feed on the residual energies of the sacrificed blood. The whispers, now a haunting lament, spoke of a darkness that sought communion with the living, defying the constraints of the ritual. The haunted dwelling, its spectral foundations shaken by the consequences of the sacrifice, stood as a conduit for the malevolent forces that sought release.

As they explored the old house, Sheila and Rob discovered cryptic symbols appearing on the walls—a manifestation of the supernatural disturbances that had been unleashed. The whispers, now a spectral symphony, guided them through the haunted corridors, conveying the urgency of a greater darkness that loomed on the horizon. The air, charged with an otherworldly energy, carried a spectral resonance that hinted at the impending confrontation with the malevolent entity.

Sheila and Rob sought the guidance of the psychic medium who had assisted them in the cleansing ritual. The whispers, now a haunting melody, seemed to echo through the secluded residence of the medium, conveying the urgency of the situation. The air, thick with the residual energies of the supernatural encounter, guided them toward a revelation that defied comprehension.

The psychic medium, aware of the consequences of the sacrifice, spoke of a greater malevolence that had been awakened—an entity that defied the boundaries of the ritual. The whispers, now a relentless drone, urged Sheila and Rob to confront the looming darkness before

it consumed the haunted dwelling. The air, heavy with the essence of the supernatural, carried a spectral resonance that transcended the mortal realm.

Determined to face the consequences of their actions, Sheila and Rob returned to the old house, armed with newfound knowledge. The whispers, now a spectral chorus, seemed to align with their resolve as they ventured into the dimly lit halls. The haunted dwelling, though momentarily quelled, awaited the final confrontation with the malevolent entity that lingered within its spectral depths.

As night settled over the old house, Sheila and Rob felt the temperature drop—a chilling sign of the entity's presence. Shadows danced on the walls, and the air vibrated with a spectral resonance that hinted at the impending confrontation. The whispers, now a haunting lament, guided them toward the heart of the spectral storm—an epicenter where the forces of the living and the supernatural converged.

In the dim light, Sheila and Rob glimpsed fleeting apparitions—manifestations of the greater darkness that had been unleashed. The whispers, now a dissonant symphony, seemed to speak of a malevolence that sought communion with the living, defying the constraints of the ritual. The haunted dwelling, its spectral foundations saturated with the essence of the supernatural, stood as a battleground where the consequences of the sacrifice unfolded in a terrifying crescendo.

Suddenly, the room quivered with unseen energies, and the temperature plummeted. The whispers, now a spectral chorus, guided Sheila and Rob toward the epicenter of the supernatural disturbance. The air, charged with an otherworldly energy, carried a spectral resonance that hinted at the imminent confrontation with the malevolent entity.

As they approached the heart of the spectral storm, Sheila and Rob felt an oppressive force—a darkness that seemed to envelop them. The whispers, now a relentless drone, seemed to echo through the haunted dwelling, urging them to confront the malevolent entity that lurked within the shadows. The old house, though momentarily quelled, stood

as a stage for the final showdown between the forces of the living and the supernatural.

In the dimly lit chamber, Sheila and Rob confronted the malevolent entity. The whispers, now a haunting melody, guided them through the spectral encounter—a dance between the living and the abyss. The haunted dwelling, its spectral foundations shaken by the consequences of the sacrifice, became a crucible where the boundaries between reality and the supernatural blurred.

The entity, a manifestation of the ancient darkness that had been awakened, spoke through the spectral symphony. The whispers, now a dissonant chorus, conveyed the grievances and malevolence of the malevolent force that sought communion with the living. The haunted dwelling, a conduit for the supernatural forces, bore silent witness to the final showdown that unfolded within its spectral corridors.

Sheila and Rob, their senses heightened by the supernatural onslaught, faced a choice—succumb to the malevolent forces or confront the entity head-on. The whispers, now a relentless drone, urged them toward a revelation that defied comprehension. The haunted dwelling, its spectral foundations saturated with the essence of the living, stood as a battleground where the forces of the living and the supernatural clashed in a terrifying crescendo.

In the dim light, Sheila and Rob glimpsed shadowy figures—apparitions of the past that materialized in the spectral realm. The whispers, now a haunting lament, spoke of the tormented souls that lingered within the haunted dwelling. The air, charged with an otherworldly energy, guided them toward the epicenter of the spectral storm—an impending confrontation with the malevolent entity.

As the entity recoiled, the whispers, now a spectral chorus, intensified. Sheila and Rob, their resolve tested by the supernatural onslaught, faced the malevolent force with determination. The haunted dwelling, its spectral foundations shaken by the consequences of the sacrifice, became a silent witness to the final confrontation between the living and the supernatural.

With an otherworldly surge of energy, Sheila and Rob confronted the entity head-on. The whispers, now a relentless drone, seemed to align with the living as the spectral encounter reached its zenith. The haunted dwelling, its foundations saturated with the essence of the supernatural, stood as a crucible where the forces of light and darkness clashed in a terrifying crescendo.

Unexpectedly, the entity recoiled—a spectral manifestation weakened by the determination of the living. The whispers, now a fading memory, left an eerie stillness in their wake. Sheila and Rob, their senses overwhelmed by the supernatural encounter, stood amidst the remnants of the spectral storm. The haunted dwelling, though momentarily quelled, seemed to sigh with a spectral resignation as if acknowledging the fleeting victory over the malevolent forces.

As Sheila and Rob emerged from the confrontation, a sense of cautious hope lingered in the air. The whispers, now a distant murmur, guided them through the dimly lit halls of the old house—the battleground where the forces of the living had triumphed over the malevolent entity. The haunted dwelling, though forever scarred by the supernatural encounter, stood as a testament to the resilience of those who dared to confront the ancient darkness that lurked within its spectral confines.

Little did Sheila and Rob know that the true horror, a revelation that would redefine their very existence, awaited in the shadows of the haunted dwelling. The whispers, now a fading memory, left the door ajar for the looming terror that awaited in the aftermath of the supernatural sacrifice. Sheila and Rob, bound by the malevolent forces that lingered within, faced an uncertain future where the horrors of the past cast a long, lingering shadow over their fragile grasp on reality.

Chapter 17: The Confrontation

In the aftermath of the supernatural encounter, Sheila and Rob found themselves standing amidst the remnants of the spectral storm that had gripped the old house. The air, heavy with the essence of the supernatural, carried a spectral resonance that hinted at the lingering

forces within the haunted dwelling. The whispers, now a distant murmur, guided them through the dimly lit halls as they grappled with the aftermath of the harrowing confrontation.

As they explored the old house, Sheila and Rob felt a palpable tension—an unsettling energy that seemed to emanate from the very walls. Shadows danced on the walls, and the air vibrated with a spectral resonance that hinted at a lingering malevolence. The whispers, now a haunting lament, guided them toward the heart of the spectral disturbance—an impending confrontation with the consequences of the sacrifice.

Unbeknownst to them, the malevolent entity, though weakened, lingered within the haunted dwelling, seeking revenge for the disruption of its spectral communion. The air, thick with the essence of the supernatural, carried an ominous energy that hinted at the impending clash between the living and the lingering darkness. Sheila and Rob, their nerves on edge, exchanged wary glances as they ventured into the dimly lit corridors.

As night fell over the old house, the spectral disturbances intensified. Objects moved mysteriously, and the whispers, now a relentless drone, seemed to echo through the haunted dwelling. The air, charged with an otherworldly energy, guided Sheila and Rob toward the epicenter of the spectral storm—a confrontation with the malevolent forces that sought release.

In the dim light, Sheila and Rob discovered cryptic symbols appearing on the walls—a manifestation of the supernatural disturbances that had been unleashed. The whispers, now a spectral symphony, intensified as they delved into the haunted corridors, conveying the urgency of a greater darkness that loomed on the horizon. The old house, though momentarily quelled, stood as a battleground where the forces of the living and the supernatural clashed in an otherworldly dance.

Sheila and Rob sought the guidance of the psychic medium who had assisted them in the cleansing ritual. The whispers, now a haunting melody, seemed to echo through the secluded residence of the medium,

conveying the urgency of the situation. The air, thick with the residual energies of the supernatural encounter, guided them toward a revelation that defied comprehension.

The psychic medium, aware of the lingering malevolence, spoke of the entity's resilience—a force that defied the boundaries of the ritual. The whispers, now a relentless drone, urged Sheila and Rob to confront the looming darkness before it consumed the haunted dwelling. The air, heavy with the essence of the supernatural, carried a spectral resonance that transcended the mortal realm.

Determined to face the consequences of their actions, Sheila and Rob returned to the old house, armed with newfound knowledge. The whispers, now a spectral chorus, seemed to align with their resolve as they ventured into the dimly lit halls. The haunted dwelling, though momentarily quelled, awaited the final confrontation with the malevolent entity that lingered within its spectral depths.

As night settled over the old house, Sheila and Rob felt the temperature drop—a chilling sign of the entity's presence. Shadows danced on the walls, and the air vibrated with a spectral resonance that hinted at the impending confrontation. The whispers, now a haunting lament, guided them toward the heart of the spectral storm—an epicenter where the forces of the living and the supernatural converged.

In the dim light, Sheila and Rob glimpsed fleeting apparitions—manifestations of the greater darkness that had been unleashed. The whispers, now a dissonant symphony, seemed to speak of a malevolence that sought communion with the living, defying the constraints of the ritual. The haunted dwelling, its spectral foundations saturated with the essence of the supernatural, stood as a battleground where the consequences of the sacrifice unfolded in a terrifying crescendo.

Suddenly, the room quivered with unseen energies, and the temperature plummeted. The whispers, now a spectral chorus, guided Sheila and Rob toward the epicenter of the supernatural disturbance. The air, charged with an otherworldly energy, carried a spectral resonance that hinted at the imminent confrontation with the malevolent entity.

As they approached the heart of the spectral storm, Sheila and Rob felt an oppressive force—a darkness that seemed to envelop them. The whispers, now a relentless drone, seemed to echo through the haunted dwelling, urging them to confront the malevolent entity that lurked within the shadows. The old house, though momentarily quelled, stood as a stage for the final showdown between the forces of the living and the supernatural.

In the dimly lit chamber, Sheila and Rob confronted the malevolent entity. The whispers, now a haunting melody, guided them through the spectral encounter—a dance between the living and the abyss. The haunted dwelling, its spectral foundations shaken by the consequences of the sacrifice, became a crucible where the boundaries between reality and the supernatural blurred.

The entity, a manifestation of the ancient darkness that had been awakened, spoke through the spectral symphony. The whispers, now a dissonant chorus, conveyed the grievances and malevolence of the malevolent force that sought communion with the living. The haunted dwelling, a conduit for the supernatural forces, bore silent witness to the final showdown that unfolded within its spectral corridors.

Sheila and Rob, their senses heightened by the supernatural on-slaught, faced a choice—succumb to the malevolent forces or confront the entity head-on. The whispers, now a relentless drone, urged them toward a revelation that defied comprehension. The haunted dwelling, its spectral foundations saturated with the essence of the living, stood as a battleground where the forces of the living and the supernatural clashed in a terrifying crescendo.

In the dim light, Sheila and Rob glimpsed shadowy figures—apparitions of the past that materialized in the spectral realm. The whispers, now a haunting lament, spoke of the tormented souls that lingered within the haunted dwelling. The air, charged with an otherworldly energy, guided them toward the epicenter of the spectral storm—an impending confrontation with the malevolent entity.

As the entity recoiled, the whispers, now a spectral chorus, intensified. Sheila and Rob, their resolve tested by the supernatural onslaught, faced the malevolent force with determination. The haunted dwelling, its spectral foundations saturated with the essence of the supernatural, stood as a crucible where the forces of light and darkness clashed in a terrifying crescendo.

Unexpectedly, the entity recoiled—a spectral manifestation weakened by the determination of the living. The whispers, now a fading memory, left an eerie stillness in their wake. Sheila and Rob, their senses overwhelmed by the supernatural encounter, stood amidst the remnants of the spectral storm. The haunted dwelling, though momentarily quelled, seemed to sigh with a spectral resignation as if acknowledging the fleeting victory over the malevolent forces.

As Sheila and Rob emerged from the confrontation, a sense of cautious hope lingered in the air. The whispers, now a distant murmur, guided them through the dimly lit halls of the old house—the battleground where the forces of the living had triumphed over the malevolent entity. The haunted dwelling, though forever scarred by the supernatural encounter, stood as a testament to the resilience of those who dared to confront the ancient darkness that lurked within its spectral confines.

Little did Sheila and Rob know that the true horror, a revelation that would redefine their very existence, awaited in the shadows of the haunted dwelling. The whispers, now a fading memory, left the door ajar for the looming terror that awaited in the aftermath of the supernatural sacrifice. Sheila and Rob, bound by the malevolent forces that lingered within, faced an uncertain future where the horrors of the past cast a long, lingering shadow over their fragile grasp on reality.

Chapter 18: The Resolution

The aftermath of the confrontation left Sheila and Rob in a state of emotional turmoil. The air, thick with the remnants of the supernatural encounter, carried a spectral resonance that seemed to linger within the haunted dwelling. The whispers, now a distant murmur, guided

them through the dimly lit halls as they grappled with the irreversible consequences of the sacrifice and the lingering darkness that clung to the old house.

As they explored the haunted corridors, Sheila and Rob discovered that the malevolent entity, though weakened, had left an indelible mark on the spectral fabric of the old house. Shadows danced on the walls, and the air vibrated with a spectral resonance that hinted at the lingering malevolence. The whispers, now a haunting lament, guided them toward the heart of the spectral disturbance—an exploration of the haunted dwelling's newfound reality.

Unbeknownst to them, the sacrifice had not only sealed the ancient evil but had woven the malevolent forces into the very fabric of the haunted dwelling. The air, heavy with the essence of the supernatural, carried an ominous energy that hinted at the spectral unrest within. Sheila and Rob, their senses heightened by the aftermath of the confrontation, exchanged wary glances as they ventured into the dimly lit corridors.

As night fell over the old house, the spectral disturbances intensified. Objects moved mysteriously, and the whispers, now a relentless drone, seemed to echo through the haunted dwelling. The air, charged with an otherworldly energy, guided Sheila and Rob toward the epicenter of the spectral storm—a realization that the malevolent forces were not entirely quelled.

In the dim light, Sheila and Rob glimpsed cryptic symbols appearing on the walls—a manifestation of the supernatural disturbances that had been woven into the spectral fabric of the old house. The whispers, now a spectral symphony, intensified as they delved into the haunted corridors, conveying the urgency of a greater darkness that loomed on the horizon. The haunted dwelling, though momentarily quelled, stood as a battleground where the forces of the living and the supernatural clashed in an otherworldly dance.

Sheila and Rob sought the guidance of the psychic medium who had assisted them in the cleansing ritual. The whispers, now a haunting

melody, seemed to echo through the secluded residence of the medium, conveying the urgency of the situation. The air, thick with the residual energies of the supernatural encounter, guided them toward a revelation that defied comprehension.

The psychic medium, aware of the lingering malevolence, spoke of the residual energies that had become entwined with the old house's spectral fabric. The whispers, now a relentless drone, urged Sheila and Rob to confront the lingering darkness before it consumed the haunted dwelling. The air, heavy with the essence of the supernatural, carried a spectral resonance that transcended the mortal realm.

Determined to face the consequences of their actions, Sheila and Rob returned to the old house, armed with newfound knowledge. The whispers, now a spectral chorus, seemed to align with their resolve as they ventured into the dimly lit halls. The haunted dwelling, though momentarily quelled, awaited the final confrontation with the residual malevolent forces that lingered within its spectral depths.

As night settled over the old house, Sheila and Rob felt the temperature drop—a chilling sign of the residual entity's presence. Shadows danced on the walls, and the air vibrated with a spectral resonance that hinted at the impending confrontation. The whispers, now a haunting lament, guided them toward the heart of the spectral storm—an epicenter where the forces of the living and the supernatural converged.

In the dim light, Sheila and Rob glimpsed fleeting apparitions—manifestations of the residual darkness that clung to the haunted dwelling. The whispers, now a dissonant symphony, seemed to speak of a malevolence that sought communion with the living, defying the constraints of the ritual. The old house, though momentarily quelled, stood as a battleground where the consequences of the sacrifice unfolded in a terrifying crescendo.

Suddenly, the room quivered with unseen energies, and the temperature plummeted. The whispers, now a spectral chorus, guided Sheila and Rob toward the epicenter of the supernatural disturbance. The air, charged with an otherworldly energy, carried a spectral resonance

that hinted at the imminent confrontation with the residual malevolent forces.

As they approached the heart of the spectral storm, Sheila and Rob felt an oppressive force—a darkness that seemed to envelop them. The whispers, now a relentless drone, seemed to echo through the haunted dwelling, urging them to confront the lingering malevolent forces that lurked within the shadows. The old house, though momentarily quelled, stood as a stage for the final showdown between the forces of the living and the residual supernatural darkness.

In the dimly lit chamber, Sheila and Rob confronted the residual malevolent forces. The whispers, now a haunting melody, guided them through the spectral encounter—a dance between the living and the lingering abyss. The haunted dwelling, its spectral foundations shaken by the consequences of the sacrifice, became a crucible where the boundaries between reality and the residual supernatural blurred.

The residual entity, a manifestation of the ancient darkness that had been entwined with the spectral fabric, spoke through the dissonant chorus. The whispers, now a relentless drone, conveyed the grievances and malevolence of the lingering force that sought communion with the living. The haunted dwelling, a conduit for the residual supernatural forces, bore silent witness to the final showdown that unfolded within its spectral corridors.

Sheila and Rob, their senses heightened by the supernatural onslaught, faced a choice—succumb to the lingering malevolent forces or confront the residual entity head-on. The whispers, now a relentless drone, urged them toward a revelation that defied comprehension. The haunted dwelling, its spectral foundations saturated with the essence of the living, stood as a battleground where the forces of the living and the residual supernatural clashed in a terrifying crescendo.

In the dim light, Sheila and Rob glimpsed shadowy figures—apparitions of the past that materialized in the spectral realm. The whispers, now a haunting lament, spoke of the tormented souls that lingered within the haunted dwelling. The air, charged with an otherworldly

energy, guided them toward the epicenter of the spectral storm—an impending confrontation with the residual malevolent entity.

As the entity recoiled, the whispers, now a spectral chorus, intensified. Sheila and Rob, their resolve tested by the supernatural onslaught, faced the residual malevolent force with determination. The haunted dwelling, its spectral foundations saturated with the essence of the supernatural, stood as a crucible where the forces of light and darkness clashed in a terrifying crescendo.

Unexpectedly, the residual entity recoiled—a spectral manifestation weakened by the determination of the living. The whispers, now a fading memory, left an eerie stillness in their wake. Sheila and Rob, their senses overwhelmed by the supernatural encounter, stood amidst the remnants of the residual spectral storm. The haunted dwelling, though momentarily quelled, seemed to sigh with a spectral resignation as if acknowledging the fleeting victory over the lingering malevolent forces.

As Sheila and Rob emerged from the confrontation, a sense of cautious hope lingered in the air. The whispers, now a distant murmur, guided them through the dimly lit halls of the old house—the battleground where the forces of the living had once again triumphed over the residual malevolent entity. The haunted dwelling, though forever scarred by the supernatural encounter, stood as a testament to the resilience of those who dared to confront the ancient darkness that lingered within its spectral confines.

Little did Sheila and Rob know that the true horror, a revelation that would redefine their very existence, awaited in the shadows of the haunted dwelling. The whispers, now a fading memory, left the door ajar for the looming terror that awaited in the aftermath of the supernatural sacrifice. Sheila and Rob, bound by the lingering forces that clung within, faced an uncertain future where the horrors of the past cast a long, lingering shadow over their fragile grasp on reality.

Chapter 19: The Awakening

As Sheila and Rob emerged from the lingering shadows of the haunted dwelling, a fragile sense of hope clung to the air. The whispers,

now a distant murmur, guided them through the dimly lit halls—the haunted battleground where they had confronted the malevolent forces and the residual darkness. However, the old house, forever scarred by the supernatural encounter, bore the weight of a haunting legacy that transcended the physical realm.

In the aftermath of the confrontation, Sheila and Rob felt a disquieting calm settle over the old house. The air, heavy with the essence of the supernatural, carried a spectral resonance that hinted at the lingering forces within the haunted dwelling. Shadows danced on the walls, and the whispers, now a fading memory, seemed to echo through the spectral corridors—an eerie reminder of the harrowing journey that had unfolded within the confines of the ancient dwelling.

Unbeknownst to them, the supernatural encounter had left an indelible mark on Sheila's soul. As night fell over the old house, a subtle shift occurred within Sheila—an awakening to a new reality that transcended the boundaries of the living. The whispers, now a distant melody, guided her through the haunted corridors, leading her toward a revelation that defied comprehension.

As they explored the old house, Sheila and Rob discovered that the residual energies had imprinted themselves onto the very fabric of Sheila's being. Shadows, now a spectral dance, seemed to weave through her existence, blurring the boundaries between the living and the supernatural. The whispers, now a haunting lament, echoed through her consciousness—an unsettling reminder that the spectral legacy lingered within.

In the dim light, Sheila and Rob witnessed cryptic symbols appearing on Sheila's skin—a manifestation of the supernatural imprint left by the ancient darkness. The whispers, now a spectral symphony, intensified as they delved into the haunted corridors, conveying the urgency of a greater awakening that loomed on the horizon. The old house, though momentarily quelled, stood as a conduit for Sheila's transformation—an evolution that defied the constraints of the mortal realm.

Sheila, grappling with the newfound reality, sought the guidance of the psychic medium who had assisted them in the cleansing ritual. The whispers, now a haunting melody, seemed to echo through the secluded residence of the medium, conveying the urgency of Sheila's awakening. The air, thick with the residual energies of the supernatural encounter, guided them toward a revelation that went beyond the haunted dwelling's spectral confines.

The psychic medium, attuned to the supernatural currents, spoke of Sheila's connection to the ancient darkness—an awakening that defied the boundaries of the ritual. The whispers, now a relentless drone, urged Sheila to embrace the spectral legacy within her. The air, heavy with the essence of the supernatural, carried a spectral resonance that transcended the mortal realm.

Determined to understand the extent of her transformation, Sheila returned to the old house, her senses heightened by the lingering supernatural energies. The whispers, now a spectral chorus, seemed to align with her evolving awareness as she ventured into the dimly lit halls. The haunted dwelling, though scarred by the supernatural encounter, awaited the next chapter in Sheila's journey—an odyssey that would redefine her very existence.

As night settled over the old house, Sheila felt the temperature drop—a chilling sign of her newfound connection to the lingering forces. Shadows danced on the walls, and the air vibrated with a spectral resonance that hinted at the awakening within her. The whispers, now a haunting lament, guided her toward the heart of the spectral storm—an epicenter where the forces of the living and the supernatural converged within her being.

In the dim light, Sheila glimpsed fleeting apparitions—manifestations of the ancient darkness that had become intertwined with her soul. The whispers, now a dissonant symphony, seemed to speak of a malevolence seeking communion with her, defying the constraints of the ritual. The old house, though momentarily quelled, stood as a

witness to Sheila's metamorphosis—an evolution that transcended the boundaries of the living.

Suddenly, the room quivered with unseen energies, and the temperature plummeted. The whispers, now a spectral chorus, intensified as Sheila confronted the epicenter of the supernatural disturbance within herself. The air, charged with an otherworldly energy, carried a spectral resonance that hinted at the imminent confrontation with the ancient darkness that had become a part of her very essence.

As Sheila approached the heart of the spectral storm within her, she felt an oppressive force—an awakening darkness that seemed to envelop her being. The whispers, now a relentless drone, echoed through her consciousness, urging her to confront the malevolent forces that lingered within the depths of her soul. Sheila, standing at the threshold of her own transformation, faced the haunting legacy that had become an integral part of her existence.

In the dimly lit chamber of her consciousness, Sheila confronted the residual malevolent forces that lingered within her. The whispers, now a haunting melody, guided her through the spectral encounter—a dance between her awakened self and the lingering abyss. The haunted dwelling, its spectral foundations shaken by the consequences of the sacrifice, became a crucible where the boundaries between Sheila's reality and the supernatural blurred.

The residual entity within Sheila, a manifestation of the ancient darkness, spoke through the spectral symphony within her soul. The whispers, now a dissonant chorus, conveyed the grievances and malevolence of the lingering force that sought communion with her. Sheila, in a surreal confrontation with her own awakening, faced the ancient darkness that had become intertwined with her very essence. The haunted dwelling, a conduit for the residual supernatural forces, bore silent witness to the final showdown within the depths of Sheila's consciousness.

As Sheila grappled with the malevolent forces within her, the whispers, now a relentless drone, urged her toward a revelation that defied comprehension. The haunted dwelling, its spectral foundations

saturated with the essence of Sheila's transformation, stood as a battleground where the forces of light and darkness clashed in a terrifying crescendo within the depths of her soul.

In the dim light, Sheila glimpsed shadowy figures—apparitions of the past that materialized in the spectral realm within her consciousness. The whispers, now a haunting lament, spoke of the tormented souls that lingered within her awakened self. The air, charged with an otherworldly energy, guided her toward the epicenter of the spectral storm—an impending confrontation with the malevolent entity that had become an integral part of her very existence.

As Sheila confronted the entity within, the whispers, now a spectral chorus, intensified. Her resolve tested by the supernatural onslaught, she faced the residual malevolent force with determination. The haunted dwelling, its spectral foundations saturated with the essence of the supernatural, stood as a crucible where the forces of light and darkness clashed in a terrifying crescendo within the depths of Sheila's soul.

Unexpectedly, the residual entity within Sheila recoiled—a spectral manifestation weakened by her determination to overcome the malevolent forces. The whispers, now a fading memory, left an eerie stillness in the chambers of her consciousness. Sheila, her senses overwhelmed by the supernatural encounter within, stood amidst the remnants of the spectral storm that had unfolded within her soul. The haunted dwelling, though momentarily quelled, seemed to sigh with a spectral resignation as if acknowledging the fleeting victory over the lingering malevolent forces.

As Sheila emerged from the depths of her own awakening, a sense of cautious hope lingered in the air. The whispers, now a distant murmur, guided her through the dimly lit halls of her own consciousness— the battleground where she had triumphed over the malevolent forces within. The haunted dwelling, forever scarred by the supernatural encounter, stood as a testament to the resilience of the human spirit and the capacity to confront the ancient darkness that lurked within one's own soul.

Little did Sheila know that her journey was far from over. The whispers, now a fading memory, left the door ajar for the looming terror that awaited in the aftermath of her awakening. Sheila, forever changed by the harrowing ordeal within herself, faced an uncertain future where the horrors of her own past cast a long, lingering shadow over her fragile grasp on reality. The haunted dwelling, a reflection of her awakened soul, awaited the next chapter in Sheila's journey—a journey that would redefine the very fabric of her existence.

Chapter 20: The Return

In the aftermath of Sheila's awakening, a deceptive calm settled over the old house. The air, thick with the remnants of the supernatural encounter within her soul, carried an unsettling resonance that hinted at the depths of her transformation. The whispers, now a distant murmur, guided Sheila through the dimly lit halls—a haunting reminder of the malevolent forces that lingered within her awakened self.

As night fell over the old house, Sheila's senses heightened, attuned to the subtle shifts in the spectral currents that surrounded her. Shadows danced on the walls, and the air vibrated with a spectral resonance that hinted at the lingering darkness within her. The whispers, now a fading memory, seemed to echo through the haunted corridors—an ominous prelude to the return of the malevolent forces that had become entwined with her very essence.

Unbeknownst to Sheila, her awakening had not only transformed her soul but had left an indelible mark on the haunted dwelling itself. The air, heavy with the essence of the supernatural, carried an ominous energy that hinted at a spectral unrest within the old house. The whispers, now a haunting lament, guided her toward the epicenter of the spectral storm—an awareness that the malevolent forces were not confined to her consciousness alone.

In the dim light, Sheila and Rob witnessed cryptic symbols reappearing on the walls—a manifestation of the malevolent forces that had returned to the spectral fabric of the old house. The whispers, now a spectral symphony, intensified as they delved into the haunted

corridors, conveying the urgency of a greater darkness that loomed on the horizon. The old house, though scarred by the supernatural encounter, stood as a stage for the malevolent forces' return—an encore that defied the constraints of the ritual.

Sheila, grappling with the resurgence of the malevolent forces, sought the guidance of the psychic medium who had assisted them in the cleansing ritual. The whispers, now a haunting melody, seemed to echo through the secluded residence of the medium, conveying the urgency of the situation. The air, thick with the residual energies of the supernatural encounter, guided them toward a revelation that went beyond the haunted dwelling's spectral confines.

The psychic medium, aware of the lingering malevolence, spoke of the malevolent forces' return—an awakening that defied the boundaries of the ritual. The whispers, now a relentless drone, urged Sheila and Rob to confront the looming darkness before it consumed the haunted dwelling. The air, heavy with the essence of the supernatural, carried a spectral resonance that transcended the mortal realm.

Determined to face the consequences of her awakening, Sheila returned to the old house, her senses heightened by the lingering supernatural energies. The whispers, now a spectral chorus, seemed to align with her evolving awareness as she ventured into the dimly lit halls. The haunted dwelling, though scarred by the supernatural encounter, awaited the next chapter in Sheila's journey—an odyssey that would test the limits of her newfound connection to the malevolent forces.

As night settled over the old house, Sheila felt the temperature drop—a chilling sign of the malevolent forces' return. Shadows danced on the walls, and the air vibrated with a spectral resonance that hinted at the impending confrontation. The whispers, now a haunting lament, guided her toward the heart of the spectral storm—an epicenter where the forces of the living and the supernatural converged within her being.

In the dim light, Sheila glimpsed fleeting apparitions—manifestations of the malevolent forces that had returned to the haunted dwelling. The whispers, now a dissonant symphony, seemed to speak of a

malevolence seeking communion with her, defying the constraints of the ritual. The old house, though momentarily quelled, stood as a witness to Sheila's confrontation with the return of the malevolent forces —an encore that echoed through the spectral corridors.

Suddenly, the room quivered with unseen energies, and the temperature plummeted. The whispers, now a spectral chorus, intensified as Sheila confronted the epicenter of the supernatural disturbance within herself. The air, charged with an otherworldly energy, carried a spectral resonance that hinted at the imminent confrontation with the malevolent forces that had returned to the old house.

As Sheila approached the heart of the spectral storm within her, she felt an oppressive force—an awakening darkness that seemed to envelop her being. The whispers, now a relentless drone, echoed through her consciousness, urging her to confront the malevolent forces that lingered within the depths of her soul. Sheila, standing at the threshold of her own transformation, faced the haunting encore that had become an integral part of her existence.

In the dimly lit chamber of her consciousness, Sheila confronted the return of the malevolent forces that lingered within her. The whispers, now a haunting melody, guided her through the spectral encounter—a dance between her awakened self and the lingering abyss. The haunted dwelling, its spectral foundations shaken by the consequences of the sacrifice, became a crucible where the boundaries between Sheila's reality and the return of the malevolent forces blurred.

The malevolent forces within Sheila, a manifestation of the ancient darkness, spoke through the spectral symphony within her soul. The whispers, now a dissonant chorus, conveyed the grievances and malevolence of the lingering force that sought communion with her. Sheila, in a surreal confrontation with the return of the malevolent forces, faced the ancient darkness that had become intertwined with her very essence. The haunted dwelling, a conduit for the malevolent supernatural forces, bore silent witness to the encore within the depths of Sheila's consciousness.

As Sheila grappled with the malevolent forces within her, the whispers, now a relentless drone, urged her toward a revelation that defied comprehension. The haunted dwelling, its spectral foundations saturated with the essence of Sheila's confrontation, stood as a battleground where the forces of light and darkness clashed in a terrifying encore within the depths of her soul.

In the dim light, Sheila glimpsed shadowy figures—apparitions of the past that materialized in the spectral realm within her consciousness. The whispers, now a haunting lament, spoke of the tormented souls that lingered within her awakened self. The air, charged with an otherworldly energy, guided her toward the epicenter of the spectral storm—an impending encore with the malevolent entity that had become an integral part of her very existence.

As Sheila confronted the entity within, the whispers, now a spectral chorus, intensified. Her resolve tested by the supernatural encore, she faced the return of the malevolent force with determination. The haunted dwelling, its spectral foundations saturated with the essence of the supernatural, stood as a crucible where the forces of light and darkness clashed in a terrifying encore within the depths of Sheila's soul.

Unexpectedly, the return of the malevolent forces within Sheila recoiled—a spectral manifestation weakened by her determination to overcome the malevolent encore. The whispers, now a fading memory, left an eerie stillness in the chambers of her consciousness. Sheila, her senses overwhelmed by the supernatural encore within, stood amidst the remnants of the spectral storm that had unfolded within her soul. The haunted dwelling, though momentarily quelled, seemed to sigh with a spectral resignation as if acknowledging the fleeting victory over the lingering malevolent forces.

As Sheila emerged from the depths of her own confrontation, a sense of cautious hope lingered in the air. The whispers, now a distant murmur, guided her through the dimly lit halls of her own consciousness—the battleground where she had triumphed over the malevolent forces within. The haunted dwelling, forever scarred by the supernatural

encore, stood as a testament to the resilience of the human spirit and the capacity to confront the ancient darkness that lurked within one's own soul.

Little did Sheila know that the return of the malevolent forces signaled a new chapter in her journey. The whispers, now a fading memory, left the door ajar for the looming terror that awaited in the aftermath of the supernatural encore. Sheila, forever changed by the harrowing ordeal within herself, faced an uncertain future where the horrors of her own past cast a long, lingering shadow over her fragile grasp on reality. The haunted dwelling, a reflection of her awakened soul, awaited the next chapter in Sheila's journey—a journey that would redefine the very fabric of her existence.

Chapter 21: The Revelation

In the wake of the malevolent forces' return, the old house stood as a silent witness to the unfolding nightmare that awaited Sheila. The air, thick with the supernatural energies that clung to her awakened soul, carried an oppressive weight that seemed to permeate every corner of the haunted dwelling. The whispers, now a distant murmur, guided Sheila through the dimly lit halls—a foreboding prelude to the revelation that awaited in the shadows.

As night fell over the old house, Sheila's senses remained on edge, attuned to the subtle shifts in the spectral currents that surrounded her. Shadows danced on the walls, and the air vibrated with a spectral resonance that hinted at the impending revelation. The whispers, now a fading memory, seemed to echo through the haunted corridors—an eerie reminder of the malevolent forces that lurked within the depths of her awakened self.

Unbeknownst to Sheila, the return of the malevolent forces had not only marked the old house but had woven a dark tapestry that transcended the physical realm. The air, heavy with the essence of the supernatural encore, carried an ominous energy that hinted at a spectral unrest within the very fabric of the haunted dwelling. The whispers, now a haunting lament, guided her toward the epicenter of

the spectral storm—an awareness that the malevolent forces sought not only communion with her soul but also a greater revelation that defied comprehension.

In the dim light, Sheila and Rob witnessed cryptic symbols reappearing on the walls—a manifestation of the malevolent forces that had returned to the spectral fabric of the old house. The whispers, now a spectral symphony, intensified as they delved into the haunted corridors, conveying the urgency of a revelation that went beyond the boundaries of the living. The old house, though momentarily quelled, stood as a stage for the malevolent forces' revelation—an unveiling that defied the constraints of the mortal realm.

Sheila, grappling with the ominous energies that clung to her awakened soul, sought the guidance of the psychic medium who had assisted them in the cleansing ritual. The whispers, now a haunting melody, seemed to echo through the secluded residence of the medium, conveying the urgency of the situation. The air, thick with the residual energies of the supernatural encore, guided them toward a revelation that transcended the haunted dwelling's spectral confines.

The psychic medium, attuned to the supernatural currents, spoke of a revelation that went beyond the malevolent forces' return—an awakening that defied the boundaries of the ritual. The whispers, now a relentless drone, urged Sheila and Rob to confront the looming darkness before it consumed not only their souls but also the very fabric of reality. The air, heavy with the essence of the supernatural, carried a spectral resonance that transcended the mortal realm.

Determined to face the consequences of the revelation, Sheila returned to the old house, her senses heightened by the lingering supernatural energies. The whispers, now a spectral chorus, seemed to align with her evolving awareness as she ventured into the dimly lit halls. The haunted dwelling, scarred by the supernatural encounter and the malevolent encore, awaited the next chapter in Sheila's journey—an odyssey that would test the limits of her newfound connection to the malevolent forces and the revelation that awaited in the shadows.

As night settled over the old house, Sheila felt the temperature drop—a chilling sign of the revelation that loomed on the horizon. Shadows danced on the walls, and the air vibrated with a spectral resonance that hinted at the impending unveiling. The whispers, now a haunting lament, guided her toward the heart of the spectral storm—an epicenter where the forces of the living and the supernatural converged within her being.

In the dim light, Sheila glimpsed fleeting apparitions—manifestations of the malevolent forces that had returned to the haunted dwelling. The whispers, now a dissonant symphony, seemed to speak of a malevolence seeking communion with her, defying the constraints of the ritual. The old house, though momentarily quelled, stood as a witness to Sheila's confrontation with the revelation—an unveiling that echoed through the spectral corridors.

Suddenly, the room quivered with unseen energies, and the temperature plummeted. The whispers, now a spectral chorus, intensified as Sheila confronted the epicenter of the supernatural disturbance within herself. The air, charged with an otherworldly energy, carried a spectral resonance that hinted at the imminent confrontation with the revelation that had become intertwined with her very essence.

As Sheila approached the heart of the spectral storm within her, she felt an oppressive force—an awakening darkness that seemed to envelop her being. The whispers, now a relentless drone, echoed through her consciousness, urging her to confront the malevolent forces and the revelation that lingered within the depths of her soul. Sheila, standing at the threshold of her own transformation, faced the haunting unveiling that had become an integral part of her existence.

In the dimly lit chamber of her consciousness, Sheila confronted the revelation that unfolded within her soul. The whispers, now a haunting melody, guided her through the spectral encounter—a dance between her awakened self and the lingering abyss. The haunted dwelling, its spectral foundations shaken by the consequences of the sacrifice and the

malevolent encore, became a crucible where the boundaries between Sheila's reality and the revelation blurred.

The revelation within Sheila, a manifestation of the ancient darkness, spoke through the spectral symphony within her soul. The whispers, now a dissonant chorus, conveyed the grievances and malevolence of the lingering force that sought communion with her. Sheila, in a surreal confrontation with the revelation, faced the ancient darkness that had become intertwined with her very essence. The haunted dwelling, a conduit for the malevolent supernatural forces and the revelation, bore silent witness to the final unveiling within the depths of Sheila's consciousness.

As Sheila grappled with the malevolent forces and the revelation within her, the whispers, now a relentless drone, urged her toward a revelation that defied comprehension. The haunted dwelling, its spectral foundations saturated with the essence of Sheila's confrontation and the revelation, stood as a battleground where the forces of light and darkness clashed in a terrifying crescendo within the depths of her soul.

In the dim light, Sheila glimpsed shadowy figures—apparitions of the past that materialized in the spectral realm within her consciousness. The whispers, now a haunting lament, spoke of the tormented souls that lingered within her awakened self. The air, charged with an otherworldly energy, guided her toward the epicenter of the spectral storm—an impending revelation with the malevolent entity that had become an integral part of her very existence.

As Sheila confronted the entity within, the whispers, now a spectral chorus, intensified. Her resolve tested by the supernatural onslaught, she faced the revelation and the return of the malevolent force with determination. The haunted dwelling, its spectral foundations saturated with the essence of the supernatural, stood as a crucible where the forces of light and darkness clashed in a terrifying crescendo within the depths of Sheila's soul.

Unexpectedly, the revelation within Sheila recoiled—a spectral manifestation weakened by her determination to overcome the malevolent

forces. The whispers, now a fading memory, left an eerie stillness in the chambers of her consciousness. Sheila, her senses overwhelmed by the supernatural encounter within and the revelation, stood amidst the remnants of the spectral storm that had unfolded within her soul. The haunted dwelling, though momentarily quelled, seemed to sigh with a spectral resignation as if acknowledging the fleeting victory over the lingering malevolent forces and the revelation.

As Sheila emerged from the depths of her own confrontation and the revelation, a sense of cautious hope lingered in the air. The whispers, now a distant murmur, guided her through the dimly lit halls of her own consciousness—the battleground where she had triumphed over the malevolent forces and the revelation within. The haunted dwelling, forever scarred by the supernatural encounter, the malevolent encore, and the revelation, stood as a testament to the resilience of the human spirit and the capacity to confront the ancient darkness that lurked within one's own soul.

Little did Sheila know that the revelation signaled a new chapter in her journey. The whispers, now a fading memory, left the door ajar for the looming terror that awaited in the aftermath of the supernatural encounter, the malevolent encore, and the revelation. Sheila, forever changed by the harrowing ordeal within herself, faced an uncertain future where the horrors of her own past cast a long, lingering shadow over her fragile grasp on reality. The haunted dwelling, a reflection of her awakened soul, awaited the next chapter in Sheila's journey—a journey that would redefine the very fabric of her existence.

Chapter 22: The Sacrifice

As Sheila emerged from the depths of the haunting revelation, an uneasy calm settled over the old house. The air, thick with the remnants of the supernatural encounter, the malevolent encore, and the revelation within her soul, carried a weight that seemed to hang in the dimly lit halls. The whispers, now a distant murmur, guided Sheila through the spectral corridors—an ominous reminder of the malevolent forces and the revelation that lingered within the shadows.

The old house, scarred by the supernatural events that had unfolded within its walls, stood as a testament to the harrowing journey Sheila had traversed. Shadows danced on the walls, and the air vibrated with a spectral resonance that hinted at the lingering darkness within her. The whispers, now a fading memory, seemed to echo through the haunted dwelling—an eerie prelude to the final chapter that awaited Sheila.

Unbeknownst to her, the malevolent forces, the revelation, and the haunting encore had left an indelible mark not only on her soul but also on the spectral fabric of the old house. The air, heavy with the essence of the supernatural, carried an ominous energy that hinted at a linger-ing presence—a spectral force that awaited the culmination of Sheila's journey. The whispers, now a haunting lament, guided her toward the epicenter of the spectral storm—an awareness that the malevolent forces and the revelation were not mere echoes of the past but a looming threat that sought a resolution.

In the dim light, Sheila and Rob observed cryptic symbols etching themselves onto the walls—a manifestation of the malevolent forces, the revelation, and the encore that had become intertwined with the haunted dwelling. The whispers, now a spectral symphony, intensified as they delved into the haunted corridors, conveying the urgency of a greater darkness that loomed on the horizon. The old house, though momentarily quelled, stood as a stage for the malevolent forces' final act—an act that defied the constraints of the ritual and hinted at a resolution that transcended the boundaries of the living.

Sheila, grappling with the weight of the revelation, sought the guid-ance of the psychic medium who had assisted them in the cleansing ritual. The whispers, now a haunting melody, seemed to echo through the secluded residence of the medium, conveying the urgency of the situation. The air, thick with the residual energies of the supernatural encounter, the malevolent encore, and the revelation, guided them to-ward a resolution that went beyond the haunted dwelling's spectral confines.

The psychic medium, aware of the lingering malevolence, spoke of a resolution that defied the boundaries of the ritual. The whispers, now a relentless drone, urged Sheila and Rob to confront the looming darkness before it consumed not only their souls but also the very fabric of reality. The air, heavy with the essence of the supernatural, carried a spectral resonance that transcended the mortal realm.

Determined to face the consequences of the supernatural events, Sheila returned to the old house, her senses heightened by the lingering energies. The whispers, now a spectral chorus, seemed to align with her evolving awareness as she ventured into the dimly lit halls. The haunted dwelling, scarred by the supernatural events and the revelation, awaited the next chapter in Sheila's journey—an odyssey that would test the limits of her newfound connection to the malevolent forces.

As night settled over the old house, Sheila felt the temperature drop—a chilling sign of the impending resolution. Shadows danced on the walls, and the air vibrated with a spectral resonance that hinted at the imminent confrontation. The whispers, now a haunting lament, guided her toward the heart of the spectral storm—an epicenter where the forces of the living and the supernatural converged within her being.

In the dim light, Sheila glimpsed fleeting apparitions—manifestations of the malevolent forces that had returned to the haunted dwelling. The whispers, now a dissonant symphony, seemed to speak of a malevolence seeking communion with her, defying the constraints of the ritual. The old house, though momentarily quelled, stood as a witness to Sheila's confrontation with the resolution—an act that echoed through the spectral corridors.

Suddenly, the room quivered with unseen energies, and the temperature plummeted. The whispers, now a spectral chorus, intensified as Sheila confronted the epicenter of the supernatural disturbance within herself. The air, charged with an otherworldly energy, carried a spectral resonance that hinted at the imminent confrontation with the resolution that had become intertwined with her very essence.

As Sheila approached the heart of the spectral storm within her, she felt an oppressive force—an awakening darkness that seemed to envelop her being. The whispers, now a relentless drone, echoed through her consciousness, urging her to confront the malevolent forces and the resolution that lingered within the depths of her soul. Sheila, standing at the threshold of her own transformation, faced the haunting resolution that had become an integral part of her existence.

In the dimly lit chamber of her consciousness, Sheila confronted the resolution that unfolded within her soul. The whispers, now a haunting melody, guided her through the spectral encounter—a dance between her awakened self and the lingering abyss. The haunted dwelling, its spectral foundations shaken by the consequences of the sacrifice, the malevolent encore, and the revelation, became a crucible where the boundaries between Sheila's reality and the resolution blurred.

The resolution within Sheila, a manifestation of the ancient darkness, spoke through the spectral symphony within her soul. The whispers, now a dissonant chorus, conveyed the grievances and malevolence of the lingering force that sought communion with her. Sheila, in a surreal confrontation with the resolution, faced the ancient darkness that had become intertwined with her very essence. The haunted dwelling, a conduit for the malevolent supernatural forces and the resolution, bore silent witness to the final act within the depths of Sheila's consciousness.

As Sheila grappled with the malevolent forces and the resolution within her, the whispers, now a relentless drone, urged her toward a resolution that defied comprehension. The haunted dwelling, its spectral foundations saturated with the essence of Sheila's confrontation, the malevolent encore, and the revelation, stood as a battleground where the forces of light and darkness clashed in a terrifying crescendo within the depths of her soul.

In the dim light, Sheila glimpsed shadowy figures—apparitions of the past that materialized in the spectral realm within her consciousness. The whispers, now a haunting lament, spoke of the tormented souls

that lingered within her awakened self. The air, charged with an other-worldly energy, guided her toward the epicenter of the spectral storm—an impending resolution with the malevolent entity that had become an integral part of her very existence.

As Sheila confronted the entity within, the whispers, now a spectral chorus, intensified. Her resolve tested by the supernatural onslaught, she faced the resolution and the return of the malevolent force with determination. The haunted dwelling, its spectral foundations saturated with the essence of the supernatural, stood as a crucible where the forces of light and darkness clashed in a terrifying crescendo within the depths of Sheila's soul.

Unexpectedly, the resolution within Sheila recoiled—a spectral manifestation weakened by her determination to overcome the malevolent forces. The whispers, now a fading memory, left an eerie stillness in the chambers of her consciousness. Sheila, her senses overwhelmed by the supernatural encounter, the malevolent encore, and the resolution, stood amidst the remnants of the spectral storm that had unfolded within her soul. The haunted dwelling, though momentarily quelled, seemed to sigh with a spectral resignation as if acknowledging the fleeting victory over the lingering malevolent forces and the resolution.

As Sheila emerged from the depths of her own confrontation and the resolution, a sense of cautious hope lingered in the air. The whispers, now a distant murmur, guided her through the dimly lit halls of her own consciousness—the battleground where she had triumphed over the malevolent forces, the revelation, and the resolution within. The haunted dwelling, forever scarred by the supernatural encounter, stood as a testament to the resilience of the human spirit and the capacity to confront the ancient darkness that lurked within one's own soul.

Little did Sheila know that the resolution marked the final chapter in her journey. The whispers, now a fading memory, left the door ajar for the looming terror that awaited in the aftermath of the supernatural encounter, the malevolent encore, and the revelation. Sheila, forever changed by the harrowing ordeal within herself, faced an uncertain

future where the horrors of her own past cast a long, lingering shadow over her fragile grasp on reality. The haunted dwelling, a reflection of her awakened soul, awaited the next chapter in Sheila's journey—a journey that would redefine the very fabric of her existence.

**The Horror Inside
The House Awaits
By
Doug Hensley
Table Of Contents**

Chapter 1: The New House - Sheila moves into a beautiful but eerie old house, noticing strange noises and feeling uneasy.

Chapter 2: The Whispers - Sheila hears faint voices whispering when alone at night, making her question her sanity.

Chapter 3: The Dark History - Sheila researches the house's past, finding a dark tale of murder and suicide. Chapter 4: The Warning - An elderly neighbor tells Sheila she must leave the house before it's too late. Sheila refuses.

Chapter 5: The Apparition - Sheila sees a ghostly figure staring at her from the hall, but it disappears before she can investigate.

Chapter 6: The Visitor - Sheila's childhood friend Rob stays the night, also experiencing unsettling events in the house.

Chapter 7: The Presence - Doors open on their own, objects move mysteriously, and Sheila feels someone watching, though Rob remains oblivious.

Chapter 8: The Message - Cryptic words are scrawled on the bathroom mirror when Sheila and Rob wake up, leaving them shaken.

Chapter 9: The History Revealed - Sheila finds an old diary explaining gruesome rituals once held in the house's basement.

Chapter 10: The Basement - Sheila and Rob find a secret door leading down to a dark basement. Going down, they trigger a cave-in, trapping them inside.

Chapter 11: The Escape - After finding ritual items in the basement, Sheila and Rob escape and block the basement door, believing the nightmare is over.

Chapter 12: The Attacks - Paranormal attacks on Sheila grow violent. Desperate, she considers holding a seance.

Chapter 13: The Seance - The seance summons malevolent spirits. One possesses Rob, forcing Sheila to take drastic measures.

Chapter 14: The Cleansing - Sheila enlists a psychic medium to cleanse the home. The process seems successful until things escalate again. Chapter 15: The Truth - Research reveals the house was built for occult rituals, with a dark energy woven into the walls. There is only one way to stop it.

Chapter 16: The Sacrifice - Sheila learns she must offer a blood sacrifice in the house to seal the evil presence. She prepares for the ritual.

Chapter 17: The Confrontation - Unexpected twists force Sheila into a final showdown with the sinister forces in the house. All seems lost until she embraces her destiny. Chapter 18: The Resolution - Sheila defeats the evil forces at great personal cost. The house is finally at peace, but so much has changed. Chapter 19: The Awakening - Sheila slowly recovers, adjusting to a new normal. For the first time in years, she feels hope.

Chapter 20: The Return - Strange events make Sheila question if the evil presence was truly eradicated. Ominous signs suggest a greater darkness.

Chapter 21: The Revelation - Sheila discovers the house's evil has corrupted her soul. She must act quickly if she hopes to save herself. Chapter 22: The Sacrifice - Sheila makes one final sacrifice, for her own sake rather than the house's. Her journey ends, for better or worse.

Chapter 1: The New House

Sheila, a young woman seeking a fresh start, moves into a beautiful yet eerie old house. Almost immediately, strange noises and an overwhelming feeling of unease settle in, setting the stage for the supernatural events that will unfold.

Chapter 2: The Whispers As Sheila settles into her new home, she begins hearing faint voices whispering to her when she's alone at night. The mysterious whispers cast doubt on her sanity and create an atmosphere of increasing tension.

Chapter 3: The Dark History Driven by curiosity and a growing sense of dread, Sheila delves into the house's past. Her research reveals a dark tale of murder and suicide, hinting at the malevolent forces that may be at play.

Chapter 4: The Warning An elderly neighbor warns Sheila of impending danger and urges her to leave the house before it's too late. Despite the ominous warning, Sheila stubbornly refuses to abandon her new home.

Chapter 5: The Apparition Sheila's fears intensify when she catches a glimpse of a ghostly figure staring at her from the hall. However, the apparition vanishes before she can investigate further, leaving her to grapple with the supernatural occurrences.

Chapter 6: The Visitor In an attempt to find solace, Sheila invites her childhood friend Rob to stay the night. Rob, too, experiences unsettling events in the house, heightening the sense of foreboding.

Chapter 7: The Presence Doors open on their own, objects move mysteriously, and Sheila senses an unseen presence watching her. Despite the escalating paranormal activity, Rob remains oblivious to the unfolding horror.

Chapter 8: The Message Sheila and Rob wake up to cryptic words scrawled on the bathroom mirror, further deepening the mystery and leaving them shaken. The supernatural forces in the house are making their presence known in unsettling ways.

Chapter 9: The History Revealed Sheila discovers an old diary in the house, unveiling the gruesome rituals that were once held in its dark

basement. The revelation adds a layer of horror to the already chilling atmosphere.

Chapter 10: The Basement Driven by the need to unravel the mysteries surrounding the house, Sheila and Rob find a secret door leading to a dark basement. Their exploration triggers a cave-in, trapping them inside and marking a point of no return.

Chapter 11: The Escape Believing the nightmare is over, Sheila and Rob manage to escape the basement and block the door, thinking they have successfully sealed away the malevolent forces. However, the worst is yet to come.

Chapter 12: The Attacks Paranormal attacks on Sheila escalate, growing increasingly violent. Desperate for answers, she contemplates holding a seance to communicate with the otherworldly entities.

Chapter 13: The Seance The seance takes a dark turn as malevolent spirits are summoned, with one possessing Rob. Sheila is forced to take drastic measures to confront the supernatural threat.

Chapter 14: The Cleansing Sheila enlists the help of a psychic medium to cleanse the home. Initially, the process appears successful, providing a false sense of security. However, the calm is short-lived as the haunting experiences resume.

Chapter 15: The Truth Through extensive research, Sheila uncovers that the house was purposefully built for occult rituals, with a dark energy woven into its very walls. The revelation leaves her with the chilling realization that only one method can put an end to the terror.

Chapter 16: The Sacrifice Sheila learns that she must make a blood sacrifice within the house to seal the evil presence once and for all. As she prepares for the ritual, the gravity of the situation weighs heavily on her.

Chapter 17: The Confrontation Unexpected twists and turns force Sheila into a final showdown with the sinister forces in the house. All seems lost until she embraces her destiny, revealing a strength she never knew she possessed.

Chapter 18: The Resolution At great personal cost, Sheila successfully defeats the evil forces within the house. While the dwelling is finally at peace, the toll on Sheila is profound, leaving her forever changed.

Chapter 19: The Awakening As Sheila slowly recovers, she must adjust to a new normal. For the first time in years, she feels a glimmer of hope, but the scars of the harrowing ordeal run deep.

Chapter 20: The Return Strange events begin to unfold, making Sheila question if the evil presence was truly eradicated. Ominous signs suggest a greater darkness that may linger, threatening to undo everything she thought she had achieved.

Chapter 21: The Revelation In a shocking discovery, Sheila realizes that the house's evil has corrupted her soul. With time running out, she must act swiftly to save herself from the malevolent forces that have taken root within her.

Chapter 22: The Sacrifice In a final, desperate act, Sheila makes one last sacrifice—this time for her own sake rather than the house's. Her journey comes to an end, leaving readers to wonder if the darkness truly dissipates or if it merely finds a new host.

Chapter 1: The New House

The creaking floorboards echoed through the empty rooms as Sheila cautiously stepped into her new home. The air felt heavy, laden with an unspoken history that sent shivers down her spine. The walls, adorned with faded wallpaper, seemed to hold secrets, and the windows allowed only a dim, feeble light to penetrate the gloom.

Sheila's belongings were scattered in disarray, yet the beauty of the old house couldn't be denied. As the sun dipped below the horizon, casting long, eerie shadows across the wooden floors, Sheila couldn't shake the feeling that she was not alone.

Night descended with a whispering chill, and Sheila settled into her bed. But as the clock struck midnight, the house came alive with strange noises. Whispers, soft and elusive, slithered through the silence, causing her heart to race. She strained her ears, catching fragmented words that left her questioning her sanity.

In the dimness, Sheila felt the presence of something unseen. It was as if the very walls held a malevolent secret, a history buried deep within the foundation. Her unease intensified as the whispers grew into an indistinct murmur that seemed to resonate with the pulse of the house.

The next day, Sheila decided to uncover the mysteries surrounding her new abode. Armed with curiosity and a sense of foreboding, she delved into the house's past. Dusty old books and faded photographs revealed a dark tale of murder and suicide that had stained the very essence of the building.

As Sheila immersed herself in the grim accounts of the past, the atmosphere in the house seemed to shift. Shadows danced along the walls, and the temperature dropped, making her breath visible in the cold air. The weight of the house's history pressed upon her, like an invisible hand tightening around her throat.

A knock on the door interrupted Sheila's unsettling discoveries. An elderly neighbor, eyes clouded with concern, warned her of the impending danger that lurked within the house. "Leave, child, before it devours your soul," the old woman pleaded, but Sheila, fueled by stubborn determination, dismissed the ominous advice.

Nightfall brought with it a ghastly apparition. Sheila, bathed in the pale glow of the moonlight, glimpsed a ghostly figure in the hallway. It stared at her with hollow eyes, sending a chill through her veins. Before she could react, the apparition dissolved into the shadows, leaving Sheila trembling in the oppressive silence.

Desperate for solace, Sheila invited her childhood friend Rob to stay the night. As the hours passed, the house unleashed its malevolent grip on them both. Objects moved of their own accord, doors swung open with an otherworldly force, and a pervasive feeling of being watched hung in the air. Yet, Rob remained oblivious to the supernatural dance unfolding around them.

Cryptic messages appeared on the bathroom mirror the following morning. Scrawled in an otherworldly hand, the words sent shivers

down Sheila's spine. The house was communicating with them, leaving an indelible mark on their reality.

With each passing day, the house's dark history unveiled itself in more sinister ways. Sheila discovered an old diary tucked away in a forgotten corner, detailing gruesome rituals held in the very basement she had yet to explore.

Determined to confront the source of the malevolence, Sheila and Rob discovered a hidden door leading to the ominous depths of the basement. The air grew thick with anticipation as they descended, unaware that they were stepping into a trap set by forces beyond their comprehension.

A sudden and violent cave-in trapped Sheila and Rob in the lightless abyss. Panic set in as the walls seemed to close in around them. Shadows danced in the dim illumination of their flashlights, and the oppressive darkness whispered promises of doom.

Hours passed before they managed to escape, their faces etched with fear. Convinced that sealing the basement door had ended the nightmare, Sheila dared to hope for a return to normalcy. Little did she know, the true horror had only just begun.

Paranormal attacks on Sheila intensified, the unseen forces growing bolder and more malevolent. Objects hurled across rooms, chilling whispers turned into guttural growls, and a sinister presence loomed over her every move.

Desperation led Sheila to consider a seance, a desperate attempt to communicate with the entities plaguing her. The air crackled with tension as she and Rob sat in a circle, hands trembling as they called out to the unknown. But the seance took a dark turn, as malevolent spirits seized the opportunity to manifest their malevolence.

Rob, overcome by an unseen force, became a vessel for the malevolent entities. Sheila, faced with a friend turned foe, had no choice but to take drastic measures. The once comforting bonds of friendship now strained under the weight of supernatural possession.

In her quest for salvation, Sheila sought the help of a psychic medium to cleanse the home. The air thickened with anticipation as the medium performed rituals to banish the malevolent entities. For a fleeting moment, the house seemed at peace, and Sheila allowed herself a breath of relief.

However, the calm proved short-lived. The house, it seemed, had only been biding its time. The cleansing had only served to agitate the dormant evil that lingered within the very fabric of the walls.

Driven by an insatiable need for the truth, Sheila's research revealed that the house was purposefully constructed for occult rituals. A dark energy, woven into the very foundation, defied any attempts to eradicate it conventionally. The realization struck her like a physical blow, and the oppressive weight of the house's malevolence pressed down on her soul.

Sheila learned of a chilling solution—one that required a blood sacrifice to seal the evil presence. The revelation sent shivers down her spine, but with unwavering resolve, she prepared for the ritual. The air in the house crackled with a palpable tension as Sheila steeled herself for the harrowing task that lay ahead.

As the appointed hour arrived, Sheila embarked on the ritual, guided by the cryptic instructions she had unearthed. The air thickened with an otherworldly energy as she treaded the fine line between the living and the supernatural. The house seemed to breathe, its walls pulsating with an unholy heartbeat.

Unexpected twists and turns forced Sheila into a final confrontation with the sinister forces that had tormented her. The battle unfolded in a crescendo of terror, with each moment pushing her to the brink of despair. All seemed lost until Sheila, drawing upon a strength she never knew she possessed, embraced her destiny and faced the malevolent entities head-on.

At great personal cost, Sheila emerged victorious. The malevolent forces were banished, and the house fell silent. But victory came at a price—Sheila was forever changed, scarred by the ordeal that had tested her sanity and resilience.

As Sheila grappled with the aftermath of the climactic events, she found herself in a house that bore the marks of the supernatural battle. The once-elegant rooms, now tinged with an otherworldly aura, stood as a testament to the horrors that had unfolded within their walls.

The awakening came slowly for Sheila. She found herself in a surreal new normal, haunted by memories of the malevolence that had once claimed her every waking moment. Yet, for the first time in years, a flicker of hope ignited within her.

But the return to normalcy proved elusive. Strange events unfolded around Sheila, casting doubt on whether the evil presence had truly been eradicated. Ominous signs, subtle yet undeniable, hinted at a darkness that lingered, threatening to unravel everything she had fought so hard to achieve.

In a shocking revelation, Sheila discovered that the house's evil had not only touched the walls but had also corrupted her very soul. Time was of the essence as she grappled with the realization that salvation required swift and decisive action.

The final sacrifice loomed before Sheila—a desperate act to save herself from the malevolent forces that sought to claim her. Her journey reached its conclusion, leaving her standing at the precipice of the unknown. Whether the darkness dissipated or found a new host remained a lingering question, echoing in the silence of the house that had become a battleground between the living and the supernatural.

Chapter 2: The Whispers

As the haunting echoes of the previous night lingered, Sheila awoke to a house cloaked in shadows. The morning light struggled to penetrate the heavy curtains, casting an eerie glow across the room. The unsettling events of the night before weighed on her mind, and a sense of trepidation settled in her chest.

Dragging herself out of bed, Sheila couldn't shake the feeling that the walls were watching her every move. The air seemed to hum with an unnatural energy, and she wondered if the house itself held memories of the whispers that had invaded her sleep.

As dusk settled once again, the atmosphere in the house shifted. The creaking floorboards beneath Sheila's tentative steps seemed to resonate with a spectral rhythm. The shadows danced in a macabre ballet, and the air took on a frigid chill that seeped into her bones.

Alone in the dimly lit living room, Sheila felt a subtle change in the air—a whispering murmur that curled around her consciousness like tendrils of smoke. A strange sensation crawled up her spine, and she strained to catch the fragmented words carried by the unseen voices.

The whispers, soft and elusive, wrapped around her mind like a ghostly embrace. Sheila couldn't discern the origin of the ethereal voices, and a growing unease settled in the pit of her stomach. The words, a dissonant symphony of indistinct muttering, seemed to weave tales of forgotten sorrows and ancient malevolence.

Torn between fear and curiosity, Sheila followed the whispers as they led her through the labyrinthine corridors of the old house. The air grew heavier, and the oppressive darkness seemed to amplify the haunting voices that echoed through the halls.

The night unfolded in a surreal dance of shadows and secrets. Sheila, guided by the mysterious whispers, wandered deeper into the heart of the house. Each step felt like a descent into a realm where reality and the supernatural coexisted in a fragile balance.

In the heart of the house, Sheila found herself standing before a weathered door. The whispers, now a cacophony of urgent voices, beckoned her to open it. Hesitant but driven by an unexplainable force, she turned the rusted doorknob.

The room beyond was shrouded in an impenetrable darkness. The air felt charged with an otherworldly energy, and the whispers reached a fevered pitch. As Sheila stepped into the room, a chilling wind swept through, extinguishing the feeble candlelight that flickered in the corners.

In the profound darkness, shapes and shadows materialized, dancing on the periphery of Sheila's vision. The whispers coalesced into a haunting chorus, a symphony of forgotten souls yearning to be heard.

Goosebumps erupted on Sheila's skin as she realized that she was not alone in the spectral gathering.

The room seemed to pulse with an unseen heartbeat, and Sheila felt a cold breath on the nape of her neck. The whispers, now mere inches away, spoke directly into her mind. Words, ancient and cryptic, intertwined with her thoughts, creating a disorienting fusion of reality and the supernatural.

Sheila, paralyzed by the ghostly communion, struggled to comprehend the weight of the revelations. The whispers spoke of long-buried secrets, of a history stained with sorrow and malevolence. The house, it seemed, held memories that transcended the boundaries of time.

In a crescendo of spectral intensity, the whispers began to echo the names of the departed, their voices rising and falling like a spectral tide. Sheila felt an overwhelming sadness wash over her as she became a vessel for the collective lament of the forgotten souls trapped within the walls.

As the spectral symphony reached its zenith, Sheila's surroundings blurred into a phantasmagoric dreamscape. Shadows danced in a macabre ballet, and ghostly apparitions materialized before her. The faces of the departed stared into her soul, their eyes reflecting an eternity of suffering.

In a sudden, jarring silence, the room plunged into darkness once more. Sheila stood alone, her breath ragged and heart pounding. The weight of the revelations pressed down on her shoulders, and the whispers, now a mere echo in the recesses of her mind, faded into the obscurity of the old house.

Sheila stumbled back into the dimly lit corridor, disoriented and shaken. The whispers, though momentarily silenced, lingered in the air like an unseen specter. The house, now charged with an unsettling energy, seemed to watch her with an intensity that transcended the physical realm.

Haunted by the night's spectral communion, Sheila retreated to the safety of her room. The whispers, though subdued, continued to echo in the corners of her mind. Sleep, an elusive sanctuary, offered no respite

as the haunting voices seeped into her dreams, intertwining reality and nightmare in a disconcerting tapestry.

Morning brought little solace as Sheila grappled with the aftermath of the spectral encounter. The once-charming house now bore the weight of its own history, and every creak and groan seemed to carry the echoes of the departed. The whispers, now a constant companion, followed her every move, leaving her sanity teetering on the edge of an abyss.

As Sheila navigated the mundane tasks of daily life, the spectral voices whispered secrets that tore at the fabric of her understanding. The house, it seemed, held a malevolent legacy that transcended the passage of time, and Sheila found herself entangled in a web of forgotten sorrows and ancient grievances.

The days blurred into a disorienting haze as Sheila, haunted by the whispers, grappled with a reality that seemed to unravel at the seams. The walls, once silent witnesses to the passage of time, now pulsed with an otherworldly energy that defied rational explanation.

In the suffocating embrace of the old house, Sheila faced a choice— succumb to the spectral whispers that threatened to unravel her sanity or confront the malevolent forces that lurked in the shadows. Little did she know that the true horror, like a dormant beast, awaited its awakening in the depths of the house's dark history. The whispers, a prelude to the malevolence that lay ahead, continued to echo through the corridors, weaving a sinister tale that intertwined with Sheila's very existence. The house, a malevolent entity in its own right, had claimed her as its unwilling conduit, a vessel through which the forgotten voices sought to rewrite the narrative of their tragic past. As night fell once again, Sheila stood at the precipice of a nightmare, the echoes of the whispers lingering like a ghostly requiem. The darkness, pregnant with unspoken horrors, awaited its chance to consume her soul. Little did Sheila know that the true terror, the culmination of the spectral whispers, loomed on the horizon, threatening to plunge her into a darkness from which there might be no escape. The whispers, a harbinger of an

ancient malevolence, echoed through the haunted corridors, signaling the beginning of a descent into the heart of terror.

Chapter 3: The Dark History

The day unfolded with a sense of oppressive anticipation as Sheila, haunted by the lingering whispers, delved into the dark history of the house. Dust-covered books, their pages brittle with age, beckoned to her from the shelves, revealing tales of sorrow and malevolence that clung to the very essence of the dwelling.

Sheila's fingers traced the words on the yellowed pages, each revelation a cold breath against her skin. The house, it seemed, bore witness to a tapestry of tragedies—a canvas painted with the blood of those long forgotten. Murmurs of untold horrors seemed to emanate from the pages, seeping into her consciousness like an insidious poison.

The sun dipped below the horizon, casting elongated shadows that danced along the walls. Sheila, now immersed in the chilling accounts of the past, couldn't escape the feeling that the very air she breathed carried the weight of the malevolent history woven into the fabric of the house.

As darkness claimed the landscape outside, Sheila's mind echoed with the stories of those who had once called the house their home. A family torn asunder by betrayal, a forbidden love that led to tragedy, and the anguished cries of lost souls echoed through the corridors, merging with the persistent whispers that lingered like a ghostly chorus.

Driven by a compulsion she couldn't fully comprehend, Sheila unearthed old photographs from a dusty box hidden in the attic. Faces frozen in time stared back at her, their eyes holding the secrets of a bygone era. She felt an inexplicable connection to these spectral visages, as if their silent pleas for remembrance echoed in the recesses of her mind.

The photographs revealed a family whose smiles hid a darker truth—a truth that the house guarded with a possessive malevolence. In one faded picture, a child's eyes seemed to bore into Sheila's soul, a silent plea etched in their depths. The whispers intensified, an unseen

hand guiding her through the labyrinth of familial tragedies that stained the house with a legacy of sorrow.

In her search for understanding, Sheila stumbled upon a hidden compartment in the attic. Within its confines lay a collection of letters, brittle with age and tinged with the desperation of the departed. The correspondence spoke of forbidden rituals and a pact sealed in blood—a pact that bound the souls of the house to an otherworldly realm.

The revelation sent shivers down Sheila's spine as the echoes of the past reverberated in the dimly lit room. The house, it seemed, was a vessel for dark forces that defied the boundaries between the living and the dead. Sheila, now an unwitting participant in the spectral drama, grappled with the weight of the malevolent history that clung to her like a suffocating shroud.

Night descended, and Sheila found herself standing before the door that led to the basement—the epicenter of the house's darkest secrets. The whispers, now a cacophony of spectral voices, urged her to descend into the abyss and confront the malevolence that lurked in the hidden recesses.

The creaking stairs groaned under her weight as Sheila descended into the subterranean realm. The air grew colder with each step, and the oppressive darkness seemed to swallow the feeble light of her flashlight. Shadows clung to the walls like spectral tendrils, and the whispers reached a fevered pitch, guiding her deeper into the heart of the supernatural abyss.

As Sheila entered the basement, a chill crawled up her spine. The room, bathed in an otherworldly gloom, revealed the remnants of forgotten rituals—a sacrificial altar, cryptic symbols etched into the walls, and a palpable malevolence that seemed to pulse with a life of its own.

Sheila's breath caught as she uncovered an old diary amidst the dust-covered artifacts. Its pages, stained with the ink of a tormented soul, detailed the ghastly rituals conducted in the name of an otherworldly entity. The diary spoke of a darkness that hungered for innocent souls, a darkness that had claimed the very foundations of the house.

With trembling hands, Sheila read aloud the incantations that had once reverberated within the cold stone walls. The air thickened with an unseen presence as the words echoed through the basement, awakening the dormant malevolence that lingered like a dormant beast.

A sudden gust of wind extinguished the feeble light, plunging Sheila into a darkness that seemed to consume her very essence. Whispers surrounded her, their voices intertwining with the oppressive silence. Shadows danced in the obscurity, and Sheila felt a spectral presence closing in around her.

As she fumbled to relight her flashlight, Sheila caught a glimpse of ghostly figures that materialized in the shadows. Eyes devoid of life stared at her, their hollow gazes filled with an insatiable hunger. The apparitions seemed to reach out from the shadows, their fingers brushing against her skin like the breath of a long-forgotten nightmare.

In the suffocating darkness, Sheila stumbled backward, her heart pounding in her chest. The whispers, now an anguished wail, reverberated through the basement, creating a dissonant symphony of horror. The malevolent forces that had slumbered within the house were now awake, hungry for the essence of the living.

In a desperate attempt to escape the spectral onslaught, Sheila retraced her steps through the labyrinthine corridors of the basement. The walls seemed to close in around her, and the air pulsed with an otherworldly energy that clung to her like a suffocating fog.

As she reached the basement stairs, a cold hand brushed against the nape of her neck. Sheila recoiled, her senses overwhelmed by the touch of unseen fingers. The whispers, now a maddening cacophony, echoed in her ears like a chorus of the damned.

With every step she climbed, the malevolence pursued her like a relentless shadow. The basement seemed to resist her escape, its unseen tendrils reaching out to claim her soul. Sheila emerged into the dimly lit corridor, gasping for breath as the weight of the supernatural encounter pressed down on her chest.

The house, now a malevolent entity awakened from its slumber, seemed to watch Sheila with an insatiable hunger. The whispers, though momentarily subdued, lingered in the air like a haunting refrain. The basement, a portal to an otherworldly realm, had unleashed a darkness that threatened to consume everything in its path.

Sheila, shaken to her core, stumbled into her room and barricaded the door as if shielding herself from the unseen forces that lurked outside. The whispers, now a persistent hum in the background, continued to echo through the walls, their spectral voices weaving a tapestry of horror that seemed to stretch across time and space.

Sleep, elusive and treacherous, offered no refuge as Sheila found herself trapped in a nightmare that transcended the boundaries of the waking world. Shadows danced on the edges of her consciousness, and ghostly apparitions lurked in the recesses of her dreams.

Morning brought little solace as Sheila awoke to a house shrouded in an oppressive silence. The whispers, though momentarily silenced, lingered like a malevolent residue. The basement, now a forbidden chasm that bridged the realms of the living and the dead, beckoned to her with an unseen gravity.

The day unfolded with a palpable tension as Sheila, now a reluctant participant in a supernatural drama, grappled with the malevolence that had been unleashed. The dark history of the house, etched into its very foundations, loomed like a specter over every room, every corridor.

The house, now a living entity that hungered for the essence of the living, seemed to watch Sheila with an insatiable appetite. The whispers, a relentless chorus that echoed through the haunted halls, hinted at a darkness that transcended the limits of her understanding.

As night descended once again, Sheila stood at the crossroads of horror, the echoes of the dark history pulsating through the very walls. The malevolent forces, awakened from their slumber, awaited their next move in a macabre dance that threatened to consume Sheila's very soul. The house, a conduit for ancient malevolence, seemed to pulse with a malevolent energy that defied all attempts at rational explanation. Little

did Sheila know that the true terror, a malevolent force that transcended the boundaries of the supernatural, awaited its moment to strike in the chilling depths of the haunted dwelling.

Chapter 4: The Warning

The oppressive weight of the malevolent history lingered in the air as Sheila, haunted by the nightmarish events in the basement, found herself thrust deeper into the clutches of the old house. The whispers, though momentarily subdued, continued to echo through the corridors like an unseen presence that refused to be silenced.

As the sun dipped below the horizon, casting long shadows that stretched like spectral fingers, Sheila roamed the dimly lit rooms in a daze. The walls, adorned with faded wallpaper, seemed to close in around her like a suffocating embrace. Every creak and groan of the aging structure resonated with the echoes of the dark history that clung to the very fabric of the dwelling.

In a feeble attempt to regain a semblance of control, Sheila decided to venture outside. The night air, cool and crisp, offered a brief respite from the oppressive atmosphere within the house. As she stepped onto the porch, the world beyond seemed to hold its breath, as if aware of the supernatural forces that pulsed within the walls.

The neighboring houses stood in stoic silence, their windows gazing like empty eyes into the night. A distant streetlamp flickered intermittently, casting eerie shadows that danced on the pavement. Sheila, shivering in the cold, felt an inexplicable sense of being watched—an unseen gaze that followed her every move.

A sudden gust of wind carried with it a spectral whisper that sent a chill down Sheila's spine. The voice, laden with urgency, seemed to carry a warning—an ethereal plea that resonated with the very core of her being. Unsettled, she turned toward the source of the whisper, but the darkness offered no clues, concealing its secrets within its velvety embrace.

Returning to the house, Sheila couldn't escape the feeling that the very air held a sense of foreboding. The whispers, now a constant

companion, seemed to guide her toward the heart of the malevolence that lurked within. As she ascended the creaking stairs, the old house seemed to creak and groan in protest, as if resisting her attempts to uncover its darkest secrets.

The attic, a repository of forgotten artifacts, drew Sheila with an irresistible gravity. The air grew thick with an otherworldly energy as she approached the door leading to the mysterious space. As she turned the doorknob, a fleeting vision of ghostly figures danced on the periphery of her vision, vanishing as quickly as they appeared.

The attic, bathed in the feeble glow of a single bulb, revealed a myriad of forgotten relics—a dusty collection of forgotten memories. Sheila's flashlight illuminated old trunks, moth-eaten clothing, and a peculiar assortment of items that seemed frozen in time. Each artifact, a silent witness to the house's twisted history, exuded an otherworldly aura that seemed to tug at the edges of Sheila's sanity.

Among the forgotten relics, Sheila discovered an old photograph album. Its pages, yellowed with age, unveiled the lives of those who had once called the house their home. Family gatherings frozen in time, celebrations tainted by an unseen darkness, and the eyes of children who seemed to peer through the veil of the past—all spoke of a history steeped in sorrow.

As Sheila flipped through the photographs, a sudden chill settled in the room. Shadows danced along the walls, and the whispers intensified, their urgency now laced with an unspoken dread. The album, like a portal to the past, beckoned her to uncover the secrets that lingered within its pages.

The images told a tale of a family whose smiles concealed a tragic fate. A mother, her eyes reflecting a haunting sadness, held her children close in a sepia-toned embrace. The father, a stern figure with a haunted gaze, seemed to carry the weight of a malevolence that transcended the boundaries of the photograph.

In one particularly unsettling image, Sheila noticed a figure standing in the background—a silhouette that seemed to merge with the

shadows, its eyes staring into the depths of her soul. The whispers, now a dissonant chorus, echoed the name of the figure—an entity known only as "The Watcher."

A sudden realization gripped Sheila—the warnings she had received, the spectral figures in the attic, and the ever-present whispers—all converged on the ominous presence of The Watcher. As she traced the figure's silhouette with her trembling finger, the air thickened with an oppressive energy that seemed to bear the weight of the malevolent entity.

Driven by a desperate need to understand, Sheila decided to consult the elderly neighbor who had issued the initial warning. With the photograph album in hand, she ventured outside once again, the night air carrying with it a sense of impending doom.

The neighbor's house, a weathered structure bathed in the glow of a flickering porch light, seemed to emanate a warmth that stood in stark contrast to the cold atmosphere within Sheila's own dwelling. The old woman, with eyes clouded by the passage of time, opened the door with a knowing look that hinted at a lifetime of secrets.

As Sheila explained the events that had transpired—the whispers, the spectral figures, and the ominous presence of The Watcher—the elderly neighbor listened in solemn silence. When Sheila showed her the photograph album, the neighbor's eyes widened in recognition, and a shiver ran down her spine.

"You've unearthed a dark legacy," the old woman murmured, her voice a hushed whisper that seemed to carry the weight of untold secrets. She invited Sheila inside, where the walls seemed to resonate with a history that had long been buried.

Seated in a dimly lit room adorned with faded tapestries, the neighbor began to weave a tale that sent shivers down Sheila's spine. The house, it seemed, had once been a haven for a family whose lives had become entwined with an otherworldly force—a force that had claimed them in a twisted dance of tragedy.

The elderly neighbor spoke of The Watcher, an entity born from forbidden rituals conducted in the very heart of the house. Its malevolence, fueled by the suffering of the past, lingered like a vengeful specter, a guardian of dark secrets that defied the boundaries between the living and the dead.

The family in the photographs, the whispers, and the spectral figures—all were linked to The Watcher's insatiable hunger for the souls of the living. The old woman's words painted a harrowing picture of a malevolent force that sought to reclaim what had been lost—an entity that fed on the essence of the unsuspecting inhabitants.

As the elderly neighbor spoke, Sheila felt the weight of The Watcher's gaze upon her. The air in the room grew dense with an unseen presence, and the whispers, now a mournful lament, echoed through the walls like a requiem for the damned.

"You must leave this place," the old woman implored, her eyes reflecting a depth of sorrow that seemed to transcend the confines of the room. "The Watcher is awakened, and its hunger knows no bounds. Your very soul is in peril."

Fear gripped Sheila's heart as the magnitude of the malevolence became apparent. The warnings, the whispers, and the dark history of the house all converged on a chilling reality—a reality in which Sheila stood on the precipice of a supernatural abyss.

Determined to confront The Watcher and unravel the malevolent forces that held the house in their clutches, Sheila returned to her home with a sense of grim resolve. The night, now heavy with the weight of unseen eyes, seemed to pulse with an otherworldly energy that hinted at the imminent confrontation.

The house, a silent witness to the unfolding horror, awaited its fate in the embrace of darkness. Sheila, armed with the knowledge of the malevolent history and the warnings of The Watcher's insatiable hunger, steeled herself for a battle that would transcend the boundaries of the living and the dead. The whispers, now a chorus of spectral voices, guided her toward the heart of the supernatural storm that awaited in

the haunted corridors of the old dwelling. Little did she know that the true terror, a confrontation with The Watcher that would redefine the very fabric of reality, loomed on the horizon, threatening to plunge her into a darkness from which there might be no escape. The night, pregnant with the weight of unspoken horrors, unfolded with a spectral symphony that echoed the malevolent legacy of The Watcher—a force that hungered for the essence of the living, a force that would stop at nothing to reclaim what had been lost in the shadows of the past.

Chapter 5: The Apparition

As Sheila braced herself for the impending confrontation with The Watcher, the house seemed to hold its breath in a malevolent silence. The air, thick with the weight of unseen eyes, pressed against her skin like a suffocating shroud. Every step she took echoed in the dimly lit corridors, the whispers guiding her toward the heart of the supernatural storm.

The attic, a spectral realm illuminated by a feeble bulb, awaited her return. The artifacts, relics of a twisted history, seemed to resonate with an otherworldly energy as Sheila ascended the creaking stairs. The photograph album, now a key to the malevolent secrets that lurked within, clutched in her trembling hands, felt like a talisman against the encroaching darkness.

The whispers, now a relentless chorus that echoed through the haunted halls, intensified as Sheila reached the attic. The air pulsed with an unseen presence, and the shadows danced on the walls in a macabre ballet. The photograph album, when opened, revealed spectral figures that seemed to move within the confines of the images—a silent procession of lost souls tethered to The Watcher's insatiable hunger.

With a heavy heart, Sheila placed the photograph album on a dusty table in the center of the attic. The air seemed to vibrate with an unseen energy, and the whispers reached a fevered pitch. A sudden gust of wind extinguished the feeble bulb, plunging the attic into darkness.

In the obscurity, Sheila felt a spectral presence closing in around her. The whispers, now an anguished wail, surrounded her like a ghostly

chorus. The air seemed charged with an otherworldly force as The Watcher's malevolence manifested in the shadows.

A cold breath brushed against Sheila's neck, and she sensed the gaze of unseen eyes upon her. The spectral figures from the photographs materialized in the darkness, their eyes reflecting a hunger that transcended the boundaries of the living and the dead.

In the suffocating darkness, Sheila felt a touch—a caress of unseen fingers that traced the contours of her face. The whispers, now a maddening cacophony, echoed through the attic, creating a dissonant symphony of horror. The Watcher, a malevolent force that defied explanation, sought to claim her soul in a spectral dance of damnation.

Desperation gripped Sheila as she fumbled for her flashlight, the feeble beam cutting through the obscurity like a beacon of fragile hope. The spectral figures, their faces twisted in silent anguish, retreated into the shadows as the light pierced the darkness.

With trembling hands, Sheila retrieved the photograph album. The images, though now devoid of spectral movement, seemed to carry the weight of the malevolent history that clung to the house. The Watcher, its presence still palpable in the obscurity, awaited its chance to strike once again.

The whispers, now a haunting melody, guided Sheila back through the labyrinthine corridors. The old house, a spectral battleground, seemed to pulse with an otherworldly energy that defied rational explanation. As she descended the creaking stairs, the weight of The Watcher's malevolence bore down on her shoulders like an unseen burden.

In the dimly lit living room, Sheila's flashlight revealed a ghostly figure standing in the hall—a silhouette that seemed to merge with the shadows. The Watcher, its form obscured by the darkness, stared at her with eyes that held the emptiness of eternity.

Fear clawed at Sheila's chest as she confronted the spectral entity that lurked within the old house. The whispers, now a mournful lament, echoed through the corridors, intertwining with the malevolent

presence that encircled her. The time for understanding was over; the time for confrontation had arrived.

Sheila, driven by a grim resolve, approached The Watcher. The air seemed to ripple with an unseen force, and the whispers reached a crescendo as she stood face to face with the malevolent entity. The Watcher, a manifestation of forgotten sorrows and ancient grievances, exuded an otherworldly aura that seemed to defy the very laws of nature.

In the spectral confrontation, Sheila felt a cold hand brush against her cheek—a touch that carried the weight of a thousand lost souls. The whispers, now an ethereal chorus, spoke words that resonated with the depths of her consciousness. The Watcher sought communion, a merging of the living and the dead in a twisted dance of supernatural entanglement.

With a surge of determination, Sheila raised the photograph album. The images, now illuminated by the feeble glow of her flashlight, held a spectral resonance that seemed to repel The Watcher. The entity recoiled, its form dissipating like mist in the face of an unseen force.

In the haunting confrontation, Sheila felt a surge of power—the power of the forgotten souls that lingered within the photographs. The whispers, now a triumphant hymn, reverberated through the haunted halls as The Watcher retreated into the shadows. The malevolent force, thwarted by the spectral energy of the past, seemed to dissipate like a fading nightmare.

The old house, once a battleground between the living and the dead, fell silent. The whispers, now a fading echo, lingered in the air like a melancholic melody. Sheila, exhausted and shaken, stood amidst the remnants of the spectral encounter, the photograph album clutched in her trembling hands.

As the oppressive atmosphere lifted, Sheila felt a profound change in the house—a sense of peace that transcended the malevolent legacy of The Watcher. The whispers, though subdued, carried a lingering gratitude, as if the forgotten souls had found solace in the spectral confrontation.

With a heavy heart, Sheila descended into the basement—the very heart of the house's dark history. The air, once thick with malevolence, now held a somber tranquility. The relics of forgotten rituals seemed frozen in time, their significance transformed by the spectral encounter.

In the dim light, Sheila uncovered the old diary—the key to the understanding of the house's twisted past. The pages, though stained with the ink of tormented souls, now bore a sense of closure. The Watcher, defeated by the power of the forgotten, had relinquished its hold on the old dwelling.

As Sheila emerged from the basement, the morning sun began to cast its gentle rays on the once-foreboding structure. The old house, no longer a haven for malevolent forces, seemed to stand in quiet reverence to the spectral encounter that had unfolded within its walls.

The whispers, now a distant echo, guided Sheila to the attic—the epicenter of the supernatural storm. The photograph album, placed back in its dusty corner, exuded a spectral resonance that seemed to linger in the air. The spectral figures within the images, their faces now frozen in peace, bore silent witness to the resolution of a malevolent legacy.

Sheila, now forever changed by the harrowing ordeal, stepped outside into the cool morning air. The neighborhood, once draped in a veil of darkness, now basked in the warmth of the rising sun. The whispers, though a mere memory, carried a final message—a farewell from the forgotten souls who had found redemption in the face of supernatural turmoil.

As Sheila walked away from the old house, the sense of normalcy slowly returned. The neighborhood, once tainted by the malevolent force that had claimed the dwelling, now stood as a testament to the triumph of the living over the specters of the past.

Little did Sheila know that the true horror, a final revelation that would redefine the very fabric of her existence, awaited in the shadows of her newfound peace. The old house, though freed from the clutches of The Watcher, held a secret that would unveil itself in a chilling twist

of fate—one that would test the limits of Sheila's resilience and plunge her into a darkness from which there might be no escape.

The whispers, now a distant memory, left the door open for the looming terror that awaited in the aftermath of the supernatural storm. The haunting melody of the forgotten lingered in the air as Sheila ventured into the uncertain future—a future where the boundaries between the living and the dead remained blurred, and the horrors of the past cast a long, lingering shadow over the new normal that awaited her.

Chapter 6: The Visitor

In the wake of the harrowing confrontation with The Watcher, Sheila grappled with the aftermath of the supernatural storm that had engulfed the old house. The whispers, now a distant echo, left an eerie silence in their wake—a silence that seemed to stretch across the haunted halls like a spectral tapestry.

As Sheila navigated the dimly lit rooms, the old house felt different. The air, once thick with malevolence, now carried a palpable tranquility. The remnants of forgotten rituals in the basement seemed frozen in time, their significance transformed by the spectral encounter. The photograph album, placed back in its dusty corner in the attic, exuded a spectral resonance that lingered like a fading memory.

Despite the apparent peace that settled over the dwelling, Sheila couldn't shake the feeling that the old house held secrets yet to be unveiled. The neighborhood, seemingly untouched by the supernatural turmoil, continued its daily rhythm. Sheila's neighbors, unaware of the malevolent force that had gripped their midst, carried on with their lives in blissful ignorance.

The morning sun cast a warm glow on the neighborhood, and Sheila decided to take a stroll outside. The fresh air, tinged with the scent of dew-kissed grass, offered a reprieve from the suffocating atmosphere within the old house. As she walked down the quiet streets, the whispers, though faint, seemed to guide her steps toward a sense of normalcy.

In the midst of the peaceful neighborhood, Sheila encountered a figure from her past—Rob, her childhood friend who had experienced the unsettling events in the house. Rob, unaware of the supernatural horrors that had transpired, greeted Sheila with a warm smile.

As they exchanged pleasantries, Sheila hesitated to divulge the haunting experiences she had faced. The whispers, now a gentle hum in the background, seemed to caution her against revealing the spectral truth that lingered within the old house. Instead, she chose to enjoy the fleeting moments of normalcy with Rob, hoping to leave the malevolent past behind.

The day unfolded with a semblance of serenity as Sheila and Rob reminisced about their shared childhood memories. Laughter echoed through the air, temporarily drowning out the lingering echoes of the supernatural encounter. The old house, its haunted corridors temporarily silenced, stood as a mere backdrop to the facade of normalcy that enveloped the neighborhood.

As night descended, Sheila invited Rob to stay the night—a decision that would unwittingly drag him into the lingering shadows of the malevolent past. The whispers, though muted, seemed to intensify as darkness cloaked the old house in an otherworldly stillness.

In the dimly lit living room, Sheila and Rob shared stories from their past, seeking refuge in the familiarity of friendship. The air, though seemingly calm, held a sense of foreboding as the whispers, now a spectral melody, intertwined with the gentle hum of the night.

As they settled in for the night, Sheila couldn't escape the feeling that The Watcher's malevolence lingered in the shadows. The spectral figures from the photographs, now etched in her memory, seemed to cast ghostly shadows on the walls. The old house, once a haven for dark forces, bore silent witness to the unsuspecting visitors who dared to cross its threshold.

The night progressed in a semblance of tranquility, the whispers fading into the background. Yet, as the clock ticked towards midnight, an unspoken tension enveloped the dwelling. Sheila, restless and haunted

by the memories of the supernatural storm, found herself drawn to the attic—the epicenter of the spectral encounter.

In the attic, the photograph album lay in its dusty corner, seemingly untouched by the passage of time. The whispers, though muted, urged Sheila to revisit the malevolent history that clung to the old house. With a heavy heart, she opened the album, its pages revealing the spectral figures that had once danced within its confines.

As Sheila traced the images with her trembling finger, a sudden gust of wind extinguished the feeble bulb, plunging the attic into darkness. The whispers, now a mournful lament, echoed through the spectral realm as the photographs seemed to come to life once again.

In the obscurity, Sheila felt a spectral presence closing in around her. The whispers, now a dissonant chorus, spoke words that seemed to reverberate with the anguished cries of the forgotten. The Watcher, its malevolence not fully vanquished, sought communion with the living in a macabre dance of supernatural entanglement.

Rob, stirred from his sleep by the eerie atmosphere, joined Sheila in the attic. The air seemed to vibrate with an unseen force as the whispers guided them toward the heart of the spectral storm. The photograph album, now a conduit to the malevolent past, exuded an otherworldly energy that drew them deeper into the supernatural abyss.

As they stood in the darkness, the spectral figures from the photographs materialized around them. Eyes devoid of life stared at Sheila and Rob, their hollow gazes filled with an insatiable hunger. The whispers, now a haunting melody, spoke of unresolved sorrows that lingered within the old house.

In the spectral confrontation, Sheila and Rob felt the weight of unseen eyes upon them. The Watcher, though seemingly thwarted, manifested in the shadows with a renewed malevolence. The whispers, now a spectral symphony, hinted at a darkness that defied the boundaries of the living and the dead.

Desperation gripped Sheila as she clutched the photograph album. The images, now illuminated by the feeble glow of Rob's flashlight,

held a spectral resonance that seemed to repel The Watcher. The entity recoiled, its form dissipating like mist in the face of an unseen force.

In the haunting confrontation, Sheila and Rob felt a surge of power—the power of the forgotten souls that lingered within the photographs. The whispers, now a triumphant hymn, reverberated through the haunted attic as The Watcher retreated into the shadows. The malevolent force, though temporarily thwarted, lingered like a specter in the lingering darkness.

The attic, once a battleground between the living and the dead, fell silent. The whispers, now a fading echo, left an eerie stillness in their wake. Sheila and Rob, exhausted and shaken, stood amidst the remnants of the spectral encounter, the photograph album a testament to the unresolved sorrows that clung to the old house.

As they descended from the attic, the old house seemed to sigh with a spectral resignation. The whispers, though subdued, lingered in the air like a melancholic melody. The night, pregnant with the weight of unspoken horrors, unfolded with a sense of uncertainty—a future where the boundaries between the living and the dead remained blurred.

Sheila and Rob, now forever entwined in the malevolent legacy of the old house, sought refuge in the dimly lit living room. The whispers, though muted, hinted at a lingering terror that awaited in the shadows. Little did they know that the true horror, a revelation that would redefine the very fabric of their existence, loomed on the horizon—a revelation that would test the limits of their resilience and plunge them into a darkness from which there might be no escape.

The whispers, now a distant murmur, left the door ajar for the looming terror that awaited in the aftermath of the spectral storm. The old house, its haunted corridors pulsating with unresolved sorrows, stood as a gateway to a supernatural abyss. Sheila and Rob, bound by the malevolent forces that lingered within, faced an uncertain future where the horrors of the past cast a long, lingering shadow over their fragile grasp on reality.

Chapter 7: The Presence

The night, once a harbinger of supernatural turmoil, descended upon the old house with an unsettling stillness. Sheila and Rob, shaken by the spectral encounter in the attic, sought solace in the dimly lit living room. The air, though seemingly calm, carried an unspoken tension—a tension that seemed to thicken with every passing moment.

As they sat in the silence, the whispers, now a muted hum, seemed to guide Sheila's attention toward the shadows that lurked in the corners of the room. The old house, a silent witness to the malevolent forces that had unfolded within its walls, exuded an otherworldly energy that defied the confines of the living and the dead.

A subtle chill crept through the air as the temperature in the room dropped. The whispers, though faint, took on a dissonant tone—a spectral melody that hinted at the lingering presence of The Watcher. Sheila and Rob, their senses heightened by the supernatural ordeal, felt an unseen gaze upon them.

In the dim light, objects in the room seemed to shift mysteriously. A picture frame trembled on the wall, and the flickering flame of a candle cast dancing shadows that defied the laws of physics. The old house, now a conduit for the residual malevolence, pulsed with an unseen force that sought communion with the living.

Unease settled over Sheila and Rob as they exchanged wary glances. The whispers, now a spectral chorus, seemed to speak of a malevolent force that had not been fully vanquished—a force that lingered in the shadows, biding its time for a resurgence. The old house, once a haven for dark rituals, held its secrets close, and the unsuspecting inhabitants stood at the mercy of the supernatural storm that raged within its walls.

In an attempt to dispel the ominous atmosphere, Sheila suggested a distraction—turning on the television to drown out the spectral whispers. As they sat on the worn-out couch, the flickering images on the screen seemed to offer a brief respite from the encroaching darkness. However, the shadows that danced in the periphery of their vision hinted at a malevolence that refused to be ignored.

The night unfolded with a deceptive calmness, the television casting a pale glow that struggled against the encroaching darkness. Sheila and Rob, though attempting to maintain a façade of normalcy, couldn't shake the feeling that The Watcher's presence lingered like a spectral specter in the room.

As the clock struck midnight, a sudden drop in temperature sent shivers down their spines. The whispers, now a mournful wail, echoed through the haunted halls, creating an ethereal symphony of dread. Sheila and Rob, bound by the malevolent legacy of the old house, felt an unseen force closing in around them.

In the dim light, a shadowy figure materialized in the hall—a silhouette that seemed to defy the laws of the physical world. The Watcher, its malevolence not fully quelled, stood as a spectral guardian in the shadows. The whispers, now a dissonant chorus, spoke of an unresolved darkness that sought to reclaim the living.

Fear gripped Sheila and Rob as The Watcher's presence manifested in the room. The air seemed charged with an otherworldly energy as the entity, now a tangible force, cast a haunting gaze upon the unsuspecting visitors. The whispers, though muted, carried a warning—an anguished plea to leave the old house before it succumbed to the malevolent forces that clung to its very foundations.

In a desperate attempt to defy the encroaching darkness, Sheila and Rob decided to leave the living room and venture into the seemingly unaffected parts of the house. The whispers, now a relentless drone, seemed to guide them toward the heart of the supernatural storm.

As they ascended the creaking stairs, the oppressive atmosphere intensified. The walls, adorned with faded wallpaper, seemed to close in around them like a suffocating embrace. The Watcher's presence, a spectral entity that defied rational explanation, pulsed with an unseen force that sought to ensnare their very souls.

In the upstairs hallway, a door creaked open on its own—a manifestation of the lingering malevolence that gripped the old house. The whispers, now a haunting lament, guided Sheila and Rob toward the

threshold of the mysteriously opened door. The room beyond, bathed in an unnatural darkness, beckoned them to confront the unresolved sorrows that lingered within.

As they entered the room, the air thickened with an oppressive energy. The temperature dropped, and the whispers reached a fevered pitch. The Watcher's presence, now an undeniable force, seemed to coalesce in the shadows—a spectral guardian that stood between the living and the abyss.

In the dim light, Sheila and Rob discovered an old mirror—a relic that seemed to hold the key to the malevolent forces that plagued the old house. The whispers, now a cacophony of spectral voices, spoke of a dark energy woven into the very fabric of the reflection.

As they stared into the mirror, their reflections seemed distorted—a ghastly image that hinted at the malevolent entity that lurked within the haunted dwelling. The Watcher, its form now a nightmarish apparition in the reflective surface, bore silent witness to the unfolding confrontation.

A sudden realization gripped Sheila—the mirror, a conduit for The Watcher's malevolence, held the key to the unresolved darkness that clung to the old house. The whispers, though chaotic, seemed to guide her toward a revelation that would redefine the boundaries between the living and the dead.

Driven by a grim resolve, Sheila and Rob decided to confront The Watcher through the mirror—a ritual that promised to unveil the malevolent forces that lurked within. The room, now bathed in an otherworldly glow, felt like a spectral battleground where the living and the dead converged in a macabre dance of supernatural entanglement.

As they stood before the mirror, the whispers reached a crescendo. The Watcher's apparition, now a nightmarish entity that defied description, materialized in the reflective surface. The air seemed to vibrate with an unseen force as Sheila and Rob prepared to confront the malevolent force that had haunted them.

The room, now a spectral realm suspended between the living and the dead, bore witness to the spectral encounter. The Watcher, its malevolence intensified by the confrontation, sought communion with the living in a ghastly manifestation that defied the laws of nature.

In the mirror's reflection, Sheila and Rob felt the weight of unseen eyes upon them. The Watcher's gaze, a haunting stare that held the emptiness of eternity, sought to penetrate the very depths of their souls. The whispers, now a mournful hymn, intertwined with the oppressive energy as the supernatural battle unfolded.

With a surge of spectral power, Sheila and Rob confronted The Watcher through the mirror. The whispers, though chaotic, seemed to align with the living, creating a dissonant symphony that echoed through the spectral realm. The Watcher, now faced with the combined resilience of the living, recoiled in the face of an unseen force.

In the haunting confrontation, the mirror shattered—an explosion of glass that seemed to reverberate through the haunted halls. The Watcher's malevolence, now fractured and dispersed, retreated into the shadows like a fading nightmare. The room, once a battleground between the living and the abyss, fell silent.

Sheila and Rob, exhausted and shaken, stood amidst the shards of the shattered mirror. The whispers, now a distant echo, carried a sense of fleeting victory. The old house, though still haunted by the malevolent forces that clung to its foundations, seemed to sigh with a spectral resignation.

The night, now heavy with the weight of supernatural turmoil, unfolded with an unsettling stillness. Sheila and Rob, their resolve tested by the spectral encounter, descended from the upstairs realm and returned to the living room. The air, though laden with the remnants of the supernatural battle, felt lighter as if a temporary reprieve had been granted.

Little did they know that the true horror, a revelation that would redefine the very fabric of their existence, awaited in the shadows of their newfound victory. The old house, though temporarily quelled, held

secrets that would unveil themselves in a chilling twist of fate—one that would test the limits of Sheila and Rob's resilience and plunge them into a darkness from which there might be no escape.

The whispers, now a fading memory, left the door ajar for the looming terror that awaited in the aftermath of the spectral storm. The old house, its haunted corridors pulsating with unresolved sorrows, stood as a gateway to a supernatural abyss. Sheila and Rob, bound by the malevolent forces that lingered within, faced an uncertain future where the horrors of the past cast a long, lingering shadow over their fragile grasp on reality.

Chapter 8: The Message

The night, now heavy with the echoes of the spectral confrontation, unfolded with an eerie stillness in the old house. Sheila and Rob, their nerves still on edge from the encounter in the haunted room, sought refuge in the dimly lit living room. The air, though seemingly calm, carried the residual tension of the supernatural battle that had unfolded within the haunted dwelling.

As they settled on the worn-out couch, the whispers, though subdued, lingered in the air like a spectral melody. The old house, once a haven for dark rituals and spectral forces, seemed to hold its breath in the aftermath of the shattered mirror. Sheila and Rob, their senses heightened by the otherworldly encounter, exchanged wary glances as they awaited the next manifestation of The Watcher's malevolence.

The television, now a mere flickering glow in the dim room, offered a semblance of normalcy. Sheila, attempting to distract herself from the lingering horrors, suggested turning on the lights to dispel the encroaching darkness. As she reached for the switch, a sudden power outage plunged the old house into complete darkness.

In the pitch-black silence, the whispers intensified. The air seemed charged with an otherworldly energy, and a sense of dread settled over Sheila and Rob like a suffocating shroud. The old house, now devoid of any artificial illumination, became a spectral realm where the living and the dead coexisted in an uneasy truce.

Amidst the darkness, an ominous presence loomed—a manifestation of The Watcher's lingering malevolence. The whispers, now a dissonant chorus, guided Sheila and Rob toward the heart of the supernatural storm. The basement, a place fraught with the echoes of forgotten rituals, beckoned them to confront the unresolved darkness that clung to the old house.

With flashlights in hand, Sheila and Rob descended into the dimly lit basement. The air, thick with the weight of unseen eyes, seemed to pulse with a spectral energy that transcended the boundaries of the living and the dead. The whispers, now a haunting murmur, guided them toward a message—a cryptic revelation that awaited in the subterranean depths.

In the basement, amidst the relics of forgotten rituals, Sheila discovered an old Ouija board—an artifact that seemed to carry the spectral residue of past seances. The whispers, now a relentless drone, urged them to communicate with the other side in a desperate attempt to unravel the malevolent mysteries that clung to the old house.

With hesitant resolve, Sheila and Rob placed their trembling hands on the planchette. The Ouija board, now a conduit for the spectral forces, seemed to come alive with an otherworldly energy. The whispers, though chaotic, aligned with the planchette's movements, guiding them through a spectral conversation with the entities that lingered in the shadows.

As they sought answers from the other side, the planchette spelled out cryptic words on the Ouija board. The whispers, now a spectral symphony, intensified as the message unfolded. "He watches," the planchette spelled out, the words etched in an otherworldly script that seemed to defy rational explanation.

A chill ran down Sheila's spine as the whispers spoke of The Watcher's insatiable hunger—an entity that observed the living with an unrelenting gaze. The message, though cryptic, hinted at a darkness that transcended the boundaries of the living and the dead. The old house,

a silent witness to the supernatural turmoil, bore witness to a revelation that would redefine the very fabric of reality.

In the dim light of the basement, Sheila and Rob felt an unseen force closing in around them. The whispers, now a haunting melody, intertwined with the spectral energy that permeated the air. The Ouija board, a conduit for the malevolent forces, seemed to carry a message from beyond—a message that foretold a greater darkness that awaited in the shadows.

With a sense of trepidation, Sheila and Rob decided to delve deeper into the basement—a place where the old house's dark history unfolded in the form of forgotten rituals and malevolent entities. The whispers, though chaotic, seemed to guide them toward an altar—a focal point of the supernatural energies that pulsed through the subterranean depths.

As they reached the heart of the basement, a cold wind swept through the air—a spectral breeze that carried with it the echoes of forgotten incantations. The whispers, now a mournful lament, spoke of a ritual that could potentially unveil the true nature of The Watcher's malevolence.

On the altar, Sheila found an ancient book—an occult tome that detailed the dark history woven into the very foundations of the old house. The whispers, though fragmented, urged her to decipher the cryptic symbols and incantations that adorned the pages. The malevolent legacy, now laid bare in the pages of the ancient book, hinted at a supernatural force that defied comprehension.

With a heavy heart, Sheila began to read aloud the incantations—a desperate attempt to commune with the entities that lingered in the shadows. The whispers, now a spectral chorus, seemed to align with the words of the ritual, creating a dissonant symphony that reverberated through the basement.

As the incantations reached a fevered pitch, the air in the basement seemed to warp and twist. Shadows danced on the walls, and the whispers, now a cacophony of spectral voices, spoke of a portal—a gateway between the living and the abyss. The old house, its spectral foundations

shaken by the unfolding ritual, became a conduit for the malevolent forces that sought communion with the living.

In the dim light, the basement transformed into a spectral realm—a place suspended between the living and the dead. The whispers, now an anguished wail, guided Sheila and Rob toward the heart of the supernatural storm. The ritual, though wrought with danger, promised to unveil the true nature of The Watcher's malevolence.

As they stood at the precipice of the ritual's culmination, a sudden gust of wind extinguished their flashlights. Darkness enveloped them, and the whispers, now a relentless drone, seemed to merge with the shadows that danced in the spectral realm. The Ouija board, the ancient book, and the altar became mere silhouettes in the obscurity—a spectral tableau that hinted at the imminent confrontation with the unknown.

In the darkness, Sheila and Rob felt a surge of supernatural energy—the very fabric of reality seemed to warp and bend. The whispers, now a spectral symphony, reached a crescendo as the ritual reached its zenith. The portal, a shimmering gateway between the living and the abyss, beckoned them to confront the malevolent forces that awaited on the other side.

With a hesitant step, Sheila and Rob crossed the threshold of the portal. The whispers, now a haunting melody, surrounded them like a ghostly chorus. The old house, its foundations shaken by the unfolding ritual, bore silent witness to the spectral encounter that transcended the boundaries of the living and the dead.

As they entered the other side, the supernatural realm unfolded with an eerie beauty. Ethereal

Chapter 9: The History Revealed

In the supernatural realm beyond the portal, Sheila and Rob found themselves surrounded by a surreal landscape. Ghostly echoes of forgotten rituals and spectral entities painted the ethereal canvas. The whispers, now a haunting melody, guided them deeper into the spectral abyss—a place where the dark history of the old house unraveled in a dissonant symphony of the supernatural.

As they ventured through the ghostly landscape, Sheila and Rob discovered fragments of the past—a spectral montage that revealed the horrors once held within the old house's walls. The whispers, though fragmented, spoke of gruesome rituals and malevolent entities that had left an indelible mark on the haunted dwelling.

Images of hooded figures engaged in forbidden ceremonies danced before their eyes. The air, thick with the scent of incense and spectral energy, carried the echoes of tormented souls who had fallen victim to the malevolent forces that once reigned in the old house. The whispers, now a mournful lament, spoke of an occult legacy woven into the very fabric of the supernatural realm.

In their spectral journey, Sheila and Rob stumbled upon an ancient diary—an artifact that seemed to hold the key to the malevolent history that plagued the old house. The diary, its pages yellowed with age, detailed the dark rituals that had once unfolded in the basement. The whispers, now a spectral chorus, urged them to read the words that revealed the origin of The Watcher's malevolence.

As Sheila deciphered the cryptic entries, the images of hooded figures engaging in occult ceremonies became vivid in her mind. The diary spoke of a cult that had once thrived within the old house, conducting rituals that sought communion with otherworldly entities. The whispers, though haunting, hinted at a darkness that transcended the boundaries of the living and the dead.

In the spectral realm, Sheila and Rob felt the weight of the forgotten souls that had fallen victim to the cult's malevolence. The air, charged with an otherworldly energy, seemed to vibrate with the echoes of tormented cries. The old house, once a haven for dark forces, bore witness to the anguished spirits that lingered within the supernatural tapestry.

As they delved deeper into the spectral landscape, the whispers guided them toward a hidden chamber—a place where the cult's rituals had reached their zenith. The air in the chamber felt oppressive, and the whispers, now a relentless drone, seemed to speak of a malevolent energy woven into the very walls of the old house.

In the chamber, Sheila and Rob discovered an altar—an ancient stone slab adorned with cryptic symbols. The whispers, now a cacophony of spectral voices, spoke of blood sacrifices and forbidden rites that had stained the altar with the anguish of the forgotten. The old house, its spectral foundations steeped in the malevolent legacy, became a witness to the horrors that had transpired within its confines.

The images in the spectral landscape became more vivid—a macabre display of hooded figures performing dark rituals in the dimly lit chamber. The whispers, now a mournful hymn, conveyed the desperation of the tormented souls who had once walked the halls of the old house. Sheila and Rob, entwined in the spectral tapestry, felt the weight of the dark history that clung to their very beings.

As they reached the climax of the spectral journey, the whispers guided them toward a hidden passage in the chamber. A secret door, concealed by centuries-old dust, beckoned them to confront the source of The Watcher's malevolence. The old house, its spectral corridors pulsating with the echoes of the past, stood as a gateway to a deeper darkness that awaited in the shadows.

With trepidation, Sheila and Rob opened the secret door, revealing a staircase that descended into the depths of the supernatural realm. The air, now thick with the energy of the forgotten, guided them toward an underground cavern—a place where the cult's rituals had once reached their zenith.

In the cavern, the whispers reached a fevered pitch. The air seemed charged with an unseen force as Sheila and Rob navigated through the dimly lit passages. The walls, adorned with ancient symbols, spoke of a dark energy that permeated the very foundations of the old house.

As they reached the heart of the cavern, a revelation unfolded—a sacrificial chamber adorned with an altar bathed in an otherworldly glow. The whispers, now a dissonant symphony, spoke of the need for a blood sacrifice to seal the malevolent forces that lingered within the old house. Sheila and Rob, bound by the supernatural forces that guided

their journey, faced an unimaginable choice that would redefine the very fabric of their existence.

The images in the cavern came to life—a spectral replay of the cult's rituals and the sacrifices that had stained the altar with the blood of the innocent. The whispers, now a haunting melody, spoke of The Watcher's insatiable hunger and the need for a final sacrifice to quell the malevolent forces.

In the cavern's depths, Sheila and Rob confronted the truth—the old house, built for occult rituals, held a dark energy woven into its very walls. The whispers, though chaotic, conveyed a revelation that transcended the boundaries of the living and the dead. The sacrificial chamber, a place where the malevolent legacy reached its zenith, became a battleground between the supernatural and the mortal.

With a heavy heart, Sheila and Rob realized the only way to seal the malevolent forces was through a blood sacrifice. The whispers, now a mournful lament, spoke of the necessity to offer a part of themselves to quell the insatiable hunger of The Watcher. The old house, its spectral foundations shaken by the revelation, stood as a testament to the price that must be paid to vanquish the malevolent legacy.

In the dim light of the sacrificial chamber, Sheila and Rob prepared for the ritual—a desperate attempt to seal the malevolent forces that clung to the old house. The whispers, now a spectral symphony, guided them through the ancient rites that had once unleashed the supernatural storm within the haunted dwelling.

As the ritual reached its climax, Sheila and Rob felt an otherworldly energy enveloping them. The air pulsed with the echoes of forgotten incantations, and the sacrificial chamber seemed to vibrate with a spectral resonance. The whispers, though haunting, guided them toward a destiny entwined with the malevolent forces that sought communion with the living.

With a surge of supernatural power, Sheila and Rob offered a part of themselves to the sacrificial chamber. The whispers, now a triumphant hymn, echoed through the cavern as their sacrifice became a beacon of

light in the spectral darkness. The old house, its foundations saturated with the essence of the living, stood at the precipice of a resolution that transcended the boundaries of the mortal realm.

In the aftermath of the ritual, the cavern fell silent. The whispers, though fading, left an eerie stillness in their wake. Sheila and Rob, exhausted and shaken, stood amidst the spectral remnants of the sacrificial chamber. The old house, though still haunted by the echoes of the past, seemed to sigh with a spectral resignation.

The supernatural realm, now devoid of the malevolent forces that once tormented the haunted dwelling, unfolded with an unsettling stillness. Sheila and Rob, their journey through the spectral abyss complete, ascended from the underground cavern and returned to the haunted halls of the old house.

As they emerged into the dim light of the old house, a sense of eerie calm settled over them. The whispers, now a distant echo, carried a semblance of victory—a fleeting reprieve from the encroaching darkness. Little did they know that the true challenge awaited in the aftermath of the ritual—a revelation that would test the limits of their resilience and plunge them into a darkness from which there might be no escape.

The old house, though temporarily quelled, bore witness to the sacrifices made to seal the malevolent forces within its spectral confines. Sheila and Rob, forever changed by the ritual, faced an uncertain future where the echoes of the past lingered like a spectral shadow. The whispers, now a fading memory, left the door ajar for the looming terror that awaited in the aftermath of the spectral storm.

In the dim light of the old house, Sheila and Rob, their spirits weighed down by the sacrifice, descended from the underground cavern and returned to the living room. The air, though laden with the remnants of the supernatural battle, felt lighter as if a temporary reprieve had been granted.

As they navigated the haunted halls, a realization gripped Sheila and Rob—the old house, though temporarily quelled, held secrets that would unveil themselves in a chilling twist of fate. The whispers, now

a fading memory, left the door ajar for the looming terror that awaited in the aftermath of the spectral storm. The old house, its foundations saturated with the essence of the living, stood as a gateway to a supernatural abyss. Sheila and Rob, bound by the malevolent forces that lingered within, faced an uncertain future where the horrors of the past cast a long, lingering shadow over their fragile grasp on reality.

Chapter 10: The Basement

After sealing the malevolent forces within the old house through the sacrificial ritual, Sheila and Rob found themselves back in the dimly lit living room. The air, though tinged with an unsettling calm, carried the echoes of the supernatural journey they had undertaken. The whispers, now a distant memory, left a spectral resonance in the haunted dwelling.

As Sheila and Rob attempted to regain their bearings, a foreboding sensation lingered in the air. The old house, once a haven for dark rituals, stood as a testament to the sacrifices made to quell the malevolent forces. Little did they know that the true test awaited in the aftermath of the ritual—a revelation that would redefine the very fabric of their existence.

In the eerie quiet, Sheila's gaze was drawn to the basement door—the same door that had led them to the depths of the supernatural realm. The whispers, though muted, seemed to guide her attention toward the subterranean depths where forgotten rituals had once unfolded. A sense of trepidation settled over her as the basement became a focal point of the encroaching darkness.

Rob, too, felt an unspoken unease as he followed Sheila's gaze toward the basement door. The air, though seemingly calm, carried a spectral energy that hinted at the unresolved mysteries lurking within the subterranean depths. The old house, though momentarily at peace, seemed to hold secrets that demanded further exploration.

Driven by an unspoken compulsion, Sheila and Rob approached the basement door. The whispers, now a faint murmur, seemed to beckon them to descend once more into the depths of the haunted dwelling. The wooden stairs creaked under their weight as they descended into

the dimly lit basement—a place where the supernatural energies still lingered, weaving a spectral tapestry of the past.

In the basement, the air felt charged with an otherworldly energy. The whispers, though subdued, guided Sheila and Rob toward the heart of the supernatural storm. The old house, its foundations saturated with the essence of the living, seemed to pulse with an unseen force that transcended the boundaries of the mortal realm.

As they ventured deeper into the basement, Sheila's flashlight revealed forgotten artifacts—relics of the occult rituals that had once held sway within the haunted dwelling. The whispers, though fragmented, spoke of a lingering malevolence that refused to be fully contained. The old house, its spectral corridors echoing with the whispers of the past, became a gateway to a darkness that awaited in the shadows.

A sudden drop in temperature signaled a change in the atmosphere. The whispers, now a haunting lament, guided Sheila and Rob toward a hidden corner of the basement. There, obscured by shadows, they discovered a mysterious door—an entrance to a forgotten chamber that had eluded their previous exploration.

With trepidation, Sheila and Rob opened the door, revealing a chamber bathed in an unnatural darkness. The air, thick with the scent of ancient incense, seemed to vibrate with the echoes of spectral energy. The whispers, now a dissonant symphony, spoke of a deeper layer of malevolence that awaited discovery.

As they entered the hidden chamber, Sheila's flashlight revealed cryptic symbols etched into the walls—a language of the occult that spoke of forbidden knowledge and ancient rites. The whispers, though chaotic, seemed to convey a message—a revelation that transcended the boundaries of the living and the dead. The old house, now a conduit for the supernatural, bore witness to the unfolding mysteries that awaited in the hidden chamber.

In the dim light, Sheila and Rob stumbled upon an ancient tome—an occult grimoire that held the secrets of the forgotten rituals. The whispers, now a spectral chorus, urged Sheila to decipher the cryptic

symbols that adorned the pages. The malevolent legacy, though temporarily quelled, seemed to find its voice in the ancient words that unfolded in the flickering light.

As Sheila read aloud the incantations, the chamber seemed to come alive with an otherworldly energy. Shadows danced on the walls, and the whispers, now a cacophony of spectral voices, spoke of a deeper darkness that had yet to be unveiled. The old house, a witness to the unfolding ritual, became a gateway to the unknown—a place where the living and the dead converged in a macabre dance.

In the spectral glow, the hidden chamber transformed into a supernatural realm—a place suspended between the living and the abyss. The whispers, now a mournful wail, guided Sheila and Rob toward a revelation that would test the limits of their resilience. The old house, its foundations shaken by the unfolding ritual, became a battleground where the supernatural and the mortal collided.

As they delved deeper into the hidden chamber, the symbols on the walls seemed to shift—a spectral language that defied comprehension. The whispers, though haunting, spoke of an ancient evil that had been awakened by their presence. Sheila and Rob, bound by the malevolent forces that lingered within the old house, faced an unforeseen challenge that awaited in the shadows.

A sudden gust of wind extinguished their flashlights, plunging the hidden chamber into complete darkness. The whispers, now a relentless drone, seemed to merge with the shadows that danced in the spectral realm. The old house, its spectral foundations saturated with the essence of the living, stood at the precipice of a new, malevolent revelation.

In the darkness, Sheila and Rob felt an unseen force closing in around them. The whispers, now a spectral symphony, guided them toward a spectral entity that awaited in the hidden corners of the chamber. The old house, a silent witness to the unfolding darkness, seemed to sigh with a spectral resignation.

With a sense of urgency, Sheila and Rob fumbled for their flashlights, attempting to pierce the veil of darkness that surrounded them.

The whispers, though chaotic, spoke of an ancient evil that sought communion with the living. The hidden chamber, now a battleground between the mortal and the supernatural, became a place where the boundaries between reality and the abyss blurred.

As their flashlights flickered to life, Sheila and Rob beheld a chilling sight—a spectral entity, its form indistinct in the shadows, stood before them. The whispers, now a haunting melody, spoke of an ancient evil that had been awakened by their presence. The old house, a conduit for the malevolent forces, bore silent witness to the spectral encounter that unfolded in the hidden chamber.

The entity, a manifestation of the ancient evil that had lingered within the old house, seemed to reach out from the shadows. The whispers, now a dissonant chorus, urged Sheila and Rob to confront the malevolent force that awaited in the spectral realm. The old house, though temporarily quelled, stood as a gateway to a darkness that defied rational explanation.

With a surge of supernatural power, the entity confronted Sheila and Rob. The whispers, now a mournful hymn, seemed to align with the malevolent force as the spectral encounter reached its zenith. The old house, its foundations saturated with the essence of the living, became a battleground where the living and the dead converged in a macabre dance of supernatural entanglement.

Sheila and Rob, entwined in the spectral tapestry, felt the weight of unseen eyes upon them. The whispers, now a relentless drone, seemed to echo through the hidden chamber—a spectral symphony that reverberated through the haunted dwelling. The old house, its spectral foundations shaken by the malevolent revelation, stood at the precipice of a new, horrifying chapter in its dark history.

As the entity reached out with spectral tendrils, Sheila and Rob, driven by an unspoken determination, faced the malevolent force with a courage born of desperation. The whispers, though chaotic, guided them through the spectral encounter—a dance between the living and the abyss. The old house, a silent witness to the unfolding darkness,

stood as a battleground where the forces of the supernatural and the mortal clashed in a terrifying crescendo.

In the dim light of the hidden chamber, a struggle unfolded—a battle between the living and the spectral entity that sought communion with the living. The whispers, now a spectral symphony, intensified as Sheila and Rob confronted the ancient evil that had been awakened by their presence. The old house, its foundations saturated with the essence of the living, became a crucible where the boundaries between reality and the abyss blurred.

With a surge of supernatural energy, Sheila and Rob channeled the remnants of the sacrificial ritual into a desperate confrontation with the entity. The whispers, now a haunting melody, seemed to align with the living as the spectral encounter reached its climax. The old house, a silent witness to the unfolding darkness, stood as a testament to the resilience of those who dared to confront the malevolent forces that lurked within its haunted halls.

As the spectral entity recoiled, the whispers, now a fading memory, left an eerie stillness in their wake. Sheila and Rob, exhausted and shaken, stood amidst the spectral remnants of the hidden chamber. The old house, though still haunted by the echoes of the past, seemed to sigh with a spectral resignation.

The supernatural realm, now devoid of the malevolent entity that had sought communion with the living, unfolded with an unsettling stillness. Sheila and Rob, their courage tested by the spectral encounter, ascended from the hidden chamber and returned to the haunted halls of the old house. The air, though laden with the remnants of the supernatural battle, felt lighter as if a temporary reprieve had been granted.

Little did they know that the true horror, a revelation that would redefine the very fabric of their existence, awaited in the shadows of their newfound victory. The old house, though temporarily quelled, held secrets that would unveil themselves in a chilling twist of fate—one that would test the limits of Sheila and Rob's resilience and plunge them into a darkness from which there might be no escape.

The whispers, now a fading memory, left the door ajar for the looming terror that awaited in the aftermath of the spectral storm. The old house, its haunted corridors pulsating with unresolved sorrows, stood as a gateway to a supernatural abyss. Sheila and Rob, bound by the malevolent forces that lingered within, faced an uncertain future where the horrors of the past cast a long, lingering shadow over their fragile grasp on reality.

Chapter 11: The Escape

Having confronted the malevolent forces in the hidden chamber, Sheila and Rob ascended from the basement, their nerves on edge from the spectral encounter. The air in the old house, though momentarily relieved of the oppressive darkness, still held a spectral tension—a silent reminder of the horrors that lurked within its haunted halls. Unbeknownst to them, a new chapter of terror awaited as the old house seemed to cling to the malevolence that had taken root in its very foundations.

As they emerged into the dim light of the living room, Sheila and Rob exchanged glances laden with unspoken fear. The whispers, though muted, seemed to linger in the air like a haunting refrain. The old house, its spectral corridors echoing with the echoes of the past, stood as a silent witness to the unfolding nightmare that awaited the unwitting inhabitants.

A sense of urgency gripped Sheila as her gaze once again fell upon the basement door—the same door that had led them to the depths of the supernatural realm. The whispers, though subdued, seemed to guide her attention toward the subterranean depths where forgotten rituals had once unfolded. The basement, now a nexus of malevolence, beckoned them to confront the unresolved mysteries that lingered within.

Rob, his nerves still raw from the spectral encounter, hesitated as Sheila approached the basement door. The air, though seemingly calm, carried a spectral resonance that hinted at the lingering darkness within the haunted dwelling. The old house, a silent observer to the unfolding

terror, seemed to pulse with an unseen force that transcended the boundaries of the living and the dead.

With a sense of trepidation, Sheila opened the basement door, revealing the wooden stairs that led to the subterranean depths. The whispers, now a faint murmur, seemed to echo through the haunted halls, guiding them toward the heart of the encroaching darkness. The old house, though momentarily quelled, held secrets that demanded further exploration—a revelation that would test the limits of Sheila and Rob's resilience.

As they descended into the dimly lit basement, the air felt heavy with an otherworldly energy. The whispers, though muted, seemed to guide Sheila and Rob toward the epicenter of the supernatural storm. The old house, its spectral foundations saturated with the essence of the living, became a conduit for the malevolent forces that sought communion with the unwitting inhabitants.

In the basement, the artifacts of forgotten rituals lay in shadowed corners, silent witnesses to the malevolence that had once thrived within the haunted dwelling. The whispers, though fragmented, spoke of a lingering darkness that refused to be fully contained. The old house, a spectral battleground, seemed to pulse with an unseen force that beckoned Sheila and Rob to delve deeper into the abyss.

As they ventured into the basement's depths, Sheila's flashlight revealed a hidden passage—a secret corridor that led to unexplored realms within the haunted dwelling. The whispers, though haunting, guided them toward a revelation that transcended the boundaries of the living and the dead. The old house, now a labyrinth of malevolence, became a spectral tapestry where the living and the abyss converged in an eerie dance.

A sudden drop in temperature signaled a shift in the atmosphere. The whispers, now a haunting lament, guided Sheila and Rob toward an ancient doorway—an entrance to a forgotten chamber that had eluded their previous exploration. The old house, though momentarily

quelled, seemed to cling to the malevolent forces that lurked within its spectral depths.

With trepidation, Sheila and Rob opened the ancient doorway, revealing a chamber bathed in an unnatural darkness. The air, thick with the scent of ancient incense, seemed to vibrate with the echoes of spectral energy. The whispers, now a dissonant symphony, spoke of a deeper layer of malevolence that awaited discovery.

In the dim light, Sheila and Rob stumbled upon an ancient altar—an occult relic that held the secrets of forbidden rituals. The whispers, though chaotic, urged Sheila to decipher the cryptic symbols that adorned the altar. The malevolent legacy, though temporarily quelled, seemed to find its voice in the ancient rites that unfolded in the flickering light.

As Sheila and Rob examined the altar, a sudden gust of wind extinguished their flashlights, plunging the chamber into complete darkness. The whispers, now a relentless drone, merged with the shadows that danced in the spectral realm. The old house, its spectral foundations saturated with the essence of the living, stood at the precipice of a new, malevolent revelation.

In the darkness, Sheila and Rob felt an unseen force closing in around them. The whispers, now a spectral symphony, guided them toward a spectral entity that awaited in the hidden corners of the chamber. The old house, a silent witness to the unfolding darkness, seemed to sigh with a spectral resignation.

With a sense of urgency, Sheila and Rob fumbled for their flashlights, attempting to pierce the veil of darkness that surrounded them. The whispers, though chaotic, spoke of an ancient evil that sought communion with the living. The hidden chamber, now a battleground between the mortal and the supernatural, became a place where the boundaries between reality and the abyss blurred.

As their flashlights flickered to life, Sheila and Rob beheld a chilling sight—a spectral entity, its form indistinct in the shadows, stood before them. The whispers, now a haunting melody, spoke of an ancient evil

that had been awakened by their presence. The old house, a conduit for the malevolent forces, bore silent witness to the spectral encounter that unfolded in the hidden chamber.

The entity, a manifestation of the ancient evil that had lingered within the old house, seemed to reach out from the shadows. The whispers, now a dissonant chorus, urged Sheila and Rob to confront the malevolent force that awaited in the spectral realm. The old house, though temporarily quelled, stood as a gateway to a darkness that defied rational explanation.

With a surge of supernatural power, the entity confronted Sheila and Rob. The whispers, now a mournful hymn, seemed to align with the malevolent force as the spectral encounter reached its zenith. The old house, its foundations saturated with the essence of the living, became a battleground where the living and the dead converged in a macabre dance.

Sheila and Rob, entwined in the spectral tapestry, felt the weight of unseen eyes upon them. The whispers, now a relentless drone, seemed to echo through the hidden chamber—a spectral symphony that reverberated through the haunted dwelling. The old house, its spectral foundations shaken by the malevolent revelation, stood at the precipice of a new, horrifying chapter in its dark history.

As the entity reached out with spectral tendrils, Sheila and Rob, driven by an unspoken determination, faced the malevolent force with a courage born of desperation. The whispers, though chaotic, guided them through the spectral encounter—a dance between the living and the abyss. The old house, a silent witness to the unfolding darkness, stood as a battleground where the forces of the supernatural and the mortal clashed in a terrifying crescendo.

In the dim light of the hidden chamber, a struggle unfolded—a battle between the living and the spectral entity that sought communion with the living. The whispers, now a spectral symphony, intensified as Sheila and Rob confronted the ancient evil that had been awakened by their presence. The old house, its foundations saturated with the essence of

the living, became a crucible where the boundaries between reality and the abyss blurred.

With a surge of supernatural energy, Sheila and Rob channeled the remnants of the sacrificial ritual into a desperate confrontation with the entity. The whispers, now a haunting melody, seemed to align with the living as the spectral encounter reached its climax. The old house, a silent witness to the unfolding darkness, stood as a testament to the resilience of those who dared to confront the malevolent forces that lurked within its haunted halls.

As the spectral entity recoiled, the whispers, now a fading memory, left an eerie stillness in their wake. Sheila and Rob, exhausted and shaken, stood amidst the spectral remnants of the hidden chamber. The old house, though still haunted by the echoes of the past, seemed to sigh with a spectral resignation.

The supernatural realm, now devoid of the malevolent entity that had sought communion with the living, unfolded with an unsettling stillness. Sheila and Rob, their courage tested by the spectral encounter, ascended from the hidden chamber and returned to the haunted halls of the old house. The air, though laden with the remnants of the supernatural battle, felt lighter as if a temporary reprieve had been granted.

Little did they know that the true horror, a revelation that would redefine the very fabric of their existence, awaited in the shadows of their newfound victory. The old house, though temporarily quelled, held secrets that would unveil themselves in a chilling twist of fate—one that would test the limits of Sheila and Rob's resilience and plunge them into a darkness from which there might be no escape.

The whispers, now a fading memory, left the door ajar for the looming terror that awaited in the aftermath of the spectral storm. The old house, its haunted corridors pulsating with unresolved sorrows, stood as a gateway to a supernatural abyss. Sheila and Rob, bound by the malevolent forces that lingered within, faced an uncertain future where the horrors of the past cast a long, lingering shadow over their fragile grasp on reality.

Chapter 12: The Attacks

As Sheila and Rob emerged from the hidden chamber, a sense of unease lingered in the air. The old house, though temporarily quelled by their confrontation with the spectral entity, exuded an eerie calm that belied the malevolence buried within its haunted corridors. Unbeknownst to the shaken inhabitants, the aftermath of the ritual had set into motion a series of paranormal attacks that would test the limits of their courage and resilience.

The whispers, though muted, seemed to carry a warning—a spectral echo of the malevolent forces that still clung to the very fabric of the old house. Sheila and Rob, their nerves raw from the supernatural encounter, exchanged wary glances as they navigated the dimly lit halls. The air, laden with the remnants of the spectral battle, became a spectral tapestry where the living and the dead converged in an unsettling dance.

As night fell over the old house, Sheila found herself alone in the living room. The whispers, now a distant murmur, seemed to beckon her toward the spectral energies that lingered within the haunted dwelling. The old house, a silent witness to the unfolding nightmare, held secrets that awaited discovery—a revelation that would thrust Sheila into a harrowing series of paranormal attacks.

The attacks began subtly—a flickering of lights, objects moving mysteriously, and an unshakable feeling of being watched. Sheila, though initially dismissive, couldn't ignore the mounting sense of dread that accompanied these strange occurrences. The whispers, now a haunting melody, seemed to intensify as if heralding the approach of an unseen malevolence.

One night, as Sheila lay in bed, the attacks escalated. Shadows danced on the walls, and an otherworldly chill permeated the room. The whispers, now a dissonant chorus, filled the air with a spectral energy that seemed to converge around her. The old house, its foundations saturated with the essence of the living, became a battleground where the forces of the supernatural sought communion with the unsuspecting inhabitants.

Sheila, gripped by a growing terror, sought solace in the presence of Rob. Together, they confronted the escalating attacks, attempting to rationalize the paranormal occurrences that defied logical explanation. The old house, though momentarily quelled, seemed to pulse with an unseen force that defied the boundaries of the mortal realm.

The attacks took a violent turn, as unseen forces hurled objects across the room and ominous shadows seemed to reach out from the spectral realm. Sheila and Rob, their nerves stretched to the breaking point, struggled to maintain their grasp on reality. The whispers, now a relentless drone, echoed through the haunted halls, guiding the malevolent forces in their torment of the unsuspecting inhabitants.

Desperate for answers, Sheila delved into her research, revisiting the ancient tome and the diary that chronicled the house's dark history. The whispers, though fragmented, seemed to offer cryptic clues that hinted at a malevolent presence seeking revenge. The old house, its haunted corridors echoing with the sorrows of the past, held the key to understanding the origins of the supernatural attacks.

In their quest for answers, Sheila and Rob enlisted the help of a local paranormal investigator. The whispers, now a spectral symphony, seemed to intensify as the investigator delved into the history of the old house. The malevolent forces, though temporarily restrained, resisted the intrusion, escalating the attacks in retaliation.

The investigator, a skeptic turned believer, witnessed the paranormal onslaught firsthand. Doors slammed shut, eerie whispers reverberated through the halls, and unseen hands seemed to grab at those who dared to venture into the haunted dwelling. The old house, now a battleground for the living and the supernatural, exuded a malevolence that defied rational explanation.

In a desperate attempt to quell the attacks, Sheila and Rob decided to hold a seance—an act that would either provide answers or further provoke the wrath of the malevolent forces. The whispers, now a haunting lament, seemed to guide them toward the living room where the seance would take place. The old house, its spectral foundations

shaken by the paranormal onslaught, awaited the unfolding ritual with a spectral resignation.

As the seance began, the air in the living room became charged with an otherworldly energy. The whispers, now a cacophony of spectral voices, spoke of the ancient evil that sought communion with the living. The old house, its haunted halls bearing witness to the unfolding ritual, seemed to sigh with a spectral anticipation.

Suddenly, the room plunged into darkness, and a chilling wind swept through the living room. The whispers, now a spectral chorus, guided Sheila and Rob toward a revelation that transcended the boundaries of the living and the dead. The old house, its foundations saturated with the essence of the living, became a conduit for the malevolent forces that sought release through the seance.

In the darkness, Sheila felt an unseen presence—the very embodiment of the malevolence that had plagued the old house. The whispers, now a mournful hymn, seemed to echo through the spectral realm as the ancient evil made itself known. The old house, a witness to the unfolding ritual, stood at the precipice of a terrifying revelation.

The entity, a manifestation of the supernatural forces, spoke through the seance—a voice that sent shivers down the spines of those present. The whispers, now a spectral symphony, conveyed the entity's grievances and the reasons behind the relentless attacks. The old house, its spectral foundations saturated with the essence of the living, became a stage for the malevolent forces to voice their unholy intentions.

As the seance reached its climax, Sheila and Rob faced a choice—succumb to the malevolent forces or confront the entity head-on. The whispers, now a haunting melody, seemed to offer a glimmer of hope amidst the overwhelming darkness. The old house, its haunted corridors pulsating with the echoes of the past, awaited the resolution of the supernatural conflict that unfolded within its spectral confines.

With determination born of desperation, Sheila and Rob confronted the entity. The whispers, now a spectral chorus, guided them through the confrontation—a dance between the living and the abyss. The old

house, a silent witness to the unfolding darkness, stood as a battleground where the forces of the supernatural and the mortal clashed in a terrifying crescendo.

As Sheila and Rob faced the entity, a surge of supernatural energy filled the room. The whispers, now a relentless drone, seemed to align with the living as the spectral encounter reached its zenith. The old house, its foundations saturated with the essence of the living, became a crucible where the boundaries between reality and the abyss blurred.

In the dim light of the living room, a struggle unfolded—a battle between the living and the malevolent entity that sought communion with the living. The whispers, now a spectral symphony, intensified as Sheila and Rob confronted the ancient evil that had been awakened by their presence. The old house, its haunted foundations shaken by the paranormal conflict, stood as a testament to the resilience of those who dared to confront the malevolent forces that lurked within its spectral halls.

As the entity recoiled, the whispers, now a fading memory, left an eerie stillness in their wake. Sheila and Rob, exhausted and shaken, stood amidst the spectral remnants of the seance. The old house, though still haunted by the echoes of the past, seemed to sigh with a spectral resignation.

The supernatural realm, now devoid of the entity that had sought communion with the living, unfolded with an unsettling stillness. Sheila and Rob, their courage tested by the spectral encounter, navigated the haunted halls of the old house. The air, though laden with the remnants of the paranormal conflict, felt lighter as if a temporary reprieve had been granted.

Little did they know that the true horror, a revelation that would redefine the very fabric of their existence, awaited in the shadows of their newfound victory. The old house, though temporarily quelled, held secrets that would unveil themselves in a chilling twist of fate—one that would test the limits of Sheila and Rob's resilience and plunge them into a darkness from which there might be no escape.

The whispers, now a fading memory, left the door ajar for the looming terror that awaited in the aftermath of the supernatural onslaught. The old house, its haunted corridors pulsating with unresolved sorrows, stood as a gateway to a supernatural abyss. Sheila and Rob, bound by the malevolent forces that lingered within, faced an uncertain future where the horrors of the past cast a long, lingering shadow over their fragile grasp on reality.

Chapter 13: The Seance

As the aftermath of the paranormal attacks lingered in the old house, Sheila and Rob, driven by a desperate need for answers, decided to delve deeper into the supernatural realm. The whispers, though diminished, seemed to guide them toward a fateful decision—the summoning of forces beyond their understanding through a seance. The old house, its haunted corridors pulsating with unresolved sorrows, awaited the unfolding ritual with a spectral anticipation.

Sheila and Rob gathered in the living room, surrounded by flickering candles and the musty scent of ancient incense. The whispers, now a distant murmur, seemed to converge around them as they prepared for the seance. The air in the room became charged with an otherworldly energy, and the old house, a silent witness to the unfolding ritual, stood at the precipice of a new, unsettling chapter.

The seance began with the chanting of incantations from an ancient tome Sheila had found in her research. The whispers, now a haunting lament, filled the room with a spectral resonance that transcended the boundaries of the living and the dead. The old house, its spectral foundations saturated with the essence of the living, became a conduit for the malevolent forces that awaited release through the ritual.

As the incantations echoed through the room, a sudden drop in temperature signaled the arrival of unseen entities. The whispers, now a spectral symphony, seemed to guide Sheila and Rob toward a revelation that defied rational explanation. The old house, its haunted halls bearing witness to the unfolding ritual, exuded a spectral energy that reached beyond the mortal realm.

In the dim light, Sheila and Rob felt an otherworldly presence—the very embodiment of the malevolence that had plagued the old house. The whispers, now a dissonant chorus, urged them to maintain their focus as the spectral entities made themselves known. The old house, a stage for the supernatural forces, stood as a gateway to a darkness that defied comprehension.

As the seance continued, the room filled with eerie whispers, shadows danced on the walls, and an unseen force seemed to grip those present. Sheila and Rob, their senses heightened by the supernatural energies, felt the weight of unseen eyes upon them. The old house, its spectral foundations shaken by the unfolding ritual, became a battleground where the living and the abyss converged in an unsettling dance.

Suddenly, the room plunged into darkness, and an otherworldly wind swept through the living room. The whispers, now a relentless drone, guided Sheila and Rob toward the epicenter of the spectral storm. The old house, though momentarily quelled, seemed to pulse with an unseen force that defied the boundaries of the mortal realm.

In the darkness, Sheila and Rob glimpsed shadowy figures—apparitions of the past that materialized in the spectral realm. The whispers, now a spectral chorus, spoke of the tormented souls that lingered within the haunted dwelling. The old house, its haunted corridors echoing with the sorrows of the past, became a tapestry of spectral entities seeking release through the seance.

As the apparitions manifested, the room resonated with their ethereal presence. The whispers, now a haunting melody, conveyed the grievances of the tormented souls that sought communion with the living. The old house, a conduit for the spectral forces, bore witness to the unfolding drama between the mortal and the supernatural.

Amidst the spectral symphony, Sheila and Rob felt a sudden shift—a malevolent entity seizing the opportunity to make its presence known. The whispers, now a dissonant chorus, guided them toward a revelation that sent shivers down their spines. The old house, its spectral

foundations saturated with the essence of the living, stood as a stage for the malevolent force that awaited confrontation.

The entity, a manifestation of the ancient evil that lingered within the old house, spoke through the seance—a voice that echoed with a chilling resonance. The whispers, now a mournful hymn, conveyed the entity's grievances and the reasons behind the relentless attacks. The old house, its haunted halls bearing witness to the unfolding ritual, seemed to sigh with a spectral anticipation.

Sheila and Rob, their senses overwhelmed by the supernatural onslaught, faced a choice—succumb to the malevolent forces or confront the entity head-on. The whispers, now a haunting melody, seemed to offer a glimmer of hope amidst the overwhelming darkness. The old house, its haunted corridors pulsating with the echoes of the past, awaited the resolution of the supernatural conflict that unfolded within its spectral confines.

With determination born of desperation, Sheila and Rob confronted the entity. The whispers, now a spectral chorus, guided them through the confrontation—a dance between the living and the abyss. The old house, a silent witness to the unfolding darkness, stood as a battleground where the forces of the supernatural and the mortal clashed in a terrifying crescendo.

As Sheila and Rob faced the entity, a surge of supernatural energy filled the room. The whispers, now a relentless drone, seemed to align with the living as the spectral encounter reached its zenith. The old house, its foundations saturated with the essence of the living, became a crucible where the boundaries between reality and the abyss blurred.

In the dim light of the living room, a struggle unfolded—a battle between the living and the malevolent entity that sought communion with the living. The whispers, now a spectral symphony, intensified as Sheila and Rob confronted the ancient evil that had been awakened by their presence. The old house, its haunted foundations shaken by the paranormal conflict, stood as a testament to the resilience of those

who dared to confront the malevolent forces that lurked within its spectral halls.

As the entity recoiled, the whispers, now a fading memory, left an eerie stillness in their wake. Sheila and Rob, exhausted and shaken, stood amidst the spectral remnants of the seance. The old house, though still haunted by the echoes of the past, seemed to sigh with a spectral resignation.

The supernatural realm, now devoid of the entity that had sought communion with the living, unfolded with an unsettling stillness. Sheila and Rob, their courage tested by the spectral encounter, navigated the haunted halls of the old house. The air, though laden with the remnants of the paranormal conflict, felt lighter as if a temporary reprieve had been granted.

Little did they know that the true horror, a revelation that would redefine the very fabric of their existence, awaited in the shadows of their newfound victory. The old house, though temporarily quelled, held secrets that would unveil themselves in a chilling twist of fate—one that would test the limits of Sheila and Rob's resilience and plunge them into a darkness from which there might be no escape.

The whispers, now a fading memory, left the door ajar for the looming terror that awaited in the aftermath of the supernatural onslaught. The old house, its haunted corridors pulsating with unresolved sorrows, stood as a gateway to a supernatural abyss. Sheila and Rob, bound by the malevolent forces that lingered within, faced an uncertain future where the horrors of the past cast a long, lingering shadow over their fragile grasp on reality.

Chapter 14: The Cleansing

In the wake of the seance, Sheila and Rob, still reeling from the otherworldly encounter, found themselves at a crossroads. The old house, though momentarily relieved of the malevolent entity's presence, exuded an eerie calm that hinted at the lingering supernatural forces within its haunted walls. Determined to put an end to the paranormal onslaught, Sheila sought the guidance of a psychic medium—an expert

in the arcane arts who might hold the key to cleansing the ancient dwelling.

The whispers, now a faint echo of the malevolence that had permeated the old house, guided Sheila and Rob toward the psychic medium's secluded residence. The air, heavy with the remnants of the spectral storm, carried a spectral resonance that seemed to converge around them. The old house, its spectral foundations saturated with the essence of the living, became a distant backdrop to the unfolding quest for purification.

The psychic medium, a mysterious figure with a demeanor that mirrored the enigmatic forces surrounding the old house, welcomed Sheila and Rob into a dimly lit room adorned with mystical artifacts. The whispers, now a haunting melody, seemed to intensify in the presence of the psychic medium. The air became charged with an otherworldly energy as the cleansing ritual began.

As the psychic medium delved into the spiritual realm, Sheila and Rob felt a shift in the atmosphere. The whispers, now a spectral symphony, guided the medium's hands as they moved through intricate gestures, channeling supernatural forces to cleanse the old house of its malevolent energies. The haunted dwelling, a silent witness to the unfolding ritual, awaited the purifying touch of the arcane.

Suddenly, the room quivered with unseen energies. Shadows danced on the walls, and the air vibrated with a spectral resonance. The whispers, now a dissonant chorus, echoed through the room, carrying the remnants of the malevolent entity's presence. The old house, though momentarily quelled, seemed to resist the cleansing as if clinging to the dark energies that had taken root within its spectral depths.

As the cleansing ritual continued, Sheila and Rob witnessed a manifestation of spectral mists swirling through the room. The whispers, now a relentless drone, seemed to speak of the ancient sorrows that clung to the old house like a malevolent shroud. The psychic medium, undeterred by the supernatural turbulence, pressed on with the purifying incantations.

In the dim light, Sheila and Rob glimpsed fleeting apparitions—the tormented souls that lingered within the old house. The whispers, now a haunting lament, carried the voices of the restless spirits seeking release through the cleansing ritual. The haunted dwelling, its spectral foundations shaken by the purifying energies, became a nexus where the living and the dead converged in an otherworldly dance.

Unexpectedly, the psychic medium's eyes glazed over, and her voice took on an otherworldly resonance. The whispers, now a mournful hymn, spoke through the medium, conveying the grievances of the ancient spirits that had been disturbed by the malevolent entity. The old house, a conduit for the spectral forces, bore silent witness to the spectral communion that unfolded in the purifying ritual.

As the psychic medium channeled the spirits, Sheila and Rob felt a surge of supernatural energy coursing through the room. The whispers, now a spectral chorus, guided them toward a revelation that transcended the boundaries of the living and the dead. The old house, though momentarily quelled, seemed to sigh with a spectral resignation as the purifying energies sought to dispel the malevolent forces that clung to its haunted corridors.

The psychic medium, still in the grip of the supernatural trance, uttered cryptic words that seemed to unlock the secrets of the old house's dark history. The whispers, now a dissonant symphony, guided Sheila and Rob toward a hidden chamber—an ancient sanctum where forgotten rituals had once unfolded. The haunted dwelling, its spectral foundations saturated with the essence of the living, became a battleground for the living and the supernatural.

As the purifying ritual reached its climax, Sheila and Rob, entranced by the spectral energies, witnessed a spectral convergence. The whispers, now a spectral melody, spoke of the ancient rituals that had bound the malevolent forces to the old house. The psychic medium, still in communion with the spirits, channeled the supernatural energies toward the heart of the spectral storm.

A sudden burst of light illuminated the room as the cleansing energies reached their zenith. The whispers, now a fading memory, left an eerie stillness in their wake. Sheila and Rob, their senses overwhelmed by the spectral convergence, stood amidst the remnants of the purifying ritual. The old house, though still haunted by the echoes of the past, seemed to sigh with a spectral resignation as if acknowledging the fleeting victory over the malevolent forces.

The psychic medium, released from the supernatural trance, conveyed the success of the cleansing ritual. The whispers, now a distant murmur, hinted at a temporary reprieve from the paranormal onslaught. The old house, its spectral foundations shaken by the purifying energies, awaited the aftermath of the cleansing—a revelation that would test the limits of Sheila and Rob's resilience and unravel the mysteries hidden within its haunted corridors.

As Sheila and Rob left the psychic medium's residence, a sense of cautious hope lingered in the air. The whispers, now a faint echo of the supernatural forces, guided them back to the old house—the battleground where the forces of the living and the dead had clashed in a spectral dance. The haunted dwelling, though momentarily relieved of the malevolent entity's presence, held secrets that awaited unraveling as the aftermath of the cleansing ritual cast a spectral light on the mysteries that lay hidden within its spectral confines.

Chapter 15: The Truth

With the cleansing ritual behind them, Sheila and Rob returned to the old house, hoping for a respite from the malevolent forces that had plagued them. The whispers, now a mere whisper of the supernatural energies that once gripped the haunted dwelling, guided them through the dimly lit halls. The air, heavy with the aftermath of the purifying ritual, carried a spectral resonance that hinted at the revelations awaiting them.

As Sheila and Rob explored the old house, a sense of cautious optimism settled over them. The whispers, though diminished, seemed to convey a temporary peace—a fragile equilibrium between the living

and the supernatural. The haunted dwelling, a silent witness to the unfolding events, exuded an eerie calm that belied the mysteries hidden within its spectral depths.

However, as night fell over the old house, an unsettling energy permeated the air. The whispers, now a distant murmur, hinted at a resurgence of the malevolent forces. Sheila and Rob, their nerves on edge, exchanged wary glances as they navigated the dimly lit corridors. The haunted dwelling, though momentarily quelled, held secrets that awaited revelation in the spectral silence of the night.

A series of cryptic symbols appeared on the walls—manifestations of the supernatural energies that lingered within the old house. The whispers, now a haunting melody, seemed to speak through the spectral symbols, conveying a message that defied rational explanation. The air, charged with an otherworldly energy, guided Sheila and Rob toward the heart of the spectral disturbance.

In the dim light, they discovered a hidden chamber—a forgotten sanctum where the malevolent rituals of the past had unfolded. The whispers, now a spectral symphony, intensified as Sheila and Rob delved into the secrets concealed within the ancient chamber. The haunted dwelling, its spectral foundations saturated with the essence of the living, became a tapestry where the past and present converged in an unsettling dance.

As they explored the hidden chamber, Sheila uncovered an old diary that chronicled the house's dark history. The whispers, now a dissonant chorus, guided her through the cryptic entries that spoke of occult rituals and malevolent forces bound to the old house. The air, thick with the residual energies of the past, carried a spectral resonance that transcended the boundaries of time.

The diary revealed a gruesome truth—the old house had been built for occult rituals, with a dark energy woven into its very walls. The whispers, now a relentless drone, conveyed the malevolent forces that had been awakened by the unwitting presence of Sheila and Rob. The haunted dwelling, a silent witness to the unfolding revelations, stood

as a testament to the ancient darkness that sought communion with the living.

As Sheila and Rob grappled with the horrifying truth, the whispers guided them toward a chilling realization—there was only one way to stop the malevolent forces that had been unleashed. The haunted dwelling, though momentarily quelled by the cleansing ritual, demanded a final sacrifice to seal the ancient evil that lurked within its spectral depths.

The revelation weighed heavily on Sheila's shoulders as she contemplated the harrowing decision that awaited her. The whispers, now a haunting lament, seemed to offer guidance through the darkness that enveloped the old house. The air, heavy with the echoes of the past, carried a spectral energy that transcended the mortal realm.

Determined to confront the malevolent forces head-on, Sheila and Rob sought counsel from the psychic medium who had guided them through the cleansing ritual. The whispers, now a spectral chorus, guided them to the medium's secluded residence, where the air buzzed with the residual energies of the supernatural encounter. The haunted dwelling, a distant backdrop to the unfolding quest, awaited the resolution of the spectral conflict that had gripped its haunted halls.

The psychic medium, aware of the lingering malevolence, spoke of the ancient ritual that could seal the evil presence within the old house. The whispers, now a spectral melody, seemed to convey the urgency of the impending sacrifice. The air, thick with the spectral energies, guided Sheila and Rob toward a path that would test the limits of their courage and resilience.

Sheila, faced with an unimaginable choice, grappled with the weight of the revelation. The whispers, now a dissonant symphony, urged her to confront the malevolent forces head-on. The haunted dwelling, its spectral foundations shaken by the impending decision, stood as a crucible where the boundaries between the living and the supernatural blurred.

As night fell over the old house, Sheila prepared for the ritual—a blood sacrifice that would bind the malevolent forces and seal the ancient evil within the spectral confines. The whispers, now a relentless drone, echoed through the haunted dwelling, guiding her toward the heart of the spectral storm. The air, heavy with the essence of the supernatural, carried a spectral resonance that transcended the mortal realm.

Rob, torn between loyalty and the impending sacrifice, stood by Sheila's side as she embraced her destiny. The whispers, now a haunting lament, seemed to offer solace in the face of the inevitable. The haunted dwelling, a silent witness to the unfolding ritual, exuded an eerie calm that belied the impending darkness.

In the dimly lit chamber, Sheila performed the ritual with a heavy heart. The whispers, now a spectral symphony, guided her through the ancient incantations that would bind the malevolent forces to the old house. The air, charged with an otherworldly energy, carried the weight of the sacrifice that would determine the fate of the haunted dwelling.

As Sheila completed the ritual, a surge of supernatural energy filled the room. The whispers, now a fading memory, left an eerie stillness in their wake. The haunted dwelling, though temporarily quelled, seemed to sigh with a spectral resignation. The air, thick with the remnants of the ritual, carried a spectral resonance that lingered in the haunted corridors.

In the aftermath of the sacrifice, Sheila and Rob, exhausted and shaken, emerged from the hidden chamber. The whispers, now a distant murmur, guided them through the dimly lit halls of the old house. The haunted dwelling, though momentarily relieved of the malevolent entity's presence, held secrets that awaited unraveling in the aftermath of the ritual.

As Sheila and Rob faced the uncertain aftermath, a chilling realization dawned upon them—the sacrifice, though sealing the ancient evil, had forever changed the fabric of their existence. The whispers, now a spectral chorus, seemed to convey the irreversible consequences of the harrowing ordeal. The haunted dwelling, a silent witness to the

unfolding aftermath, stood as a testament to the sacrifices made in the name of sealing the ancient darkness within its spectral confines.

Little did they know that the true horror, a revelation that would redefine their very existence, awaited in the shadows of the haunted dwelling. The whispers, now a fading memory, left the door ajar for the looming terror that awaited in the aftermath of the supernatural sacrifice. Sheila and Rob, bound by the malevolent forces that lingered within, faced an uncertain future where the horrors of the past cast a long, lingering shadow over their fragile grasp on reality.

Chapter 16: The Sacrifice

With the echoes of the ritual still reverberating through the old house, Sheila and Rob grappled with the aftermath of the harrowing sacrifice. The air, thick with the remnants of supernatural energies, carried a spectral resonance that seemed to linger in the haunted dwelling. The whispers, now a distant murmur, guided them through the dimly lit halls as they confronted the irreversible consequences of sealing the ancient evil within the spectral confines.

As Sheila and Rob emerged from the hidden chamber, an unsettling stillness enveloped the old house. The whispers, now a fading memory, left an eerie calm in their wake. The haunted dwelling, though momentarily relieved of the malevolent entity's presence, stood as a silent witness to the sacrifices made in the name of sealing the ancient darkness within its spectral corridors.

However, the calm was deceptive, for a greater malevolence seemed to seep through the very walls of the old house. The air, heavy with the essence of the supernatural, carried an ominous energy that hinted at the lingering darkness within. Sheila and Rob, their senses heightened by the aftermath of the sacrifice, exchanged wary glances as they navigated the dimly lit corridors.

Unbeknownst to them, the sacrifice had unleashed unforeseen consequences—unsettling manifestations that defied rational explanation. Shadows danced on the walls, and whispers, now a dissonant symphony, seemed to echo through the haunted dwelling, conveying a spectral

unrest that transcended the mortal realm. The old house, though momentarily quelled, stood as a battleground where the forces of the living and the supernatural clashed in an otherworldly dance.

As night fell over the old house, the spectral disturbances intensified. Objects moved mysteriously, and the air vibrated with a spectral resonance that hinted at a malevolent force lingering within the haunted dwelling. The whispers, now a relentless drone, guided Sheila and Rob toward the heart of the spectral storm—an impending confrontation with the consequences of the sacrifice.

In the dim light, Sheila and Rob felt an otherworldly presence—an entity that seemed to feed on the residual energies of the sacrificed blood. The whispers, now a haunting lament, spoke of a darkness that sought communion with the living, defying the constraints of the ritual. The haunted dwelling, its spectral foundations shaken by the consequences of the sacrifice, stood as a conduit for the malevolent forces that sought release.

As they explored the old house, Sheila and Rob discovered cryptic symbols appearing on the walls—a manifestation of the supernatural disturbances that had been unleashed. The whispers, now a spectral symphony, guided them through the haunted corridors, conveying the urgency of a greater darkness that loomed on the horizon. The air, charged with an otherworldly energy, carried a spectral resonance that hinted at the impending confrontation with the malevolent entity.

Sheila and Rob sought the guidance of the psychic medium who had assisted them in the cleansing ritual. The whispers, now a haunting melody, seemed to echo through the secluded residence of the medium, conveying the urgency of the situation. The air, thick with the residual energies of the supernatural encounter, guided them toward a revelation that defied comprehension.

The psychic medium, aware of the consequences of the sacrifice, spoke of a greater malevolence that had been awakened—an entity that defied the boundaries of the ritual. The whispers, now a relentless drone, urged Sheila and Rob to confront the looming darkness before

it consumed the haunted dwelling. The air, heavy with the essence of the supernatural, carried a spectral resonance that transcended the mortal realm.

Determined to face the consequences of their actions, Sheila and Rob returned to the old house, armed with newfound knowledge. The whispers, now a spectral chorus, seemed to align with their resolve as they ventured into the dimly lit halls. The haunted dwelling, though momentarily quelled, awaited the final confrontation with the malevolent entity that lingered within its spectral depths.

As night settled over the old house, Sheila and Rob felt the temperature drop—a chilling sign of the entity's presence. Shadows danced on the walls, and the air vibrated with a spectral resonance that hinted at the impending confrontation. The whispers, now a haunting lament, guided them toward the heart of the spectral storm—an epicenter where the forces of the living and the supernatural converged.

In the dim light, Sheila and Rob glimpsed fleeting apparitions—manifestations of the greater darkness that had been unleashed. The whispers, now a dissonant symphony, seemed to speak of a malevolence that sought communion with the living, defying the constraints of the ritual. The haunted dwelling, its spectral foundations saturated with the essence of the supernatural, stood as a battleground where the consequences of the sacrifice unfolded in a terrifying crescendo.

Suddenly, the room quivered with unseen energies, and the temperature plummeted. The whispers, now a spectral chorus, guided Sheila and Rob toward the epicenter of the supernatural disturbance. The air, charged with an otherworldly energy, carried a spectral resonance that hinted at the imminent confrontation with the malevolent entity.

As they approached the heart of the spectral storm, Sheila and Rob felt an oppressive force—a darkness that seemed to envelop them. The whispers, now a relentless drone, seemed to echo through the haunted dwelling, urging them to confront the malevolent entity that lurked within the shadows. The old house, though momentarily quelled, stood

as a stage for the final showdown between the forces of the living and the supernatural.

In the dimly lit chamber, Sheila and Rob confronted the malevolent entity. The whispers, now a haunting melody, guided them through the spectral encounter—a dance between the living and the abyss. The haunted dwelling, its spectral foundations shaken by the consequences of the sacrifice, became a crucible where the boundaries between reality and the supernatural blurred.

The entity, a manifestation of the ancient darkness that had been awakened, spoke through the spectral symphony. The whispers, now a dissonant chorus, conveyed the grievances and malevolence of the malevolent force that sought communion with the living. The haunted dwelling, a conduit for the supernatural forces, bore silent witness to the final showdown that unfolded within its spectral corridors.

Sheila and Rob, their senses heightened by the supernatural onslaught, faced a choice—succumb to the malevolent forces or confront the entity head-on. The whispers, now a relentless drone, urged them toward a revelation that defied comprehension. The haunted dwelling, its spectral foundations saturated with the essence of the living, stood as a battleground where the forces of the living and the supernatural clashed in a terrifying crescendo.

In the dim light, Sheila and Rob glimpsed shadowy figures—apparitions of the past that materialized in the spectral realm. The whispers, now a haunting lament, spoke of the tormented souls that lingered within the haunted dwelling. The air, charged with an otherworldly energy, guided them toward the epicenter of the spectral storm—an impending confrontation with the malevolent entity.

As the entity recoiled, the whispers, now a spectral chorus, intensified. Sheila and Rob, their resolve tested by the supernatural onslaught, faced the malevolent force with determination. The haunted dwelling, its spectral foundations shaken by the consequences of the sacrifice, became a silent witness to the final confrontation between the living and the supernatural.

With an otherworldly surge of energy, Sheila and Rob confronted the entity head-on. The whispers, now a relentless drone, seemed to align with the living as the spectral encounter reached its zenith. The haunted dwelling, its foundations saturated with the essence of the supernatural, stood as a crucible where the forces of light and darkness clashed in a terrifying crescendo.

Unexpectedly, the entity recoiled—a spectral manifestation weakened by the determination of the living. The whispers, now a fading memory, left an eerie stillness in their wake. Sheila and Rob, their senses overwhelmed by the supernatural encounter, stood amidst the remnants of the spectral storm. The haunted dwelling, though momentarily quelled, seemed to sigh with a spectral resignation as if acknowledging the fleeting victory over the malevolent forces.

As Sheila and Rob emerged from the confrontation, a sense of cautious hope lingered in the air. The whispers, now a distant murmur, guided them through the dimly lit halls of the old house—the battleground where the forces of the living had triumphed over the malevolent entity. The haunted dwelling, though forever scarred by the supernatural encounter, stood as a testament to the resilience of those who dared to confront the ancient darkness that lurked within its spectral confines.

Little did Sheila and Rob know that the true horror, a revelation that would redefine their very existence, awaited in the shadows of the haunted dwelling. The whispers, now a fading memory, left the door ajar for the looming terror that awaited in the aftermath of the supernatural sacrifice. Sheila and Rob, bound by the malevolent forces that lingered within, faced an uncertain future where the horrors of the past cast a long, lingering shadow over their fragile grasp on reality.

Chapter 17: The Confrontation

In the aftermath of the supernatural encounter, Sheila and Rob found themselves standing amidst the remnants of the spectral storm that had gripped the old house. The air, heavy with the essence of the supernatural, carried a spectral resonance that hinted at the lingering

forces within the haunted dwelling. The whispers, now a distant murmur, guided them through the dimly lit halls as they grappled with the aftermath of the harrowing confrontation.

As they explored the old house, Sheila and Rob felt a palpable tension—an unsettling energy that seemed to emanate from the very walls. Shadows danced on the walls, and the air vibrated with a spectral resonance that hinted at a lingering malevolence. The whispers, now a haunting lament, guided them toward the heart of the spectral disturbance—an impending confrontation with the consequences of the sacrifice.

Unbeknownst to them, the malevolent entity, though weakened, lingered within the haunted dwelling, seeking revenge for the disruption of its spectral communion. The air, thick with the essence of the supernatural, carried an ominous energy that hinted at the impending clash between the living and the lingering darkness. Sheila and Rob, their nerves on edge, exchanged wary glances as they ventured into the dimly lit corridors.

As night fell over the old house, the spectral disturbances intensified. Objects moved mysteriously, and the whispers, now a relentless drone, seemed to echo through the haunted dwelling. The air, charged with an otherworldly energy, guided Sheila and Rob toward the epicenter of the spectral storm—a confrontation with the malevolent forces that sought release.

In the dim light, Sheila and Rob discovered cryptic symbols appearing on the walls—a manifestation of the supernatural disturbances that had been unleashed. The whispers, now a spectral symphony, intensified as they delved into the haunted corridors, conveying the urgency of a greater darkness that loomed on the horizon. The old house, though momentarily quelled, stood as a battleground where the forces of the living and the supernatural clashed in an otherworldly dance.

Sheila and Rob sought the guidance of the psychic medium who had assisted them in the cleansing ritual. The whispers, now a haunting melody, seemed to echo through the secluded residence of the medium,

conveying the urgency of the situation. The air, thick with the residual energies of the supernatural encounter, guided them toward a revelation that defied comprehension.

The psychic medium, aware of the lingering malevolence, spoke of the entity's resilience—a force that defied the boundaries of the ritual. The whispers, now a relentless drone, urged Sheila and Rob to confront the looming darkness before it consumed the haunted dwelling. The air, heavy with the essence of the supernatural, carried a spectral resonance that transcended the mortal realm.

Determined to face the consequences of their actions, Sheila and Rob returned to the old house, armed with newfound knowledge. The whispers, now a spectral chorus, seemed to align with their resolve as they ventured into the dimly lit halls. The haunted dwelling, though momentarily quelled, awaited the final confrontation with the malevolent entity that lingered within its spectral depths.

As night settled over the old house, Sheila and Rob felt the temperature drop—a chilling sign of the entity's presence. Shadows danced on the walls, and the air vibrated with a spectral resonance that hinted at the impending confrontation. The whispers, now a haunting lament, guided them toward the heart of the spectral storm—an epicenter where the forces of the living and the supernatural converged.

In the dim light, Sheila and Rob glimpsed fleeting apparitions—manifestations of the greater darkness that had been unleashed. The whispers, now a dissonant symphony, seemed to speak of a malevolence that sought communion with the living, defying the constraints of the ritual. The haunted dwelling, its spectral foundations saturated with the essence of the supernatural, stood as a battleground where the consequences of the sacrifice unfolded in a terrifying crescendo.

Suddenly, the room quivered with unseen energies, and the temperature plummeted. The whispers, now a spectral chorus, guided Sheila and Rob toward the epicenter of the supernatural disturbance. The air, charged with an otherworldly energy, carried a spectral resonance that hinted at the imminent confrontation with the malevolent entity.

As they approached the heart of the spectral storm, Sheila and Rob felt an oppressive force—a darkness that seemed to envelop them. The whispers, now a relentless drone, seemed to echo through the haunted dwelling, urging them to confront the malevolent entity that lurked within the shadows. The old house, though momentarily quelled, stood as a stage for the final showdown between the forces of the living and the supernatural.

In the dimly lit chamber, Sheila and Rob confronted the malevolent entity. The whispers, now a haunting melody, guided them through the spectral encounter—a dance between the living and the abyss. The haunted dwelling, its spectral foundations shaken by the consequences of the sacrifice, became a crucible where the boundaries between reality and the supernatural blurred.

The entity, a manifestation of the ancient darkness that had been awakened, spoke through the spectral symphony. The whispers, now a dissonant chorus, conveyed the grievances and malevolence of the malevolent force that sought communion with the living. The haunted dwelling, a conduit for the supernatural forces, bore silent witness to the final showdown that unfolded within its spectral corridors.

Sheila and Rob, their senses heightened by the supernatural on-slaught, faced a choice—succumb to the malevolent forces or confront the entity head-on. The whispers, now a relentless drone, urged them toward a revelation that defied comprehension. The haunted dwelling, its spectral foundations saturated with the essence of the living, stood as a battleground where the forces of the living and the supernatural clashed in a terrifying crescendo.

In the dim light, Sheila and Rob glimpsed shadowy figures—apparitions of the past that materialized in the spectral realm. The whispers, now a haunting lament, spoke of the tormented souls that lingered within the haunted dwelling. The air, charged with an otherworldly energy, guided them toward the epicenter of the spectral storm—an impending confrontation with the malevolent entity.

As the entity recoiled, the whispers, now a spectral chorus, intensified. Sheila and Rob, their resolve tested by the supernatural onslaught, faced the malevolent force with determination. The haunted dwelling, its spectral foundations saturated with the essence of the supernatural, stood as a crucible where the forces of light and darkness clashed in a terrifying crescendo.

Unexpectedly, the entity recoiled—a spectral manifestation weakened by the determination of the living. The whispers, now a fading memory, left an eerie stillness in their wake. Sheila and Rob, their senses overwhelmed by the supernatural encounter, stood amidst the remnants of the spectral storm. The haunted dwelling, though momentarily quelled, seemed to sigh with a spectral resignation as if acknowledging the fleeting victory over the malevolent forces.

As Sheila and Rob emerged from the confrontation, a sense of cautious hope lingered in the air. The whispers, now a distant murmur, guided them through the dimly lit halls of the old house—the battleground where the forces of the living had triumphed over the malevolent entity. The haunted dwelling, though forever scarred by the supernatural encounter, stood as a testament to the resilience of those who dared to confront the ancient darkness that lurked within its spectral confines.

Little did Sheila and Rob know that the true horror, a revelation that would redefine their very existence, awaited in the shadows of the haunted dwelling. The whispers, now a fading memory, left the door ajar for the looming terror that awaited in the aftermath of the supernatural sacrifice. Sheila and Rob, bound by the malevolent forces that lingered within, faced an uncertain future where the horrors of the past cast a long, lingering shadow over their fragile grasp on reality.

Chapter 18: The Resolution

The aftermath of the confrontation left Sheila and Rob in a state of emotional turmoil. The air, thick with the remnants of the supernatural encounter, carried a spectral resonance that seemed to linger within the haunted dwelling. The whispers, now a distant murmur, guided

them through the dimly lit halls as they grappled with the irreversible consequences of the sacrifice and the lingering darkness that clung to the old house.

As they explored the haunted corridors, Sheila and Rob discovered that the malevolent entity, though weakened, had left an indelible mark on the spectral fabric of the old house. Shadows danced on the walls, and the air vibrated with a spectral resonance that hinted at the lingering malevolence. The whispers, now a haunting lament, guided them toward the heart of the spectral disturbance—an exploration of the haunted dwelling's newfound reality.

Unbeknownst to them, the sacrifice had not only sealed the ancient evil but had woven the malevolent forces into the very fabric of the haunted dwelling. The air, heavy with the essence of the supernatural, carried an ominous energy that hinted at the spectral unrest within. Sheila and Rob, their senses heightened by the aftermath of the confrontation, exchanged wary glances as they ventured into the dimly lit corridors.

As night fell over the old house, the spectral disturbances intensified. Objects moved mysteriously, and the whispers, now a relentless drone, seemed to echo through the haunted dwelling. The air, charged with an otherworldly energy, guided Sheila and Rob toward the epicenter of the spectral storm—a realization that the malevolent forces were not entirely quelled.

In the dim light, Sheila and Rob glimpsed cryptic symbols appearing on the walls—a manifestation of the supernatural disturbances that had been woven into the spectral fabric of the old house. The whispers, now a spectral symphony, intensified as they delved into the haunted corridors, conveying the urgency of a greater darkness that loomed on the horizon. The haunted dwelling, though momentarily quelled, stood as a battleground where the forces of the living and the supernatural clashed in an otherworldly dance.

Sheila and Rob sought the guidance of the psychic medium who had assisted them in the cleansing ritual. The whispers, now a haunting

melody, seemed to echo through the secluded residence of the medium, conveying the urgency of the situation. The air, thick with the residual energies of the supernatural encounter, guided them toward a revelation that defied comprehension.

The psychic medium, aware of the lingering malevolence, spoke of the residual energies that had become entwined with the old house's spectral fabric. The whispers, now a relentless drone, urged Sheila and Rob to confront the lingering darkness before it consumed the haunted dwelling. The air, heavy with the essence of the supernatural, carried a spectral resonance that transcended the mortal realm.

Determined to face the consequences of their actions, Sheila and Rob returned to the old house, armed with newfound knowledge. The whispers, now a spectral chorus, seemed to align with their resolve as they ventured into the dimly lit halls. The haunted dwelling, though momentarily quelled, awaited the final confrontation with the residual malevolent forces that lingered within its spectral depths.

As night settled over the old house, Sheila and Rob felt the temperature drop—a chilling sign of the residual entity's presence. Shadows danced on the walls, and the air vibrated with a spectral resonance that hinted at the impending confrontation. The whispers, now a haunting lament, guided them toward the heart of the spectral storm—an epicenter where the forces of the living and the supernatural converged.

In the dim light, Sheila and Rob glimpsed fleeting apparitions—manifestations of the residual darkness that clung to the haunted dwelling. The whispers, now a dissonant symphony, seemed to speak of a malevolence that sought communion with the living, defying the constraints of the ritual. The old house, though momentarily quelled, stood as a battleground where the consequences of the sacrifice unfolded in a terrifying crescendo.

Suddenly, the room quivered with unseen energies, and the temperature plummeted. The whispers, now a spectral chorus, guided Sheila and Rob toward the epicenter of the supernatural disturbance. The air, charged with an otherworldly energy, carried a spectral resonance

that hinted at the imminent confrontation with the residual malevolent forces.

As they approached the heart of the spectral storm, Sheila and Rob felt an oppressive force—a darkness that seemed to envelop them. The whispers, now a relentless drone, seemed to echo through the haunted dwelling, urging them to confront the lingering malevolent forces that lurked within the shadows. The old house, though momentarily quelled, stood as a stage for the final showdown between the forces of the living and the residual supernatural darkness.

In the dimly lit chamber, Sheila and Rob confronted the residual malevolent forces. The whispers, now a haunting melody, guided them through the spectral encounter—a dance between the living and the lingering abyss. The haunted dwelling, its spectral foundations shaken by the consequences of the sacrifice, became a crucible where the boundaries between reality and the residual supernatural blurred.

The residual entity, a manifestation of the ancient darkness that had been entwined with the spectral fabric, spoke through the dissonant chorus. The whispers, now a relentless drone, conveyed the grievances and malevolence of the lingering force that sought communion with the living. The haunted dwelling, a conduit for the residual supernatural forces, bore silent witness to the final showdown that unfolded within its spectral corridors.

Sheila and Rob, their senses heightened by the supernatural on-slaught, faced a choice—succumb to the lingering malevolent forces or confront the residual entity head-on. The whispers, now a relentless drone, urged them toward a revelation that defied comprehension. The haunted dwelling, its spectral foundations saturated with the essence of the living, stood as a battleground where the forces of the living and the residual supernatural clashed in a terrifying crescendo.

In the dim light, Sheila and Rob glimpsed shadowy figures—appa-ritions of the past that materialized in the spectral realm. The whispers, now a haunting lament, spoke of the tormented souls that lingered within the haunted dwelling. The air, charged with an otherworldly

energy, guided them toward the epicenter of the spectral storm—an impending confrontation with the residual malevolent entity.

As the entity recoiled, the whispers, now a spectral chorus, intensified. Sheila and Rob, their resolve tested by the supernatural onslaught, faced the residual malevolent force with determination. The haunted dwelling, its spectral foundations saturated with the essence of the supernatural, stood as a crucible where the forces of light and darkness clashed in a terrifying crescendo.

Unexpectedly, the residual entity recoiled—a spectral manifestation weakened by the determination of the living. The whispers, now a fading memory, left an eerie stillness in their wake. Sheila and Rob, their senses overwhelmed by the supernatural encounter, stood amidst the remnants of the residual spectral storm. The haunted dwelling, though momentarily quelled, seemed to sigh with a spectral resignation as if acknowledging the fleeting victory over the lingering malevolent forces.

As Sheila and Rob emerged from the confrontation, a sense of cautious hope lingered in the air. The whispers, now a distant murmur, guided them through the dimly lit halls of the old house—the battleground where the forces of the living had once again triumphed over the residual malevolent entity. The haunted dwelling, though forever scarred by the supernatural encounter, stood as a testament to the resilience of those who dared to confront the ancient darkness that lingered within its spectral confines.

Little did Sheila and Rob know that the true horror, a revelation that would redefine their very existence, awaited in the shadows of the haunted dwelling. The whispers, now a fading memory, left the door ajar for the looming terror that awaited in the aftermath of the supernatural sacrifice. Sheila and Rob, bound by the lingering forces that clung within, faced an uncertain future where the horrors of the past cast a long, lingering shadow over their fragile grasp on reality.

Chapter 19: The Awakening

As Sheila and Rob emerged from the lingering shadows of the haunted dwelling, a fragile sense of hope clung to the air. The whispers,

now a distant murmur, guided them through the dimly lit halls—the haunted battleground where they had confronted the malevolent forces and the residual darkness. However, the old house, forever scarred by the supernatural encounter, bore the weight of a haunting legacy that transcended the physical realm.

In the aftermath of the confrontation, Sheila and Rob felt a disquieting calm settle over the old house. The air, heavy with the essence of the supernatural, carried a spectral resonance that hinted at the lingering forces within the haunted dwelling. Shadows danced on the walls, and the whispers, now a fading memory, seemed to echo through the spectral corridors—an eerie reminder of the harrowing journey that had unfolded within the confines of the ancient dwelling.

Unbeknownst to them, the supernatural encounter had left an indelible mark on Sheila's soul. As night fell over the old house, a subtle shift occurred within Sheila—an awakening to a new reality that transcended the boundaries of the living. The whispers, now a distant melody, guided her through the haunted corridors, leading her toward a revelation that defied comprehension.

As they explored the old house, Sheila and Rob discovered that the residual energies had imprinted themselves onto the very fabric of Sheila's being. Shadows, now a spectral dance, seemed to weave through her existence, blurring the boundaries between the living and the supernatural. The whispers, now a haunting lament, echoed through her consciousness—an unsettling reminder that the spectral legacy lingered within.

In the dim light, Sheila and Rob witnessed cryptic symbols appearing on Sheila's skin—a manifestation of the supernatural imprint left by the ancient darkness. The whispers, now a spectral symphony, intensified as they delved into the haunted corridors, conveying the urgency of a greater awakening that loomed on the horizon. The old house, though momentarily quelled, stood as a conduit for Sheila's transformation—an evolution that defied the constraints of the mortal realm.

Sheila, grappling with the newfound reality, sought the guidance of the psychic medium who had assisted them in the cleansing ritual. The whispers, now a haunting melody, seemed to echo through the secluded residence of the medium, conveying the urgency of Sheila's awakening. The air, thick with the residual energies of the supernatural encounter, guided them toward a revelation that went beyond the haunted dwelling's spectral confines.

The psychic medium, attuned to the supernatural currents, spoke of Sheila's connection to the ancient darkness—an awakening that defied the boundaries of the ritual. The whispers, now a relentless drone, urged Sheila to embrace the spectral legacy within her. The air, heavy with the essence of the supernatural, carried a spectral resonance that transcended the mortal realm.

Determined to understand the extent of her transformation, Sheila returned to the old house, her senses heightened by the lingering supernatural energies. The whispers, now a spectral chorus, seemed to align with her evolving awareness as she ventured into the dimly lit halls. The haunted dwelling, though scarred by the supernatural encounter, awaited the next chapter in Sheila's journey—an odyssey that would redefine her very existence.

As night settled over the old house, Sheila felt the temperature drop—a chilling sign of her newfound connection to the lingering forces. Shadows danced on the walls, and the air vibrated with a spectral resonance that hinted at the awakening within her. The whispers, now a haunting lament, guided her toward the heart of the spectral storm—an epicenter where the forces of the living and the supernatural converged within her being.

In the dim light, Sheila glimpsed fleeting apparitions—manifestations of the ancient darkness that had become intertwined with her soul. The whispers, now a dissonant symphony, seemed to speak of a malevolence seeking communion with her, defying the constraints of the ritual. The old house, though momentarily quelled, stood as a

witness to Sheila's metamorphosis—an evolution that transcended the boundaries of the living.

Suddenly, the room quivered with unseen energies, and the temperature plummeted. The whispers, now a spectral chorus, intensified as Sheila confronted the epicenter of the supernatural disturbance within herself. The air, charged with an otherworldly energy, carried a spectral resonance that hinted at the imminent confrontation with the ancient darkness that had become a part of her very essence.

As Sheila approached the heart of the spectral storm within her, she felt an oppressive force—an awakening darkness that seemed to envelop her being. The whispers, now a relentless drone, echoed through her consciousness, urging her to confront the malevolent forces that lingered within the depths of her soul. Sheila, standing at the threshold of her own transformation, faced the haunting legacy that had become an integral part of her existence.

In the dimly lit chamber of her consciousness, Sheila confronted the residual malevolent forces that lingered within her. The whispers, now a haunting melody, guided her through the spectral encounter—a dance between her awakened self and the lingering abyss. The haunted dwelling, its spectral foundations shaken by the consequences of the sacrifice, became a crucible where the boundaries between Sheila's reality and the supernatural blurred.

The residual entity within Sheila, a manifestation of the ancient darkness, spoke through the spectral symphony within her soul. The whispers, now a dissonant chorus, conveyed the grievances and malevolence of the lingering force that sought communion with her. Sheila, in a surreal confrontation with her own awakening, faced the ancient darkness that had become intertwined with her very essence. The haunted dwelling, a conduit for the residual supernatural forces, bore silent witness to the final showdown within the depths of Sheila's consciousness.

As Sheila grappled with the malevolent forces within her, the whispers, now a relentless drone, urged her toward a revelation that defied comprehension. The haunted dwelling, its spectral foundations

saturated with the essence of Sheila's transformation, stood as a battleground where the forces of light and darkness clashed in a terrifying crescendo within the depths of her soul.

In the dim light, Sheila glimpsed shadowy figures—apparitions of the past that materialized in the spectral realm within her consciousness. The whispers, now a haunting lament, spoke of the tormented souls that lingered within her awakened self. The air, charged with an otherworldly energy, guided her toward the epicenter of the spectral storm—an impending confrontation with the malevolent entity that had become an integral part of her very existence.

As Sheila confronted the entity within, the whispers, now a spectral chorus, intensified. Her resolve tested by the supernatural onslaught, she faced the residual malevolent force with determination. The haunted dwelling, its spectral foundations saturated with the essence of the supernatural, stood as a crucible where the forces of light and darkness clashed in a terrifying crescendo within the depths of Sheila's soul.

Unexpectedly, the residual entity within Sheila recoiled—a spectral manifestation weakened by her determination to overcome the malevolent forces. The whispers, now a fading memory, left an eerie stillness in the chambers of her consciousness. Sheila, her senses overwhelmed by the supernatural encounter within, stood amidst the remnants of the spectral storm that had unfolded within her soul. The haunted dwelling, though momentarily quelled, seemed to sigh with a spectral resignation as if acknowledging the fleeting victory over the lingering malevolent forces.

As Sheila emerged from the depths of her own awakening, a sense of cautious hope lingered in the air. The whispers, now a distant murmur, guided her through the dimly lit halls of her own consciousness— the battleground where she had triumphed over the malevolent forces within. The haunted dwelling, forever scarred by the supernatural encounter, stood as a testament to the resilience of the human spirit and the capacity to confront the ancient darkness that lurked within one's own soul.

Little did Sheila know that her journey was far from over. The whispers, now a fading memory, left the door ajar for the looming terror that awaited in the aftermath of her awakening. Sheila, forever changed by the harrowing ordeal within herself, faced an uncertain future where the horrors of her own past cast a long, lingering shadow over her fragile grasp on reality. The haunted dwelling, a reflection of her awakened soul, awaited the next chapter in Sheila's journey—a journey that would redefine the very fabric of her existence.

Chapter 20: The Return

In the aftermath of Sheila's awakening, a deceptive calm settled over the old house. The air, thick with the remnants of the supernatural encounter within her soul, carried an unsettling resonance that hinted at the depths of her transformation. The whispers, now a distant murmur, guided Sheila through the dimly lit halls—a haunting reminder of the malevolent forces that lingered within her awakened self.

As night fell over the old house, Sheila's senses heightened, attuned to the subtle shifts in the spectral currents that surrounded her. Shadows danced on the walls, and the air vibrated with a spectral resonance that hinted at the lingering darkness within her. The whispers, now a fading memory, seemed to echo through the haunted corridors—an ominous prelude to the return of the malevolent forces that had become entwined with her very essence.

Unbeknownst to Sheila, her awakening had not only transformed her soul but had left an indelible mark on the haunted dwelling itself. The air, heavy with the essence of the supernatural, carried an ominous energy that hinted at a spectral unrest within the old house. The whispers, now a haunting lament, guided her toward the epicenter of the spectral storm—an awareness that the malevolent forces were not confined to her consciousness alone.

In the dim light, Sheila and Rob witnessed cryptic symbols reappearing on the walls—a manifestation of the malevolent forces that had returned to the spectral fabric of the old house. The whispers, now a spectral symphony, intensified as they delved into the haunted

corridors, conveying the urgency of a greater darkness that loomed on the horizon. The old house, though scarred by the supernatural encounter, stood as a stage for the malevolent forces' return—an encore that defied the constraints of the ritual.

Sheila, grappling with the resurgence of the malevolent forces, sought the guidance of the psychic medium who had assisted them in the cleansing ritual. The whispers, now a haunting melody, seemed to echo through the secluded residence of the medium, conveying the urgency of the situation. The air, thick with the residual energies of the supernatural encounter, guided them toward a revelation that went beyond the haunted dwelling's spectral confines.

The psychic medium, aware of the lingering malevolence, spoke of the malevolent forces' return—an awakening that defied the boundaries of the ritual. The whispers, now a relentless drone, urged Sheila and Rob to confront the looming darkness before it consumed the haunted dwelling. The air, heavy with the essence of the supernatural, carried a spectral resonance that transcended the mortal realm.

Determined to face the consequences of her awakening, Sheila returned to the old house, her senses heightened by the lingering supernatural energies. The whispers, now a spectral chorus, seemed to align with her evolving awareness as she ventured into the dimly lit halls. The haunted dwelling, though scarred by the supernatural encounter, awaited the next chapter in Sheila's journey—an odyssey that would test the limits of her newfound connection to the malevolent forces.

As night settled over the old house, Sheila felt the temperature drop—a chilling sign of the malevolent forces' return. Shadows danced on the walls, and the air vibrated with a spectral resonance that hinted at the impending confrontation. The whispers, now a haunting lament, guided her toward the heart of the spectral storm—an epicenter where the forces of the living and the supernatural converged within her being.

In the dim light, Sheila glimpsed fleeting apparitions—manifestations of the malevolent forces that had returned to the haunted dwelling. The whispers, now a dissonant symphony, seemed to speak of a

malevolence seeking communion with her, defying the constraints of the ritual. The old house, though momentarily quelled, stood as a witness to Sheila's confrontation with the return of the malevolent forces —an encore that echoed through the spectral corridors.

Suddenly, the room quivered with unseen energies, and the temperature plummeted. The whispers, now a spectral chorus, intensified as Sheila confronted the epicenter of the supernatural disturbance within herself. The air, charged with an otherworldly energy, carried a spectral resonance that hinted at the imminent confrontation with the malevolent forces that had returned to the old house.

As Sheila approached the heart of the spectral storm within her, she felt an oppressive force—an awakening darkness that seemed to envelop her being. The whispers, now a relentless drone, echoed through her consciousness, urging her to confront the malevolent forces that lingered within the depths of her soul. Sheila, standing at the threshold of her own transformation, faced the haunting encore that had become an integral part of her existence.

In the dimly lit chamber of her consciousness, Sheila confronted the return of the malevolent forces that lingered within her. The whispers, now a haunting melody, guided her through the spectral encounter—a dance between her awakened self and the lingering abyss. The haunted dwelling, its spectral foundations shaken by the consequences of the sacrifice, became a crucible where the boundaries between Sheila's reality and the return of the malevolent forces blurred.

The malevolent forces within Sheila, a manifestation of the ancient darkness, spoke through the spectral symphony within her soul. The whispers, now a dissonant chorus, conveyed the grievances and malevolence of the lingering force that sought communion with her. Sheila, in a surreal confrontation with the return of the malevolent forces, faced the ancient darkness that had become intertwined with her very essence. The haunted dwelling, a conduit for the malevolent supernatural forces, bore silent witness to the encore within the depths of Sheila's consciousness.

As Sheila grappled with the malevolent forces within her, the whispers, now a relentless drone, urged her toward a revelation that defied comprehension. The haunted dwelling, its spectral foundations saturated with the essence of Sheila's confrontation, stood as a battleground where the forces of light and darkness clashed in a terrifying encore within the depths of her soul.

In the dim light, Sheila glimpsed shadowy figures—apparitions of the past that materialized in the spectral realm within her consciousness. The whispers, now a haunting lament, spoke of the tormented souls that lingered within her awakened self. The air, charged with an otherworldly energy, guided her toward the epicenter of the spectral storm—an impending encore with the malevolent entity that had become an integral part of her very existence.

As Sheila confronted the entity within, the whispers, now a spectral chorus, intensified. Her resolve tested by the supernatural encore, she faced the return of the malevolent force with determination. The haunted dwelling, its spectral foundations saturated with the essence of the supernatural, stood as a crucible where the forces of light and darkness clashed in a terrifying encore within the depths of Sheila's soul.

Unexpectedly, the return of the malevolent forces within Sheila recoiled—a spectral manifestation weakened by her determination to overcome the malevolent encore. The whispers, now a fading memory, left an eerie stillness in the chambers of her consciousness. Sheila, her senses overwhelmed by the supernatural encore within, stood amidst the remnants of the spectral storm that had unfolded within her soul. The haunted dwelling, though momentarily quelled, seemed to sigh with a spectral resignation as if acknowledging the fleeting victory over the lingering malevolent forces.

As Sheila emerged from the depths of her own confrontation, a sense of cautious hope lingered in the air. The whispers, now a distant murmur, guided her through the dimly lit halls of her own consciousness—the battleground where she had triumphed over the malevolent forces within. The haunted dwelling, forever scarred by the supernatural

encore, stood as a testament to the resilience of the human spirit and the capacity to confront the ancient darkness that lurked within one's own soul.

Little did Sheila know that the return of the malevolent forces signaled a new chapter in her journey. The whispers, now a fading memory, left the door ajar for the looming terror that awaited in the aftermath of the supernatural encore. Sheila, forever changed by the harrowing ordeal within herself, faced an uncertain future where the horrors of her own past cast a long, lingering shadow over her fragile grasp on reality. The haunted dwelling, a reflection of her awakened soul, awaited the next chapter in Sheila's journey—a journey that would redefine the very fabric of her existence.

Chapter 21: The Revelation

In the wake of the malevolent forces' return, the old house stood as a silent witness to the unfolding nightmare that awaited Sheila. The air, thick with the supernatural energies that clung to her awakened soul, carried an oppressive weight that seemed to permeate every corner of the haunted dwelling. The whispers, now a distant murmur, guided Sheila through the dimly lit halls—a foreboding prelude to the revelation that awaited in the shadows.

As night fell over the old house, Sheila's senses remained on edge, attuned to the subtle shifts in the spectral currents that surrounded her. Shadows danced on the walls, and the air vibrated with a spectral resonance that hinted at the impending revelation. The whispers, now a fading memory, seemed to echo through the haunted corridors—an eerie reminder of the malevolent forces that lurked within the depths of her awakened self.

Unbeknownst to Sheila, the return of the malevolent forces had not only marked the old house but had woven a dark tapestry that transcended the physical realm. The air, heavy with the essence of the supernatural encore, carried an ominous energy that hinted at a spectral unrest within the very fabric of the haunted dwelling. The whispers, now a haunting lament, guided her toward the epicenter of

the spectral storm—an awareness that the malevolent forces sought not only communion with her soul but also a greater revelation that defied comprehension.

In the dim light, Sheila and Rob witnessed cryptic symbols reappearing on the walls—a manifestation of the malevolent forces that had returned to the spectral fabric of the old house. The whispers, now a spectral symphony, intensified as they delved into the haunted corridors, conveying the urgency of a revelation that went beyond the boundaries of the living. The old house, though momentarily quelled, stood as a stage for the malevolent forces' revelation—an unveiling that defied the constraints of the mortal realm.

Sheila, grappling with the ominous energies that clung to her awakened soul, sought the guidance of the psychic medium who had assisted them in the cleansing ritual. The whispers, now a haunting melody, seemed to echo through the secluded residence of the medium, conveying the urgency of the situation. The air, thick with the residual energies of the supernatural encore, guided them toward a revelation that transcended the haunted dwelling's spectral confines.

The psychic medium, attuned to the supernatural currents, spoke of a revelation that went beyond the malevolent forces' return—an awakening that defied the boundaries of the ritual. The whispers, now a relentless drone, urged Sheila and Rob to confront the looming darkness before it consumed not only their souls but also the very fabric of reality. The air, heavy with the essence of the supernatural, carried a spectral resonance that transcended the mortal realm.

Determined to face the consequences of the revelation, Sheila returned to the old house, her senses heightened by the lingering supernatural energies. The whispers, now a spectral chorus, seemed to align with her evolving awareness as she ventured into the dimly lit halls. The haunted dwelling, scarred by the supernatural encounter and the malevolent encore, awaited the next chapter in Sheila's journey—an odyssey that would test the limits of her newfound connection to the malevolent forces and the revelation that awaited in the shadows.

As night settled over the old house, Sheila felt the temperature drop—a chilling sign of the revelation that loomed on the horizon. Shadows danced on the walls, and the air vibrated with a spectral resonance that hinted at the impending unveiling. The whispers, now a haunting lament, guided her toward the heart of the spectral storm—an epicenter where the forces of the living and the supernatural converged within her being.

In the dim light, Sheila glimpsed fleeting apparitions—manifestations of the malevolent forces that had returned to the haunted dwelling. The whispers, now a dissonant symphony, seemed to speak of a malevolence seeking communion with her, defying the constraints of the ritual. The old house, though momentarily quelled, stood as a witness to Sheila's confrontation with the revelation—an unveiling that echoed through the spectral corridors.

Suddenly, the room quivered with unseen energies, and the temperature plummeted. The whispers, now a spectral chorus, intensified as Sheila confronted the epicenter of the supernatural disturbance within herself. The air, charged with an otherworldly energy, carried a spectral resonance that hinted at the imminent confrontation with the revelation that had become intertwined with her very essence.

As Sheila approached the heart of the spectral storm within her, she felt an oppressive force—an awakening darkness that seemed to envelop her being. The whispers, now a relentless drone, echoed through her consciousness, urging her to confront the malevolent forces and the revelation that lingered within the depths of her soul. Sheila, standing at the threshold of her own transformation, faced the haunting unveiling that had become an integral part of her existence.

In the dimly lit chamber of her consciousness, Sheila confronted the revelation that unfolded within her soul. The whispers, now a haunting melody, guided her through the spectral encounter—a dance between her awakened self and the lingering abyss. The haunted dwelling, its spectral foundations shaken by the consequences of the sacrifice and the

malevolent encore, became a crucible where the boundaries between Sheila's reality and the revelation blurred.

The revelation within Sheila, a manifestation of the ancient darkness, spoke through the spectral symphony within her soul. The whispers, now a dissonant chorus, conveyed the grievances and malevolence of the lingering force that sought communion with her. Sheila, in a surreal confrontation with the revelation, faced the ancient darkness that had become intertwined with her very essence. The haunted dwelling, a conduit for the malevolent supernatural forces and the revelation, bore silent witness to the final unveiling within the depths of Sheila's consciousness.

As Sheila grappled with the malevolent forces and the revelation within her, the whispers, now a relentless drone, urged her toward a revelation that defied comprehension. The haunted dwelling, its spectral foundations saturated with the essence of Sheila's confrontation and the revelation, stood as a battleground where the forces of light and darkness clashed in a terrifying crescendo within the depths of her soul.

In the dim light, Sheila glimpsed shadowy figures—apparitions of the past that materialized in the spectral realm within her consciousness. The whispers, now a haunting lament, spoke of the tormented souls that lingered within her awakened self. The air, charged with an otherworldly energy, guided her toward the epicenter of the spectral storm— an impending revelation with the malevolent entity that had become an integral part of her very existence.

As Sheila confronted the entity within, the whispers, now a spectral chorus, intensified. Her resolve tested by the supernatural onslaught, she faced the revelation and the return of the malevolent force with determination. The haunted dwelling, its spectral foundations saturated with the essence of the supernatural, stood as a crucible where the forces of light and darkness clashed in a terrifying crescendo within the depths of Sheila's soul.

Unexpectedly, the revelation within Sheila recoiled—a spectral manifestation weakened by her determination to overcome the malevolent

forces. The whispers, now a fading memory, left an eerie stillness in the chambers of her consciousness. Sheila, her senses overwhelmed by the supernatural encounter within and the revelation, stood amidst the remnants of the spectral storm that had unfolded within her soul. The haunted dwelling, though momentarily quelled, seemed to sigh with a spectral resignation as if acknowledging the fleeting victory over the lingering malevolent forces and the revelation.

As Sheila emerged from the depths of her own confrontation and the revelation, a sense of cautious hope lingered in the air. The whispers, now a distant murmur, guided her through the dimly lit halls of her own consciousness—the battleground where she had triumphed over the malevolent forces and the revelation within. The haunted dwelling, forever scarred by the supernatural encounter, the malevolent encore, and the revelation, stood as a testament to the resilience of the human spirit and the capacity to confront the ancient darkness that lurked within one's own soul.

Little did Sheila know that the revelation signaled a new chapter in her journey. The whispers, now a fading memory, left the door ajar for the looming terror that awaited in the aftermath of the supernatural encounter, the malevolent encore, and the revelation. Sheila, forever changed by the harrowing ordeal within herself, faced an uncertain future where the horrors of her own past cast a long, lingering shadow over her fragile grasp on reality. The haunted dwelling, a reflection of her awakened soul, awaited the next chapter in Sheila's journey—a journey that would redefine the very fabric of her existence.

Chapter 22: The Sacrifice

As Sheila emerged from the depths of the haunting revelation, an uneasy calm settled over the old house. The air, thick with the remnants of the supernatural encounter, the malevolent encore, and the revelation within her soul, carried a weight that seemed to hang in the dimly lit halls. The whispers, now a distant murmur, guided Sheila through the spectral corridors—an ominous reminder of the malevolent forces and the revelation that lingered within the shadows.

The old house, scarred by the supernatural events that had unfolded within its walls, stood as a testament to the harrowing journey Sheila had traversed. Shadows danced on the walls, and the air vibrated with a spectral resonance that hinted at the lingering darkness within her. The whispers, now a fading memory, seemed to echo through the haunted dwelling—an eerie prelude to the final chapter that awaited Sheila.

Unbeknownst to her, the malevolent forces, the revelation, and the haunting encore had left an indelible mark not only on her soul but also on the spectral fabric of the old house. The air, heavy with the essence of the supernatural, carried an ominous energy that hinted at a lingering presence—a spectral force that awaited the culmination of Sheila's journey. The whispers, now a haunting lament, guided her toward the epicenter of the spectral storm—an awareness that the malevolent forces and the revelation were not mere echoes of the past but a looming threat that sought a resolution.

In the dim light, Sheila and Rob observed cryptic symbols etching themselves onto the walls—a manifestation of the malevolent forces, the revelation, and the encore that had become intertwined with the haunted dwelling. The whispers, now a spectral symphony, intensified as they delved into the haunted corridors, conveying the urgency of a greater darkness that loomed on the horizon. The old house, though momentarily quelled, stood as a stage for the malevolent forces' final act—an act that defied the constraints of the ritual and hinted at a resolution that transcended the boundaries of the living.

Sheila, grappling with the weight of the revelation, sought the guidance of the psychic medium who had assisted them in the cleansing ritual. The whispers, now a haunting melody, seemed to echo through the secluded residence of the medium, conveying the urgency of the situation. The air, thick with the residual energies of the supernatural encounter, the malevolent encore, and the revelation, guided them toward a resolution that went beyond the haunted dwelling's spectral confines.

The psychic medium, aware of the lingering malevolence, spoke of a resolution that defied the boundaries of the ritual. The whispers, now a relentless drone, urged Sheila and Rob to confront the looming darkness before it consumed not only their souls but also the very fabric of reality. The air, heavy with the essence of the supernatural, carried a spectral resonance that transcended the mortal realm.

Determined to face the consequences of the supernatural events, Sheila returned to the old house, her senses heightened by the lingering energies. The whispers, now a spectral chorus, seemed to align with her evolving awareness as she ventured into the dimly lit halls. The haunted dwelling, scarred by the supernatural events and the revelation, awaited the next chapter in Sheila's journey—an odyssey that would test the limits of her newfound connection to the malevolent forces.

As night settled over the old house, Sheila felt the temperature drop—a chilling sign of the impending resolution. Shadows danced on the walls, and the air vibrated with a spectral resonance that hinted at the imminent confrontation. The whispers, now a haunting lament, guided her toward the heart of the spectral storm—an epicenter where the forces of the living and the supernatural converged within her being.

In the dim light, Sheila glimpsed fleeting apparitions—manifestations of the malevolent forces that had returned to the haunted dwelling. The whispers, now a dissonant symphony, seemed to speak of a malevolence seeking communion with her, defying the constraints of the ritual. The old house, though momentarily quelled, stood as a witness to Sheila's confrontation with the resolution—an act that echoed through the spectral corridors.

Suddenly, the room quivered with unseen energies, and the temperature plummeted. The whispers, now a spectral chorus, intensified as Sheila confronted the epicenter of the supernatural disturbance within herself. The air, charged with an otherworldly energy, carried a spectral resonance that hinted at the imminent confrontation with the resolution that had become intertwined with her very essence.

As Sheila approached the heart of the spectral storm within her, she felt an oppressive force—an awakening darkness that seemed to envelop her being. The whispers, now a relentless drone, echoed through her consciousness, urging her to confront the malevolent forces and the resolution that lingered within the depths of her soul. Sheila, standing at the threshold of her own transformation, faced the haunting resolution that had become an integral part of her existence.

In the dimly lit chamber of her consciousness, Sheila confronted the resolution that unfolded within her soul. The whispers, now a haunting melody, guided her through the spectral encounter—a dance between her awakened self and the lingering abyss. The haunted dwelling, its spectral foundations shaken by the consequences of the sacrifice, the malevolent encore, and the revelation, became a crucible where the boundaries between Sheila's reality and the resolution blurred.

The resolution within Sheila, a manifestation of the ancient darkness, spoke through the spectral symphony within her soul. The whispers, now a dissonant chorus, conveyed the grievances and malevolence of the lingering force that sought communion with her. Sheila, in a surreal confrontation with the resolution, faced the ancient darkness that had become intertwined with her very essence. The haunted dwelling, a conduit for the malevolent supernatural forces and the resolution, bore silent witness to the final act within the depths of Sheila's consciousness.

As Sheila grappled with the malevolent forces and the resolution within her, the whispers, now a relentless drone, urged her toward a resolution that defied comprehension. The haunted dwelling, its spectral foundations saturated with the essence of Sheila's confrontation, the malevolent encore, and the revelation, stood as a battleground where the forces of light and darkness clashed in a terrifying crescendo within the depths of her soul.

In the dim light, Sheila glimpsed shadowy figures—apparitions of the past that materialized in the spectral realm within her consciousness. The whispers, now a haunting lament, spoke of the tormented souls

that lingered within her awakened self. The air, charged with an other-worldly energy, guided her toward the epicenter of the spectral storm—an impending resolution with the malevolent entity that had become an integral part of her very existence.

As Sheila confronted the entity within, the whispers, now a spectral chorus, intensified. Her resolve tested by the supernatural onslaught, she faced the resolution and the return of the malevolent force with determination. The haunted dwelling, its spectral foundations saturated with the essence of the supernatural, stood as a crucible where the forces of light and darkness clashed in a terrifying crescendo within the depths of Sheila's soul.

Unexpectedly, the resolution within Sheila recoiled—a spectral manifestation weakened by her determination to overcome the malevolent forces. The whispers, now a fading memory, left an eerie stillness in the chambers of her consciousness. Sheila, her senses overwhelmed by the supernatural encounter, the malevolent encore, and the resolution, stood amidst the remnants of the spectral storm that had unfolded within her soul. The haunted dwelling, though momentarily quelled, seemed to sigh with a spectral resignation as if acknowledging the fleeting victory over the lingering malevolent forces and the resolution.

As Sheila emerged from the depths of her own confrontation and the resolution, a sense of cautious hope lingered in the air. The whispers, now a distant murmur, guided her through the dimly lit halls of her own consciousness—the battleground where she had triumphed over the malevolent forces, the revelation, and the resolution within. The haunted dwelling, forever scarred by the supernatural encounter, stood as a testament to the resilience of the human spirit and the capacity to confront the ancient darkness that lurked within one's own soul.

Little did Sheila know that the resolution marked the final chapter in her journey. The whispers, now a fading memory, left the door ajar for the looming terror that awaited in the aftermath of the supernatural encounter, the malevolent encore, and the revelation. Sheila, forever changed by the harrowing ordeal within herself, faced an uncertain

future where the horrors of her own past cast a long, lingering shadow over her fragile grasp on reality. The haunted dwelling, a reflection of her awakened soul, awaited the next chapter in Sheila's journey—a journey that would redefine the very fabric of her existence.

**The Horror Inside
The House Awaits
By
Doug Hensley
Table Of Contents**

Chapter 1: The New House - Sheila moves into a beautiful but eerie old house, noticing strange noises and feeling uneasy.

Chapter 2: The Whispers - Sheila hears faint voices whispering when alone at night, making her question her sanity.

Chapter 3: The Dark History - Sheila researches the house's past, finding a dark tale of murder and suicide. Chapter 4: The Warning - An elderly neighbor tells Sheila she must leave the house before it's too late. Sheila refuses.

Chapter 5: The Apparition - Sheila sees a ghostly figure staring at her from the hall, but it disappears before she can investigate.

Chapter 6: The Visitor - Sheila's childhood friend Rob stays the night, also experiencing unsettling events in the house.

Chapter 7: The Presence - Doors open on their own, objects move mysteriously, and Sheila feels someone watching, though Rob remains oblivious.

Chapter 8: The Message - Cryptic words are scrawled on the bathroom mirror when Sheila and Rob wake up, leaving them shaken.

Chapter 9: The History Revealed - Sheila finds an old diary explaining gruesome rituals once held in the house's basement.

Chapter 10: The Basement - Sheila and Rob find a secret door leading down to a dark basement. Going down, they trigger a cave-in, trapping them inside.

Chapter 11: The Escape - After finding ritual items in the basement, Sheila and Rob escape and block the basement door, believing the nightmare is over.

Chapter 12: The Attacks - Paranormal attacks on Sheila grow violent. Desperate, she considers holding a seance.

Chapter 13: The Seance - The seance summons malevolent spirits. One possesses Rob, forcing Sheila to take drastic measures.

Chapter 14: The Cleansing - Sheila enlists a psychic medium to cleanse the home. The process seems successful until things escalate again. Chapter 15: The Truth - Research reveals the house was built for occult rituals, with a dark energy woven into the walls. There is only one way to stop it.

Chapter 16: The Sacrifice - Sheila learns she must offer a blood sacrifice in the house to seal the evil presence. She prepares for the ritual.

Chapter 17: The Confrontation - Unexpected twists force Sheila into a final showdown with the sinister forces in the house. All seems lost until she embraces her destiny. Chapter 18: The Resolution - Sheila defeats the evil forces at great personal cost. The house is finally at peace, but so much has changed. Chapter 19: The Awakening - Sheila slowly recovers, adjusting to a new normal. For the first time in years, she feels hope.

Chapter 20: The Return - Strange events make Sheila question if the evil presence was truly eradicated. Ominous signs suggest a greater darkness.

Chapter 21: The Revelation - Sheila discovers the house's evil has corrupted her soul. She must act quickly if she hopes to save herself. Chapter 22: The Sacrifice - Sheila makes one final sacrifice, for her own sake rather than the house's. Her journey ends, for better or worse.

Chapter 1: The New House

Sheila, a young woman seeking a fresh start, moves into a beautiful yet eerie old house. Almost immediately, strange noises and an overwhelming feeling of unease settle in, setting the stage for the supernatural events that will unfold.

Chapter 2: The Whispers As Sheila settles into her new home, she begins hearing faint voices whispering to her when she's alone at night. The mysterious whispers cast doubt on her sanity and create an atmosphere of increasing tension.

Chapter 3: The Dark History Driven by curiosity and a growing sense of dread, Sheila delves into the house's past. Her research reveals a dark tale of murder and suicide, hinting at the malevolent forces that may be at play.

Chapter 4: The Warning An elderly neighbor warns Sheila of impending danger and urges her to leave the house before it's too late. Despite the ominous warning, Sheila stubbornly refuses to abandon her new home.

Chapter 5: The Apparition Sheila's fears intensify when she catches a glimpse of a ghostly figure staring at her from the hall. However, the apparition vanishes before she can investigate further, leaving her to grapple with the supernatural occurrences.

Chapter 6: The Visitor In an attempt to find solace, Sheila invites her childhood friend Rob to stay the night. Rob, too, experiences unsettling events in the house, heightening the sense of foreboding.

Chapter 7: The Presence Doors open on their own, objects move mysteriously, and Sheila senses an unseen presence watching her. Despite the escalating paranormal activity, Rob remains oblivious to the unfolding horror.

Chapter 8: The Message Sheila and Rob wake up to cryptic words scrawled on the bathroom mirror, further deepening the mystery and leaving them shaken. The supernatural forces in the house are making their presence known in unsettling ways.

Chapter 9: The History Revealed Sheila discovers an old diary in the house, unveiling the gruesome rituals that were once held in its dark

basement. The revelation adds a layer of horror to the already chilling atmosphere.

Chapter 10: The Basement Driven by the need to unravel the mysteries surrounding the house, Sheila and Rob find a secret door leading to a dark basement. Their exploration triggers a cave-in, trapping them inside and marking a point of no return.

Chapter 11: The Escape Believing the nightmare is over, Sheila and Rob manage to escape the basement and block the door, thinking they have successfully sealed away the malevolent forces. However, the worst is yet to come.

Chapter 12: The Attacks Paranormal attacks on Sheila escalate, growing increasingly violent. Desperate for answers, she contemplates holding a seance to communicate with the otherworldly entities.

Chapter 13: The Seance The seance takes a dark turn as malevolent spirits are summoned, with one possessing Rob. Sheila is forced to take drastic measures to confront the supernatural threat.

Chapter 14: The Cleansing Sheila enlists the help of a psychic medium to cleanse the home. Initially, the process appears successful, providing a false sense of security. However, the calm is short-lived as the haunting experiences resume.

Chapter 15: The Truth Through extensive research, Sheila uncovers that the house was purposefully built for occult rituals, with a dark energy woven into its very walls. The revelation leaves her with the chilling realization that only one method can put an end to the terror.

Chapter 16: The Sacrifice Sheila learns that she must make a blood sacrifice within the house to seal the evil presence once and for all. As she prepares for the ritual, the gravity of the situation weighs heavily on her.

Chapter 17: The Confrontation Unexpected twists and turns force Sheila into a final showdown with the sinister forces in the house. All seems lost until she embraces her destiny, revealing a strength she never knew she possessed.

Chapter 18: The Resolution At great personal cost, Sheila successfully defeats the evil forces within the house. While the dwelling is finally at peace, the toll on Sheila is profound, leaving her forever changed.

Chapter 19: The Awakening As Sheila slowly recovers, she must adjust to a new normal. For the first time in years, she feels a glimmer of hope, but the scars of the harrowing ordeal run deep.

Chapter 20: The Return Strange events begin to unfold, making Sheila question if the evil presence was truly eradicated. Ominous signs suggest a greater darkness that may linger, threatening to undo everything she thought she had achieved.

Chapter 21: The Revelation In a shocking discovery, Sheila realizes that the house's evil has corrupted her soul. With time running out, she must act swiftly to save herself from the malevolent forces that have taken root within her.

Chapter 22: The Sacrifice In a final, desperate act, Sheila makes one last sacrifice—this time for her own sake rather than the house's. Her journey comes to an end, leaving readers to wonder if the darkness truly dissipates or if it merely finds a new host.

Chapter 1: The New House

The creaking floorboards echoed through the empty rooms as Sheila cautiously stepped into her new home. The air felt heavy, laden with an unspoken history that sent shivers down her spine. The walls, adorned with faded wallpaper, seemed to hold secrets, and the windows allowed only a dim, feeble light to penetrate the gloom.

Sheila's belongings were scattered in disarray, yet the beauty of the old house couldn't be denied. As the sun dipped below the horizon, casting long, eerie shadows across the wooden floors, Sheila couldn't shake the feeling that she was not alone.

Night descended with a whispering chill, and Sheila settled into her bed. But as the clock struck midnight, the house came alive with strange noises. Whispers, soft and elusive, slithered through the silence, causing her heart to race. She strained her ears, catching fragmented words that left her questioning her sanity.

In the dimness, Sheila felt the presence of something unseen. It was as if the very walls held a malevolent secret, a history buried deep within the foundation. Her unease intensified as the whispers grew into an indistinct murmur that seemed to resonate with the pulse of the house.

The next day, Sheila decided to uncover the mysteries surrounding her new abode. Armed with curiosity and a sense of foreboding, she delved into the house's past. Dusty old books and faded photographs revealed a dark tale of murder and suicide that had stained the very essence of the building.

As Sheila immersed herself in the grim accounts of the past, the atmosphere in the house seemed to shift. Shadows danced along the walls, and the temperature dropped, making her breath visible in the cold air. The weight of the house's history pressed upon her, like an invisible hand tightening around her throat.

A knock on the door interrupted Sheila's unsettling discoveries. An elderly neighbor, eyes clouded with concern, warned her of the impending danger that lurked within the house. "Leave, child, before it devours your soul," the old woman pleaded, but Sheila, fueled by stubborn determination, dismissed the ominous advice.

Nightfall brought with it a ghastly apparition. Sheila, bathed in the pale glow of the moonlight, glimpsed a ghostly figure in the hallway. It stared at her with hollow eyes, sending a chill through her veins. Before she could react, the apparition dissolved into the shadows, leaving Sheila trembling in the oppressive silence.

Desperate for solace, Sheila invited her childhood friend Rob to stay the night. As the hours passed, the house unleashed its malevolent grip on them both. Objects moved of their own accord, doors swung open with an otherworldly force, and a pervasive feeling of being watched hung in the air. Yet, Rob remained oblivious to the supernatural dance unfolding around them.

Cryptic messages appeared on the bathroom mirror the following morning. Scrawled in an otherworldly hand, the words sent shivers

down Sheila's spine. The house was communicating with them, leaving an indelible mark on their reality.

With each passing day, the house's dark history unveiled itself in more sinister ways. Sheila discovered an old diary tucked away in a forgotten corner, detailing gruesome rituals held in the very basement she had yet to explore.

Determined to confront the source of the malevolence, Sheila and Rob discovered a hidden door leading to the ominous depths of the basement. The air grew thick with anticipation as they descended, unaware that they were stepping into a trap set by forces beyond their comprehension.

A sudden and violent cave-in trapped Sheila and Rob in the lightless abyss. Panic set in as the walls seemed to close in around them. Shadows danced in the dim illumination of their flashlights, and the oppressive darkness whispered promises of doom.

Hours passed before they managed to escape, their faces etched with fear. Convinced that sealing the basement door had ended the nightmare, Sheila dared to hope for a return to normalcy. Little did she know, the true horror had only just begun.

Paranormal attacks on Sheila intensified, the unseen forces growing bolder and more malevolent. Objects hurled across rooms, chilling whispers turned into guttural growls, and a sinister presence loomed over her every move.

Desperation led Sheila to consider a seance, a desperate attempt to communicate with the entities plaguing her. The air crackled with tension as she and Rob sat in a circle, hands trembling as they called out to the unknown. But the seance took a dark turn, as malevolent spirits seized the opportunity to manifest their malevolence.

Rob, overcome by an unseen force, became a vessel for the malevolent entities. Sheila, faced with a friend turned foe, had no choice but to take drastic measures. The once comforting bonds of friendship now strained under the weight of supernatural possession.

In her quest for salvation, Sheila sought the help of a psychic medium to cleanse the home. The air thickened with anticipation as the medium performed rituals to banish the malevolent entities. For a fleeting moment, the house seemed at peace, and Sheila allowed herself a breath of relief.

However, the calm proved short-lived. The house, it seemed, had only been biding its time. The cleansing had only served to agitate the dormant evil that lingered within the very fabric of the walls.

Driven by an insatiable need for the truth, Sheila's research revealed that the house was purposefully constructed for occult rituals. A dark energy, woven into the very foundation, defied any attempts to eradicate it conventionally. The realization struck her like a physical blow, and the oppressive weight of the house's malevolence pressed down on her soul.

Sheila learned of a chilling solution—one that required a blood sacrifice to seal the evil presence. The revelation sent shivers down her spine, but with unwavering resolve, she prepared for the ritual. The air in the house crackled with a palpable tension as Sheila steeled herself for the harrowing task that lay ahead.

As the appointed hour arrived, Sheila embarked on the ritual, guided by the cryptic instructions she had unearthed. The air thickened with an otherworldly energy as she treaded the fine line between the living and the supernatural. The house seemed to breathe, its walls pulsating with an unholy heartbeat.

Unexpected twists and turns forced Sheila into a final confrontation with the sinister forces that had tormented her. The battle unfolded in a crescendo of terror, with each moment pushing her to the brink of despair. All seemed lost until Sheila, drawing upon a strength she never knew she possessed, embraced her destiny and faced the malevolent entities head-on.

At great personal cost, Sheila emerged victorious. The malevolent forces were banished, and the house fell silent. But victory came at a price—Sheila was forever changed, scarred by the ordeal that had tested her sanity and resilience.

As Sheila grappled with the aftermath of the climactic events, she found herself in a house that bore the marks of the supernatural battle. The once-elegant rooms, now tinged with an otherworldly aura, stood as a testament to the horrors that had unfolded within their walls.

The awakening came slowly for Sheila. She found herself in a surreal new normal, haunted by memories of the malevolence that had once claimed her every waking moment. Yet, for the first time in years, a flicker of hope ignited within her.

But the return to normalcy proved elusive. Strange events unfolded around Sheila, casting doubt on whether the evil presence had truly been eradicated. Ominous signs, subtle yet undeniable, hinted at a darkness that lingered, threatening to unravel everything she had fought so hard to achieve.

In a shocking revelation, Sheila discovered that the house's evil had not only touched the walls but had also corrupted her very soul. Time was of the essence as she grappled with the realization that salvation required swift and decisive action.

The final sacrifice loomed before Sheila—a desperate act to save herself from the malevolent forces that sought to claim her. Her journey reached its conclusion, leaving her standing at the precipice of the unknown. Whether the darkness dissipated or found a new host remained a lingering question, echoing in the silence of the house that had become a battleground between the living and the supernatural.

Chapter 2: The Whispers

As the haunting echoes of the previous night lingered, Sheila awoke to a house cloaked in shadows. The morning light struggled to penetrate the heavy curtains, casting an eerie glow across the room. The unsettling events of the night before weighed on her mind, and a sense of trepidation settled in her chest.

Dragging herself out of bed, Sheila couldn't shake the feeling that the walls were watching her every move. The air seemed to hum with an unnatural energy, and she wondered if the house itself held memories of the whispers that had invaded her sleep.

As dusk settled once again, the atmosphere in the house shifted. The creaking floorboards beneath Sheila's tentative steps seemed to resonate with a spectral rhythm. The shadows danced in a macabre ballet, and the air took on a frigid chill that seeped into her bones.

Alone in the dimly lit living room, Sheila felt a subtle change in the air—a whispering murmur that curled around her consciousness like tendrils of smoke. A strange sensation crawled up her spine, and she strained to catch the fragmented words carried by the unseen voices.

The whispers, soft and elusive, wrapped around her mind like a ghostly embrace. Sheila couldn't discern the origin of the ethereal voices, and a growing unease settled in the pit of her stomach. The words, a dissonant symphony of indistinct muttering, seemed to weave tales of forgotten sorrows and ancient malevolence.

Torn between fear and curiosity, Sheila followed the whispers as they led her through the labyrinthine corridors of the old house. The air grew heavier, and the oppressive darkness seemed to amplify the haunting voices that echoed through the halls.

The night unfolded in a surreal dance of shadows and secrets. Sheila, guided by the mysterious whispers, wandered deeper into the heart of the house. Each step felt like a descent into a realm where reality and the supernatural coexisted in a fragile balance.

In the heart of the house, Sheila found herself standing before a weathered door. The whispers, now a cacophony of urgent voices, beckoned her to open it. Hesitant but driven by an unexplainable force, she turned the rusted doorknob.

The room beyond was shrouded in an impenetrable darkness. The air felt charged with an otherworldly energy, and the whispers reached a fevered pitch. As Sheila stepped into the room, a chilling wind swept through, extinguishing the feeble candlelight that flickered in the corners.

In the profound darkness, shapes and shadows materialized, dancing on the periphery of Sheila's vision. The whispers coalesced into a haunting chorus, a symphony of forgotten souls yearning to be heard.

Goosebumps erupted on Sheila's skin as she realized that she was not alone in the spectral gathering.

The room seemed to pulse with an unseen heartbeat, and Sheila felt a cold breath on the nape of her neck. The whispers, now mere inches away, spoke directly into her mind. Words, ancient and cryptic, intertwined with her thoughts, creating a disorienting fusion of reality and the supernatural.

Sheila, paralyzed by the ghostly communion, struggled to comprehend the weight of the revelations. The whispers spoke of long-buried secrets, of a history stained with sorrow and malevolence. The house, it seemed, held memories that transcended the boundaries of time.

In a crescendo of spectral intensity, the whispers began to echo the names of the departed, their voices rising and falling like a spectral tide. Sheila felt an overwhelming sadness wash over her as she became a vessel for the collective lament of the forgotten souls trapped within the walls.

As the spectral symphony reached its zenith, Sheila's surroundings blurred into a phantasmagoric dreamscape. Shadows danced in a macabre ballet, and ghostly apparitions materialized before her. The faces of the departed stared into her soul, their eyes reflecting an eternity of suffering.

In a sudden, jarring silence, the room plunged into darkness once more. Sheila stood alone, her breath ragged and heart pounding. The weight of the revelations pressed down on her shoulders, and the whispers, now a mere echo in the recesses of her mind, faded into the obscurity of the old house.

Sheila stumbled back into the dimly lit corridor, disoriented and shaken. The whispers, though momentarily silenced, lingered in the air like an unseen specter. The house, now charged with an unsettling energy, seemed to watch her with an intensity that transcended the physical realm.

Haunted by the night's spectral communion, Sheila retreated to the safety of her room. The whispers, though subdued, continued to echo in the corners of her mind. Sleep, an elusive sanctuary, offered no respite

as the haunting voices seeped into her dreams, intertwining reality and nightmare in a disconcerting tapestry.

Morning brought little solace as Sheila grappled with the aftermath of the spectral encounter. The once-charming house now bore the weight of its own history, and every creak and groan seemed to carry the echoes of the departed. The whispers, now a constant companion, followed her every move, leaving her sanity teetering on the edge of an abyss.

As Sheila navigated the mundane tasks of daily life, the spectral voices whispered secrets that tore at the fabric of her understanding. The house, it seemed, held a malevolent legacy that transcended the passage of time, and Sheila found herself entangled in a web of forgotten sorrows and ancient grievances.

The days blurred into a disorienting haze as Sheila, haunted by the whispers, grappled with a reality that seemed to unravel at the seams. The walls, once silent witnesses to the passage of time, now pulsed with an otherworldly energy that defied rational explanation.

In the suffocating embrace of the old house, Sheila faced a choice—succumb to the spectral whispers that threatened to unravel her sanity or confront the malevolent forces that lurked in the shadows. Little did she know that the true horror, like a dormant beast, awaited its awakening in the depths of the house's dark history. The whispers, a prelude to the malevolence that lay ahead, continued to echo through the corridors, weaving a sinister tale that intertwined with Sheila's very existence. The house, a malevolent entity in its own right, had claimed her as its unwilling conduit, a vessel through which the forgotten voices sought to rewrite the narrative of their tragic past. As night fell once again, Sheila stood at the precipice of a nightmare, the echoes of the whispers lingering like a ghostly requiem. The darkness, pregnant with unspoken horrors, awaited its chance to consume her soul. Little did Sheila know that the true terror, the culmination of the spectral whispers, loomed on the horizon, threatening to plunge her into a darkness from which there might be no escape. The whispers, a harbinger of an

ancient malevolence, echoed through the haunted corridors, signaling the beginning of a descent into the heart of terror.

Chapter 3: The Dark History

The day unfolded with a sense of oppressive anticipation as Sheila, haunted by the lingering whispers, delved into the dark history of the house. Dust-covered books, their pages brittle with age, beckoned to her from the shelves, revealing tales of sorrow and malevolence that clung to the very essence of the dwelling.

Sheila's fingers traced the words on the yellowed pages, each revelation a cold breath against her skin. The house, it seemed, bore witness to a tapestry of tragedies—a canvas painted with the blood of those long forgotten. Murmurs of untold horrors seemed to emanate from the pages, seeping into her consciousness like an insidious poison.

The sun dipped below the horizon, casting elongated shadows that danced along the walls. Sheila, now immersed in the chilling accounts of the past, couldn't escape the feeling that the very air she breathed carried the weight of the malevolent history woven into the fabric of the house.

As darkness claimed the landscape outside, Sheila's mind echoed with the stories of those who had once called the house their home. A family torn asunder by betrayal, a forbidden love that led to tragedy, and the anguished cries of lost souls echoed through the corridors, merging with the persistent whispers that lingered like a ghostly chorus.

Driven by a compulsion she couldn't fully comprehend, Sheila unearthed old photographs from a dusty box hidden in the attic. Faces frozen in time stared back at her, their eyes holding the secrets of a bygone era. She felt an inexplicable connection to these spectral visages, as if their silent pleas for remembrance echoed in the recesses of her mind.

The photographs revealed a family whose smiles hid a darker truth—a truth that the house guarded with a possessive malevolence. In one faded picture, a child's eyes seemed to bore into Sheila's soul, a silent plea etched in their depths. The whispers intensified, an unseen

hand guiding her through the labyrinth of familial tragedies that stained the house with a legacy of sorrow.

In her search for understanding, Sheila stumbled upon a hidden compartment in the attic. Within its confines lay a collection of letters, brittle with age and tinged with the desperation of the departed. The correspondence spoke of forbidden rituals and a pact sealed in blood—a pact that bound the souls of the house to an otherworldly realm.

The revelation sent shivers down Sheila's spine as the echoes of the past reverberated in the dimly lit room. The house, it seemed, was a vessel for dark forces that defied the boundaries between the living and the dead. Sheila, now an unwitting participant in the spectral drama, grappled with the weight of the malevolent history that clung to her like a suffocating shroud.

Night descended, and Sheila found herself standing before the door that led to the basement—the epicenter of the house's darkest secrets. The whispers, now a cacophony of spectral voices, urged her to descend into the abyss and confront the malevolence that lurked in the hidden recesses.

The creaking stairs groaned under her weight as Sheila descended into the subterranean realm. The air grew colder with each step, and the oppressive darkness seemed to swallow the feeble light of her flashlight. Shadows clung to the walls like spectral tendrils, and the whispers reached a fevered pitch, guiding her deeper into the heart of the supernatural abyss.

As Sheila entered the basement, a chill crawled up her spine. The room, bathed in an otherworldly gloom, revealed the remnants of forgotten rituals—a sacrificial altar, cryptic symbols etched into the walls, and a palpable malevolence that seemed to pulse with a life of its own.

Sheila's breath caught as she uncovered an old diary amidst the dust-covered artifacts. Its pages, stained with the ink of a tormented soul, detailed the ghastly rituals conducted in the name of an otherworldly entity. The diary spoke of a darkness that hungered for innocent souls, a darkness that had claimed the very foundations of the house.

With trembling hands, Sheila read aloud the incantations that had once reverberated within the cold stone walls. The air thickened with an unseen presence as the words echoed through the basement, awakening the dormant malevolence that lingered like a dormant beast.

A sudden gust of wind extinguished the feeble light, plunging Sheila into a darkness that seemed to consume her very essence. Whispers surrounded her, their voices intertwining with the oppressive silence. Shadows danced in the obscurity, and Sheila felt a spectral presence closing in around her.

As she fumbled to relight her flashlight, Sheila caught a glimpse of ghostly figures that materialized in the shadows. Eyes devoid of life stared at her, their hollow gazes filled with an insatiable hunger. The apparitions seemed to reach out from the shadows, their fingers brushing against her skin like the breath of a long-forgotten nightmare.

In the suffocating darkness, Sheila stumbled backward, her heart pounding in her chest. The whispers, now an anguished wail, reverberated through the basement, creating a dissonant symphony of horror. The malevolent forces that had slumbered within the house were now awake, hungry for the essence of the living.

In a desperate attempt to escape the spectral onslaught, Sheila retraced her steps through the labyrinthine corridors of the basement. The walls seemed to close in around her, and the air pulsed with an otherworldly energy that clung to her like a suffocating fog.

As she reached the basement stairs, a cold hand brushed against the nape of her neck. Sheila recoiled, her senses overwhelmed by the touch of unseen fingers. The whispers, now a maddening cacophony, echoed in her ears like a chorus of the damned.

With every step she climbed, the malevolence pursued her like a relentless shadow. The basement seemed to resist her escape, its unseen tendrils reaching out to claim her soul. Sheila emerged into the dimly lit corridor, gasping for breath as the weight of the supernatural encounter pressed down on her chest.

The house, now a malevolent entity awakened from its slumber, seemed to watch Sheila with an insatiable hunger. The whispers, though momentarily subdued, lingered in the air like a haunting refrain. The basement, a portal to an otherworldly realm, had unleashed a darkness that threatened to consume everything in its path.

Sheila, shaken to her core, stumbled into her room and barricaded the door as if shielding herself from the unseen forces that lurked outside. The whispers, now a persistent hum in the background, continued to echo through the walls, their spectral voices weaving a tapestry of horror that seemed to stretch across time and space.

Sleep, elusive and treacherous, offered no refuge as Sheila found herself trapped in a nightmare that transcended the boundaries of the waking world. Shadows danced on the edges of her consciousness, and ghostly apparitions lurked in the recesses of her dreams.

Morning brought little solace as Sheila awoke to a house shrouded in an oppressive silence. The whispers, though momentarily silenced, lingered like a malevolent residue. The basement, now a forbidden chasm that bridged the realms of the living and the dead, beckoned to her with an unseen gravity.

The day unfolded with a palpable tension as Sheila, now a reluctant participant in a supernatural drama, grappled with the malevolence that had been unleashed. The dark history of the house, etched into its very foundations, loomed like a specter over every room, every corridor.

The house, now a living entity that hungered for the essence of the living, seemed to watch Sheila with an insatiable appetite. The whispers, a relentless chorus that echoed through the haunted halls, hinted at a darkness that transcended the limits of her understanding.

As night descended once again, Sheila stood at the crossroads of horror, the echoes of the dark history pulsating through the very walls. The malevolent forces, awakened from their slumber, awaited their next move in a macabre dance that threatened to consume Sheila's very soul. The house, a conduit for ancient malevolence, seemed to pulse with a malevolent energy that defied all attempts at rational explanation. Little

did Sheila know that the true terror, a malevolent force that transcended the boundaries of the supernatural, awaited its moment to strike in the chilling depths of the haunted dwelling.

Chapter 4: The Warning

The oppressive weight of the malevolent history lingered in the air as Sheila, haunted by the nightmarish events in the basement, found herself thrust deeper into the clutches of the old house. The whispers, though momentarily subdued, continued to echo through the corridors like an unseen presence that refused to be silenced.

As the sun dipped below the horizon, casting long shadows that stretched like spectral fingers, Sheila roamed the dimly lit rooms in a daze. The walls, adorned with faded wallpaper, seemed to close in around her like a suffocating embrace. Every creak and groan of the aging structure resonated with the echoes of the dark history that clung to the very fabric of the dwelling.

In a feeble attempt to regain a semblance of control, Sheila decided to venture outside. The night air, cool and crisp, offered a brief respite from the oppressive atmosphere within the house. As she stepped onto the porch, the world beyond seemed to hold its breath, as if aware of the supernatural forces that pulsed within the walls.

The neighboring houses stood in stoic silence, their windows gazing like empty eyes into the night. A distant streetlamp flickered intermittently, casting eerie shadows that danced on the pavement. Sheila, shivering in the cold, felt an inexplicable sense of being watched—an unseen gaze that followed her every move.

A sudden gust of wind carried with it a spectral whisper that sent a chill down Sheila's spine. The voice, laden with urgency, seemed to carry a warning—an ethereal plea that resonated with the very core of her being. Unsettled, she turned toward the source of the whisper, but the darkness offered no clues, concealing its secrets within its velvety embrace.

Returning to the house, Sheila couldn't escape the feeling that the very air held a sense of foreboding. The whispers, now a constant

companion, seemed to guide her toward the heart of the malevolence that lurked within. As she ascended the creaking stairs, the old house seemed to creak and groan in protest, as if resisting her attempts to uncover its darkest secrets.

The attic, a repository of forgotten artifacts, drew Sheila with an irresistible gravity. The air grew thick with an otherworldly energy as she approached the door leading to the mysterious space. As she turned the doorknob, a fleeting vision of ghostly figures danced on the periphery of her vision, vanishing as quickly as they appeared.

The attic, bathed in the feeble glow of a single bulb, revealed a myriad of forgotten relics—a dusty collection of forgotten memories. Sheila's flashlight illuminated old trunks, moth-eaten clothing, and a peculiar assortment of items that seemed frozen in time. Each artifact, a silent witness to the house's twisted history, exuded an otherworldly aura that seemed to tug at the edges of Sheila's sanity.

Among the forgotten relics, Sheila discovered an old photograph album. Its pages, yellowed with age, unveiled the lives of those who had once called the house their home. Family gatherings frozen in time, celebrations tainted by an unseen darkness, and the eyes of children who seemed to peer through the veil of the past—all spoke of a history steeped in sorrow.

As Sheila flipped through the photographs, a sudden chill settled in the room. Shadows danced along the walls, and the whispers intensified, their urgency now laced with an unspoken dread. The album, like a portal to the past, beckoned her to uncover the secrets that lingered within its pages.

The images told a tale of a family whose smiles concealed a tragic fate. A mother, her eyes reflecting a haunting sadness, held her children close in a sepia-toned embrace. The father, a stern figure with a haunted gaze, seemed to carry the weight of a malevolence that transcended the boundaries of the photograph.

In one particularly unsettling image, Sheila noticed a figure standing in the background—a silhouette that seemed to merge with the

shadows, its eyes staring into the depths of her soul. The whispers, now a dissonant chorus, echoed the name of the figure—an entity known only as "The Watcher."

A sudden realization gripped Sheila—the warnings she had received, the spectral figures in the attic, and the ever-present whispers—all converged on the ominous presence of The Watcher. As she traced the figure's silhouette with her trembling finger, the air thickened with an oppressive energy that seemed to bear the weight of the malevolent entity.

Driven by a desperate need to understand, Sheila decided to consult the elderly neighbor who had issued the initial warning. With the photograph album in hand, she ventured outside once again, the night air carrying with it a sense of impending doom.

The neighbor's house, a weathered structure bathed in the glow of a flickering porch light, seemed to emanate a warmth that stood in stark contrast to the cold atmosphere within Sheila's own dwelling. The old woman, with eyes clouded by the passage of time, opened the door with a knowing look that hinted at a lifetime of secrets.

As Sheila explained the events that had transpired—the whispers, the spectral figures, and the ominous presence of The Watcher—the elderly neighbor listened in solemn silence. When Sheila showed her the photograph album, the neighbor's eyes widened in recognition, and a shiver ran down her spine.

"You've unearthed a dark legacy," the old woman murmured, her voice a hushed whisper that seemed to carry the weight of untold secrets. She invited Sheila inside, where the walls seemed to resonate with a history that had long been buried.

Seated in a dimly lit room adorned with faded tapestries, the neighbor began to weave a tale that sent shivers down Sheila's spine. The house, it seemed, had once been a haven for a family whose lives had become entwined with an otherworldly force—a force that had claimed them in a twisted dance of tragedy.

The elderly neighbor spoke of The Watcher, an entity born from forbidden rituals conducted in the very heart of the house. Its malevolence, fueled by the suffering of the past, lingered like a vengeful specter, a guardian of dark secrets that defied the boundaries between the living and the dead.

The family in the photographs, the whispers, and the spectral figures —all were linked to The Watcher's insatiable hunger for the souls of the living. The old woman's words painted a harrowing picture of a malevolent force that sought to reclaim what had been lost—an entity that fed on the essence of the unsuspecting inhabitants.

As the elderly neighbor spoke, Sheila felt the weight of The Watcher's gaze upon her. The air in the room grew dense with an unseen presence, and the whispers, now a mournful lament, echoed through the walls like a requiem for the damned.

"You must leave this place," the old woman implored, her eyes reflecting a depth of sorrow that seemed to transcend the confines of the room. "The Watcher is awakened, and its hunger knows no bounds. Your very soul is in peril."

Fear gripped Sheila's heart as the magnitude of the malevolence became apparent. The warnings, the whispers, and the dark history of the house all converged on a chilling reality—a reality in which Sheila stood on the precipice of a supernatural abyss.

Determined to confront The Watcher and unravel the malevolent forces that held the house in their clutches, Sheila returned to her home with a sense of grim resolve. The night, now heavy with the weight of unseen eyes, seemed to pulse with an otherworldly energy that hinted at the imminent confrontation.

The house, a silent witness to the unfolding horror, awaited its fate in the embrace of darkness. Sheila, armed with the knowledge of the malevolent history and the warnings of The Watcher's insatiable hunger, steeled herself for a battle that would transcend the boundaries of the living and the dead. The whispers, now a chorus of spectral voices, guided her toward the heart of the supernatural storm that awaited in

the haunted corridors of the old dwelling. Little did she know that the true terror, a confrontation with The Watcher that would redefine the very fabric of reality, loomed on the horizon, threatening to plunge her into a darkness from which there might be no escape. The night, pregnant with the weight of unspoken horrors, unfolded with a spectral symphony that echoed the malevolent legacy of The Watcher—a force that hungered for the essence of the living, a force that would stop at nothing to reclaim what had been lost in the shadows of the past.

Chapter 5: The Apparition

As Sheila braced herself for the impending confrontation with The Watcher, the house seemed to hold its breath in a malevolent silence. The air, thick with the weight of unseen eyes, pressed against her skin like a suffocating shroud. Every step she took echoed in the dimly lit corridors, the whispers guiding her toward the heart of the supernatural storm.

The attic, a spectral realm illuminated by a feeble bulb, awaited her return. The artifacts, relics of a twisted history, seemed to resonate with an otherworldly energy as Sheila ascended the creaking stairs. The photograph album, now a key to the malevolent secrets that lurked within, clutched in her trembling hands, felt like a talisman against the encroaching darkness.

The whispers, now a relentless chorus that echoed through the haunted halls, intensified as Sheila reached the attic. The air pulsed with an unseen presence, and the shadows danced on the walls in a macabre ballet. The photograph album, when opened, revealed spectral figures that seemed to move within the confines of the images—a silent procession of lost souls tethered to The Watcher's insatiable hunger.

With a heavy heart, Sheila placed the photograph album on a dusty table in the center of the attic. The air seemed to vibrate with an unseen energy, and the whispers reached a fevered pitch. A sudden gust of wind extinguished the feeble bulb, plunging the attic into darkness.

In the obscurity, Sheila felt a spectral presence closing in around her. The whispers, now an anguished wail, surrounded her like a ghostly

chorus. The air seemed charged with an otherworldly force as The Watcher's malevolence manifested in the shadows.

A cold breath brushed against Sheila's neck, and she sensed the gaze of unseen eyes upon her. The spectral figures from the photographs materialized in the darkness, their eyes reflecting a hunger that transcended the boundaries of the living and the dead.

In the suffocating darkness, Sheila felt a touch—a caress of unseen fingers that traced the contours of her face. The whispers, now a maddening cacophony, echoed through the attic, creating a dissonant symphony of horror. The Watcher, a malevolent force that defied explanation, sought to claim her soul in a spectral dance of damnation.

Desperation gripped Sheila as she fumbled for her flashlight, the feeble beam cutting through the obscurity like a beacon of fragile hope. The spectral figures, their faces twisted in silent anguish, retreated into the shadows as the light pierced the darkness.

With trembling hands, Sheila retrieved the photograph album. The images, though now devoid of spectral movement, seemed to carry the weight of the malevolent history that clung to the house. The Watcher, its presence still palpable in the obscurity, awaited its chance to strike once again.

The whispers, now a haunting melody, guided Sheila back through the labyrinthine corridors. The old house, a spectral battleground, seemed to pulse with an otherworldly energy that defied rational explanation. As she descended the creaking stairs, the weight of The Watcher's malevolence bore down on her shoulders like an unseen burden.

In the dimly lit living room, Sheila's flashlight revealed a ghostly figure standing in the hall—a silhouette that seemed to merge with the shadows. The Watcher, its form obscured by the darkness, stared at her with eyes that held the emptiness of eternity.

Fear clawed at Sheila's chest as she confronted the spectral entity that lurked within the old house. The whispers, now a mournful lament, echoed through the corridors, intertwining with the malevolent

presence that encircled her. The time for understanding was over; the time for confrontation had arrived.

Sheila, driven by a grim resolve, approached The Watcher. The air seemed to ripple with an unseen force, and the whispers reached a crescendo as she stood face to face with the malevolent entity. The Watcher, a manifestation of forgotten sorrows and ancient grievances, exuded an otherworldly aura that seemed to defy the very laws of nature.

In the spectral confrontation, Sheila felt a cold hand brush against her cheek—a touch that carried the weight of a thousand lost souls. The whispers, now an ethereal chorus, spoke words that resonated with the depths of her consciousness. The Watcher sought communion, a merging of the living and the dead in a twisted dance of supernatural entanglement.

With a surge of determination, Sheila raised the photograph album. The images, now illuminated by the feeble glow of her flashlight, held a spectral resonance that seemed to repel The Watcher. The entity recoiled, its form dissipating like mist in the face of an unseen force.

In the haunting confrontation, Sheila felt a surge of power—the power of the forgotten souls that lingered within the photographs. The whispers, now a triumphant hymn, reverberated through the haunted halls as The Watcher retreated into the shadows. The malevolent force, thwarted by the spectral energy of the past, seemed to dissipate like a fading nightmare.

The old house, once a battleground between the living and the dead, fell silent. The whispers, now a fading echo, lingered in the air like a melancholic melody. Sheila, exhausted and shaken, stood amidst the remnants of the spectral encounter, the photograph album clutched in her trembling hands.

As the oppressive atmosphere lifted, Sheila felt a profound change in the house—a sense of peace that transcended the malevolent legacy of The Watcher. The whispers, though subdued, carried a lingering gratitude, as if the forgotten souls had found solace in the spectral confrontation.

With a heavy heart, Sheila descended into the basement—the very heart of the house's dark history. The air, once thick with malevolence, now held a somber tranquility. The relics of forgotten rituals seemed frozen in time, their significance transformed by the spectral encounter.

In the dim light, Sheila uncovered the old diary—the key to the understanding of the house's twisted past. The pages, though stained with the ink of tormented souls, now bore a sense of closure. The Watcher, defeated by the power of the forgotten, had relinquished its hold on the old dwelling.

As Sheila emerged from the basement, the morning sun began to cast its gentle rays on the once-foreboding structure. The old house, no longer a haven for malevolent forces, seemed to stand in quiet reverence to the spectral encounter that had unfolded within its walls.

The whispers, now a distant echo, guided Sheila to the attic—the epicenter of the supernatural storm. The photograph album, placed back in its dusty corner, exuded a spectral resonance that seemed to linger in the air. The spectral figures within the images, their faces now frozen in peace, bore silent witness to the resolution of a malevolent legacy.

Sheila, now forever changed by the harrowing ordeal, stepped outside into the cool morning air. The neighborhood, once draped in a veil of darkness, now basked in the warmth of the rising sun. The whispers, though a mere memory, carried a final message—a farewell from the forgotten souls who had found redemption in the face of supernatural turmoil.

As Sheila walked away from the old house, the sense of normalcy slowly returned. The neighborhood, once tainted by the malevolent force that had claimed the dwelling, now stood as a testament to the triumph of the living over the specters of the past.

Little did Sheila know that the true horror, a final revelation that would redefine the very fabric of her existence, awaited in the shadows of her newfound peace. The old house, though freed from the clutches of The Watcher, held a secret that would unveil itself in a chilling twist

of fate—one that would test the limits of Sheila's resilience and plunge her into a darkness from which there might be no escape.

The whispers, now a distant memory, left the door open for the looming terror that awaited in the aftermath of the supernatural storm. The haunting melody of the forgotten lingered in the air as Sheila ventured into the uncertain future—a future where the boundaries between the living and the dead remained blurred, and the horrors of the past cast a long, lingering shadow over the new normal that awaited her.

Chapter 6: The Visitor

In the wake of the harrowing confrontation with The Watcher, Sheila grappled with the aftermath of the supernatural storm that had engulfed the old house. The whispers, now a distant echo, left an eerie silence in their wake—a silence that seemed to stretch across the haunted halls like a spectral tapestry.

As Sheila navigated the dimly lit rooms, the old house felt different. The air, once thick with malevolence, now carried a palpable tranquility. The remnants of forgotten rituals in the basement seemed frozen in time, their significance transformed by the spectral encounter. The photograph album, placed back in its dusty corner in the attic, exuded a spectral resonance that lingered like a fading memory.

Despite the apparent peace that settled over the dwelling, Sheila couldn't shake the feeling that the old house held secrets yet to be unveiled. The neighborhood, seemingly untouched by the supernatural turmoil, continued its daily rhythm. Sheila's neighbors, unaware of the malevolent force that had gripped their midst, carried on with their lives in blissful ignorance.

The morning sun cast a warm glow on the neighborhood, and Sheila decided to take a stroll outside. The fresh air, tinged with the scent of dew-kissed grass, offered a reprieve from the suffocating atmosphere within the old house. As she walked down the quiet streets, the whispers, though faint, seemed to guide her steps toward a sense of normalcy.

In the midst of the peaceful neighborhood, Sheila encountered a figure from her past—Rob, her childhood friend who had experienced the unsettling events in the house. Rob, unaware of the supernatural horrors that had transpired, greeted Sheila with a warm smile.

As they exchanged pleasantries, Sheila hesitated to divulge the haunting experiences she had faced. The whispers, now a gentle hum in the background, seemed to caution her against revealing the spectral truth that lingered within the old house. Instead, she chose to enjoy the fleeting moments of normalcy with Rob, hoping to leave the malevolent past behind.

The day unfolded with a semblance of serenity as Sheila and Rob reminisced about their shared childhood memories. Laughter echoed through the air, temporarily drowning out the lingering echoes of the supernatural encounter. The old house, its haunted corridors temporarily silenced, stood as a mere backdrop to the facade of normalcy that enveloped the neighborhood.

As night descended, Sheila invited Rob to stay the night—a decision that would unwittingly drag him into the lingering shadows of the malevolent past. The whispers, though muted, seemed to intensify as darkness cloaked the old house in an otherworldly stillness.

In the dimly lit living room, Sheila and Rob shared stories from their past, seeking refuge in the familiarity of friendship. The air, though seemingly calm, held a sense of foreboding as the whispers, now a spectral melody, intertwined with the gentle hum of the night.

As they settled in for the night, Sheila couldn't escape the feeling that The Watcher's malevolence lingered in the shadows. The spectral figures from the photographs, now etched in her memory, seemed to cast ghostly shadows on the walls. The old house, once a haven for dark forces, bore silent witness to the unsuspecting visitors who dared to cross its threshold.

The night progressed in a semblance of tranquility, the whispers fading into the background. Yet, as the clock ticked towards midnight, an unspoken tension enveloped the dwelling. Sheila, restless and haunted

by the memories of the supernatural storm, found herself drawn to the attic—the epicenter of the spectral encounter.

In the attic, the photograph album lay in its dusty corner, seemingly untouched by the passage of time. The whispers, though muted, urged Sheila to revisit the malevolent history that clung to the old house. With a heavy heart, she opened the album, its pages revealing the spectral figures that had once danced within its confines.

As Sheila traced the images with her trembling finger, a sudden gust of wind extinguished the feeble bulb, plunging the attic into darkness. The whispers, now a mournful lament, echoed through the spectral realm as the photographs seemed to come to life once again.

In the obscurity, Sheila felt a spectral presence closing in around her. The whispers, now a dissonant chorus, spoke words that seemed to reverberate with the anguished cries of the forgotten. The Watcher, its malevolence not fully vanquished, sought communion with the living in a macabre dance of supernatural entanglement.

Rob, stirred from his sleep by the eerie atmosphere, joined Sheila in the attic. The air seemed to vibrate with an unseen force as the whispers guided them toward the heart of the spectral storm. The photograph album, now a conduit to the malevolent past, exuded an otherworldly energy that drew them deeper into the supernatural abyss.

As they stood in the darkness, the spectral figures from the photographs materialized around them. Eyes devoid of life stared at Sheila and Rob, their hollow gazes filled with an insatiable hunger. The whispers, now a haunting melody, spoke of unresolved sorrows that lingered within the old house.

In the spectral confrontation, Sheila and Rob felt the weight of unseen eyes upon them. The Watcher, though seemingly thwarted, manifested in the shadows with a renewed malevolence. The whispers, now a spectral symphony, hinted at a darkness that defied the boundaries of the living and the dead.

Desperation gripped Sheila as she clutched the photograph album. The images, now illuminated by the feeble glow of Rob's flashlight,

held a spectral resonance that seemed to repel The Watcher. The entity recoiled, its form dissipating like mist in the face of an unseen force.

In the haunting confrontation, Sheila and Rob felt a surge of power—the power of the forgotten souls that lingered within the photographs. The whispers, now a triumphant hymn, reverberated through the haunted attic as The Watcher retreated into the shadows. The malevolent force, though temporarily thwarted, lingered like a specter in the lingering darkness.

The attic, once a battleground between the living and the dead, fell silent. The whispers, now a fading echo, left an eerie stillness in their wake. Sheila and Rob, exhausted and shaken, stood amidst the remnants of the spectral encounter, the photograph album a testament to the unresolved sorrows that clung to the old house.

As they descended from the attic, the old house seemed to sigh with a spectral resignation. The whispers, though subdued, lingered in the air like a melancholic melody. The night, pregnant with the weight of unspoken horrors, unfolded with a sense of uncertainty—a future where the boundaries between the living and the dead remained blurred.

Sheila and Rob, now forever entwined in the malevolent legacy of the old house, sought refuge in the dimly lit living room. The whispers, though muted, hinted at a lingering terror that awaited in the shadows. Little did they know that the true horror, a revelation that would redefine the very fabric of their existence, loomed on the horizon—a revelation that would test the limits of their resilience and plunge them into a darkness from which there might be no escape.

The whispers, now a distant murmur, left the door ajar for the looming terror that awaited in the aftermath of the spectral storm. The old house, its haunted corridors pulsating with unresolved sorrows, stood as a gateway to a supernatural abyss. Sheila and Rob, bound by the malevolent forces that lingered within, faced an uncertain future where the horrors of the past cast a long, lingering shadow over their fragile grasp on reality.

Chapter 7: The Presence

The night, once a harbinger of supernatural turmoil, descended upon the old house with an unsettling stillness. Sheila and Rob, shaken by the spectral encounter in the attic, sought solace in the dimly lit living room. The air, though seemingly calm, carried an unspoken tension—a tension that seemed to thicken with every passing moment.

As they sat in the silence, the whispers, now a muted hum, seemed to guide Sheila's attention toward the shadows that lurked in the corners of the room. The old house, a silent witness to the malevolent forces that had unfolded within its walls, exuded an otherworldly energy that defied the confines of the living and the dead.

A subtle chill crept through the air as the temperature in the room dropped. The whispers, though faint, took on a dissonant tone—a spectral melody that hinted at the lingering presence of The Watcher. Sheila and Rob, their senses heightened by the supernatural ordeal, felt an unseen gaze upon them.

In the dim light, objects in the room seemed to shift mysteriously. A picture frame trembled on the wall, and the flickering flame of a candle cast dancing shadows that defied the laws of physics. The old house, now a conduit for the residual malevolence, pulsed with an unseen force that sought communion with the living.

Unease settled over Sheila and Rob as they exchanged wary glances. The whispers, now a spectral chorus, seemed to speak of a malevolent force that had not been fully vanquished—a force that lingered in the shadows, biding its time for a resurgence. The old house, once a haven for dark rituals, held its secrets close, and the unsuspecting inhabitants stood at the mercy of the supernatural storm that raged within its walls.

In an attempt to dispel the ominous atmosphere, Sheila suggested a distraction—turning on the television to drown out the spectral whispers. As they sat on the worn-out couch, the flickering images on the screen seemed to offer a brief respite from the encroaching darkness. However, the shadows that danced in the periphery of their vision hinted at a malevolence that refused to be ignored.

The night unfolded with a deceptive calmness, the television casting a pale glow that struggled against the encroaching darkness. Sheila and Rob, though attempting to maintain a façade of normalcy, couldn't shake the feeling that The Watcher's presence lingered like a spectral specter in the room.

As the clock struck midnight, a sudden drop in temperature sent shivers down their spines. The whispers, now a mournful wail, echoed through the haunted halls, creating an ethereal symphony of dread. Sheila and Rob, bound by the malevolent legacy of the old house, felt an unseen force closing in around them.

In the dim light, a shadowy figure materialized in the hall—a silhouette that seemed to defy the laws of the physical world. The Watcher, its malevolence not fully quelled, stood as a spectral guardian in the shadows. The whispers, now a dissonant chorus, spoke of an unresolved darkness that sought to reclaim the living.

Fear gripped Sheila and Rob as The Watcher's presence manifested in the room. The air seemed charged with an otherworldly energy as the entity, now a tangible force, cast a haunting gaze upon the unsuspecting visitors. The whispers, though muted, carried a warning—an anguished plea to leave the old house before it succumbed to the malevolent forces that clung to its very foundations.

In a desperate attempt to defy the encroaching darkness, Sheila and Rob decided to leave the living room and venture into the seemingly unaffected parts of the house. The whispers, now a relentless drone, seemed to guide them toward the heart of the supernatural storm.

As they ascended the creaking stairs, the oppressive atmosphere intensified. The walls, adorned with faded wallpaper, seemed to close in around them like a suffocating embrace. The Watcher's presence, a spectral entity that defied rational explanation, pulsed with an unseen force that sought to ensnare their very souls.

In the upstairs hallway, a door creaked open on its own—a manifestation of the lingering malevolence that gripped the old house. The whispers, now a haunting lament, guided Sheila and Rob toward the

threshold of the mysteriously opened door. The room beyond, bathed in an unnatural darkness, beckoned them to confront the unresolved sorrows that lingered within.

As they entered the room, the air thickened with an oppressive energy. The temperature dropped, and the whispers reached a fevered pitch. The Watcher's presence, now an undeniable force, seemed to coalesce in the shadows—a spectral guardian that stood between the living and the abyss.

In the dim light, Sheila and Rob discovered an old mirror—a relic that seemed to hold the key to the malevolent forces that plagued the old house. The whispers, now a cacophony of spectral voices, spoke of a dark energy woven into the very fabric of the reflection.

As they stared into the mirror, their reflections seemed distorted—a ghastly image that hinted at the malevolent entity that lurked within the haunted dwelling. The Watcher, its form now a nightmarish apparition in the reflective surface, bore silent witness to the unfolding confrontation.

A sudden realization gripped Sheila—the mirror, a conduit for The Watcher's malevolence, held the key to the unresolved darkness that clung to the old house. The whispers, though chaotic, seemed to guide her toward a revelation that would redefine the boundaries between the living and the dead.

Driven by a grim resolve, Sheila and Rob decided to confront The Watcher through the mirror—a ritual that promised to unveil the malevolent forces that lurked within. The room, now bathed in an otherworldly glow, felt like a spectral battleground where the living and the dead converged in a macabre dance of supernatural entanglement.

As they stood before the mirror, the whispers reached a crescendo. The Watcher's apparition, now a nightmarish entity that defied description, materialized in the reflective surface. The air seemed to vibrate with an unseen force as Sheila and Rob prepared to confront the malevolent force that had haunted them.

The room, now a spectral realm suspended between the living and the dead, bore witness to the spectral encounter. The Watcher, its malevolence intensified by the confrontation, sought communion with the living in a ghastly manifestation that defied the laws of nature.

In the mirror's reflection, Sheila and Rob felt the weight of unseen eyes upon them. The Watcher's gaze, a haunting stare that held the emptiness of eternity, sought to penetrate the very depths of their souls. The whispers, now a mournful hymn, intertwined with the oppressive energy as the supernatural battle unfolded.

With a surge of spectral power, Sheila and Rob confronted The Watcher through the mirror. The whispers, though chaotic, seemed to align with the living, creating a dissonant symphony that echoed through the spectral realm. The Watcher, now faced with the combined resilience of the living, recoiled in the face of an unseen force.

In the haunting confrontation, the mirror shattered—an explosion of glass that seemed to reverberate through the haunted halls. The Watcher's malevolence, now fractured and dispersed, retreated into the shadows like a fading nightmare. The room, once a battleground between the living and the abyss, fell silent.

Sheila and Rob, exhausted and shaken, stood amidst the shards of the shattered mirror. The whispers, now a distant echo, carried a sense of fleeting victory. The old house, though still haunted by the malevolent forces that clung to its foundations, seemed to sigh with a spectral resignation.

The night, now heavy with the weight of supernatural turmoil, unfolded with an unsettling stillness. Sheila and Rob, their resolve tested by the spectral encounter, descended from the upstairs realm and returned to the living room. The air, though laden with the remnants of the supernatural battle, felt lighter as if a temporary reprieve had been granted.

Little did they know that the true horror, a revelation that would redefine the very fabric of their existence, awaited in the shadows of their newfound victory. The old house, though temporarily quelled, held

secrets that would unveil themselves in a chilling twist of fate—one that would test the limits of Sheila and Rob's resilience and plunge them into a darkness from which there might be no escape.

The whispers, now a fading memory, left the door ajar for the looming terror that awaited in the aftermath of the spectral storm. The old house, its haunted corridors pulsating with unresolved sorrows, stood as a gateway to a supernatural abyss. Sheila and Rob, bound by the malevolent forces that lingered within, faced an uncertain future where the horrors of the past cast a long, lingering shadow over their fragile grasp on reality.

Chapter 8: The Message

The night, now heavy with the echoes of the spectral confrontation, unfolded with an eerie stillness in the old house. Sheila and Rob, their nerves still on edge from the encounter in the haunted room, sought refuge in the dimly lit living room. The air, though seemingly calm, carried the residual tension of the supernatural battle that had unfolded within the haunted dwelling.

As they settled on the worn-out couch, the whispers, though subdued, lingered in the air like a spectral melody. The old house, once a haven for dark rituals and spectral forces, seemed to hold its breath in the aftermath of the shattered mirror. Sheila and Rob, their senses heightened by the otherworldly encounter, exchanged wary glances as they awaited the next manifestation of The Watcher's malevolence.

The television, now a mere flickering glow in the dim room, offered a semblance of normalcy. Sheila, attempting to distract herself from the lingering horrors, suggested turning on the lights to dispel the encroaching darkness. As she reached for the switch, a sudden power outage plunged the old house into complete darkness.

In the pitch-black silence, the whispers intensified. The air seemed charged with an otherworldly energy, and a sense of dread settled over Sheila and Rob like a suffocating shroud. The old house, now devoid of any artificial illumination, became a spectral realm where the living and the dead coexisted in an uneasy truce.

Amidst the darkness, an ominous presence loomed—a manifestation of The Watcher's lingering malevolence. The whispers, now a dissonant chorus, guided Sheila and Rob toward the heart of the supernatural storm. The basement, a place fraught with the echoes of forgotten rituals, beckoned them to confront the unresolved darkness that clung to the old house.

With flashlights in hand, Sheila and Rob descended into the dimly lit basement. The air, thick with the weight of unseen eyes, seemed to pulse with a spectral energy that transcended the boundaries of the living and the dead. The whispers, now a haunting murmur, guided them toward a message—a cryptic revelation that awaited in the subterranean depths.

In the basement, amidst the relics of forgotten rituals, Sheila discovered an old Ouija board—an artifact that seemed to carry the spectral residue of past seances. The whispers, now a relentless drone, urged them to communicate with the other side in a desperate attempt to unravel the malevolent mysteries that clung to the old house.

With hesitant resolve, Sheila and Rob placed their trembling hands on the planchette. The Ouija board, now a conduit for the spectral forces, seemed to come alive with an otherworldly energy. The whispers, though chaotic, aligned with the planchette's movements, guiding them through a spectral conversation with the entities that lingered in the shadows.

As they sought answers from the other side, the planchette spelled out cryptic words on the Ouija board. The whispers, now a spectral symphony, intensified as the message unfolded. "He watches," the planchette spelled out, the words etched in an otherworldly script that seemed to defy rational explanation.

A chill ran down Sheila's spine as the whispers spoke of The Watcher's insatiable hunger—an entity that observed the living with an unrelenting gaze. The message, though cryptic, hinted at a darkness that transcended the boundaries of the living and the dead. The old house,

a silent witness to the supernatural turmoil, bore witness to a revelation that would redefine the very fabric of reality.

In the dim light of the basement, Sheila and Rob felt an unseen force closing in around them. The whispers, now a haunting melody, intertwined with the spectral energy that permeated the air. The Ouija board, a conduit for the malevolent forces, seemed to carry a message from beyond—a message that foretold a greater darkness that awaited in the shadows.

With a sense of trepidation, Sheila and Rob decided to delve deeper into the basement—a place where the old house's dark history unfolded in the form of forgotten rituals and malevolent entities. The whispers, though chaotic, seemed to guide them toward an altar—a focal point of the supernatural energies that pulsed through the subterranean depths.

As they reached the heart of the basement, a cold wind swept through the air—a spectral breeze that carried with it the echoes of forgotten incantations. The whispers, now a mournful lament, spoke of a ritual that could potentially unveil the true nature of The Watcher's malevolence.

On the altar, Sheila found an ancient book—an occult tome that detailed the dark history woven into the very foundations of the old house. The whispers, though fragmented, urged her to decipher the cryptic symbols and incantations that adorned the pages. The malevolent legacy, now laid bare in the pages of the ancient book, hinted at a supernatural force that defied comprehension.

With a heavy heart, Sheila began to read aloud the incantations—a desperate attempt to commune with the entities that lingered in the shadows. The whispers, now a spectral chorus, seemed to align with the words of the ritual, creating a dissonant symphony that reverberated through the basement.

As the incantations reached a fevered pitch, the air in the basement seemed to warp and twist. Shadows danced on the walls, and the whispers, now a cacophony of spectral voices, spoke of a portal—a gateway between the living and the abyss. The old house, its spectral foundations

shaken by the unfolding ritual, became a conduit for the malevolent forces that sought communion with the living.

In the dim light, the basement transformed into a spectral realm—a place suspended between the living and the dead. The whispers, now an anguished wail, guided Sheila and Rob toward the heart of the supernatural storm. The ritual, though wrought with danger, promised to unveil the true nature of The Watcher's malevolence.

As they stood at the precipice of the ritual's culmination, a sudden gust of wind extinguished their flashlights. Darkness enveloped them, and the whispers, now a relentless drone, seemed to merge with the shadows that danced in the spectral realm. The Ouija board, the ancient book, and the altar became mere silhouettes in the obscurity—a spectral tableau that hinted at the imminent confrontation with the unknown.

In the darkness, Sheila and Rob felt a surge of supernatural energy—the very fabric of reality seemed to warp and bend. The whispers, now a spectral symphony, reached a crescendo as the ritual reached its zenith. The portal, a shimmering gateway between the living and the abyss, beckoned them to confront the malevolent forces that awaited on the other side.

With a hesitant step, Sheila and Rob crossed the threshold of the portal. The whispers, now a haunting melody, surrounded them like a ghostly chorus. The old house, its foundations shaken by the unfolding ritual, bore silent witness to the spectral encounter that transcended the boundaries of the living and the dead.

As they entered the other side, the supernatural realm unfolded with an eerie beauty. Ethereal

Chapter 9: The History Revealed

In the supernatural realm beyond the portal, Sheila and Rob found themselves surrounded by a surreal landscape. Ghostly echoes of forgotten rituals and spectral entities painted the ethereal canvas. The whispers, now a haunting melody, guided them deeper into the spectral abyss—a place where the dark history of the old house unraveled in a dissonant symphony of the supernatural.

As they ventured through the ghostly landscape, Sheila and Rob discovered fragments of the past—a spectral montage that revealed the horrors once held within the old house's walls. The whispers, though fragmented, spoke of gruesome rituals and malevolent entities that had left an indelible mark on the haunted dwelling.

Images of hooded figures engaged in forbidden ceremonies danced before their eyes. The air, thick with the scent of incense and spectral energy, carried the echoes of tormented souls who had fallen victim to the malevolent forces that once reigned in the old house. The whispers, now a mournful lament, spoke of an occult legacy woven into the very fabric of the supernatural realm.

In their spectral journey, Sheila and Rob stumbled upon an ancient diary—an artifact that seemed to hold the key to the malevolent history that plagued the old house. The diary, its pages yellowed with age, detailed the dark rituals that had once unfolded in the basement. The whispers, now a spectral chorus, urged them to read the words that revealed the origin of The Watcher's malevolence.

As Sheila deciphered the cryptic entries, the images of hooded figures engaging in occult ceremonies became vivid in her mind. The diary spoke of a cult that had once thrived within the old house, conducting rituals that sought communion with otherworldly entities. The whispers, though haunting, hinted at a darkness that transcended the boundaries of the living and the dead.

In the spectral realm, Sheila and Rob felt the weight of the forgotten souls that had fallen victim to the cult's malevolence. The air, charged with an otherworldly energy, seemed to vibrate with the echoes of tormented cries. The old house, once a haven for dark forces, bore witness to the anguished spirits that lingered within the supernatural tapestry.

As they delved deeper into the spectral landscape, the whispers guided them toward a hidden chamber—a place where the cult's rituals had reached their zenith. The air in the chamber felt oppressive, and the whispers, now a relentless drone, seemed to speak of a malevolent energy woven into the very walls of the old house.

In the chamber, Sheila and Rob discovered an altar—an ancient stone slab adorned with cryptic symbols. The whispers, now a cacophony of spectral voices, spoke of blood sacrifices and forbidden rites that had stained the altar with the anguish of the forgotten. The old house, its spectral foundations steeped in the malevolent legacy, became a witness to the horrors that had transpired within its confines.

The images in the spectral landscape became more vivid—a macabre display of hooded figures performing dark rituals in the dimly lit chamber. The whispers, now a mournful hymn, conveyed the desperation of the tormented souls who had once walked the halls of the old house. Sheila and Rob, entwined in the spectral tapestry, felt the weight of the dark history that clung to their very beings.

As they reached the climax of the spectral journey, the whispers guided them toward a hidden passage in the chamber. A secret door, concealed by centuries-old dust, beckoned them to confront the source of The Watcher's malevolence. The old house, its spectral corridors pulsating with the echoes of the past, stood as a gateway to a deeper darkness that awaited in the shadows.

With trepidation, Sheila and Rob opened the secret door, revealing a staircase that descended into the depths of the supernatural realm. The air, now thick with the energy of the forgotten, guided them toward an underground cavern—a place where the cult's rituals had once reached their zenith.

In the cavern, the whispers reached a fevered pitch. The air seemed charged with an unseen force as Sheila and Rob navigated through the dimly lit passages. The walls, adorned with ancient symbols, spoke of a dark energy that permeated the very foundations of the old house.

As they reached the heart of the cavern, a revelation unfolded—a sacrificial chamber adorned with an altar bathed in an otherworldly glow. The whispers, now a dissonant symphony, spoke of the need for a blood sacrifice to seal the malevolent forces that lingered within the old house. Sheila and Rob, bound by the supernatural forces that guided

their journey, faced an unimaginable choice that would redefine the very fabric of their existence.

The images in the cavern came to life—a spectral replay of the cult's rituals and the sacrifices that had stained the altar with the blood of the innocent. The whispers, now a haunting melody, spoke of The Watcher's insatiable hunger and the need for a final sacrifice to quell the malevolent forces.

In the cavern's depths, Sheila and Rob confronted the truth—the old house, built for occult rituals, held a dark energy woven into its very walls. The whispers, though chaotic, conveyed a revelation that transcended the boundaries of the living and the dead. The sacrificial chamber, a place where the malevolent legacy reached its zenith, became a battleground between the supernatural and the mortal.

With a heavy heart, Sheila and Rob realized the only way to seal the malevolent forces was through a blood sacrifice. The whispers, now a mournful lament, spoke of the necessity to offer a part of themselves to quell the insatiable hunger of The Watcher. The old house, its spectral foundations shaken by the revelation, stood as a testament to the price that must be paid to vanquish the malevolent legacy.

In the dim light of the sacrificial chamber, Sheila and Rob prepared for the ritual—a desperate attempt to seal the malevolent forces that clung to the old house. The whispers, now a spectral symphony, guided them through the ancient rites that had once unleashed the supernatural storm within the haunted dwelling.

As the ritual reached its climax, Sheila and Rob felt an otherworldly energy enveloping them. The air pulsed with the echoes of forgotten incantations, and the sacrificial chamber seemed to vibrate with a spectral resonance. The whispers, though haunting, guided them toward a destiny entwined with the malevolent forces that sought communion with the living.

With a surge of supernatural power, Sheila and Rob offered a part of themselves to the sacrificial chamber. The whispers, now a triumphant hymn, echoed through the cavern as their sacrifice became a beacon of

light in the spectral darkness. The old house, its foundations saturated with the essence of the living, stood at the precipice of a resolution that transcended the boundaries of the mortal realm.

In the aftermath of the ritual, the cavern fell silent. The whispers, though fading, left an eerie stillness in their wake. Sheila and Rob, exhausted and shaken, stood amidst the spectral remnants of the sacrificial chamber. The old house, though still haunted by the echoes of the past, seemed to sigh with a spectral resignation.

The supernatural realm, now devoid of the malevolent forces that once tormented the haunted dwelling, unfolded with an unsettling stillness. Sheila and Rob, their journey through the spectral abyss complete, ascended from the underground cavern and returned to the haunted halls of the old house.

As they emerged into the dim light of the old house, a sense of eerie calm settled over them. The whispers, now a distant echo, carried a semblance of victory—a fleeting reprieve from the encroaching darkness. Little did they know that the true challenge awaited in the aftermath of the ritual—a revelation that would test the limits of their resilience and plunge them into a darkness from which there might be no escape.

The old house, though temporarily quelled, bore witness to the sacrifices made to seal the malevolent forces within its spectral confines. Sheila and Rob, forever changed by the ritual, faced an uncertain future where the echoes of the past lingered like a spectral shadow. The whispers, now a fading memory, left the door ajar for the looming terror that awaited in the aftermath of the spectral storm.

In the dim light of the old house, Sheila and Rob, their spirits weighed down by the sacrifice, descended from the underground cavern and returned to the living room. The air, though laden with the remnants of the supernatural battle, felt lighter as if a temporary reprieve had been granted.

As they navigated the haunted halls, a realization gripped Sheila and Rob—the old house, though temporarily quelled, held secrets that would unveil themselves in a chilling twist of fate. The whispers, now

a fading memory, left the door ajar for the looming terror that awaited in the aftermath of the spectral storm. The old house, its foundations saturated with the essence of the living, stood as a gateway to a supernatural abyss. Sheila and Rob, bound by the malevolent forces that lingered within, faced an uncertain future where the horrors of the past cast a long, lingering shadow over their fragile grasp on reality.

Chapter 10: The Basement

After sealing the malevolent forces within the old house through the sacrificial ritual, Sheila and Rob found themselves back in the dimly lit living room. The air, though tinged with an unsettling calm, carried the echoes of the supernatural journey they had undertaken. The whispers, now a distant memory, left a spectral resonance in the haunted dwelling.

As Sheila and Rob attempted to regain their bearings, a foreboding sensation lingered in the air. The old house, once a haven for dark rituals, stood as a testament to the sacrifices made to quell the malevolent forces. Little did they know that the true test awaited in the aftermath of the ritual—a revelation that would redefine the very fabric of their existence.

In the eerie quiet, Sheila's gaze was drawn to the basement door—the same door that had led them to the depths of the supernatural realm. The whispers, though muted, seemed to guide her attention toward the subterranean depths where forgotten rituals had once unfolded. A sense of trepidation settled over her as the basement became a focal point of the encroaching darkness.

Rob, too, felt an unspoken unease as he followed Sheila's gaze toward the basement door. The air, though seemingly calm, carried a spectral energy that hinted at the unresolved mysteries lurking within the subterranean depths. The old house, though momentarily at peace, seemed to hold secrets that demanded further exploration.

Driven by an unspoken compulsion, Sheila and Rob approached the basement door. The whispers, now a faint murmur, seemed to beckon them to descend once more into the depths of the haunted dwelling. The wooden stairs creaked under their weight as they descended into

the dimly lit basement—a place where the supernatural energies still lingered, weaving a spectral tapestry of the past.

In the basement, the air felt charged with an otherworldly energy. The whispers, though subdued, guided Sheila and Rob toward the heart of the supernatural storm. The old house, its foundations saturated with the essence of the living, seemed to pulse with an unseen force that transcended the boundaries of the mortal realm.

As they ventured deeper into the basement, Sheila's flashlight revealed forgotten artifacts—relics of the occult rituals that had once held sway within the haunted dwelling. The whispers, though fragmented, spoke of a lingering malevolence that refused to be fully contained. The old house, its spectral corridors echoing with the whispers of the past, became a gateway to a darkness that awaited in the shadows.

A sudden drop in temperature signaled a change in the atmosphere. The whispers, now a haunting lament, guided Sheila and Rob toward a hidden corner of the basement. There, obscured by shadows, they discovered a mysterious door—an entrance to a forgotten chamber that had eluded their previous exploration.

With trepidation, Sheila and Rob opened the door, revealing a chamber bathed in an unnatural darkness. The air, thick with the scent of ancient incense, seemed to vibrate with the echoes of spectral energy. The whispers, now a dissonant symphony, spoke of a deeper layer of malevolence that awaited discovery.

As they entered the hidden chamber, Sheila's flashlight revealed cryptic symbols etched into the walls—a language of the occult that spoke of forbidden knowledge and ancient rites. The whispers, though chaotic, seemed to convey a message—a revelation that transcended the boundaries of the living and the dead. The old house, now a conduit for the supernatural, bore witness to the unfolding mysteries that awaited in the hidden chamber.

In the dim light, Sheila and Rob stumbled upon an ancient tome— an occult grimoire that held the secrets of the forgotten rituals. The whispers, now a spectral chorus, urged Sheila to decipher the cryptic

symbols that adorned the pages. The malevolent legacy, though temporarily quelled, seemed to find its voice in the ancient words that unfolded in the flickering light.

As Sheila read aloud the incantations, the chamber seemed to come alive with an otherworldly energy. Shadows danced on the walls, and the whispers, now a cacophony of spectral voices, spoke of a deeper darkness that had yet to be unveiled. The old house, a witness to the unfolding ritual, became a gateway to the unknown—a place where the living and the dead converged in a macabre dance.

In the spectral glow, the hidden chamber transformed into a supernatural realm—a place suspended between the living and the abyss. The whispers, now a mournful wail, guided Sheila and Rob toward a revelation that would test the limits of their resilience. The old house, its foundations shaken by the unfolding ritual, became a battleground where the supernatural and the mortal collided.

As they delved deeper into the hidden chamber, the symbols on the walls seemed to shift—a spectral language that defied comprehension. The whispers, though haunting, spoke of an ancient evil that had been awakened by their presence. Sheila and Rob, bound by the malevolent forces that lingered within the old house, faced an unforeseen challenge that awaited in the shadows.

A sudden gust of wind extinguished their flashlights, plunging the hidden chamber into complete darkness. The whispers, now a relentless drone, seemed to merge with the shadows that danced in the spectral realm. The old house, its spectral foundations saturated with the essence of the living, stood at the precipice of a new, malevolent revelation.

In the darkness, Sheila and Rob felt an unseen force closing in around them. The whispers, now a spectral symphony, guided them toward a spectral entity that awaited in the hidden corners of the chamber. The old house, a silent witness to the unfolding darkness, seemed to sigh with a spectral resignation.

With a sense of urgency, Sheila and Rob fumbled for their flashlights, attempting to pierce the veil of darkness that surrounded them.

The whispers, though chaotic, spoke of an ancient evil that sought communion with the living. The hidden chamber, now a battleground between the mortal and the supernatural, became a place where the boundaries between reality and the abyss blurred.

As their flashlights flickered to life, Sheila and Rob beheld a chilling sight—a spectral entity, its form indistinct in the shadows, stood before them. The whispers, now a haunting melody, spoke of an ancient evil that had been awakened by their presence. The old house, a conduit for the malevolent forces, bore silent witness to the spectral encounter that unfolded in the hidden chamber.

The entity, a manifestation of the ancient evil that had lingered within the old house, seemed to reach out from the shadows. The whispers, now a dissonant chorus, urged Sheila and Rob to confront the malevolent force that awaited in the spectral realm. The old house, though temporarily quelled, stood as a gateway to a darkness that defied rational explanation.

With a surge of supernatural power, the entity confronted Sheila and Rob. The whispers, now a mournful hymn, seemed to align with the malevolent force as the spectral encounter reached its zenith. The old house, its foundations saturated with the essence of the living, became a battleground where the living and the dead converged in a macabre dance of supernatural entanglement.

Sheila and Rob, entwined in the spectral tapestry, felt the weight of unseen eyes upon them. The whispers, now a relentless drone, seemed to echo through the hidden chamber—a spectral symphony that reverberated through the haunted dwelling. The old house, its spectral foundations shaken by the malevolent revelation, stood at the precipice of a new, horrifying chapter in its dark history.

As the entity reached out with spectral tendrils, Sheila and Rob, driven by an unspoken determination, faced the malevolent force with a courage born of desperation. The whispers, though chaotic, guided them through the spectral encounter—a dance between the living and the abyss. The old house, a silent witness to the unfolding darkness,

stood as a battleground where the forces of the supernatural and the mortal clashed in a terrifying crescendo.

In the dim light of the hidden chamber, a struggle unfolded—a battle between the living and the spectral entity that sought communion with the living. The whispers, now a spectral symphony, intensified as Sheila and Rob confronted the ancient evil that had been awakened by their presence. The old house, its foundations saturated with the essence of the living, became a crucible where the boundaries between reality and the abyss blurred.

With a surge of supernatural energy, Sheila and Rob channeled the remnants of the sacrificial ritual into a desperate confrontation with the entity. The whispers, now a haunting melody, seemed to align with the living as the spectral encounter reached its climax. The old house, a silent witness to the unfolding darkness, stood as a testament to the resilience of those who dared to confront the malevolent forces that lurked within its haunted halls.

As the spectral entity recoiled, the whispers, now a fading memory, left an eerie stillness in their wake. Sheila and Rob, exhausted and shaken, stood amidst the spectral remnants of the hidden chamber. The old house, though still haunted by the echoes of the past, seemed to sigh with a spectral resignation.

The supernatural realm, now devoid of the malevolent entity that had sought communion with the living, unfolded with an unsettling stillness. Sheila and Rob, their courage tested by the spectral encounter, ascended from the hidden chamber and returned to the haunted halls of the old house. The air, though laden with the remnants of the supernatural battle, felt lighter as if a temporary reprieve had been granted.

Little did they know that the true horror, a revelation that would redefine the very fabric of their existence, awaited in the shadows of their newfound victory. The old house, though temporarily quelled, held secrets that would unveil themselves in a chilling twist of fate—one that would test the limits of Sheila and Rob's resilience and plunge them into a darkness from which there might be no escape.

The whispers, now a fading memory, left the door ajar for the looming terror that awaited in the aftermath of the spectral storm. The old house, its haunted corridors pulsating with unresolved sorrows, stood as a gateway to a supernatural abyss. Sheila and Rob, bound by the malevolent forces that lingered within, faced an uncertain future where the horrors of the past cast a long, lingering shadow over their fragile grasp on reality.

Chapter 11: The Escape

Having confronted the malevolent forces in the hidden chamber, Sheila and Rob ascended from the basement, their nerves on edge from the spectral encounter. The air in the old house, though momentarily relieved of the oppressive darkness, still held a spectral tension—a silent reminder of the horrors that lurked within its haunted halls. Unbeknownst to them, a new chapter of terror awaited as the old house seemed to cling to the malevolence that had taken root in its very foundations.

As they emerged into the dim light of the living room, Sheila and Rob exchanged glances laden with unspoken fear. The whispers, though muted, seemed to linger in the air like a haunting refrain. The old house, its spectral corridors echoing with the echoes of the past, stood as a silent witness to the unfolding nightmare that awaited the unwitting inhabitants.

A sense of urgency gripped Sheila as her gaze once again fell upon the basement door—the same door that had led them to the depths of the supernatural realm. The whispers, though subdued, seemed to guide her attention toward the subterranean depths where forgotten rituals had once unfolded. The basement, now a nexus of malevolence, beckoned them to confront the unresolved mysteries that lingered within.

Rob, his nerves still raw from the spectral encounter, hesitated as Sheila approached the basement door. The air, though seemingly calm, carried a spectral resonance that hinted at the lingering darkness within the haunted dwelling. The old house, a silent observer to the unfolding

terror, seemed to pulse with an unseen force that transcended the boundaries of the living and the dead.

With a sense of trepidation, Sheila opened the basement door, revealing the wooden stairs that led to the subterranean depths. The whispers, now a faint murmur, seemed to echo through the haunted halls, guiding them toward the heart of the encroaching darkness. The old house, though momentarily quelled, held secrets that demanded further exploration—a revelation that would test the limits of Sheila and Rob's resilience.

As they descended into the dimly lit basement, the air felt heavy with an otherworldly energy. The whispers, though muted, seemed to guide Sheila and Rob toward the epicenter of the supernatural storm. The old house, its spectral foundations saturated with the essence of the living, became a conduit for the malevolent forces that sought communion with the unwitting inhabitants.

In the basement, the artifacts of forgotten rituals lay in shadowed corners, silent witnesses to the malevolence that had once thrived within the haunted dwelling. The whispers, though fragmented, spoke of a lingering darkness that refused to be fully contained. The old house, a spectral battleground, seemed to pulse with an unseen force that beckoned Sheila and Rob to delve deeper into the abyss.

As they ventured into the basement's depths, Sheila's flashlight revealed a hidden passage—a secret corridor that led to unexplored realms within the haunted dwelling. The whispers, though haunting, guided them toward a revelation that transcended the boundaries of the living and the dead. The old house, now a labyrinth of malevolence, became a spectral tapestry where the living and the abyss converged in an eerie dance.

A sudden drop in temperature signaled a shift in the atmosphere. The whispers, now a haunting lament, guided Sheila and Rob toward an ancient doorway—an entrance to a forgotten chamber that had eluded their previous exploration. The old house, though momentarily

quelled, seemed to cling to the malevolent forces that lurked within its spectral depths.

With trepidation, Sheila and Rob opened the ancient doorway, revealing a chamber bathed in an unnatural darkness. The air, thick with the scent of ancient incense, seemed to vibrate with the echoes of spectral energy. The whispers, now a dissonant symphony, spoke of a deeper layer of malevolence that awaited discovery.

In the dim light, Sheila and Rob stumbled upon an ancient altar—an occult relic that held the secrets of forbidden rituals. The whispers, though chaotic, urged Sheila to decipher the cryptic symbols that adorned the altar. The malevolent legacy, though temporarily quelled, seemed to find its voice in the ancient rites that unfolded in the flickering light.

As Sheila and Rob examined the altar, a sudden gust of wind extinguished their flashlights, plunging the chamber into complete darkness. The whispers, now a relentless drone, merged with the shadows that danced in the spectral realm. The old house, its spectral foundations saturated with the essence of the living, stood at the precipice of a new, malevolent revelation.

In the darkness, Sheila and Rob felt an unseen force closing in around them. The whispers, now a spectral symphony, guided them toward a spectral entity that awaited in the hidden corners of the chamber. The old house, a silent witness to the unfolding darkness, seemed to sigh with a spectral resignation.

With a sense of urgency, Sheila and Rob fumbled for their flashlights, attempting to pierce the veil of darkness that surrounded them. The whispers, though chaotic, spoke of an ancient evil that sought communion with the living. The hidden chamber, now a battleground between the mortal and the supernatural, became a place where the boundaries between reality and the abyss blurred.

As their flashlights flickered to life, Sheila and Rob beheld a chilling sight—a spectral entity, its form indistinct in the shadows, stood before them. The whispers, now a haunting melody, spoke of an ancient evil

that had been awakened by their presence. The old house, a conduit for the malevolent forces, bore silent witness to the spectral encounter that unfolded in the hidden chamber.

The entity, a manifestation of the ancient evil that had lingered within the old house, seemed to reach out from the shadows. The whispers, now a dissonant chorus, urged Sheila and Rob to confront the malevolent force that awaited in the spectral realm. The old house, though temporarily quelled, stood as a gateway to a darkness that defied rational explanation.

With a surge of supernatural power, the entity confronted Sheila and Rob. The whispers, now a mournful hymn, seemed to align with the malevolent force as the spectral encounter reached its zenith. The old house, its foundations saturated with the essence of the living, became a battleground where the living and the dead converged in a macabre dance.

Sheila and Rob, entwined in the spectral tapestry, felt the weight of unseen eyes upon them. The whispers, now a relentless drone, seemed to echo through the hidden chamber—a spectral symphony that reverberated through the haunted dwelling. The old house, its spectral foundations shaken by the malevolent revelation, stood at the precipice of a new, horrifying chapter in its dark history.

As the entity reached out with spectral tendrils, Sheila and Rob, driven by an unspoken determination, faced the malevolent force with a courage born of desperation. The whispers, though chaotic, guided them through the spectral encounter—a dance between the living and the abyss. The old house, a silent witness to the unfolding darkness, stood as a battleground where the forces of the supernatural and the mortal clashed in a terrifying crescendo.

In the dim light of the hidden chamber, a struggle unfolded—a battle between the living and the spectral entity that sought communion with the living. The whispers, now a spectral symphony, intensified as Sheila and Rob confronted the ancient evil that had been awakened by their presence. The old house, its foundations saturated with the essence of

the living, became a crucible where the boundaries between reality and the abyss blurred.

With a surge of supernatural energy, Sheila and Rob channeled the remnants of the sacrificial ritual into a desperate confrontation with the entity. The whispers, now a haunting melody, seemed to align with the living as the spectral encounter reached its climax. The old house, a silent witness to the unfolding darkness, stood as a testament to the resilience of those who dared to confront the malevolent forces that lurked within its haunted halls.

As the spectral entity recoiled, the whispers, now a fading memory, left an eerie stillness in their wake. Sheila and Rob, exhausted and shaken, stood amidst the spectral remnants of the hidden chamber. The old house, though still haunted by the echoes of the past, seemed to sigh with a spectral resignation.

The supernatural realm, now devoid of the malevolent entity that had sought communion with the living, unfolded with an unsettling stillness. Sheila and Rob, their courage tested by the spectral encounter, ascended from the hidden chamber and returned to the haunted halls of the old house. The air, though laden with the remnants of the supernatural battle, felt lighter as if a temporary reprieve had been granted.

Little did they know that the true horror, a revelation that would redefine the very fabric of their existence, awaited in the shadows of their newfound victory. The old house, though temporarily quelled, held secrets that would unveil themselves in a chilling twist of fate—one that would test the limits of Sheila and Rob's resilience and plunge them into a darkness from which there might be no escape.

The whispers, now a fading memory, left the door ajar for the looming terror that awaited in the aftermath of the spectral storm. The old house, its haunted corridors pulsating with unresolved sorrows, stood as a gateway to a supernatural abyss. Sheila and Rob, bound by the malevolent forces that lingered within, faced an uncertain future where the horrors of the past cast a long, lingering shadow over their fragile grasp on reality.

Chapter 12: The Attacks

As Sheila and Rob emerged from the hidden chamber, a sense of unease lingered in the air. The old house, though temporarily quelled by their confrontation with the spectral entity, exuded an eerie calm that belied the malevolence buried within its haunted corridors. Unbeknownst to the shaken inhabitants, the aftermath of the ritual had set into motion a series of paranormal attacks that would test the limits of their courage and resilience.

The whispers, though muted, seemed to carry a warning—a spectral echo of the malevolent forces that still clung to the very fabric of the old house. Sheila and Rob, their nerves raw from the supernatural encounter, exchanged wary glances as they navigated the dimly lit halls. The air, laden with the remnants of the spectral battle, became a spectral tapestry where the living and the dead converged in an unsettling dance.

As night fell over the old house, Sheila found herself alone in the living room. The whispers, now a distant murmur, seemed to beckon her toward the spectral energies that lingered within the haunted dwelling. The old house, a silent witness to the unfolding nightmare, held secrets that awaited discovery—a revelation that would thrust Sheila into a harrowing series of paranormal attacks.

The attacks began subtly—a flickering of lights, objects moving mysteriously, and an unshakable feeling of being watched. Sheila, though initially dismissive, couldn't ignore the mounting sense of dread that accompanied these strange occurrences. The whispers, now a haunting melody, seemed to intensify as if heralding the approach of an unseen malevolence.

One night, as Sheila lay in bed, the attacks escalated. Shadows danced on the walls, and an otherworldly chill permeated the room. The whispers, now a dissonant chorus, filled the air with a spectral energy that seemed to converge around her. The old house, its foundations saturated with the essence of the living, became a battleground where the forces of the supernatural sought communion with the unsuspecting inhabitants.

Sheila, gripped by a growing terror, sought solace in the presence of Rob. Together, they confronted the escalating attacks, attempting to rationalize the paranormal occurrences that defied logical explanation. The old house, though momentarily quelled, seemed to pulse with an unseen force that defied the boundaries of the mortal realm.

The attacks took a violent turn, as unseen forces hurled objects across the room and ominous shadows seemed to reach out from the spectral realm. Sheila and Rob, their nerves stretched to the breaking point, struggled to maintain their grasp on reality. The whispers, now a relentless drone, echoed through the haunted halls, guiding Rob the malevolent forces in their torment of the unsuspecting inhabitants.

Desperate for answers, Sheila delved into her research, revisiting the ancient tome and the diary that chronicled the house's dark history. The whispers, though fragmented, seemed to offer cryptic clues that hinted at a malevolent presence seeking revenge. The old house, its haunted corridors echoing with the sorrows of the past, held the key to understanding the origins of the supernatural attacks.

In their quest for answers, Sheila and Rob enlisted the help of a local paranormal investigator. The whispers, now a spectral symphony, seemed to intensify as the investigator delved into the history of the old house. The malevolent forces, though temporarily restrained, resisted the intrusion, escalating the attacks in retaliation.

The investigator, a skeptic turned believer, witnessed the paranormal onslaught firsthand. Doors slammed shut, eerie whispers reverberated through the halls, and unseen hands seemed to grab at those who dared to venture into the haunted dwelling. The old house, now a battleground for the living and the supernatural, exuded a malevolence that defied rational explanation.

In a desperate attempt to quell the attacks, Sheila and Rob decided to hold a seance—an act that would either provide answers or further provoke the wrath of the malevolent forces. The whispers, now a haunting lament, seemed to guide them toward the living room where the seance would take place. The old house, its spectral foundations

shaken by the paranormal onslaught, awaited the unfolding ritual with a spectral resignation.

As the seance began, the air in the living room became charged with an otherworldly energy. The whispers, now a cacophony of spectral voices, spoke of the ancient evil that sought communion with the living. The old house, its haunted halls bearing witness to the unfolding ritual, seemed to sigh with a spectral anticipation.

Suddenly, the room plunged into darkness, and a chilling wind swept through the living room. The whispers, now a spectral chorus, guided Sheila and Rob toward a revelation that transcended the boundaries of the living and the dead. The old house, its foundations saturated with the essence of the living, became a conduit for the malevolent forces that sought release through the seance.

In the darkness, Sheila felt an unseen presence—the very embodiment of the malevolence that had plagued the old house. The whispers, now a mournful hymn, seemed to echo through the spectral realm as the ancient evil made itself known. The old house, a witness to the unfolding ritual, stood at the precipice of a terrifying revelation.

The entity, a manifestation of the supernatural forces, spoke through the seance—a voice that sent shivers down the spines of those present. The whispers, now a spectral symphony, conveyed the entity's grievances and the reasons behind the relentless attacks. The old house, its spectral foundations saturated with the essence of the living, became a stage for the malevolent forces to voice their unholy intentions.

As the seance reached its climax, Sheila and Rob faced a choice—succumb to the malevolent forces or confront the entity head-on. The whispers, now a haunting melody, seemed to offer a glimmer of hope amidst the overwhelming darkness. The old house, its haunted corridors pulsating with the echoes of the past, awaited the resolution of the supernatural conflict that unfolded within its spectral confines.

With determination born of desperation, Sheila and Rob confronted the entity. The whispers, now a spectral chorus, guided them through the confrontation—a dance between the living and the abyss. The old

house, a silent witness to the unfolding darkness, stood as a battleground where the forces of the supernatural and the mortal clashed in a terrifying crescendo.

As Sheila and Rob faced the entity, a surge of supernatural energy filled the room. The whispers, now a relentless drone, seemed to align with the living as the spectral encounter reached its zenith. The old house, its foundations saturated with the essence of the living, became a crucible where the boundaries between reality and the abyss blurred.

In the dim light of the living room, a struggle unfolded—a battle between the living and the malevolent entity that sought communion with the living. The whispers, now a spectral symphony, intensified as Sheila and Rob confronted the ancient evil that had been awakened by their presence. The old house, its haunted foundations shaken by the paranormal conflict, stood as a testament to the resilience of those who dared to confront the malevolent forces that lurked within its spectral halls.

As the entity recoiled, the whispers, now a fading memory, left an eerie stillness in their wake. Sheila and Rob, exhausted and shaken, stood amidst the spectral remnants of the seance. The old house, though still haunted by the echoes of the past, seemed to sigh with a spectral resignation.

The supernatural realm, now devoid of the entity that had sought communion with the living, unfolded with an unsettling stillness. Sheila and Rob, their courage tested by the spectral encounter, navigated the haunted halls of the old house. The air, though laden with the remnants of the paranormal conflict, felt lighter as if a temporary reprieve had been granted.

Little did they know that the true horror, a revelation that would redefine the very fabric of their existence, awaited in the shadows of their newfound victory. The old house, though temporarily quelled, held secrets that would unveil themselves in a chilling twist of fate—one that would test the limits of Sheila and Rob's resilience and plunge them into a darkness from which there might be no escape.

The whispers, now a fading memory, left the door ajar for the looming terror that awaited in the aftermath of the supernatural onslaught. The old house, its haunted corridors pulsating with unresolved sorrows, stood as a gateway to a supernatural abyss. Sheila and Rob, bound by the malevolent forces that lingered within, faced an uncertain future where the horrors of the past cast a long, lingering shadow over their fragile grasp on reality.

Chapter 13: The Seance

As the aftermath of the paranormal attacks lingered in the old house, Sheila and Rob, driven by a desperate need for answers, decided to delve deeper into the supernatural realm. The whispers, though diminished, seemed to guide them toward a fateful decision—the summoning of forces beyond their understanding through a seance. The old house, its haunted corridors pulsating with unresolved sorrows, awaited the unfolding ritual with a spectral anticipation.

Sheila and Rob gathered in the living room, surrounded by flickering candles and the musty scent of ancient incense. The whispers, now a distant murmur, seemed to converge around them as they prepared for the seance. The air in the room became charged with an otherworldly energy, and the old house, a silent witness to the unfolding ritual, stood at the precipice of a new, unsettling chapter.

The seance began with the chanting of incantations from an ancient tome Sheila had found in her research. The whispers, now a haunting lament, filled the room with a spectral resonance that transcended the boundaries of the living and the dead. The old house, its spectral foundations saturated with the essence of the living, became a conduit for the malevolent forces that awaited release through the ritual.

As the incantations echoed through the room, a sudden drop in temperature signaled the arrival of unseen entities. The whispers, now a spectral symphony, seemed to guide Sheila and Rob toward a revelation that defied rational explanation. The old house, its haunted halls bearing witness to the unfolding ritual, exuded a spectral energy that reached beyond the mortal realm.

In the dim light, Sheila and Rob felt an otherworldly presence—the very embodiment of the malevolence that had plagued the old house. The whispers, now a dissonant chorus, urged them to maintain their focus as the spectral entities made themselves known. The old house, a stage for the supernatural forces, stood as a gateway to a darkness that defied comprehension.

As the seance continued, the room filled with eerie whispers, shadows danced on the walls, and an unseen force seemed to grip those present. Sheila and Rob, their senses heightened by the supernatural energies, felt the weight of unseen eyes upon them. The old house, its spectral foundations shaken by the unfolding ritual, became a battleground where the living and the abyss converged in an unsettling dance.

Suddenly, the room plunged into darkness, and an otherworldly wind swept through the living room. The whispers, now a relentless drone, guided Sheila and Rob toward the epicenter of the spectral storm. The old house, though momentarily quelled, seemed to pulse with an unseen force that defied the boundaries of the mortal realm.

In the darkness, Sheila and Rob glimpsed shadowy figures—apparitions of the past that materialized in the spectral realm. The whispers, now a spectral chorus, spoke of the tormented souls that lingered within the haunted dwelling. The old house, its haunted corridors echoing with the sorrows of the past, became a tapestry of spectral entities seeking release through the seance.

As the apparitions manifested, the room resonated with their ethereal presence. The whispers, now a haunting melody, conveyed the grievances of the tormented souls that sought communion with the living. The old house, a conduit for the spectral forces, bore witness to the unfolding drama between the mortal and the supernatural.

Amidst the spectral symphony, Sheila and Rob felt a sudden shift—a malevolent entity seizing the opportunity to make its presence known. The whispers, now a dissonant chorus, guided them toward a revelation that sent shivers down their spines. The old house, its spectral

foundations saturated with the essence of the living, stood as a stage for the malevolent force that awaited confrontation.

The entity, a manifestation of the ancient evil that lingered within the old house, spoke through the seance—a voice that echoed with a chilling resonance. The whispers, now a mournful hymn, conveyed the entity's grievances and the reasons behind the relentless attacks. The old house, its haunted halls bearing witness to the unfolding ritual, seemed to sigh with a spectral anticipation.

Sheila and Rob, their senses overwhelmed by the supernatural onslaught, faced a choice—succumb to the malevolent forces or confront the entity head-on. The whispers, now a haunting melody, seemed to offer a glimmer of hope amidst the overwhelming darkness. The old house, its haunted corridors pulsating with the echoes of the past, awaited the resolution of the supernatural conflict that unfolded within its spectral confines.

With determination born of desperation, Sheila and Rob confronted the entity. The whispers, now a spectral chorus, guided them through the confrontation—a dance between the living and the abyss. The old house, a silent witness to the unfolding darkness, stood as a battleground where the forces of the supernatural and the mortal clashed in a terrifying crescendo.

As Sheila and Rob faced the entity, a surge of supernatural energy filled the room. The whispers, now a relentless drone, seemed to align with the living as the spectral encounter reached its zenith. The old house, its foundations saturated with the essence of the living, became a crucible where the boundaries between reality and the abyss blurred.

In the dim light of the living room, a struggle unfolded—a battle between the living and the malevolent entity that sought communion with the living. The whispers, now a spectral symphony, intensified as Sheila and Rob confronted the ancient evil that had been awakened by their presence. The old house, its haunted foundations shaken by the paranormal conflict, stood as a testament to the resilience of those

who dared to confront the malevolent forces that lurked within its spectral halls.

As the entity recoiled, the whispers, now a fading memory, left an eerie stillness in their wake. Sheila and Rob, exhausted and shaken, stood amidst the spectral remnants of the seance. The old house, though still haunted by the echoes of the past, seemed to sigh with a spectral resignation.

The supernatural realm, now devoid of the entity that had sought communion with the living, unfolded with an unsettling stillness. Sheila and Rob, their courage tested by the spectral encounter, navigated the haunted halls of the old house. The air, though laden with the remnants of the paranormal conflict, felt lighter as if a temporary reprieve had been granted.

Little did they know that the true horror, a revelation that would redefine the very fabric of their existence, awaited in the shadows of their newfound victory. The old house, though temporarily quelled, held secrets that would unveil themselves in a chilling twist of fate—one that would test the limits of Sheila and Rob's resilience and plunge them into a darkness from which there might be no escape.

The whispers, now a fading memory, left the door ajar for the looming terror that awaited in the aftermath of the supernatural onslaught. The old house, its haunted corridors pulsating with unresolved sorrows, stood as a gateway to a supernatural abyss. Sheila and Rob, bound by the malevolent forces that lingered within, faced an uncertain future where the horrors of the past cast a long, lingering shadow over their fragile grasp on reality.

Chapter 14: The Cleansing

In the wake of the seance, Sheila and Rob, still reeling from the otherworldly encounter, found themselves at a crossroads. The old house, though momentarily relieved of the malevolent entity's presence, exuded an eerie calm that hinted at the lingering supernatural forces within its haunted walls. Determined to put an end to the paranormal onslaught, Sheila sought the guidance of a psychic medium—an expert

in the arcane arts who might hold the key to cleansing the ancient dwelling.

The whispers, now a faint echo of the malevolence that had permeated the old house, guided Sheila and Rob toward the psychic medium's secluded residence. The air, heavy with the remnants of the spectral storm, carried a spectral resonance that seemed to converge around them. The old house, its spectral foundations saturated with the essence of the living, became a distant backdrop to the unfolding quest for purification.

The psychic medium, a mysterious figure with a demeanor that mirrored the enigmatic forces surrounding the old house, welcomed Sheila and Rob into a dimly lit room adorned with mystical artifacts. The whispers, now a haunting melody, seemed to intensify in the presence of the psychic medium. The air became charged with an otherworldly energy as the cleansing ritual began.

As the psychic medium delved into the spiritual realm, Sheila and Rob felt a shift in the atmosphere. The whispers, now a spectral symphony, guided the medium's hands as they moved through intricate gestures, channeling supernatural forces to cleanse the old house of its malevolent energies. The haunted dwelling, a silent witness to the unfolding ritual, awaited the purifying touch of the arcane.

Suddenly, the room quivered with unseen energies. Shadows danced on the walls, and the air vibrated with a spectral resonance. The whispers, now a dissonant chorus, echoed through the room, carrying the remnants of the malevolent entity's presence. The old house, though momentarily quelled, seemed to resist the cleansing as if clinging to the dark energies that had taken root within its spectral depths.

As the cleansing ritual continued, Sheila and Rob witnessed a manifestation of spectral mists swirling through the room. The whispers, now a relentless drone, seemed to speak of the ancient sorrows that clung to the old house like a malevolent shroud. The psychic medium, undeterred by the supernatural turbulence, pressed on with the purifying incantations.

In the dim light, Sheila and Rob glimpsed fleeting apparitions—the tormented souls that lingered within the old house. The whispers, now a haunting lament, carried the voices of the restless spirits seeking release through the cleansing ritual. The haunted dwelling, its spectral foundations shaken by the purifying energies, became a nexus where the living and the dead converged in an otherworldly dance.

Unexpectedly, the psychic medium's eyes glazed over, and her voice took on an otherworldly resonance. The whispers, now a mournful hymn, spoke through the medium, conveying the grievances of the ancient spirits that had been disturbed by the malevolent entity. The old house, a conduit for the spectral forces, bore silent witness to the spectral communion that unfolded in the purifying ritual.

As the psychic medium channeled the spirits, Sheila and Rob felt a surge of supernatural energy coursing through the room. The whispers, now a spectral chorus, guided them toward a revelation that transcended the boundaries of the living and the dead. The old house, though momentarily quelled, seemed to sigh with a spectral resignation as the purifying energies sought to dispel the malevolent forces that clung to its haunted corridors.

The psychic medium, still in the grip of the supernatural trance, uttered cryptic words that seemed to unlock the secrets of the old house's dark history. The whispers, now a dissonant symphony, guided Sheila and Rob toward a hidden chamber—an ancient sanctum where forgotten rituals had once unfolded. The haunted dwelling, its spectral foundations saturated with the essence of the living, became a battleground for the living and the supernatural.

As the purifying ritual reached its climax, Sheila and Rob, entranced by the spectral energies, witnessed a spectral convergence. The whispers, now a spectral melody, spoke of the ancient rituals that had bound the malevolent forces to the old house. The psychic medium, still in communion with the spirits, channeled the supernatural energies toward the heart of the spectral storm.

A sudden burst of light illuminated the room as the cleansing energies reached their zenith. The whispers, now a fading memory, left an eerie stillness in their wake. Sheila and Rob, their senses overwhelmed by the spectral convergence, stood amidst the remnants of the purifying ritual. The old house, though still haunted by the echoes of the past, seemed to sigh with a spectral resignation as if acknowledging the fleeting victory over the malevolent forces.

The psychic medium, released from the supernatural trance, conveyed the success of the cleansing ritual. The whispers, now a distant murmur, hinted at a temporary reprieve from the paranormal onslaught. The old house, its spectral foundations shaken by the purifying energies, awaited the aftermath of the cleansing—a revelation that would test the limits of Sheila and Rob's resilience and unravel the mysteries hidden within its haunted corridors.

As Sheila and Rob left the psychic medium's residence, a sense of cautious hope lingered in the air. The whispers, now a faint echo of the supernatural forces, guided them back to the old house—the battleground where the forces of the living and the dead had clashed in a spectral dance. The haunted dwelling, though momentarily relieved of the malevolent entity's presence, held secrets that awaited unraveling as the aftermath of the cleansing ritual cast a spectral light on the mysteries that lay hidden within its spectral confines.

Chapter 15: The Truth

With the cleansing ritual behind them, Sheila and Rob returned to the old house, hoping for a respite from the malevolent forces that had plagued them. The whispers, now a mere whisper of the supernatural energies that once gripped the haunted dwelling, guided them through the dimly lit halls. The air, heavy with the aftermath of the purifying ritual, carried a spectral resonance that hinted at the revelations awaiting them.

As Sheila and Rob explored the old house, a sense of cautious optimism settled over them. The whispers, though diminished, seemed to convey a temporary peace—a fragile equilibrium between the living

and the supernatural. The haunted dwelling, a silent witness to the unfolding events, exuded an eerie calm that belied the mysteries hidden within its spectral depths.

However, as night fell over the old house, an unsettling energy permeated the air. The whispers, now a distant murmur, hinted at a resurgence of the malevolent forces. Sheila and Rob, their nerves on edge, exchanged wary glances as they navigated the dimly lit corridors. The haunted dwelling, though momentarily quelled, held secrets that awaited revelation in the spectral silence of the night.

A series of cryptic symbols appeared on the walls—manifestations of the supernatural energies that lingered within the old house. The whispers, now a haunting melody, seemed to speak through the spectral symbols, conveying a message that defied rational explanation. The air, charged with an otherworldly energy, guided Sheila and Rob toward the heart of the spectral disturbance.

In the dim light, they discovered a hidden chamber—a forgotten sanctum where the malevolent rituals of the past had unfolded. The whispers, now a spectral symphony, intensified as Sheila and Rob delved into the secrets concealed within the ancient chamber. The haunted dwelling, its spectral foundations saturated with the essence of the living, became a tapestry where the past and present converged in an unsettling dance.

As they explored the hidden chamber, Sheila uncovered an old diary that chronicled the house's dark history. The whispers, now a dissonant chorus, guided her through the cryptic entries that spoke of occult rituals and malevolent forces bound to the old house. The air, thick with the residual energies of the past, carried a spectral resonance that transcended the boundaries of time.

The diary revealed a gruesome truth—the old house had been built for occult rituals, with a dark energy woven into its very walls. The whispers, now a relentless drone, conveyed the malevolent forces that had been awakened by the unwitting presence of Sheila and Rob. The haunted dwelling, a silent witness to the unfolding revelations, stood

as a testament to the ancient darkness that sought communion with the living.

As Sheila and Rob grappled with the horrifying truth, the whispers guided them toward a chilling realization—there was only one way to stop the malevolent forces that had been unleashed. The haunted dwelling, though momentarily quelled by the cleansing ritual, demanded a final sacrifice to seal the ancient evil that lurked within its spectral depths.

The revelation weighed heavily on Sheila's shoulders as she contemplated the harrowing decision that awaited her. The whispers, now a haunting lament, seemed to offer guidance through the darkness that enveloped the old house. The air, heavy with the echoes of the past, carried a spectral energy that transcended the mortal realm.

Determined to confront the malevolent forces head-on, Sheila and Rob sought counsel from the psychic medium who had guided them through the cleansing ritual. The whispers, now a spectral chorus, guided them to the medium's secluded residence, where the air buzzed with the residual energies of the supernatural encounter. The haunted dwelling, a distant backdrop to the unfolding quest, awaited the resolution of the spectral conflict that had gripped its haunted halls.

The psychic medium, aware of the lingering malevolence, spoke of the ancient ritual that could seal the evil presence within the old house. The whispers, now a spectral melody, seemed to convey the urgency of the impending sacrifice. The air, thick with the spectral energies, guided Sheila and Rob toward a path that would test the limits of their courage and resilience.

Sheila, faced with an unimaginable choice, grappled with the weight of the revelation. The whispers, now a dissonant symphony, urged her to confront the malevolent forces head-on. The haunted dwelling, its spectral foundations shaken by the impending decision, stood as a crucible where the boundaries between the living and the supernatural blurred.

As night fell over the old house, Sheila prepared for the ritual—a blood sacrifice that would bind the malevolent forces and seal the ancient evil within the spectral confines. The whispers, now a relentless drone, echoed through the haunted dwelling, guiding her toward the heart of the spectral storm. The air, heavy with the essence of the supernatural, carried a spectral resonance that transcended the mortal realm.

Rob, torn between loyalty and the impending sacrifice, stood by Sheila's side as she embraced her destiny. The whispers, now a haunting lament, seemed to offer solace in the face of the inevitable. The haunted dwelling, a silent witness to the unfolding ritual, exuded an eerie calm that belied the impending darkness.

In the dimly lit chamber, Sheila performed the ritual with a heavy heart. The whispers, now a spectral symphony, guided her through the ancient incantations that would bind the malevolent forces to the old house. The air, charged with an otherworldly energy, carried the weight of the sacrifice that would determine the fate of the haunted dwelling.

As Sheila completed the ritual, a surge of supernatural energy filled the room. The whispers, now a fading memory, left an eerie stillness in their wake. The haunted dwelling, though temporarily quelled, seemed to sigh with a spectral resignation. The air, thick with the remnants of the ritual, carried a spectral resonance that lingered in the haunted corridors.

In the aftermath of the sacrifice, Sheila and Rob, exhausted and shaken, emerged from the hidden chamber. The whispers, now a distant murmur, guided them through the dimly lit halls of the old house. The haunted dwelling, though momentarily relieved of the malevolent entity's presence, held secrets that awaited unraveling in the aftermath of the ritual.

As Sheila and Rob faced the uncertain aftermath, a chilling realization dawned upon them—the sacrifice, though sealing the ancient evil, had forever changed the fabric of their existence. The whispers, now a spectral chorus, seemed to convey the irreversible consequences of the harrowing ordeal. The haunted dwelling, a silent witness to the

unfolding aftermath, stood as a testament to the sacrifices made in the name of sealing the ancient darkness within its spectral confines.

Little did they know that the true horror, a revelation that would redefine their very existence, awaited in the shadows of the haunted dwelling. The whispers, now a fading memory, left the door ajar for the looming terror that awaited in the aftermath of the supernatural sacrifice. Sheila and Rob, bound by the malevolent forces that lingered within, faced an uncertain future where the horrors of the past cast a long, lingering shadow over their fragile grasp on reality.

Chapter 16: The Sacrifice

With the echoes of the ritual still reverberating through the old house, Sheila and Rob grappled with the aftermath of the harrowing sacrifice. The air, thick with the remnants of supernatural energies, carried a spectral resonance that seemed to linger in the haunted dwelling. The whispers, now a distant murmur, guided them through the dimly lit halls as they confronted the irreversible consequences of sealing the ancient evil within the spectral confines.

As Sheila and Rob emerged from the hidden chamber, an unsettling stillness enveloped the old house. The whispers, now a fading memory, left an eerie calm in their wake. The haunted dwelling, though momentarily relieved of the malevolent entity's presence, stood as a silent witness to the sacrifices made in the name of sealing the ancient darkness within its spectral corridors.

However, the calm was deceptive, for a greater malevolence seemed to seep through the very walls of the old house. The air, heavy with the essence of the supernatural, carried an ominous energy that hinted at the lingering darkness within. Sheila and Rob, their senses heightened by the aftermath of the sacrifice, exchanged wary glances as they navigated the dimly lit corridors.

Unbeknownst to them, the sacrifice had unleashed unforeseen consequences—unsettling manifestations that defied rational explanation. Shadows danced on the walls, and whispers, now a dissonant symphony, seemed to echo through the haunted dwelling, conveying a spectral

unrest that transcended the mortal realm. The old house, though momentarily quelled, stood as a battleground where the forces of the living and the supernatural clashed in an otherworldly dance.

As night fell over the old house, the spectral disturbances intensified. Objects moved mysteriously, and the air vibrated with a spectral resonance that hinted at a malevolent force lingering within the haunted dwelling. The whispers, now a relentless drone, guided Sheila and Rob toward the heart of the spectral storm—an impending confrontation with the consequences of the sacrifice.

In the dim light, Sheila and Rob felt an otherworldly presence—an entity that seemed to feed on the residual energies of the sacrificed blood. The whispers, now a haunting lament, spoke of a darkness that sought communion with the living, defying the constraints of the ritual. The haunted dwelling, its spectral foundations shaken by the consequences of the sacrifice, stood as a conduit for the malevolent forces that sought release.

As they explored the old house, Sheila and Rob discovered cryptic symbols appearing on the walls—a manifestation of the supernatural disturbances that had been unleashed. The whispers, now a spectral symphony, guided them through the haunted corridors, conveying the urgency of a greater darkness that loomed on the horizon. The air, charged with an otherworldly energy, carried a spectral resonance that hinted at the impending confrontation with the malevolent entity.

Sheila and Rob sought the guidance of the psychic medium who had assisted them in the cleansing ritual. The whispers, now a haunting melody, seemed to echo through the secluded residence of the medium, conveying the urgency of the situation. The air, thick with the residual energies of the supernatural encounter, guided them toward a revelation that defied comprehension.

The psychic medium, aware of the consequences of the sacrifice, spoke of a greater malevolence that had been awakened—an entity that defied the boundaries of the ritual. The whispers, now a relentless drone, urged Sheila and Rob to confront the looming darkness before

it consumed the haunted dwelling. The air, heavy with the essence of the supernatural, carried a spectral resonance that transcended the mortal realm.

Determined to face the consequences of their actions, Sheila and Rob returned to the old house, armed with newfound knowledge. The whispers, now a spectral chorus, seemed to align with their resolve as they ventured into the dimly lit halls. The haunted dwelling, though momentarily quelled, awaited the final confrontation with the malevolent entity that lingered within its spectral depths.

As night settled over the old house, Sheila and Rob felt the temperature drop—a chilling sign of the entity's presence. Shadows danced on the walls, and the air vibrated with a spectral resonance that hinted at the impending confrontation. The whispers, now a haunting lament, guided them toward the heart of the spectral storm—an epicenter where the forces of the living and the supernatural converged.

In the dim light, Sheila and Rob glimpsed fleeting apparitions—manifestations of the greater darkness that had been unleashed. The whispers, now a dissonant symphony, seemed to speak of a malevolence that sought communion with the living, defying the constraints of the ritual. The haunted dwelling, its spectral foundations saturated with the essence of the supernatural, stood as a battleground where the consequences of the sacrifice unfolded in a terrifying crescendo.

Suddenly, the room quivered with unseen energies, and the temperature plummeted. The whispers, now a spectral chorus, guided Sheila and Rob toward the epicenter of the supernatural disturbance. The air, charged with an otherworldly energy, carried a spectral resonance that hinted at the imminent confrontation with the malevolent entity.

As they approached the heart of the spectral storm, Sheila and Rob felt an oppressive force—a darkness that seemed to envelop them. The whispers, now a relentless drone, seemed to echo through the haunted dwelling, urging them to confront the malevolent entity that lurked within the shadows. The old house, though momentarily quelled, stood

as a stage for the final showdown between the forces of the living and the supernatural.

In the dimly lit chamber, Sheila and Rob confronted the malevolent entity. The whispers, now a haunting melody, guided them through the spectral encounter—a dance between the living and the abyss. The haunted dwelling, its spectral foundations shaken by the consequences of the sacrifice, became a crucible where the boundaries between reality and the supernatural blurred.

The entity, a manifestation of the ancient darkness that had been awakened, spoke through the spectral symphony. The whispers, now a dissonant chorus, conveyed the grievances and malevolence of the malevolent force that sought communion with the living. The haunted dwelling, a conduit for the supernatural forces, bore silent witness to the final showdown that unfolded within its spectral corridors.

Sheila and Rob, their senses heightened by the supernatural onslaught, faced a choice—succumb to the malevolent forces or confront the entity head-on. The whispers, now a relentless drone, urged them toward a revelation that defied comprehension. The haunted dwelling, its spectral foundations saturated with the essence of the living, stood as a battleground where the forces of the living and the supernatural clashed in a terrifying crescendo.

In the dim light, Sheila and Rob glimpsed shadowy figures—apparitions of the past that materialized in the spectral realm. The whispers, now a haunting lament, spoke of the tormented souls that lingered within the haunted dwelling. The air, charged with an otherworldly energy, guided them toward the epicenter of the spectral storm—an impending confrontation with the malevolent entity.

As the entity recoiled, the whispers, now a spectral chorus, intensified. Sheila and Rob, their resolve tested by the supernatural onslaught, faced the malevolent force with determination. The haunted dwelling, its spectral foundations shaken by the consequences of the sacrifice, became a silent witness to the final confrontation between the living and the supernatural.

With an otherworldly surge of energy, Sheila and Rob confronted the entity head-on. The whispers, now a relentless drone, seemed to align with the living as the spectral encounter reached its zenith. The haunted dwelling, its foundations saturated with the essence of the supernatural, stood as a crucible where the forces of light and darkness clashed in a terrifying crescendo.

Unexpectedly, the entity recoiled—a spectral manifestation weakened by the determination of the living. The whispers, now a fading memory, left an eerie stillness in their wake. Sheila and Rob, their senses overwhelmed by the supernatural encounter, stood amidst the remnants of the spectral storm. The haunted dwelling, though momentarily quelled, seemed to sigh with a spectral resignation as if acknowledging the fleeting victory over the malevolent forces.

As Sheila and Rob emerged from the confrontation, a sense of cautious hope lingered in the air. The whispers, now a distant murmur, guided them through the dimly lit halls of the old house—the battleground where the forces of the living had triumphed over the malevolent entity. The haunted dwelling, though forever scarred by the supernatural encounter, stood as a testament to the resilience of those who dared to confront the ancient darkness that lurked within its spectral confines.

Little did Sheila and Rob know that the true horror, a revelation that would redefine their very existence, awaited in the shadows of the haunted dwelling. The whispers, now a fading memory, left the door ajar for the looming terror that awaited in the aftermath of the supernatural sacrifice. Sheila and Rob, bound by the malevolent forces that lingered within, faced an uncertain future where the horrors of the past cast a long, lingering shadow over their fragile grasp on reality.

Chapter 17: The Confrontation

In the aftermath of the supernatural encounter, Sheila and Rob found themselves standing amidst the remnants of the spectral storm that had gripped the old house. The air, heavy with the essence of the supernatural, carried a spectral resonance that hinted at the lingering

forces within the haunted dwelling. The whispers, now a distant murmur, guided them through the dimly lit halls as they grappled with the aftermath of the harrowing confrontation.

As they explored the old house, Sheila and Rob felt a palpable tension—an unsettling energy that seemed to emanate from the very walls. Shadows danced on the walls, and the air vibrated with a spectral resonance that hinted at a lingering malevolence. The whispers, now a haunting lament, guided them toward the heart of the spectral disturbance—an impending confrontation with the consequences of the sacrifice.

Unbeknownst to them, the malevolent entity, though weakened, lingered within the haunted dwelling, seeking revenge for the disruption of its spectral communion. The air, thick with the essence of the supernatural, carried an ominous energy that hinted at the impending clash between the living and the lingering darkness. Sheila and Rob, their nerves on edge, exchanged wary glances as they ventured into the dimly lit corridors.

As night fell over the old house, the spectral disturbances intensified. Objects moved mysteriously, and the whispers, now a relentless drone, seemed to echo through the haunted dwelling. The air, charged with an otherworldly energy, guided Sheila and Rob toward the epicenter of the spectral storm—a confrontation with the malevolent forces that sought release.

In the dim light, Sheila and Rob discovered cryptic symbols appearing on the walls—a manifestation of the supernatural disturbances that had been unleashed. The whispers, now a spectral symphony, intensified as they delved into the haunted corridors, conveying the urgency of a greater darkness that loomed on the horizon. The old house, though momentarily quelled, stood as a battleground where the forces of the living and the supernatural clashed in an otherworldly dance.

Sheila and Rob sought the guidance of the psychic medium who had assisted them in the cleansing ritual. The whispers, now a haunting melody, seemed to echo through the secluded residence of the medium,

conveying the urgency of the situation. The air, thick with the residual energies of the supernatural encounter, guided them toward a revelation that defied comprehension.

The psychic medium, aware of the lingering malevolence, spoke of the entity's resilience—a force that defied the boundaries of the ritual. The whispers, now a relentless drone, urged Sheila and Rob to confront the looming darkness before it consumed the haunted dwelling. The air, heavy with the essence of the supernatural, carried a spectral resonance that transcended the mortal realm.

Determined to face the consequences of their actions, Sheila and Rob returned to the old house, armed with newfound knowledge. The whispers, now a spectral chorus, seemed to align with their resolve as they ventured into the dimly lit halls. The haunted dwelling, though momentarily quelled, awaited the final confrontation with the malevolent entity that lingered within its spectral depths.

As night settled over the old house, Sheila and Rob felt the temperature drop—a chilling sign of the entity's presence. Shadows danced on the walls, and the air vibrated with a spectral resonance that hinted at the impending confrontation. The whispers, now a haunting lament, guided them toward the heart of the spectral storm—an epicenter where the forces of the living and the supernatural converged.

In the dim light, Sheila and Rob glimpsed fleeting apparitions—manifestations of the greater darkness that had been unleashed. The whispers, now a dissonant symphony, seemed to speak of a malevolence that sought communion with the living, defying the constraints of the ritual. The haunted dwelling, its spectral foundations saturated with the essence of the supernatural, stood as a battleground where the consequences of the sacrifice unfolded in a terrifying crescendo.

Suddenly, the room quivered with unseen energies, and the temperature plummeted. The whispers, now a spectral chorus, guided Sheila and Rob toward the epicenter of the supernatural disturbance. The air, charged with an otherworldly energy, carried a spectral resonance that hinted at the imminent confrontation with the malevolent entity.

As they approached the heart of the spectral storm, Sheila and Rob felt an oppressive force—a darkness that seemed to envelop them. The whispers, now a relentless drone, seemed to echo through the haunted dwelling, urging them to confront the malevolent entity that lurked within the shadows. The old house, though momentarily quelled, stood as a stage for the final showdown between the forces of the living and the supernatural.

In the dimly lit chamber, Sheila and Rob confronted the malevolent entity. The whispers, now a haunting melody, guided them through the spectral encounter—a dance between the living and the abyss. The haunted dwelling, its spectral foundations shaken by the consequences of the sacrifice, became a crucible where the boundaries between reality and the supernatural blurred.

The entity, a manifestation of the ancient darkness that had been awakened, spoke through the spectral symphony. The whispers, now a dissonant chorus, conveyed the grievances and malevolence of the malevolent force that sought communion with the living. The haunted dwelling, a conduit for the supernatural forces, bore silent witness to the final showdown that unfolded within its spectral corridors.

Sheila and Rob, their senses heightened by the supernatural onslaught, faced a choice—succumb to the malevolent forces or confront the entity head-on. The whispers, now a relentless drone, urged them toward a revelation that defied comprehension. The haunted dwelling, its spectral foundations saturated with the essence of the living, stood as a battleground where the forces of the living and the supernatural clashed in a terrifying crescendo.

In the dim light, Sheila and Rob glimpsed shadowy figures—apparitions of the past that materialized in the spectral realm. The whispers, now a haunting lament, spoke of the tormented souls that lingered within the haunted dwelling. The air, charged with an otherworldly energy, guided them toward the epicenter of the spectral storm—an impending confrontation with the malevolent entity.

As the entity recoiled, the whispers, now a spectral chorus, intensified. Sheila and Rob, their resolve tested by the supernatural onslaught, faced the malevolent force with determination. The haunted dwelling, its spectral foundations saturated with the essence of the supernatural, stood as a crucible where the forces of light and darkness clashed in a terrifying crescendo.

Unexpectedly, the entity recoiled—a spectral manifestation weakened by the determination of the living. The whispers, now a fading memory, left an eerie stillness in their wake. Sheila and Rob, their senses overwhelmed by the supernatural encounter, stood amidst the remnants of the spectral storm. The haunted dwelling, though momentarily quelled, seemed to sigh with a spectral resignation as if acknowledging the fleeting victory over the malevolent forces.

As Sheila and Rob emerged from the confrontation, a sense of cautious hope lingered in the air. The whispers, now a distant murmur, guided them through the dimly lit halls of the old house—the battleground where the forces of the living had triumphed over the malevolent entity. The haunted dwelling, though forever scarred by the supernatural encounter, stood as a testament to the resilience of those who dared to confront the ancient darkness that lurked within its spectral confines.

Little did Sheila and Rob know that the true horror, a revelation that would redefine their very existence, awaited in the shadows of the haunted dwelling. The whispers, now a fading memory, left the door ajar for the looming terror that awaited in the aftermath of the supernatural sacrifice. Sheila and Rob, bound by the malevolent forces that lingered within, faced an uncertain future where the horrors of the past cast a long, lingering shadow over their fragile grasp on reality.

Chapter 18: The Resolution

The aftermath of the confrontation left Sheila and Rob in a state of emotional turmoil. The air, thick with the remnants of the supernatural encounter, carried a spectral resonance that seemed to linger within the haunted dwelling. The whispers, now a distant murmur, guided

them through the dimly lit halls as they grappled with the irreversible consequences of the sacrifice and the lingering darkness that clung to the old house.

As they explored the haunted corridors, Sheila and Rob discovered that the malevolent entity, though weakened, had left an indelible mark on the spectral fabric of the old house. Shadows danced on the walls, and the air vibrated with a spectral resonance that hinted at the lingering malevolence. The whispers, now a haunting lament, guided them toward the heart of the spectral disturbance—an exploration of the haunted dwelling's newfound reality.

Unbeknownst to them, the sacrifice had not only sealed the ancient evil but had woven the malevolent forces into the very fabric of the haunted dwelling. The air, heavy with the essence of the supernatural, carried an ominous energy that hinted at the spectral unrest within. Sheila and Rob, their senses heightened by the aftermath of the confrontation, exchanged wary glances as they ventured into the dimly lit corridors.

As night fell over the old house, the spectral disturbances intensified. Objects moved mysteriously, and the whispers, now a relentless drone, seemed to echo through the haunted dwelling. The air, charged with an otherworldly energy, guided Sheila and Rob toward the epicenter of the spectral storm—a realization that the malevolent forces were not entirely quelled.

In the dim light, Sheila and Rob glimpsed cryptic symbols appearing on the walls—a manifestation of the supernatural disturbances that had been woven into the spectral fabric of the old house. The whispers, now a spectral symphony, intensified as they delved into the haunted corridors, conveying the urgency of a greater darkness that loomed on the horizon. The haunted dwelling, though momentarily quelled, stood as a battleground where the forces of the living and the supernatural clashed in an otherworldly dance.

Sheila and Rob sought the guidance of the psychic medium who had assisted them in the cleansing ritual. The whispers, now a haunting

melody, seemed to echo through the secluded residence of the medium, conveying the urgency of the situation. The air, thick with the residual energies of the supernatural encounter, guided them toward a revelation that defied comprehension.

The psychic medium, aware of the lingering malevolence, spoke of the residual energies that had become entwined with the old house's spectral fabric. The whispers, now a relentless drone, urged Sheila and Rob to confront the lingering darkness before it consumed the haunted dwelling. The air, heavy with the essence of the supernatural, carried a spectral resonance that transcended the mortal realm.

Determined to face the consequences of their actions, Sheila and Rob returned to the old house, armed with newfound knowledge. The whispers, now a spectral chorus, seemed to align with their resolve as they ventured into the dimly lit halls. The haunted dwelling, though momentarily quelled, awaited the final confrontation with the residual malevolent forces that lingered within its spectral depths.

As night settled over the old house, Sheila and Rob felt the temperature drop—a chilling sign of the residual entity's presence. Shadows danced on the walls, and the air vibrated with a spectral resonance that hinted at the impending confrontation. The whispers, now a haunting lament, guided them toward the heart of the spectral storm—an epicenter where the forces of the living and the supernatural converged.

In the dim light, Sheila and Rob glimpsed fleeting apparitions—manifestations of the residual darkness that clung to the haunted dwelling. The whispers, now a dissonant symphony, seemed to speak of a malevolence that sought communion with the living, defying the constraints of the ritual. The old house, though momentarily quelled, stood as a battleground where the consequences of the sacrifice unfolded in a terrifying crescendo.

Suddenly, the room quivered with unseen energies, and the temperature plummeted. The whispers, now a spectral chorus, guided Sheila and Rob toward the epicenter of the supernatural disturbance. The air, charged with an otherworldly energy, carried a spectral resonance

that hinted at the imminent confrontation with the residual malevolent forces.

As they approached the heart of the spectral storm, Sheila and Rob felt an oppressive force—a darkness that seemed to envelop them. The whispers, now a relentless drone, seemed to echo through the haunted dwelling, urging them to confront the lingering malevolent forces that lurked within the shadows. The old house, though momentarily quelled, stood as a stage for the final showdown between the forces of the living and the residual supernatural darkness.

In the dimly lit chamber, Sheila and Rob confronted the residual malevolent forces. The whispers, now a haunting melody, guided them through the spectral encounter—a dance between the living and the lingering abyss. The haunted dwelling, its spectral foundations shaken by the consequences of the sacrifice, became a crucible where the boundaries between reality and the residual supernatural blurred.

The residual entity, a manifestation of the ancient darkness that had been entwined with the spectral fabric, spoke through the dissonant chorus. The whispers, now a relentless drone, conveyed the grievances and malevolence of the lingering force that sought communion with the living. The haunted dwelling, a conduit for the residual supernatural forces, bore silent witness to the final showdown that unfolded within its spectral corridors.

Sheila and Rob, their senses heightened by the supernatural on-slaught, faced a choice—succumb to the lingering malevolent forces or confront the residual entity head-on. The whispers, now a relentless drone, urged them toward a revelation that defied comprehension. The haunted dwelling, its spectral foundations saturated with the essence of the living, stood as a battleground where the forces of the living and the residual supernatural clashed in a terrifying crescendo.

In the dim light, Sheila and Rob glimpsed shadowy figures—appa-ritions of the past that materialized in the spectral realm. The whispers, now a haunting lament, spoke of the tormented souls that lingered within the haunted dwelling. The air, charged with an otherworldly

energy, guided them toward the epicenter of the spectral storm—an impending confrontation with the residual malevolent entity.

As the entity recoiled, the whispers, now a spectral chorus, intensified. Sheila and Rob, their resolve tested by the supernatural onslaught, faced the residual malevolent force with determination. The haunted dwelling, its spectral foundations saturated with the essence of the supernatural, stood as a crucible where the forces of light and darkness clashed in a terrifying crescendo.

Unexpectedly, the residual entity recoiled—a spectral manifestation weakened by the determination of the living. The whispers, now a fading memory, left an eerie stillness in their wake. Sheila and Rob, their senses overwhelmed by the supernatural encounter, stood amidst the remnants of the residual spectral storm. The haunted dwelling, though momentarily quelled, seemed to sigh with a spectral resignation as if acknowledging the fleeting victory over the lingering malevolent forces.

As Sheila and Rob emerged from the confrontation, a sense of cautious hope lingered in the air. The whispers, now a distant murmur, guided them through the dimly lit halls of the old house—the battleground where the forces of the living had once again triumphed over the residual malevolent entity. The haunted dwelling, though forever scarred by the supernatural encounter, stood as a testament to the resilience of those who dared to confront the ancient darkness that lingered within its spectral confines.

Little did Sheila and Rob know that the true horror, a revelation that would redefine their very existence, awaited in the shadows of the haunted dwelling. The whispers, now a fading memory, left the door ajar for the looming terror that awaited in the aftermath of the supernatural sacrifice. Sheila and Rob, bound by the lingering forces that clung within, faced an uncertain future where the horrors of the past cast a long, lingering shadow over their fragile grasp on reality.

Chapter 19: The Awakening

As Sheila and Rob emerged from the lingering shadows of the haunted dwelling, a fragile sense of hope clung to the air. The whispers,

now a distant murmur, guided them through the dimly lit halls—the haunted battleground where they had confronted the malevolent forces and the residual darkness. However, the old house, forever scarred by the supernatural encounter, bore the weight of a haunting legacy that transcended the physical realm.

In the aftermath of the confrontation, Sheila and Rob felt a disquieting calm settle over the old house. The air, heavy with the essence of the supernatural, carried a spectral resonance that hinted at the lingering forces within the haunted dwelling. Shadows danced on the walls, and the whispers, now a fading memory, seemed to echo through the spectral corridors—an eerie reminder of the harrowing journey that had unfolded within the confines of the ancient dwelling.

Unbeknownst to them, the supernatural encounter had left an indelible mark on Sheila's soul. As night fell over the old house, a subtle shift occurred within Sheila—an awakening to a new reality that transcended the boundaries of the living. The whispers, now a distant melody, guided her through the haunted corridors, leading her toward a revelation that defied comprehension.

As they explored the old house, Sheila and Rob discovered that the residual energies had imprinted themselves onto the very fabric of Sheila's being. Shadows, now a spectral dance, seemed to weave through her existence, blurring the boundaries between the living and the supernatural. The whispers, now a haunting lament, echoed through her consciousness—an unsettling reminder that the spectral legacy lingered within.

In the dim light, Sheila and Rob witnessed cryptic symbols appearing on Sheila's skin—a manifestation of the supernatural imprint left by the ancient darkness. The whispers, now a spectral symphony, intensified as they delved into the haunted corridors, conveying the urgency of a greater awakening that loomed on the horizon. The old house, though momentarily quelled, stood as a conduit for Sheila's transformation—an evolution that defied the constraints of the mortal realm.

Sheila, grappling with the newfound reality, sought the guidance of the psychic medium who had assisted them in the cleansing ritual. The whispers, now a haunting melody, seemed to echo through the secluded residence of the medium, conveying the urgency of Sheila's awakening. The air, thick with the residual energies of the supernatural encounter, guided them toward a revelation that went beyond the haunted dwelling's spectral confines.

The psychic medium, attuned to the supernatural currents, spoke of Sheila's connection to the ancient darkness—an awakening that defied the boundaries of the ritual. The whispers, now a relentless drone, urged Sheila to embrace the spectral legacy within her. The air, heavy with the essence of the supernatural, carried a spectral resonance that transcended the mortal realm.

Determined to understand the extent of her transformation, Sheila returned to the old house, her senses heightened by the lingering supernatural energies. The whispers, now a spectral chorus, seemed to align with her evolving awareness as she ventured into the dimly lit halls. The haunted dwelling, though scarred by the supernatural encounter, awaited the next chapter in Sheila's journey—an odyssey that would redefine her very existence.

As night settled over the old house, Sheila felt the temperature drop—a chilling sign of her newfound connection to the lingering forces. Shadows danced on the walls, and the air vibrated with a spectral resonance that hinted at the awakening within her. The whispers, now a haunting lament, guided her toward the heart of the spectral storm—an epicenter where the forces of the living and the supernatural converged within her being.

In the dim light, Sheila glimpsed fleeting apparitions—manifestations of the ancient darkness that had become intertwined with her soul. The whispers, now a dissonant symphony, seemed to speak of a malevolence seeking communion with her, defying the constraints of the ritual. The old house, though momentarily quelled, stood as a

witness to Sheila's metamorphosis—an evolution that transcended the boundaries of the living.

Suddenly, the room quivered with unseen energies, and the temperature plummeted. The whispers, now a spectral chorus, intensified as Sheila confronted the epicenter of the supernatural disturbance within herself. The air, charged with an otherworldly energy, carried a spectral resonance that hinted at the imminent confrontation with the ancient darkness that had become a part of her very essence.

As Sheila approached the heart of the spectral storm within her, she felt an oppressive force—an awakening darkness that seemed to envelop her being. The whispers, now a relentless drone, echoed through her consciousness, urging her to confront the malevolent forces that lingered within the depths of her soul. Sheila, standing at the threshold of her own transformation, faced the haunting legacy that had become an integral part of her existence.

In the dimly lit chamber of her consciousness, Sheila confronted the residual malevolent forces that lingered within her. The whispers, now a haunting melody, guided her through the spectral encounter—a dance between her awakened self and the lingering abyss. The haunted dwelling, its spectral foundations shaken by the consequences of the sacrifice, became a crucible where the boundaries between Sheila's reality and the supernatural blurred.

The residual entity within Sheila, a manifestation of the ancient darkness, spoke through the spectral symphony within her soul. The whispers, now a dissonant chorus, conveyed the grievances and malevolence of the lingering force that sought communion with her. Sheila, in a surreal confrontation with her own awakening, faced the ancient darkness that had become intertwined with her very essence. The haunted dwelling, a conduit for the residual supernatural forces, bore silent witness to the final showdown within the depths of Sheila's consciousness.

As Sheila grappled with the malevolent forces within her, the whispers, now a relentless drone, urged her toward a revelation that defied comprehension. The haunted dwelling, its spectral foundations

saturated with the essence of Sheila's transformation, stood as a battleground where the forces of light and darkness clashed in a terrifying crescendo within the depths of her soul.

In the dim light, Sheila glimpsed shadowy figures—apparitions of the past that materialized in the spectral realm within her consciousness. The whispers, now a haunting lament, spoke of the tormented souls that lingered within her awakened self. The air, charged with an otherworldly energy, guided her toward the epicenter of the spectral storm—an impending confrontation with the malevolent entity that had become an integral part of her very existence.

As Sheila confronted the entity within, the whispers, now a spectral chorus, intensified. Her resolve tested by the supernatural onslaught, she faced the residual malevolent force with determination. The haunted dwelling, its spectral foundations saturated with the essence of the supernatural, stood as a crucible where the forces of light and darkness clashed in a terrifying crescendo within the depths of Sheila's soul.

Unexpectedly, the residual entity within Sheila recoiled—a spectral manifestation weakened by her determination to overcome the malevolent forces. The whispers, now a fading memory, left an eerie stillness in the chambers of her consciousness. Sheila, her senses overwhelmed by the supernatural encounter within, stood amidst the remnants of the spectral storm that had unfolded within her soul. The haunted dwelling, though momentarily quelled, seemed to sigh with a spectral resignation as if acknowledging the fleeting victory over the lingering malevolent forces.

As Sheila emerged from the depths of her own awakening, a sense of cautious hope lingered in the air. The whispers, now a distant murmur, guided her through the dimly lit halls of her own consciousness— the battleground where she had triumphed over the malevolent forces within. The haunted dwelling, forever scarred by the supernatural encounter, stood as a testament to the resilience of the human spirit and the capacity to confront the ancient darkness that lurked within one's own soul.

Little did Sheila know that her journey was far from over. The whispers, now a fading memory, left the door ajar for the looming terror that awaited in the aftermath of her awakening. Sheila, forever changed by the harrowing ordeal within herself, faced an uncertain future where the horrors of her own past cast a long, lingering shadow over her fragile grasp on reality. The haunted dwelling, a reflection of her awakened soul, awaited the next chapter in Sheila's journey—a journey that would redefine the very fabric of her existence.

Chapter 20: The Return

In the aftermath of Sheila's awakening, a deceptive calm settled over the old house. The air, thick with the remnants of the supernatural encounter within her soul, carried an unsettling resonance that hinted at the depths of her transformation. The whispers, now a distant murmur, guided Sheila through the dimly lit halls—a haunting reminder of the malevolent forces that lingered within her awakened self.

As night fell over the old house, Sheila's senses heightened, attuned to the subtle shifts in the spectral currents that surrounded her. Shadows danced on the walls, and the air vibrated with a spectral resonance that hinted at the lingering darkness within her. The whispers, now a fading memory, seemed to echo through the haunted corridors—an ominous prelude to the return of the malevolent forces that had become entwined with her very essence.

Unbeknownst to Sheila, her awakening had not only transformed her soul but had left an indelible mark on the haunted dwelling itself. The air, heavy with the essence of the supernatural, carried an ominous energy that hinted at a spectral unrest within the old house. The whispers, now a haunting lament, guided her toward the epicenter of the spectral storm—an awareness that the malevolent forces were not confined to her consciousness alone.

In the dim light, Sheila and Rob witnessed cryptic symbols reappearing on the walls—a manifestation of the malevolent forces that had returned to the spectral fabric of the old house. The whispers, now a spectral symphony, intensified as they delved into the haunted

corridors, conveying the urgency of a greater darkness that loomed on the horizon. The old house, though scarred by the supernatural encounter, stood as a stage for the malevolent forces' return—an encore that defied the constraints of the ritual.

Sheila, grappling with the resurgence of the malevolent forces, sought the guidance of the psychic medium who had assisted them in the cleansing ritual. The whispers, now a haunting melody, seemed to echo through the secluded residence of the medium, conveying the urgency of the situation. The air, thick with the residual energies of the supernatural encounter, guided them toward a revelation that went beyond the haunted dwelling's spectral confines.

The psychic medium, aware of the lingering malevolence, spoke of the malevolent forces' return—an awakening that defied the boundaries of the ritual. The whispers, now a relentless drone, urged Sheila and Rob to confront the looming darkness before it consumed the haunted dwelling. The air, heavy with the essence of the supernatural, carried a spectral resonance that transcended the mortal realm.

Determined to face the consequences of her awakening, Sheila returned to the old house, her senses heightened by the lingering supernatural energies. The whispers, now a spectral chorus, seemed to align with her evolving awareness as she ventured into the dimly lit halls. The haunted dwelling, though scarred by the supernatural encounter, awaited the next chapter in Sheila's journey—an odyssey that would test the limits of her newfound connection to the malevolent forces.

As night settled over the old house, Sheila felt the temperature drop—a chilling sign of the malevolent forces' return. Shadows danced on the walls, and the air vibrated with a spectral resonance that hinted at the impending confrontation. The whispers, now a haunting lament, guided her toward the heart of the spectral storm—an epicenter where the forces of the living and the supernatural converged within her being.

In the dim light, Sheila glimpsed fleeting apparitions—manifestations of the malevolent forces that had returned to the haunted dwelling. The whispers, now a dissonant symphony, seemed to speak of a

malevolence seeking communion with her, defying the constraints of the ritual. The old house, though momentarily quelled, stood as a witness to Sheila's confrontation with the return of the malevolent forces —an encore that echoed through the spectral corridors.

Suddenly, the room quivered with unseen energies, and the temperature plummeted. The whispers, now a spectral chorus, intensified as Sheila confronted the epicenter of the supernatural disturbance within herself. The air, charged with an otherworldly energy, carried a spectral resonance that hinted at the imminent confrontation with the malevolent forces that had returned to the old house.

As Sheila approached the heart of the spectral storm within her, she felt an oppressive force—an awakening darkness that seemed to envelop her being. The whispers, now a relentless drone, echoed through her consciousness, urging her to confront the malevolent forces that lingered within the depths of her soul. Sheila, standing at the threshold of her own transformation, faced the haunting encore that had become an integral part of her existence.

In the dimly lit chamber of her consciousness, Sheila confronted the return of the malevolent forces that lingered within her. The whispers, now a haunting melody, guided her through the spectral encounter—a dance between her awakened self and the lingering abyss. The haunted dwelling, its spectral foundations shaken by the consequences of the sacrifice, became a crucible where the boundaries between Sheila's reality and the return of the malevolent forces blurred.

The malevolent forces within Sheila, a manifestation of the ancient darkness, spoke through the spectral symphony within her soul. The whispers, now a dissonant chorus, conveyed the grievances and malevolence of the lingering force that sought communion with her. Sheila, in a surreal confrontation with the return of the malevolent forces, faced the ancient darkness that had become intertwined with her very essence. The haunted dwelling, a conduit for the malevolent supernatural forces, bore silent witness to the encore within the depths of Sheila's consciousness.

As Sheila grappled with the malevolent forces within her, the whispers, now a relentless drone, urged her toward a revelation that defied comprehension. The haunted dwelling, its spectral foundations saturated with the essence of Sheila's confrontation, stood as a battleground where the forces of light and darkness clashed in a terrifying encore within the depths of her soul.

In the dim light, Sheila glimpsed shadowy figures—apparitions of the past that materialized in the spectral realm within her consciousness. The whispers, now a haunting lament, spoke of the tormented souls that lingered within her awakened self. The air, charged with an otherworldly energy, guided her toward the epicenter of the spectral storm— an impending encore with the malevolent entity that had become an integral part of her very existence.

As Sheila confronted the entity within, the whispers, now a spectral chorus, intensified. Her resolve tested by the supernatural encore, she faced the return of the malevolent force with determination. The haunted dwelling, its spectral foundations saturated with the essence of the supernatural, stood as a crucible where the forces of light and darkness clashed in a terrifying encore within the depths of Sheila's soul.

Unexpectedly, the return of the malevolent forces within Sheila recoiled—a spectral manifestation weakened by her determination to overcome the malevolent encore. The whispers, now a fading memory, left an eerie stillness in the chambers of her consciousness. Sheila, her senses overwhelmed by the supernatural encore within, stood amidst the remnants of the spectral storm that had unfolded within her soul. The haunted dwelling, though momentarily quelled, seemed to sigh with a spectral resignation as if acknowledging the fleeting victory over the lingering malevolent forces.

As Sheila emerged from the depths of her own confrontation, a sense of cautious hope lingered in the air. The whispers, now a distant murmur, guided her through the dimly lit halls of her own consciousness—the battleground where she had triumphed over the malevolent forces within. The haunted dwelling, forever scarred by the supernatural

encore, stood as a testament to the resilience of the human spirit and the capacity to confront the ancient darkness that lurked within one's own soul.

Little did Sheila know that the return of the malevolent forces signaled a new chapter in her journey. The whispers, now a fading memory, left the door ajar for the looming terror that awaited in the aftermath of the supernatural encore. Sheila, forever changed by the harrowing ordeal within herself, faced an uncertain future where the horrors of her own past cast a long, lingering shadow over her fragile grasp on reality. The haunted dwelling, a reflection of her awakened soul, awaited the next chapter in Sheila's journey—a journey that would redefine the very fabric of her existence.

Chapter 21: The Revelation

In the wake of the malevolent forces' return, the old house stood as a silent witness to the unfolding nightmare that awaited Sheila. The air, thick with the supernatural energies that clung to her awakened soul, carried an oppressive weight that seemed to permeate every corner of the haunted dwelling. The whispers, now a distant murmur, guided Sheila through the dimly lit halls—a foreboding prelude to the revelation that awaited in the shadows.

As night fell over the old house, Sheila's senses remained on edge, attuned to the subtle shifts in the spectral currents that surrounded her. Shadows danced on the walls, and the air vibrated with a spectral resonance that hinted at the impending revelation. The whispers, now a fading memory, seemed to echo through the haunted corridors—an eerie reminder of the malevolent forces that lurked within the depths of her awakened self.

Unbeknownst to Sheila, the return of the malevolent forces had not only marked the old house but had woven a dark tapestry that transcended the physical realm. The air, heavy with the essence of the supernatural encore, carried an ominous energy that hinted at a spectral unrest within the very fabric of the haunted dwelling. The whispers, now a haunting lament, guided her toward the epicenter of

the spectral storm—an awareness that the malevolent forces sought not only communion with her soul but also a greater revelation that defied comprehension.

In the dim light, Sheila and Rob witnessed cryptic symbols reappearing on the walls—a manifestation of the malevolent forces that had returned to the spectral fabric of the old house. The whispers, now a spectral symphony, intensified as they delved into the haunted corridors, conveying the urgency of a revelation that went beyond the boundaries of the living. The old house, though momentarily quelled, stood as a stage for the malevolent forces' revelation—an unveiling that defied the constraints of the mortal realm.

Sheila, grappling with the ominous energies that clung to her awakened soul, sought the guidance of the psychic medium who had assisted them in the cleansing ritual. The whispers, now a haunting melody, seemed to echo through the secluded residence of the medium, conveying the urgency of the situation. The air, thick with the residual energies of the supernatural encore, guided them toward a revelation that transcended the haunted dwelling's spectral confines.

The psychic medium, attuned to the supernatural currents, spoke of a revelation that went beyond the malevolent forces' return—an awakening that defied the boundaries of the ritual. The whispers, now a relentless drone, urged Sheila and Rob to confront the looming darkness before it consumed not only their souls but also the very fabric of reality. The air, heavy with the essence of the supernatural, carried a spectral resonance that transcended the mortal realm.

Determined to face the consequences of the revelation, Sheila returned to the old house, her senses heightened by the lingering supernatural energies. The whispers, now a spectral chorus, seemed to align with her evolving awareness as she ventured into the dimly lit halls. The haunted dwelling, scarred by the supernatural encounter and the malevolent encore, awaited the next chapter in Sheila's journey—an odyssey that would test the limits of her newfound connection to the malevolent forces and the revelation that awaited in the shadows.

As night settled over the old house, Sheila felt the temperature drop—a chilling sign of the revelation that loomed on the horizon. Shadows danced on the walls, and the air vibrated with a spectral resonance that hinted at the impending unveiling. The whispers, now a haunting lament, guided her toward the heart of the spectral storm—an epicenter where the forces of the living and the supernatural converged within her being.

In the dim light, Sheila glimpsed fleeting apparitions—manifestations of the malevolent forces that had returned to the haunted dwelling. The whispers, now a dissonant symphony, seemed to speak of a malevolence seeking communion with her, defying the constraints of the ritual. The old house, though momentarily quelled, stood as a witness to Sheila's confrontation with the revelation—an unveiling that echoed through the spectral corridors.

Suddenly, the room quivered with unseen energies, and the temperature plummeted. The whispers, now a spectral chorus, intensified as Sheila confronted the epicenter of the supernatural disturbance within herself. The air, charged with an otherworldly energy, carried a spectral resonance that hinted at the imminent confrontation with the revelation that had become intertwined with her very essence.

As Sheila approached the heart of the spectral storm within her, she felt an oppressive force—an awakening darkness that seemed to envelop her being. The whispers, now a relentless drone, echoed through her consciousness, urging her to confront the malevolent forces and the revelation that lingered within the depths of her soul. Sheila, standing at the threshold of her own transformation, faced the haunting unveiling that had become an integral part of her existence.

In the dimly lit chamber of her consciousness, Sheila confronted the revelation that unfolded within her soul. The whispers, now a haunting melody, guided her through the spectral encounter—a dance between her awakened self and the lingering abyss. The haunted dwelling, its spectral foundations shaken by the consequences of the sacrifice and the

malevolent encore, became a crucible where the boundaries between Sheila's reality and the revelation blurred.

The revelation within Sheila, a manifestation of the ancient darkness, spoke through the spectral symphony within her soul. The whispers, now a dissonant chorus, conveyed the grievances and malevolence of the lingering force that sought communion with her. Sheila, in a surreal confrontation with the revelation, faced the ancient darkness that had become intertwined with her very essence. The haunted dwelling, a conduit for the malevolent supernatural forces and the revelation, bore silent witness to the final unveiling within the depths of Sheila's consciousness.

As Sheila grappled with the malevolent forces and the revelation within her, the whispers, now a relentless drone, urged her toward a revelation that defied comprehension. The haunted dwelling, its spectral foundations saturated with the essence of Sheila's confrontation and the revelation, stood as a battleground where the forces of light and darkness clashed in a terrifying crescendo within the depths of her soul.

In the dim light, Sheila glimpsed shadowy figures—apparitions of the past that materialized in the spectral realm within her consciousness. The whispers, now a haunting lament, spoke of the tormented souls that lingered within her awakened self. The air, charged with an otherworldly energy, guided her toward the epicenter of the spectral storm— an impending revelation with the malevolent entity that had become an integral part of her very existence.

As Sheila confronted the entity within, the whispers, now a spectral chorus, intensified. Her resolve tested by the supernatural onslaught, she faced the revelation and the return of the malevolent force with determination. The haunted dwelling, its spectral foundations saturated with the essence of the supernatural, stood as a crucible where the forces of light and darkness clashed in a terrifying crescendo within the depths of Sheila's soul.

Unexpectedly, the revelation within Sheila recoiled—a spectral manifestation weakened by her determination to overcome the malevolent

forces. The whispers, now a fading memory, left an eerie stillness in the chambers of her consciousness. Sheila, her senses overwhelmed by the supernatural encounter within and the revelation, stood amidst the remnants of the spectral storm that had unfolded within her soul. The haunted dwelling, though momentarily quelled, seemed to sigh with a spectral resignation as if acknowledging the fleeting victory over the lingering malevolent forces and the revelation.

As Sheila emerged from the depths of her own confrontation and the revelation, a sense of cautious hope lingered in the air. The whispers, now a distant murmur, guided her through the dimly lit halls of her own consciousness—the battleground where she had triumphed over the malevolent forces and the revelation within. The haunted dwelling, forever scarred by the supernatural encounter, the malevolent encore, and the revelation, stood as a testament to the resilience of the human spirit and the capacity to confront the ancient darkness that lurked within one's own soul.

Little did Sheila know that the revelation signaled a new chapter in her journey. The whispers, now a fading memory, left the door ajar for the looming terror that awaited in the aftermath of the supernatural encounter, the malevolent encore, and the revelation. Sheila, forever changed by the harrowing ordeal within herself, faced an uncertain future where the horrors of her own past cast a long, lingering shadow over her fragile grasp on reality. The haunted dwelling, a reflection of her awakened soul, awaited the next chapter in Sheila's journey—a journey that would redefine the very fabric of her existence.

Chapter 22: The Sacrifice

As Sheila emerged from the depths of the haunting revelation, an uneasy calm settled over the old house. The air, thick with the remnants of the supernatural encounter, the malevolent encore, and the revelation within her soul, carried a weight that seemed to hang in the dimly lit halls. The whispers, now a distant murmur, guided Sheila through the spectral corridors—an ominous reminder of the malevolent forces and the revelation that lingered within the shadows.

The old house, scarred by the supernatural events that had unfolded within its walls, stood as a testament to the harrowing journey Sheila had traversed. Shadows danced on the walls, and the air vibrated with a spectral resonance that hinted at the lingering darkness within her. The whispers, now a fading memory, seemed to echo through the haunted dwelling—an eerie prelude to the final chapter that awaited Sheila.

Unbeknownst to her, the malevolent forces, the revelation, and the haunting encore had left an indelible mark not only on her soul but also on the spectral fabric of the old house. The air, heavy with the essence of the supernatural, carried an ominous energy that hinted at a lingering presence—a spectral force that awaited the culmination of Sheila's journey. The whispers, now a haunting lament, guided her toward the epicenter of the spectral storm—an awareness that the malevolent forces and the revelation were not mere echoes of the past but a looming threat that sought a resolution.

In the dim light, Sheila and Rob observed cryptic symbols etching themselves onto the walls—a manifestation of the malevolent forces, the revelation, and the encore that had become intertwined with the haunted dwelling. The whispers, now a spectral symphony, intensified as they delved into the haunted corridors, conveying the urgency of a greater darkness that loomed on the horizon. The old house, though momentarily quelled, stood as a stage for the malevolent forces' final act—an act that defied the constraints of the ritual and hinted at a resolution that transcended the boundaries of the living.

Sheila, grappling with the weight of the revelation, sought the guidance of the psychic medium who had assisted them in the cleansing ritual. The whispers, now a haunting melody, seemed to echo through the secluded residence of the medium, conveying the urgency of the situation. The air, thick with the residual energies of the supernatural encounter, the malevolent encore, and the revelation, guided them toward a resolution that went beyond the haunted dwelling's spectral confines.

The psychic medium, aware of the lingering malevolence, spoke of a resolution that defied the boundaries of the ritual. The whispers, now a relentless drone, urged Sheila and Rob to confront the looming darkness before it consumed not only their souls but also the very fabric of reality. The air, heavy with the essence of the supernatural, carried a spectral resonance that transcended the mortal realm.

Determined to face the consequences of the supernatural events, Sheila returned to the old house, her senses heightened by the lingering energies. The whispers, now a spectral chorus, seemed to align with her evolving awareness as she ventured into the dimly lit halls. The haunted dwelling, scarred by the supernatural events and the revelation, awaited the next chapter in Sheila's journey—an odyssey that would test the limits of her newfound connection to the malevolent forces.

As night settled over the old house, Sheila felt the temperature drop—a chilling sign of the impending resolution. Shadows danced on the walls, and the air vibrated with a spectral resonance that hinted at the imminent confrontation. The whispers, now a haunting lament, guided her toward the heart of the spectral storm—an epicenter where the forces of the living and the supernatural converged within her being.

In the dim light, Sheila glimpsed fleeting apparitions—manifestations of the malevolent forces that had returned to the haunted dwelling. The whispers, now a dissonant symphony, seemed to speak of a malevolence seeking communion with her, defying the constraints of the ritual. The old house, though momentarily quelled, stood as a witness to Sheila's confrontation with the resolution—an act that echoed through the spectral corridors.

Suddenly, the room quivered with unseen energies, and the temperature plummeted. The whispers, now a spectral chorus, intensified as Sheila confronted the epicenter of the supernatural disturbance within herself. The air, charged with an otherworldly energy, carried a spectral resonance that hinted at the imminent confrontation with the resolution that had become intertwined with her very essence.

As Sheila approached the heart of the spectral storm within her, she felt an oppressive force—an awakening darkness that seemed to envelop her being. The whispers, now a relentless drone, echoed through her consciousness, urging her to confront the malevolent forces and the resolution that lingered within the depths of her soul. Sheila, standing at the threshold of her own transformation, faced the haunting resolution that had become an integral part of her existence.

In the dimly lit chamber of her consciousness, Sheila confronted the resolution that unfolded within her soul. The whispers, now a haunting melody, guided her through the spectral encounter—a dance between her awakened self and the lingering abyss. The haunted dwelling, its spectral foundations shaken by the consequences of the sacrifice, the malevolent encore, and the revelation, became a crucible where the boundaries between Sheila's reality and the resolution blurred.

The resolution within Sheila, a manifestation of the ancient darkness, spoke through the spectral symphony within her soul. The whispers, now a dissonant chorus, conveyed the grievances and malevolence of the lingering force that sought communion with her. Sheila, in a surreal confrontation with the resolution, faced the ancient darkness that had become intertwined with her very essence. The haunted dwelling, a conduit for the malevolent supernatural forces and the resolution, bore silent witness to the final act within the depths of Sheila's consciousness.

As Sheila grappled with the malevolent forces and the resolution within her, the whispers, now a relentless drone, urged her toward a resolution that defied comprehension. The haunted dwelling, its spectral foundations saturated with the essence of Sheila's confrontation, the malevolent encore, and the revelation, stood as a battleground where the forces of light and darkness clashed in a terrifying crescendo within the depths of her soul.

In the dim light, Sheila glimpsed shadowy figures—apparitions of the past that materialized in the spectral realm within her consciousness. The whispers, now a haunting lament, spoke of the tormented souls

that lingered within her awakened self. The air, charged with an otherworldly energy, guided her toward the epicenter of the spectral storm—an impending resolution with the malevolent entity that had become an integral part of her very existence.

As Sheila confronted the entity within, the whispers, now a spectral chorus, intensified. Her resolve tested by the supernatural onslaught, she faced the resolution and the return of the malevolent force with determination. The haunted dwelling, its spectral foundations saturated with the essence of the supernatural, stood as a crucible where the forces of light and darkness clashed in a terrifying crescendo within the depths of Sheila's soul.

Unexpectedly, the resolution within Sheila recoiled—a spectral manifestation weakened by her determination to overcome the malevolent forces. The whispers, now a fading memory, left an eerie stillness in the chambers of her consciousness. Sheila, her senses overwhelmed by the supernatural encounter, the malevolent encore, and the resolution, stood amidst the remnants of the spectral storm that had unfolded within her soul. The haunted dwelling, though momentarily quelled, seemed to sigh with a spectral resignation as if acknowledging the fleeting victory over the lingering malevolent forces and the resolution.

As Sheila emerged from the depths of her own confrontation and the resolution, a sense of cautious hope lingered in the air. The whispers, now a distant murmur, guided her through the dimly lit halls of her own consciousness—the battleground where she had triumphed over the malevolent forces, the revelation, and the resolution within. The haunted dwelling, forever scarred by the supernatural encounter, stood as a testament to the resilience of the human spirit and the capacity to confront the ancient darkness that lurked within one's own soul.

Little did Sheila know that the resolution marked the final chapter in her journey. The whispers, now a fading memory, left the door ajar for the looming terror that awaited in the aftermath of the supernatural encounter, the malevolent encore, and the revelation. Sheila, forever changed by the harrowing ordeal within herself, faced an uncertain

future where the horrors of her own past cast a long, lingering shadow over her fragile grasp on reality. The haunted dwelling, a reflection of her awakened soul, awaited the next chapter in Sheila's journey—a journey that would redefine the very fabric of her existence.